PERSIAN IN USE
An Elementary Textbook of Language and Culture

Iranian Studies Series

The Iranian Studies Series publishes high-quality scholarship on various aspects of Iranian civilization, covering both contemporary and classical cultures of the Persian cultural area. The contemporary Persian-speaking area includes Iran, Afghanistan, Tajikistan, and Central Asia, while classical societies using Persian as a literary and cultural language were located in Anatolia, Caucasus, Central Asia and the Indo-Pakistani subcontinent. The objective of the series is to foster studies of the literary, historical, religious and linguistic products in Iranian languages. In addition to research monographs and reference works, the series publishes English-Persian critical text-editions of important texts. The series intends to publish resources and original research and make them accessible to a wide audience.

PERSIAN IN USE

An Elementary Textbook of Language and Culture

Anousha Sedighi

Leiden University Press

First edition, 2015
Second edition, 2015
Third edition, 2016
Fourth edition, 2017
Fifth edition, 2018

Companion website: www.persianinuse.com
Graphic design, lay-out, and illustrations: Maryam Keyvan
Cover design: Tarek Atrissi Design

ISBN: 978 90 8728 217 2
e-ISBN: 978 94 0060 193 2 (epdf)
e-ISBN: 978 94 0060 194 9 (epub)

CONTENTS

Introduction

The Writing System
Alphabet & Sounds:

Group I
Group II
Group III
Group IV
Group V
Group VI
Group VII (Includes additional symbols)

Review
Review Exercises
Basic Numbers
Parts of Speech
Useful Words & Phrases

Lesson 1: Greetings & Introductions

Communication Objectives

Greetings and Farewells
Introducing Yourself
Using Written and Spoken Forms
Using Formal and Informal Forms
Asking Yes/No Questions
Talking about Your Nationality, Hometown, and Profession
Describing People and Things

Contents

Written & Spoken Forms
Interactive Dialogue 1: How are You Mina? (Informal)
Interactive Dialogue 2: How are You Mr. Parsa? (Formal)
Formal & Informal Forms
Interactive Dialogue 3: Are You a Professor?
Interactive Dialogue 4: I am Iranian-American
In-class Reading: My name is Kamran
Grammar 1: Present Tense of "To Be" (Long & Short Forms)

Lesson 2: About You   89

Communication Objectives

Talking about Your Family
Talking about Your Courses
Talking about Your Age
Identifying Class Objects and People
Expressing Likes, Dislikes, Needs, and Possession
Counting and Calculating

Contents

Lesson 5: Shopping

Communication Objectives
Talking about Price of Products
Using Shopping-related Terms
Describing Products
Expressing Quantities
Negotiating the Price
Giving Commands
Talking about What You "Want" to Do or "Have" to Do

Contents
Interactive Dialogue 1: Do You Have a Student Discount?
Interactive Dialogue 2: I Want to Buy a Nice Rug
In-class Reading: The School Principal is Sick
Grammar 1: Imperative
Grammar 2: Present Subjunctive
    Subjunctive as an Independent Verb
    Subjunctive vs. Imperative
Let's Learn More: Clothes
    Short Dialogues about Shopping
    Technology-related Words
Review Corner

Poem from شاهنامه by Ferdowsi
Song: جانِ مریم (Singer: Mohammad Nouri)
Cultural Note: Bargaining Brings Prosperity!
    Traditional Bazaars
Proverb
Thematic Review of New Vocabulary

Lesson 6: Geography & Weather

Communication Objectives

Talking about Iran's Geography: Cities, Provinces, Mountains, Seas, Neighbors, etc.

Talking about Past Events

Talking about Past Events that Happened in a Time-frame

Expressing Opinions

Making Comparisons

Talking about the Weather and the Seasons

Contents

Interactive Dialogue 1: Shiraz is More Beautiful than Tehran!

Interactive Dialogue 2: Good Old Days!

In-class Reading 1: Parsa Family's Trip

Let's Learn More: Adverbs of Time

Grammar 1: Simple Past Tense

Grammar 2: Past Continuous Tense

Let's Learn More: Geography-related Words
Directions & Continents

In-class Reading 2: The Country of Iran

Let's Learn More: Seasons
Weather

Grammar 3: Comparative Adjectives

Grammar 4: Superlative Adjectives

Let's Learn More: Extended Family

Reading from a Novel: دایی‌جان ناپلئون by Iraj Pezeshkzad

Review Corner

Poem: درآمد by Hamid Mossadegh

Song: دو ماهی (Singer: Googoosh)

Cultural Note: Iran's Ancient Sites

Proverb

Thematic Review of New Vocabulary

7. Food & Special Occasions

Communication Objectives

Talking about Different Kinds of Persian Food

Talking about Serving Food

Interacting at a Restaurant: Ordering Food, Asking for the Bill, etc.

Talking about Special Occasions: Birthday, Wedding, Funeral, etc.

Planning for Parties and Responding to Invitations

Expressing Congratulations and Condolences

Expressing Sensations and Feelings

Contents

Interactive Dialogue 1: I am Hungry and Thirsty, Mom!

Interactive Dialogue 2: Welcome to the Persepolis Restaurant!

In-class Reading: Ladan's Birthday

Grammar 1: Psychological Verbs

Let's Learn More: Fruits & Vegetables

8. Schooling & Holidays

Communication Objectives
Talking about the Education System in Iran
Talking about Traditional Celebrations and Festivals
Talking about Recent Events and Events in Progress
Requesting and Giving Information about the Date
Filling Out an Application
Reporting an Incident
Talking about the Persian Calendar and Months
Using Idiomatic Expressions and Street Talk

Contents

9. Visiting Iran

Communication Objectives

Making Reservations: Plane Ticket, Hotel Room, etc.
Interacting at the Iranian Airport
Making a Complaint
Asking for Directions
Finding Directions on a Map
Narrating Stories Situated in Time
Talking about Iranian Currency
Using Polite & Modest Forms

Contents

Interactive Dialogue 1: Both my Passports have Expired!
Interactive Dialogue 2: At Mehrabad Airport
Interactive Dialogue 3: Our Hotel Room is Very Noisy!
Interactive Dialogue 4: How Can I Get to Arya Handicraft Store?
Let's Learn More: Persian Handicrafts
Grammar 1: Present Perfect Tense
Grammar 2: Past Perfect Tense
Reading 1: Iran Air Instructions
Map of Esfahan
Let's Learn More: Money & Currency
Reading 2: Cyrus the Great
Let's Learn More: Polite, Default, & Modest Forms
Reading 3: The Abbasi Hotel
Review Corner
Poem by Rumi
Song: گل یخ (Singer: Kourosh Yaghmaei)
Cultural Note: Tips on Traveling to Iran
Proverb

Thematic Review of New Vocabulary

10. Sports & Leisure

Communication Objectives

Talking about Popular Iranian Sports
Talking about Iranian Cinema
Talking about Favorite Hobbies
Talking about Events Taking Place in the Future
Using Slang & Street Talk

Contents

Interactive Dialogue 1: Are You a Fan of Persepolis or Esteghlal?
Interactive Dialogue 2: Can We Get Tickets for the Fajr Film Festival?
In-class Reading: The International Roshd Film Festival
Grammar 1: Future Tense
Reading from a Play: آرش (written by Bahram Beyzai)
Let's Learn More: What's Your Favorite Sport?
Grammar 2: Uses of که
Grammar 3: Uses of تا

Reading from a Film Script: علی سَنتوری (written by Dariush
                                        Mehrjui & Vahidéa Mohammadi)
Let's Learn More: What is Your Favorite Hobby?
                    Calligraphy & Handwriting
Review Exercises
Review Corner
Poem: بازگشت by Kazem Kazemi
Song: یادگار دوست (Singer: Shahram Nazeri)
Cultural Note: Ancient Iranian Sport & Zurkhāneh
                Iranian Cinema
Proverb
Thematic Review of New Vocabulary

ACKNOWLEDGEMENTS

There are so many people who have helped throughout the production of this work and I am sure I will miss some of them out. First and foremost, I would like to thank the organizations that have supported this project. In chronological order, I would like to acknowledge the Faculty Enhancement Grant from Portland State University for 2008, the Fellowship from Roshan Cultural Heritage Institute for 2010, the Faculty Research Grant of the PARSA Community Foundation for 2011, and the Faculty Enhancement Grant from Portland State University for 2014.

I would like to thank Marjan Moosavi for teaching from this book in her class and for providing valuable comments and suggestions that have enriched it. Thanks are due to the students of Portland State University (2009-2016) and York University (2013-2014) for their invaluable comments and feedback. In the shaping of this book, I learned the most from students. They taught me how to teach them and what they needed to be taught.

Many others have provided feedback in the form of reading chapters and giving input or in the form of general discussions and guidance that have helped in shaping this book. In no specific order, I would like to thank Christian Lagadec, Dr. Mehdi Marashi (University of Utah), Dr. Ahmad Karimi-Hakkak (University of Maryland), Dr. Latifeh Hagigi (UCLA), Dr. Kamran Talattof (University of Arizona), Dr. Asghar Seyed-Gohrab (Leiden University), Dr. Farima Mostowfi (Georgetown University), Dr. Sima Paribakht (University of Ottawa), Dr. Nahal Akbari-Saneh (University of Maryland), Dr. Mehdi Khorrami (New York University), Dr. Jaleh Pirnazar (UC Berkley), Dr. Ali Reza Abasi (University of Maryland), Drs. Sandra Freels, Jennifer Perlmutter, and Eva Núñez Méndez (Portland State University), Dr. Elahe Omidyar Mir-Djalali (Roshan Cultural Heritage Institute), Kris Kern, Jill Emery, Samira Rezaie, Zhubin Najafi, Albert Barrow, Dirk Hutchins, and Arad Mojtahedi. I am grateful to the anonymous reviewers of Leiden University Press for their valuable comments and suggestions. All errors are solely mine. Thanks are also due to Maryam Keyvan for her artistic graphic design work.

On a more personal note, I express my gratitude to my parents, Ladan Rahiminia and Dr. Ahmad Sedighi for providing financial support in order to hire the graphic designer for the book. My father also read the chapters and provided valuable feedback. I would also like to thank my husband Farzin who had to put up with my haphazard contributions at home during the time I was working on this book. Last but not least, I would like to thank my wonderful son Kourosh whose presence has brightened my life tremendously and to whom this book is dedicated.

PREFACE

FEATURE SUMMARY:

• Colorful and lively design with over 200 illustrations and images and over 1200 words and phrases including high-frequency idioms, slang, and proverbs • New vocabulary is summarized thematically/lexically to help students engage in the accompanying communicative activities • Interactive dialogues from everyday life in both spoken and written forms introduce students to contemporary usage • Straightforward explanations of the grammatical features • Includes samples of literary texts, poems, plays, film scripts, and pop songs • Engaging classroom activities and homework exercises with the integration of all four skills • Relevant and practical cultural notes • Appendices include verb charts, language glossary, and grammar review • Companion website with audio files and authentic video clips from Iran • Corresponds to two semesters/three quarters of elementary college-level study as recommended by the *American Council on the Teaching of Foreign Languages*.

ABOUT THE BOOK:

Persian in Use is an elementary Persian language and culture textbook designed for first-year Persian language students at college level. It offers a thematically organized and integrative approach to the Persian language and culture. *Persian in Use* includes ten lessons and three appendices. The writing system is taught in the introduction and covers both the alphabet and the sound system. Both written and spoken varieties are introduced from the outset. *Persian in Use* covers approximately 120-140 contact hours of instruction corresponding to one year (two semesters/three quarters) of academic study.

Each lesson includes the following components:

- 2-4 Preparatory vocabulary lists
- 2-4 Interactive dialogues presented in both spoken and written forms
- 1-2 Reading passages used as part of the actual lesson (not an exercise)
- 2-4 Grammatical points that are already used in the dialogues and the passage
- Approximately 30 exercises that are specifically designed and labeled to enhance all four skills
- A short poem that is carefully selected to contain the grammatical point introduced in the lesson and to provide exposure to Persian literature.
- Lyrics of a song that is carefully selected to contain the grammatical point introduced in the lesson and to provide exposure to Iranian pop culture
- Cultural notes related to the topic of the lesson
- A proverb that utilizes the vocabulary or the grammatical structure used in that lesson
- Review of the new vocabulary presented thematically/lexically

Persian in Use includes three appendices: a list of verbs and their corresponding stems and prepositions, a complete language glossary, and a concise grammar review. Lessons are accompanied by audio files available at the companion website. *Persian in Use* has been piloted in different universities for five years and the feedback from students and instructors has played a major role in shaping it.

PEDOGOGICAL FEATURES:

Persian in Use is organized around high-frequency topics, contains a clear set of communication goals, integrates all four skills (reading, writing, listening, and speaking) from the outset, and employs all three communicative modes (interpersonal, interpretive, and presentational). *Persian in Use* is not based on a single approach or method. Rather, it implements multiple methodologies and approaches to meet the needs of current college-level students pursuing Persian. As such, the book includes a variety of activities such as drilling, dictation, filling in the blanks, picture description, cloze tests, matching, free writing, summarizing, locating information, role-playing, interviewing, discussion, presentation, and minimal translation. Students are required to perform a variety of tasks such as filling out an authentic questionnaire or making travel plans to visit Iranian cities. *Persian in Use* offers frequent instances of chunk learning at different levels (lexis, grammar, and discourse). A focus on performing functional tasks, the use of authentic material, promotion of cooperation between students, and raising cultural awareness remain the core goals of the book.

Persian in Use follows the ACTFL National Standards, as outlined in the *Standards for Foreign Language Learning in the 21st Century*. Thus the 5 Cs (Communication, Cultures, Connections, Comparisons, and Communities) are specifically implemented and taken into account. *Persian in Use* provides a solid foundation for meaningful communication and offers constant cultural input in each lesson. It provides many opportunities for students to connect together and compare their world with that of Persian-speaking people. Tasks such as ordering food from a restaurant in Tehran or writing an email to an Iranian pen pal link the students to the actual Communities of Iran.

LEARNING GOALS:

By the end of this book, students will have acquired the following skills:

- The ability to speak about themselves, their family and friends, their daily activities, etc. They will be able to initiate and sustain conversations (with reasonable accuracy) about basic daily life interactions with sympathetic interlocutors accustomed to non-native speech.
- The ability to read texts of elementary level difficulty (on familiar topics) so that they understand the main ideas and have the ability to guess the meaning of new words from context.
- The ability to write with reasonable accuracy simple notes, paragraphs, and short letters on familiar topics related to daily life.
- Familiarity with sounds and the differences between written and spoken forms of Persian.
- A general understanding of aspects of Iranian culture related to everyday life, society, values, traditions, history, literature, pop culture, etc.

KEY FEATURES OF *PERSIAN IN USE*

1. **New vocabulary includes diacritics**

   Short vowels in Persian are written as diacritics, which are often omitted in writing as native speakers automatically know the pronunciation of the word. Most Persian textbooks fail to place the diacritics on the new vocabulary. This causes frustration for students. In this book, the first time a new vocabulary is introduced the diacritics are included. Students are expected to learn the pronunciation afterwards and the diacritics are removed in the subsequent usages.

2. **Thematic review of new vocabulary**

   Persian in Use summarizes new vocabulary based on a specific theme (such as *"Means of Transportation"* or *"About Eating"*) or lexical category (*"Nouns & Adjectives"*) in order to make the process of vocabulary acquisition by students more meaningful.

3. **The content is organized thematically**

   Each lesson is designed around a core theme. In order to ensure authenticity, other themes may be briefly introduced in each lesson. For instance, Lesson 8 is about "Education". Since the Persian New Year occurs within the academic year, and its holidays last for two weeks till "Sizdah be-dar", the topic of "National Celebrations" is also discussed in the same lesson. So while some lessons may seem to have two unrelated themes, the content of the lesson provides the connection between the two themes.

4. **Both written and spoken forms are introduced from the outset**

   Persian in Use introduces both varieties of written and spoken language for the new vocabulary and dialogues. In the audio files, the dialogues are recorded in spoken form and the reading passages are recorded in written form. *Persian in Use* provides many opportunities for students to practice the differences between the written and spoken forms in order to gain a strong command of both.

5. **Content and exercises include authentic and level-appropriate material**

   The interactive dialogues, reading passages, and exercises are carefully selected to include authentic and level-appropriate material, yet follow a specific apparatus and maintain cohesiveness and readability. New material builds on students' existing knowledge and no linguistic form remains unexplained.

6. **Activities are specifically designed for the integration of all four skills**

   Activities and tasks are designed to reinforce all four skills. Each exercise is labeled with graphic symbols to demonstrate which skill is promoted in that exercise: *Headphone* (for listening), *Pencil* (for writing), *Book* (for reading), *People talking* (for speaking), and *Mouth* (for pronunciation). Pair/group exercises and classroom activities promote cooperation between students and reinforce communication.

16

7. Includes a variety of registers

In an effort to capture the way the language is used by native speakers, *Persian in Use* offers a variety of language styles such as the modest and polite forms, proverbs, idioms, slang, street talk, and even some derogatory words. This feature makes the book an excellent resource for those interested in learning how the language is used among the younger generations and on the streets.

8. "Common Mistakes"

One of the unique features of *Persian in Use* is the notes on "Common Mistakes". These notes address the frequent mistakes of students, especially those whose first language is English. Students often transfer/expand the grammar rules of English into Persian which usually results in ill-formed constructions. Based on many years of teaching experience and linguistic knowledge *Persian in Use* discusses the potential mistakes and helps students avoid them.

9. Cultural notes provide students with information about the culture

Persian in Use brings a fresh zest to the task of introducing the culture by providing practical tips such as a simple note on using bathrooms in Iran. Other cultural notes include information about currency, tourist information, history, values, society, cinema, food, sports, etc.

10. Supplemental materials include classical/modern poetry and lyrics of pop songs

Listening to music and reading poetry have proven to be essential tools for learning a foreign language. Thus, *Persian in Use* offers supplemental materials that include a poem and the lyrics of a song in which the new grammatical feature of the lesson is utilized. The actual songs are all available on YouTube. Students will not be evaluated on the supplemental material as they serve as a resource for students' cultural exposure. In an effort to provide level-appropriate content, the poem and song may not be about the theme of the lesson, but they are specifically chosen to include the grammatical point introduced in that lesson.

11. Appendices include a glossary, grammar review, and user-friendly verb charts

Persian in Use includes a complete language glossary as well as a list of frequently used verbs, their present and past stems, and their prepositions. The grammar review section summarizes all the tenses covered throughout the book.

12. Lively and clear layout with authentic images from Iran

Persian in Use contains a delightful layout and authentic images of Iran. Illustrations have been specifically drawn for this book and make the learning experience enjoyable and clear.

TO THE STUDENT

In order to achieve proficiency in Persian through this book you need to focus on the following four Ps: **Preparation**, **Participation**, **Practice**, and **Patience**. You need to come to class prepared, actively participate in the class activities, practice Persian outside class on a daily basis (in a group or alone), and more importantly, you need to be patient and not give up! When it comes to learning a language, pro-activeness is a huge plus! The more you participate in class, the faster you will be able to communicate in Persian. Don't be shy and afraid of making mistakes as constant trial and error is part of the process of language learning. It is normal to feel overwhelmed at times. Having group study sessions outside class will definitely help. You can share your learning experience with your classmates and learn from each other.

Learning the Persian writing system requires visual observation and constant practice in writing the new words. Remember that once is not enough! You need to listen to the audio files available at the companion website, pronounce the new letter/word and write it numerous times. This is because you are training your brain and your muscles to do new things and this process requires lots of practice. Some students think that just by looking at a new word they can learn how to write it. This is not true. Research shows that the initial process of duplication is very important in learning how to write and read in a foreign language. You need to copy the new letter or word at least 5-8 times until you can produce it comfortably. Remember to pronounce the words as you write.

The new vocabulary of each lesson is reviewed at the end of the lesson under "Thematic Review of New Vocabulary" where the new words are grouped based on their meaning or function for easier and more meaningful learning. Personalizing the new words or making your own flashcards are helpful ways to learn the new vocabulary faster. The new vocabulary should be reviewed and practiced regularly and eventually all of the words in the book should be learned. It is a good idea to learn the functional words such as pronouns (*I, you, he, she, it*), and the functional phrases such as courtesy words. The introduction chapter includes a list of "Useful Words & Phrases" which needs to be learned early on. This list provides the initial key phrases and sentences such as *"Please repeat"* and *"I don't' understand"*, etc.

The supplemental activities (Poem & Song) in each lesson are excellent resources for additional input. The actual songs are available on YouTube so you can listen to them in your leisure time. Even though you may not understand everything, you will still be exposed to the Persian language and you will learn a whole lot about the culture. In addition to the songs featured in your book, you can find many online sources for listening to music and watching movies.

Each lesson contains a self-assessment chart that helps you reflect on the lesson you have just learned and see which areas still need more work and how you plan to address these needs. Make sure to keep up your momentum and stay motivated although things may get hard at times. Try to have fun, do the best you can, and don't be too hard on yourself! ☺

TO THE INSTRUCTOR

Persian in Use is designed to cover one academic year of college level study. The breakdown of this book for semester-based instruction and quarter-based instruction is calculated as below:

Quarter System

Fall Quarter	Winter Quarter	Spring Quarter
Alphabet	Lesson 3	Lesson 7
	Lesson 4	Lesson 8
Lesson 1	Lesson 5	Lesson 9
Lesson 2	Lesson 6	Lesson 10

Semester System

Winter Term	Spring Term
Alphabet	Lesson 5
	Lesson 6
Lesson 1	Lesson 7
Lesson 2	Lesson 8
Lesson 3	Lesson 9
Lesson 4	Lesson 10

THE INTRODUCTION

The writing system is taught in the introduction. The alphabet and sounds are grouped together for easier instruction. Each group should be taught in one session (the first group is taught on the first day of class). Thus, the entire writing system will be covered in 7 sessions and session 8 will be assigned to the "Review Exercises", "Parts of Speech" and "Basic Numbers". When a new letter is introduced, the instructor writes the letter and the provided examples on the board, pronounces them several times and asks the students to repeat each word several times. The instructor then asks students to copy each word several times and monitors their hand writing one by one. The homework is re-writing each word 4-5 times. The instructor collects the homework of the previous session and corrects it (no grade is necessary).

After teaching each group of the alphabet, a spelling/dictation quiz will be assigned for the following session. This dictation quiz covers only the words that have been covered in the new group. Each dictation quiz consists of 10 words and each word is worth 2 points (total 20). The dictation quiz should be performed at the beginning of each session and should take no more than 10 minutes. After a while, students will get used to the routine and have their blank paper ready for dictation when you enter the class!

A short dialogue at the end of each group is practiced and role played the same session. At the end of each session, a couple of words from "Useful Words & Phrases" (at the end of the Introduction) can be introduced and practiced. "Parts of Speech" will be covered in session 8 after the alphabet is covered; there is no need to spend time on it. You can ask students to work on it at home and correct them together in class. This will prepare the students for understanding the part of speech in Persian a little easier. There is no need for a dictation quiz on numbers. If your sessions are shorter than an hour and a half and your class meets more than twice a day, you may need more than one session to cover each group of the alphabet and sounds. Always encourage your students to listen to the audio files available at the companion website at home to prepare for the quizzes.

LESSONS ONE THROUGH TEN

Vocabulary: The instructor should read the new vocabulary in class and ask the students to repeat it several times. The new vocabulary needs to be accompanied by a dictation quiz the following session. The meaning of each word will also be included in the dictation. You can assign 2-3 vocabulary lists for each dictation quiz. The quiz will be performed at the beginning of the following session and should not take more than 10 minutes. The dictation quiz consists of 10 words that students need to write and translate. Each correct word has 1 point and the correct translation has another point (total 20 points). Certain vocabulary lists such as cardinal and ordinal numbers (Lessons 1 & 4), technology-related words (Lesson 5), instruction of exercises (Lesson 8), or idioms and street talk (Lesson 8) do not need to be included in the dictation quizzes as they may be overwhelming for students. Only the written form of the words will be used in the spelling quiz.

Interactive Dialogues: Each lesson begins with a set of interactive dialogues. In order to keep the students engaged, the dialogues include missing words that need to be filled in with the new vocabulary. It is best if the students are first asked to close their books and listen to the dialogue. The instructor then can briefly ask questions about what the students have just heard. For instance: *Where is this dialogue taking place? What were the names of the dialogue participants?* or a question about the gist such as *what did you get out of the dialogue?* This process does not need to take a lot of time. After that, students can open their books and listen to the instructor reading the dialogue again. If a line has missing words, the students need to find the missing information from the new vocabulary list. Students are then asked to read the dialogue and help the instructor translate the line that was just read. This way, the dialogue will be learned in an interactive way as opposed to a passive way. Dialogues are provided in spoken form and are followed by their written form. The instructor can draw students' attention to the changes between written and spoken forms which are provided in red. The written forms also include missing information that needs to be filled in. Students then practice reading each dialogue in pairs or as a class (and possibly role play them). The instructor should advise students to use the spoken form when speaking and use the written form when writing.

In-class Reading: The "In-class Reading" texts are part of the actual lesson and are not an exercise. They need to be taught in class as part of the lesson. Some instructors prefer to teach the "In-class Reading" after teaching the grammar section. This is definitely a possibility especially if you feel that you have been doing similar tasks for both dialogues and in-class reading. If you want, you can cover the first grammatical point and then go back and cover the in-class reading.

Grammar: Each grammar section provides usages of a certain grammatical point that is already introduced in the context of the interactive dialogues or the "In-class Reading". The grammatical feature needs to be explained to the students and practiced. The grammar section includes "Writing & Pronunciation" rules which are intended to function as a grammar resource. Some of the "Writing and Pronunciation" rules are frequently used and need to be learned by students. However, some of these rules (such as in Lesson 5) may appear somewhat confusing for students so they can be briefly discussed, but students are not required to learned them as they may overwhelm them. The instructor can briefly mention them and move on.

Exercises: *Persian in Use* contains a variety of activities and exercises such as drilling, dictation, filling in the blanks, picture description, cloze tests, matching, free writing, locating information, tasks, and translation. Activities are designed to reinforce all four skills. Each exercise is labeled with graphic symbols to demonstrate which skill is promoted in that exercise. In addition to the "In-class Reading", Lessons 5-10 include additional authentic reading texts that function as a reading comprehension exercise or a cloze exercise to provide additional reinforcement of new vocabulary or grammatical points covered in that lesson. These texts are mainly authentic and different in nature. There are samples of a novel (دایی‌جان ناپلئون) in Lesson 6), film script (علی سَنتوری) in Lesson 10), or a play (آرش) in Lesson 10). The exercises are intentionally not labeled as "Home" or "Classroom" so that teachers have more freedom in choosing which exercise is to be done when, based on students' needs and background.

Cultural Points: Cultural points are provided in English so that students can read them on their own and they do not need to be covered during class time. However, certain cultural points such as Ta'ārof require more explanation and practice.

Supplemental Material (Poem & Song): At the end of the lessons, a short poem and the lyrics of a song are introduced. The supplemental materials do not need to be covered in class as they function as cultural enrichment material. In an effort to provide level-appropriate content, the poem and song may not be about the theme of the lesson, but they are specifically chosen to include the grammatical point introduced in that lesson. This will provide a further opportunity for students to see how the grammatical points they have learned are used in real-life authentic content.

Poems and song lyrics can serve as an excellent source for differentiated instruction. If you are teaching a class with heritage students who have prior knowledge of the language, poems and songs can be assigned to heritage learners as additional homework. While L2 learners are not required to work on the poem and song as homework, in order to provide a differentiated and more advanced curriculum to the heritage students you can ask them to work on the poem and songs. Heritage students can recite them, memorize them, analyze them, or simply translate them into English.

Self-assessment Chart: At the end of each lesson, a self-assessment chart is provided that enables students to look back and reflect on the lesson to see which areas still need more work and how they plan to address their needs in order to fully master that lesson.

ACTIVITY TYPE

As previously mentioned, all the activities of *Persian in Use* are labeled to reflect the skills that are reinforced through them. The following chart illustrates and explains these symbols and their purpose.

Headphone	**Listening**	This icon indicates that the content is available as an audio file on the companion website and students are required to listen to it.
Mouth	**Pronunciation**	This icon indicates that students are required to pronounce the content aloud.
People talking	**Speaking**	This icon indicates that students are required to speak in Persian, either as a pair or a group.
Book	**Reading**	This icon indicates that students are required to read the content.
Pencil	**Writing**	This icon indicates that students are required to write.

SCOPE & SEQUENCE

Lesson	Communication Objectives	Structure
1 **Greetings & Introductions**	Greetings and Farewells Introducing Yourself Using Written and Spoken Forms Using Formal and Informal Forms Asking Yes/No questions Talking about Your Nationality, Hometown, and Profession Describing People and Things	Present Tense of "To Be" (Long & Short Forms) Pronouns Verb agreement Sentence Structure (Part 1) Stress & Intonation The Ezāfe Construction
2 **About You**	Talking about Your Family Talking about Your Courses Talking about Your Age Identifying Class Objects and People Expressing Likes, Dislikes, Needs, and Possession Counting and Calculating	Present Tense of "To Have" Conjunction with *va* Demonstrative Pronouns Nouns: Specific, Non-specific, & Generic Specific Direct Object Marker Possessive Pronouns with *māl*
3 **Daily Activities**	Talking about Daily Activities and the Weekly Schedule Talking about Means of Transportation Talking about Actions Taking Place in the Near Future Talking about Knowing Someone vs. Something Using Common Courtesies Saying Where Things Are	Simple Present Tense Compound Verbs Plurals Sentence Structure (Part 2)
4 **Housing & Living**	Talking about Your House and Belongings Inquiring about a Rental Apartment Talking about Time and Being Late Requesting Information on the Phone Asking Questions Using Question Words	Suffix Pronouns Questions Words
5 **Shopping**	Talking about the Price of Products Using Shopping-related Terms Describing Products Expressing Quantities Negotiating the Price Giving Commands Talking about What You "Want" to Do or "Have" to Do	Imperative Subjective Subjunctive as an Independent Verb Subjunctive vs. Simple Present Subjunctive vs. Imperative

SCOPE & SEQUENCE

Vocabulary	*Poem, Song, & More*	*Culture*
Greeting Words & Phrases Farewell Words & Phrases Nationalities & Hometowns Professions Adjectives	Written vs. Spoken Forms Poem: درگلستانه by Sohrab Sepehri Proverb	Formal vs. Informal Forms First Interactions How to Address People Properly
Family Members Fields of Study Class Objects Numbers (1-100) Age-related Words Arithmetic Words	Poem: کتاب خوب by Abbas Yamini- Sharif Proverb	Diverse Iran Persian-speaking World Persian vs. Farsi
Times of the Day Means of Transportation Languages Common Courtesies Days of the Week Prepositions of Location	Poem: بَنی آدم by Sa'di Song: سیب (Singer: Simin Ghanem) Proverb	Ta'ārof: The Social Etiquette
Housing-related Words Words to Tell the Time Numbers (100-1,000,000,000) Colors Body Parts Pets	Poem: پرنده مُردنی است by Forough Farrokhzad Song: گلِ سنگم (Singer: Hayedeh) Proverb	Using Body Parts in Expressions
Shopping-related Words Clothes Technology-related Words Health-related Words Places for Shopping	Poem from شاهنامه by Ferdowsi Song: جان مریم (Singer: Mohammad Nouri) Proverb	Bargaining brings prosperity! Traditional Bazaars

SCOPE & SEQUENCE

Lesson	Communication Objectives	Structure
6 **Geography & Weather**	Talking about Iran's Geography: Cities, Provinces, Mountains, Seast, Neighbors, etc. Talking about Past Events and Events that Happened in a Time-frame Expressing Opinions Making Comparisons Talking about the Weather and the Seasons	Simple Past Tense Continuous Past Tense Comparatives Adjectives Superlative Adjectives
7 **Food & Special Occasions**	Talking about Different Kinds of Persian Food Talking about Serving Food Interacting at a Restaurant: Ordering Food, Asking for the Bill, etc. Talking about Special Occasions: Birthday, Wedding, Funeral, etc. Planning for Parties and Responding to Invitations Expressing Congratulations and Condolences Expressing Sensations and Feelings	Psychological Verbs Uses of *ham* Reflexive Pronouns
8 **Schooling & Holidays**	Talking about the Education System in Iran Talking about Traditional Celebrations and Festivals Talking about Recent Events and Events in Progress Requesting and Giving Information about the Date Filling Out an Application Reporting an Incident Talking about the Persian Calendar & Months Using Idiomatic Expressions and Street Talk	Present Progressive Past Progressive Prefixes & Suffixes
9 **Visiting Iran**	Making Reservations: Plane Ticket, Hotel Room, etc. Interacting at the Iranian Airport Making a Complaint Asking for Directions Finding Directions on a Map Narrating Stories Situated in Time Talking about Iranian Currency Using Polite & Modest Forms	Present Perfect Past Perfect
10 **Sports & Leisure**	Talking about Popular Iranian Sports Talking about Iranian Cinema Talking about Favorite Hobbies Talking about Events Taking Place in the Future Using Slang & Street Talk	Future Tense Uses of که Uses of تا

Vocabulary	*Poem, Song, & More*	*Culture*
Geography-related Words Iran's Neighbors Continents Directions Seasons & Weather Extended Family Adverbs of Time	Novel: دایی‌جان ناپلئون by Iraj Pezeshkzad Poem: درآمد by Hamid Mossadegh Song: دو ماهی (Singer: Googoosh) Proverb	Iran's Ancient Sites: Chogha Zanbil Persepolis Bisotun
Eating-related Words Fruits & Vegetables Dairy & Meat Pastry & Persian Bread Tastes & Food Portions Phrases for Special Occasions: Birthday, Wedding, Funeral	Short Story: قصّه‌ی آه by Samad Behrangi Poem: پَریا by Ahmad Shamloo Song: دست‌های تو (Singer: Dariyush) Proverb	Persian Cuisine Food Temperament
Education-related Words Academic Degrees Iranian Calendar Iranian Months Idioms, Street Talk, and Derogatory Words	Song: کودکانه (Singer: Farhad) Poem by Omar Khayyam Proverb	National Celebrations & Festivities
Traveling-related Words: (Reservations, Flight, Hotel, etc.) Asking for Directions Persian Handicrafts Money & Currency-related Words Polite, Default, & Modest Forms	Poem by Rumi Song: گل یخ (Singer: Kourosh Yaghmaei) Proverb	Cyrus the Great Tips on Traveling to Iran More about Iranian Money
Sports-related Words Cinema-related Words Slang Hobbies Handwriting and Calligraphy	Play: آرش (written by Bahram Beyzai) Film Script: علی سَنتوری (written by Dariush Mehrjui & Vahidéa Mohammadi) Poem: بازگشت by Kazem Kazemi Song: یادگار دوست (Singer: Shahrām Nazeri)	Ancient Iranian Sport: Bāstāni Iranian Cinema Film Festivals

مقدّمه
Introduction

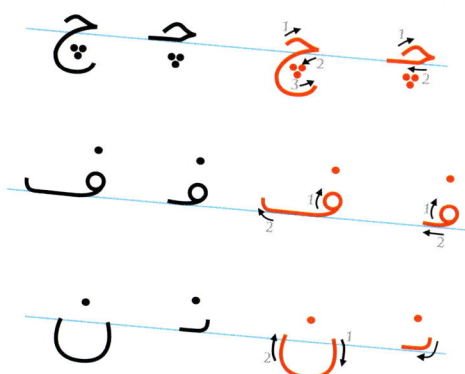

Introduction

The Writing System
Alphabet & Sounds:

THE WRITING SYSTEM

Before we learn about the writing system and sounds of Persian, let's go through some basic information quickly:

1. Persian is written from right to left.

2. There are 32 letters in the Persian alphabet. They are shown below in free standing position.

English word	Phonetic symbol	Letter	Name	English word	Phonetic symbol	Letter	Name
Sam	/s/	ص	sād	-	varies	ا	alef
Zoo	/z/	ض	zād	Bee	/b/	ب	be
Tom	/t/	ط	tā	Pam	/p/	پ	pe
Zoo	/z/	ظ	zā	Tom	/t/	ت	te
Uh-oh	/ʔ/	ع	eyn	Sam	/s/	ث	se
-	/gh/	غ	gheyn	Jim	/j/	ج	jim
Frank	/f/	ف	fe	Chair	/ch/	چ	che
-	/gh/	ق	ghāf	Ham	/h/	ح	he (jimi)
Kylo	/k/	ک	kāf	-	/kh/	خ	khe
Gang	/g/	گ	gāf	Dan	/d/	د	dāl
Lab	/l/	ل	lām	Zoo	/z/	ذ	zāl
Man	/m/	م	mim	Run	/r/	ر	re
No	/n/	ن	nun	Zoo	/z/	ز	ze
Victor	/v/	و	vāv	Garage	/zh/	ژ	zhe
Ham	/h/	ه	he (do cheshm)	Sam	/s/	س	sin
Yellow	/y/	ى	ye	Shane	/sh/	ش	shin

As can be seen in the above chart, several letters have the same pronunciation in Persian. Hence, the letters *te* and *tā* have the same sound /t/, the letters *se*, *sin*, and *sād* have the same sound /s/, the letters *zāl*, *ze*, and *zād* have the same sound /z/, the letters *he (jimi or hotti)* and *he (do cheshm or havvaz)* have the same sound /h/, and finally the letters *ghāf (or qāf)* and *gheyn* have the same sound /gh/. We will learn more about these letters soon.

3. There is no concept of capital letters in Persian.

4. Based on its location in a word, the shape of a letter changes. A letter may have different shapes in the **initial**, **medial**, or **final** position in a word.

5. In Persian, some letters connect to the **next** letter and some letters do not connect to the **next** letter. If a letter connects to the next letter, we call it a "Connector" and if a letter does not connect to the next letter, we call it a "Non-connector". This is a rather confusing concept so make sure you spend some time trying to absorb it! ☺

6. Persian has 6 vowels: 3 short vowels and 3 long vowels. The vowels function as the peaks of syllables.

Vowels

English Word	Phonetic symbol	English word	Phonetic Symbol	English word	Phonetic Symbol	
Orange	/o/	Egg	/e/	Apple	/a/	**Short**
Oops	/u/	Seen	/i/	Awesome	/ā/	**Long**

7. The three short vowels (/a/, /e/, and /o/) are diacritical and are placed above or below the consonant they follow. These diacritics are typically omitted in writing and only appear when it is necessary to assist the reader in pronunciation. In this book, each time a new word is introduced, the diacritics are included. Students are required to learn their spelling and pronunciation. The diacritics are removed after the first exposure.

8. Persian has two diphthongs. A diphthong is a combination of two vowels. The following English examples contain diphthongs: "tow", "oil", "rate", and "cow".

Persian Diphthongs

English example	Persian example	Phonetic symbol
Tow	jow (Barley)	/ow/
Hey	ney (Reed)	/ey/

9. Generally, stress falls on the final syllable of a word. Certain verb tenses, conjunctions, and interjections are exceptions in which the stress falls on the initial syllable. Examples are [bále] (*yes*), and [mérsi] (*thanks*).

10. Usually the structure of Persian words is CV, CVC, or CVCC. This means that there is usually a vowel after each consonant.

11. In Persian, when a word ends with a consonant, that consonant is pronounced very gently/mildly. This means that a foreign learner may not hear the final consonant.

12. Similar to English, the hand-written shape of a letter may look different from the way it is typed. For instance, in English, "a" and "g" are written as .... and .... Fill in the blanks.

13. Similar to English, in Persian, a **letter** may correspond to more than one **sound** and a **sound** may correspond to more than one **letter**. Let's look at some English examples:

One letter corresponds to more than one sound

Letter C			
City /s/	Cat /k/	Malicious /sh/	Science --

One sound corresponds to more than one letter

Sound /k/			
Cat /k/	Kilo /k/	Scheme /k/	Quiet /k/

Exercise 1:

a) Choose an English letter and find at least three corresponding sounds for it:

b) Choose an English sound and find at least three corresponding letters for it:

14. Similar to English, Persian has **homonym** and **homograph** words.

Exercise 2:

Find out what it means to be **homonym** and **homograph** and find some English examples for each concept.

15. Last but not least, learning the Persian alphabet is very tricky! At first, they seem very easy but as the letters accumulate they get confusing, and if you miss a session or two it is almost impossible to catch up unless you have prior exposure to this alphabet.

ALPHABET & SOUNDS

As mentioned earlier, in Persian one letter may correspond to more than one sound. Thus, we will learn the alphabet and sounds together. They will be introduced in groups based on the similarity of their shapes.

Group I

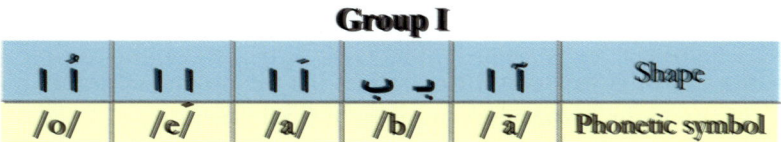

اُ	اِ	اَ	ب بـ	آ	Shape
/o/	/e/	/a/	/b/	/ā/	Phonetic symbol

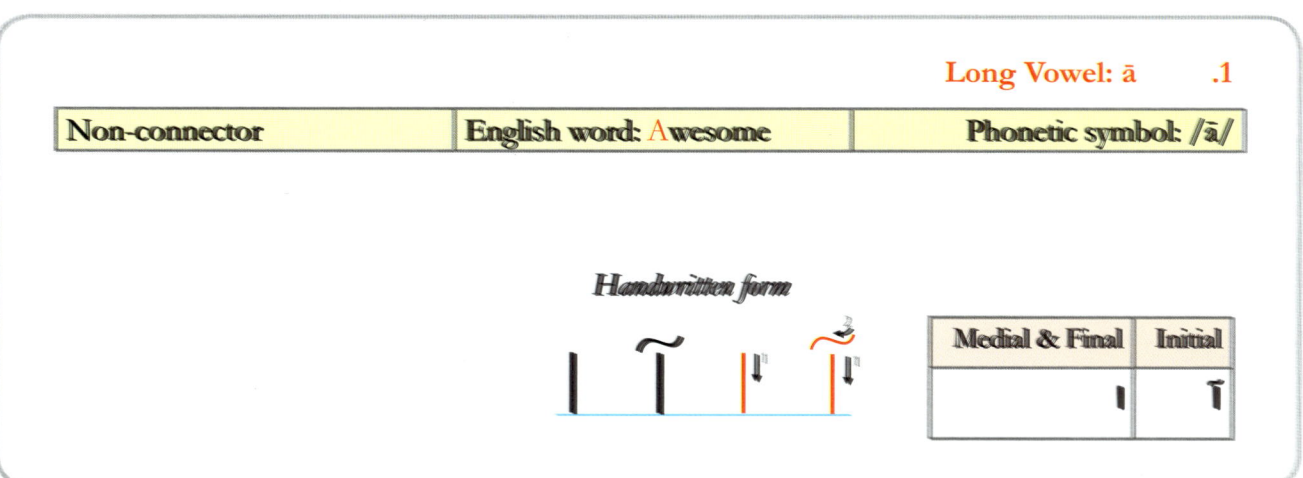

	Long Vowel: ā	.1
Non-connector	English word: Awesome	Phonetic symbol: /ā/

Handwritten form

Medial & Final	Initial
ا	آ

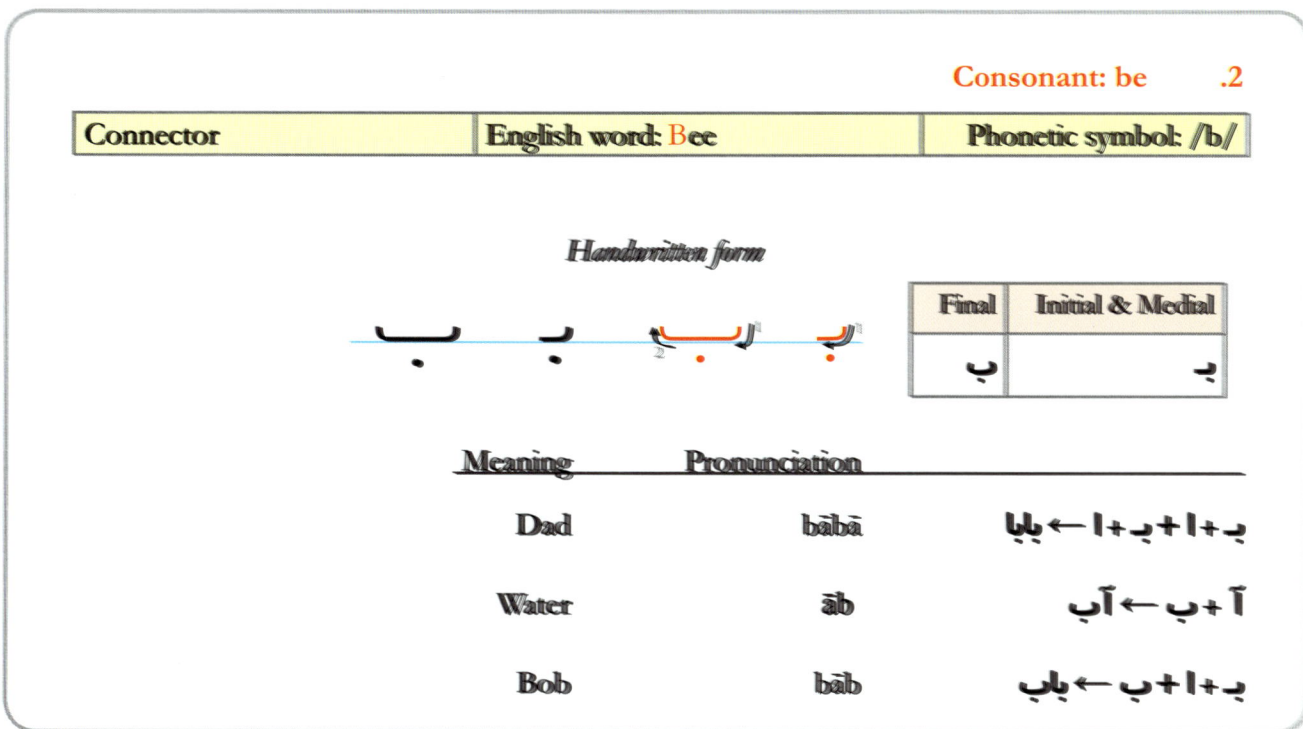

	Consonant: be	.2
Connector	English word: Bee	Phonetic symbol: /b/

Handwritten form

Final	Initial & Medial
ـب	بـ

Meaning	Pronunciation	
Dad	bābā	بابا ← ب + ا + ب + ا
Water	āb	آب ← آ + ب
Bob	bāb	باب ← ب + ا + ب

| Group I: | اُ | اِ | اَ | ب بـ | آ |

Exercise 3: Listen to the audio file and pronounce each word while looking at its spelling. Then write it several times based on the handwritten form. Follow the direction of the arrows.

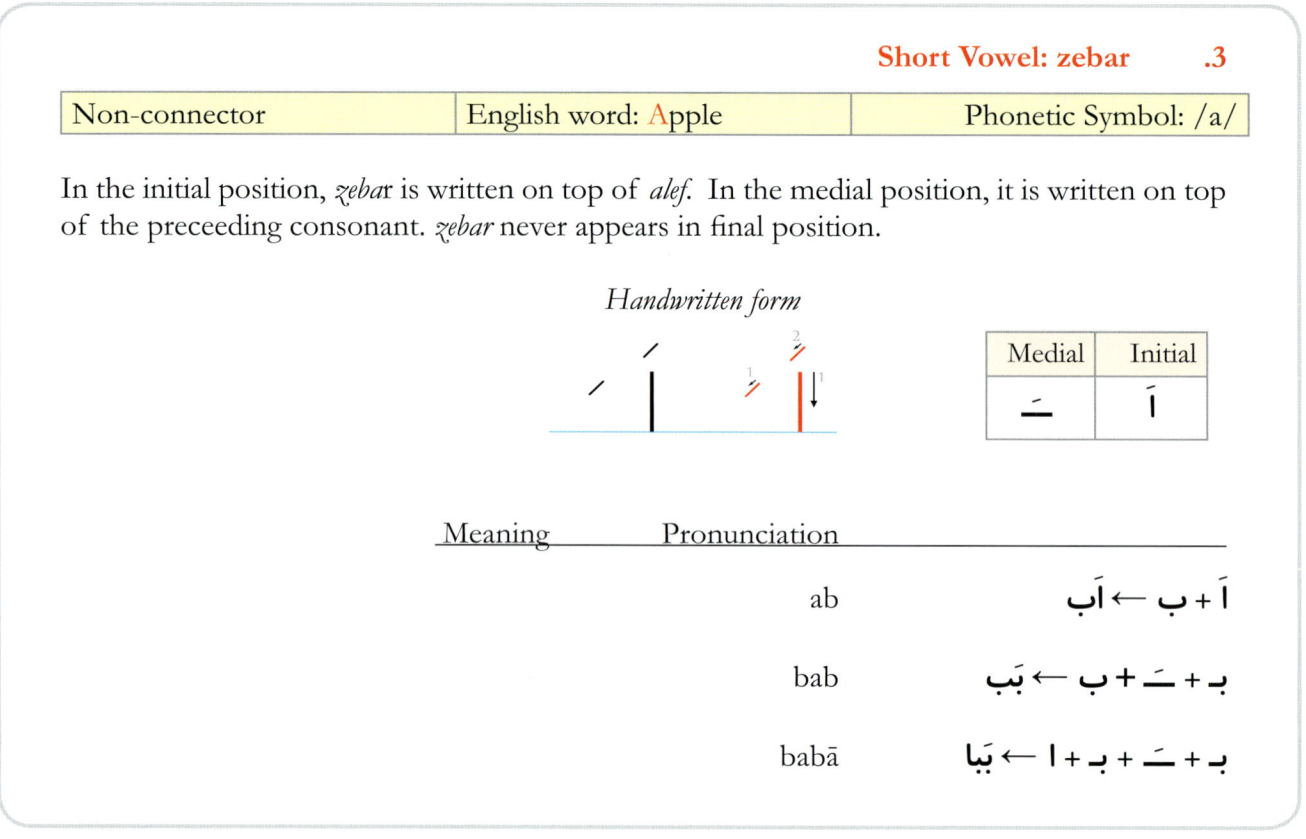

Exercise 4: Listen to the audio file and pronounce each word while looking at its spelling. Then write it several times based on the handwritten form. Follow the direction of the arrows.

> **Note:** /ā/ and /a/ must be clearly distinguished as English speakers tend to confuse these sounds frequently. If you pronounce the /a/ sound like /ā/, you will sound like Arnold Schwarzenegger speaking English! It may also change the meaning of the word entirely!

Exercise 5: Listen to the audio file and read the following words aloud:

/ā/ vs. /a/

English	Persian	English	Persian	English	Persian	English	Persian
Bad	bad	*Wet*	tar	*Head*	Sar	*Shit*	an
Wind	bād	*A musical instrument*	tār	*A bird*	Sār	*That*	ān

Group I: | ﺍ ﺍ | ﺍ ﺍ | ﺍ ﺍَ | ﺏ ﺏ | ﺍ آ |

Short Vowel: zir   .4

Non-connector	English word: Elephant	Phonetic symbol: /e/

In the initial position, /e/ is written below *alef*. In the medial position, it is written under the preceeding consonant. *zir* does not appear in final position.

Handwritten form

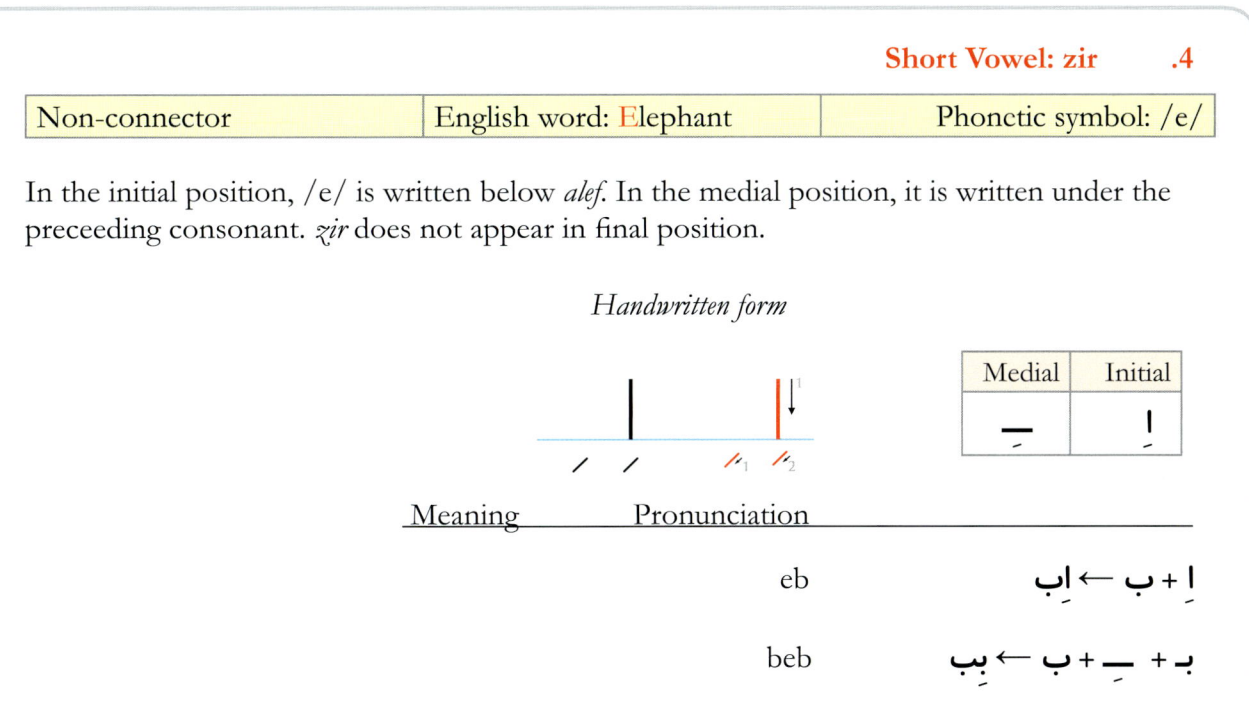

Meaning	Pronunciation	
	eb	اِ + ب ← اِب
	beb	بِ + ب + ــِـ ← بِب
	bebā	بِ + ب + ــِـ + ا ← بِبا

Exercise 6: Listen to the audio file and pronounce each word while looking at its spelling. Then write it several times based on the handwritten form. Follow the direction of the arrows.

Short Vowel: pish   .5

Non-connector	English word: Orange	Phonetic symbol: /o/

In the initial position, /o/ is written on top of *alef*. In the medial position, /o/ is written on the preceeding consonant. *pish* never appears in final position.

Handwritten form

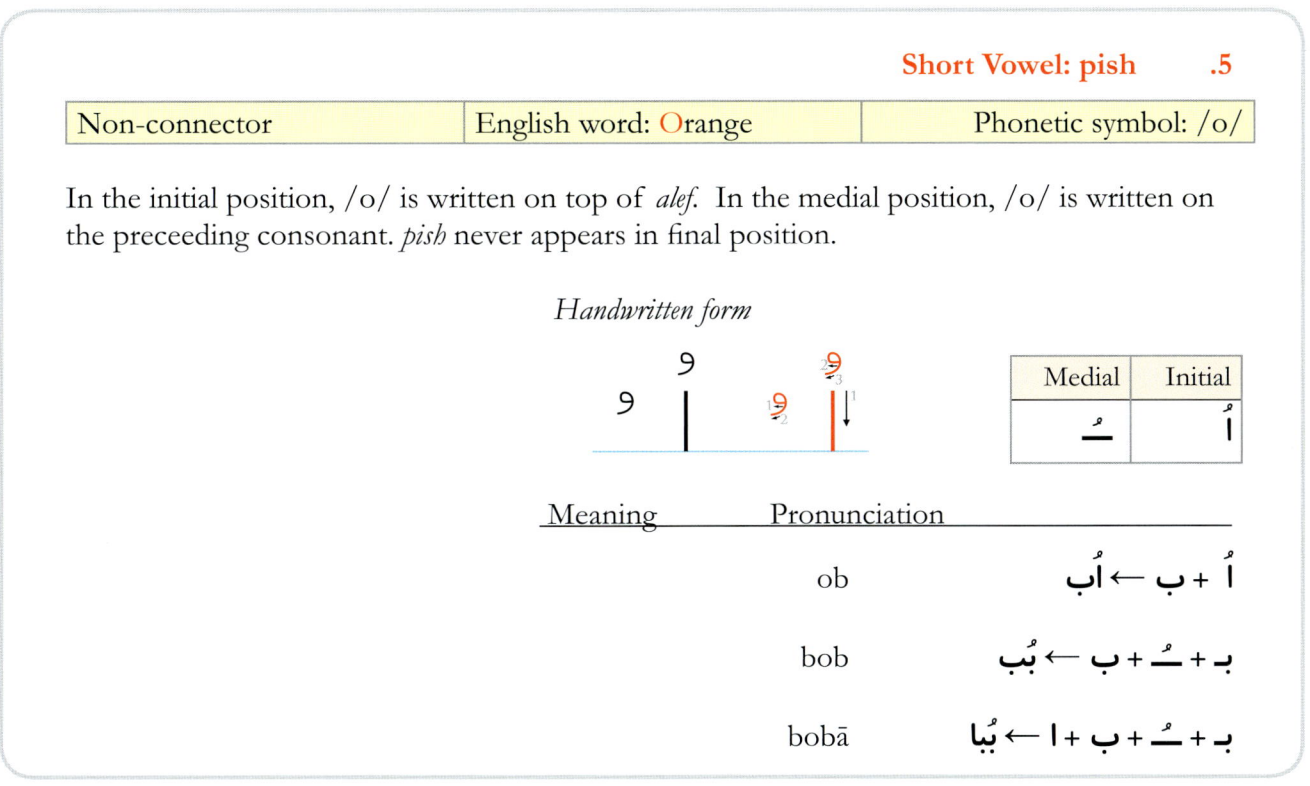

Meaning	Pronunciation	
	ob	اُ + ب ← اُب
	bob	بُ + ــُـ + ب ← بُب
	bobā	بُ + ــُـ + ب + ا ← بُبا

Group I: اُ ا   اِ ا   اَ ا   بـ ب   آ ا

Exercise 7: Listen to the audio file and pronounce each word while looking at its spelling. Then write it several times based on the handwritten form. Follow the direction of the arrows.

Review

		Medial	Initial
Long vowel	ā	ا	آ
Short vowel	a	ﹷ	اَ
Short vowel	e	ﹻ	اِ
Short vowel	o	ﹹ	اُ

Exercise 8: Practice writing the following combinations. Pronounce them as your write.

آ‐‐‐اَ‐‐‐اِ‐‐‐اُ‐‐‐

با‐‐‐بَ‐‐‐بِ‐‐‐بُ‐‐

Dialogue 1	
A. salām.	*Hello.*
B. salām.	*Hello.*
A. chetowri?	*How are you?*
B. khub, mersi.	*Fine. Thanks.*

Group I:	اُ ا	اِ ا	اَ ا	بَ بـ	آ ا

Group II

خ خ	ح ح	چ چ	ج ج	ث ث	پ پ	ت ت	Shape
/kh/	/h/	/ch/	/j/	/s/	/p/	/t/	Phonetic symbol

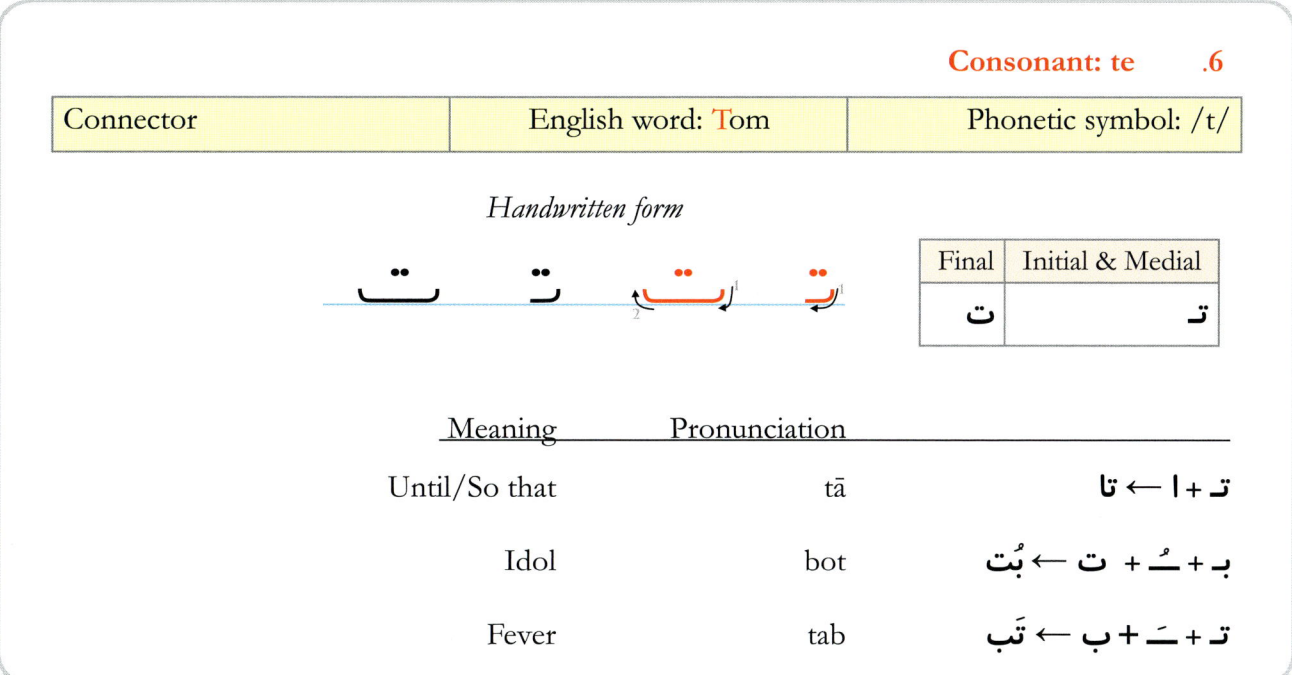

Consonant: te 6.

Connector	English word: Tom	Phonetic symbol: /t/

Handwritten form

Final	Initial & Medial
ت	ت

	Meaning	Pronunciation	
Until/So that	tā	تـ + ا ← تا
Idol	bot	بـ + ـُـ + ت ← بُت
Fever	tab	تـ + ـَـ + ب ← تَب

Exercise 9: Listen to the audio file and pronounce each word while looking at its spelling. Then write it several times based on the handwritten form. Follow the direction of the arrows.

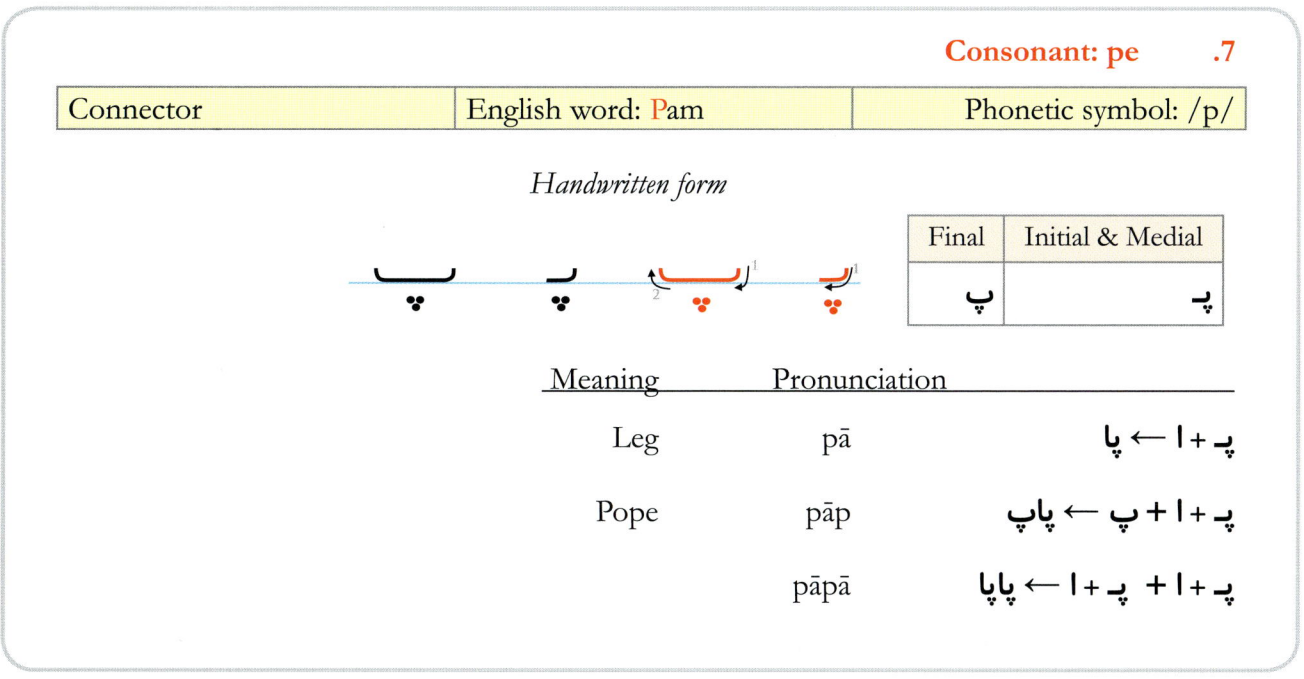

Consonant: pe 7.

Connector	English word: Pam	Phonetic symbol: /p/

Handwritten form

Final	Initial & Medial
پ	پـ

Meaning	Pronunciation	
Leg	pā	پـ + ا ← پا
Pope	pāp	پـ + ا + پ ← پاپ
	pāpā	پـ + ا + پـ + ا ← پاپا

Group II:	خ خ	ح ح	چ چ	ج ج	ث ث	پ پ	ت ت

Exercise 10: Listen to the audio file and pronounce each word while looking at its spelling. Then write it several times based on the handwritten form. Follow the direction of the arrows.

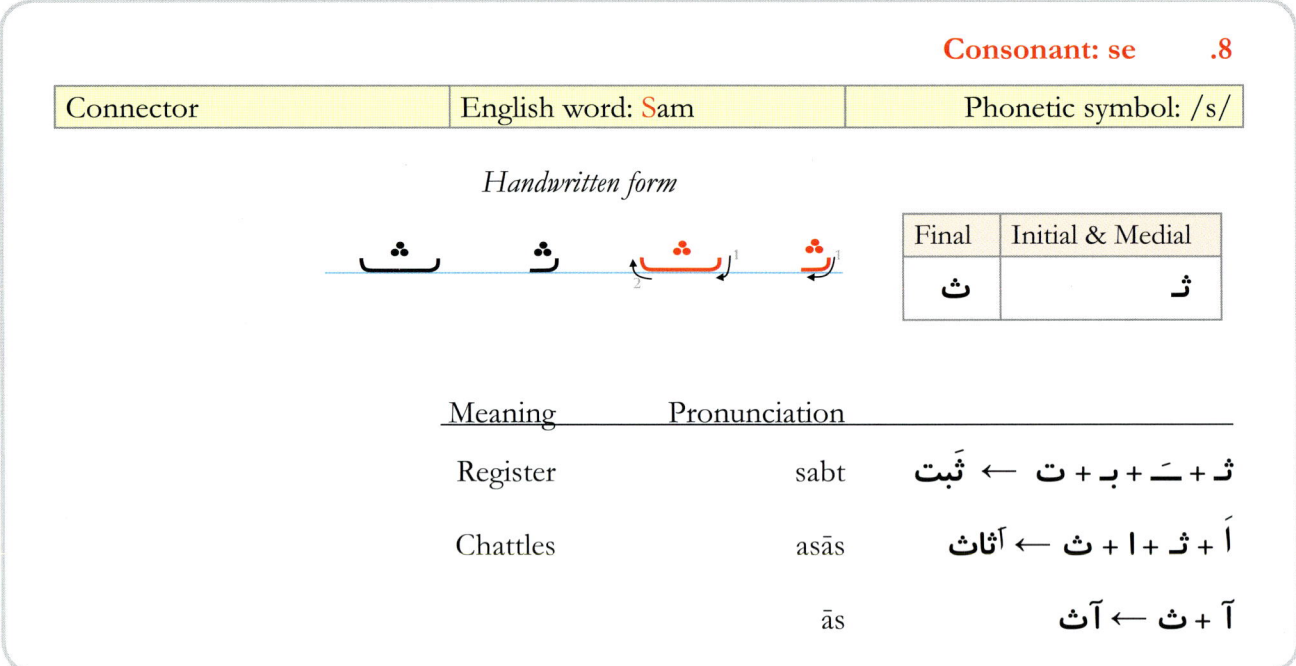

Consonant: se .8

| Connector | English word: **S**am | Phonetic symbol: /s/ |

Handwritten form

Final	Initial & Medial
ث	ﺛ

Meaning	Pronunciation	
Register	sabt	ثـ + ـَ + ﺑـ + ت ← ثَبت
Chattles	asās	أ + ثـ + ا + ث ← آثاث
	ās	آ + ث ← آث

Exercise 11: Listen to the audio file and pronounce each word while looking at its spelling. Then write it several times based on the handwritten form. Follow the direction of the arrows.

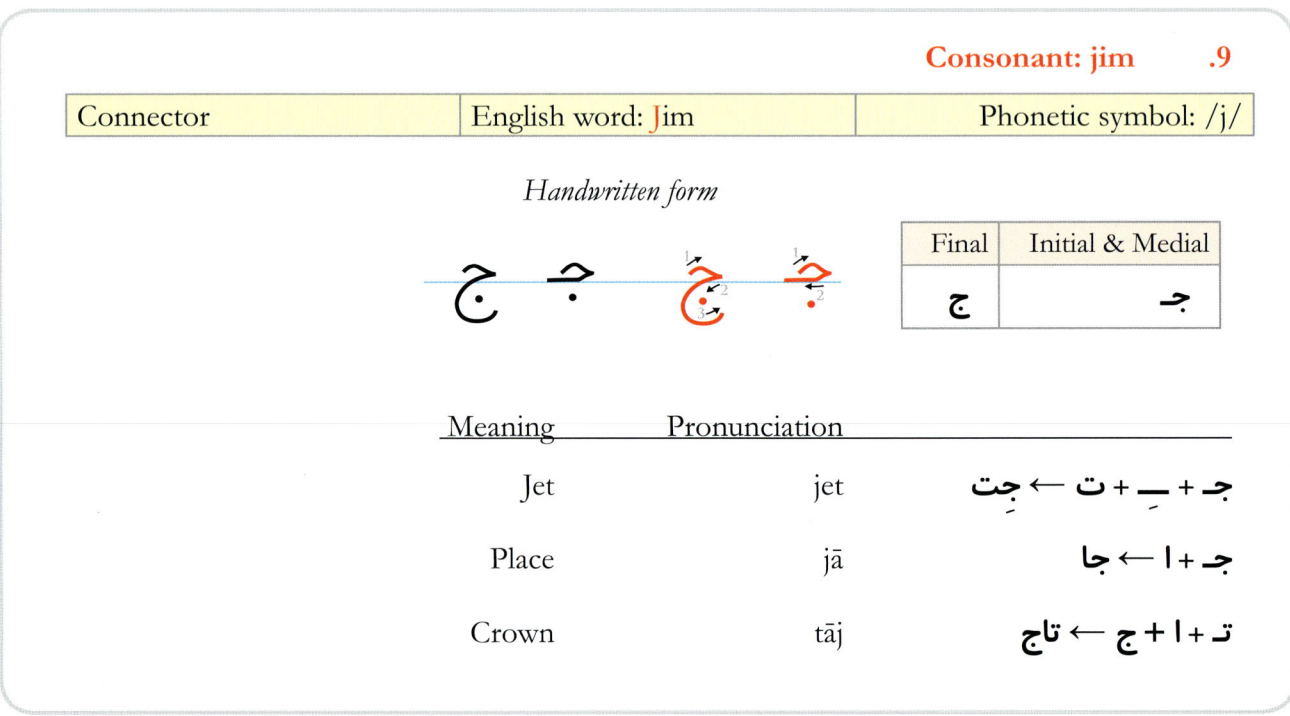

Consonant: jim .9

| Connector | English word: **J**im | Phonetic symbol: /j/ |

Handwritten form

Final	Initial & Medial
ج	ﺟ

Meaning	Pronunciation	
Jet	jet	جـ + ـِ + ت ← جِت
Place	jā	جـ + ا ← جا
Crown	tāj	تـ + ا + ج ← تاج

Exercise 12: Listen to the audio file and pronounce each word while looking at its spelling. Then write it several times based on the handwritten form. Follow the direction of the arrows.

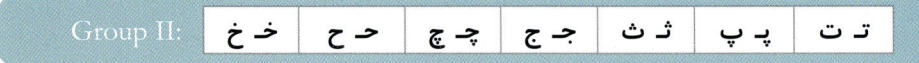

| Group II: | ت ت | پ پ | ثـ ث | جـ ج | چـ چ | حـ ح | خـ خ |

36

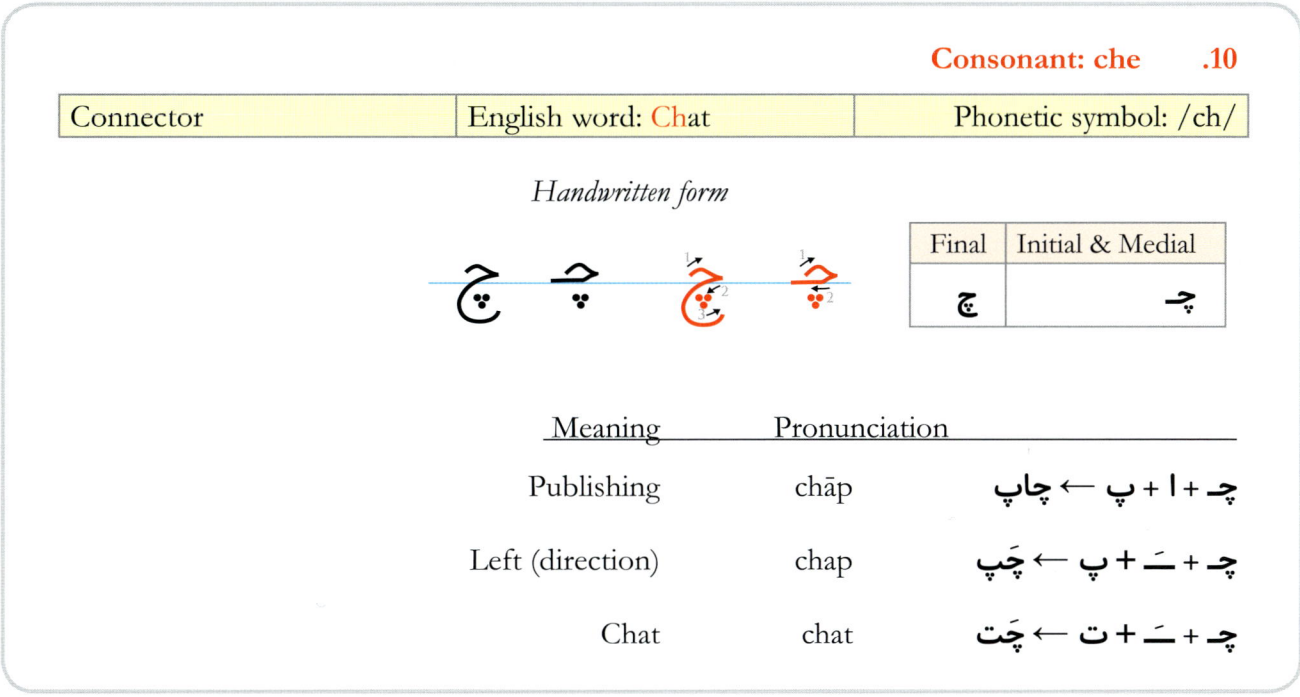

Consonant: che .10

Connector	English word: Chat	Phonetic symbol: /ch/

Handwritten form

	Final	Initial & Medial
	چ	چ

Meaning	Pronunciation	
Publishing	chāp	چ + ا + پ ← چاپ
Left (direction)	chap	چ + ـَ + پ ← چَپ
Chat	chat	چ + ـَ + ت ← چَت

Exercise 13: Listen to the audio file and pronounce each word while looking at its spelling. Then write it several times based on the handwritten form. Follow the direction of the arrows.

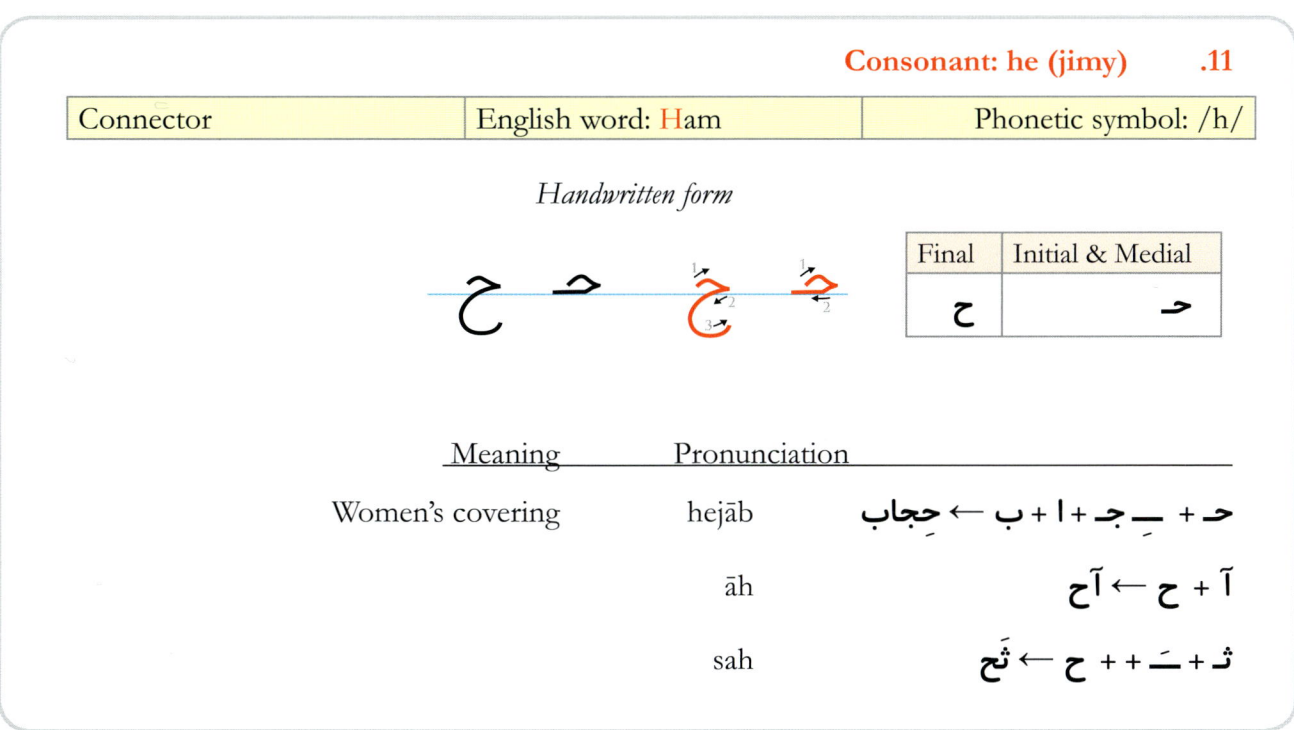

Consonant: he (jimy) .11

Connector	English word: Ham	Phonetic symbol: /h/

Handwritten form

	Final	Initial & Medial
	ح	ح

Meaning	Pronunciation	
Women's covering	hejāb	ح + ـِ + ج + ا + ب ← حِجاب
	āh	آ + ح ← آح
	sah	ث + ـَ + ح ← ثَح

Exercise 14: Listen to the audio file and pronounce each word while looking at its spelling. Then write it several times based on the handwritten form. Follow the direction of the arrows.

Group II:	خ خ	ح ح	چ چ	ج ج	ث ث	پ پ	ت ت

37

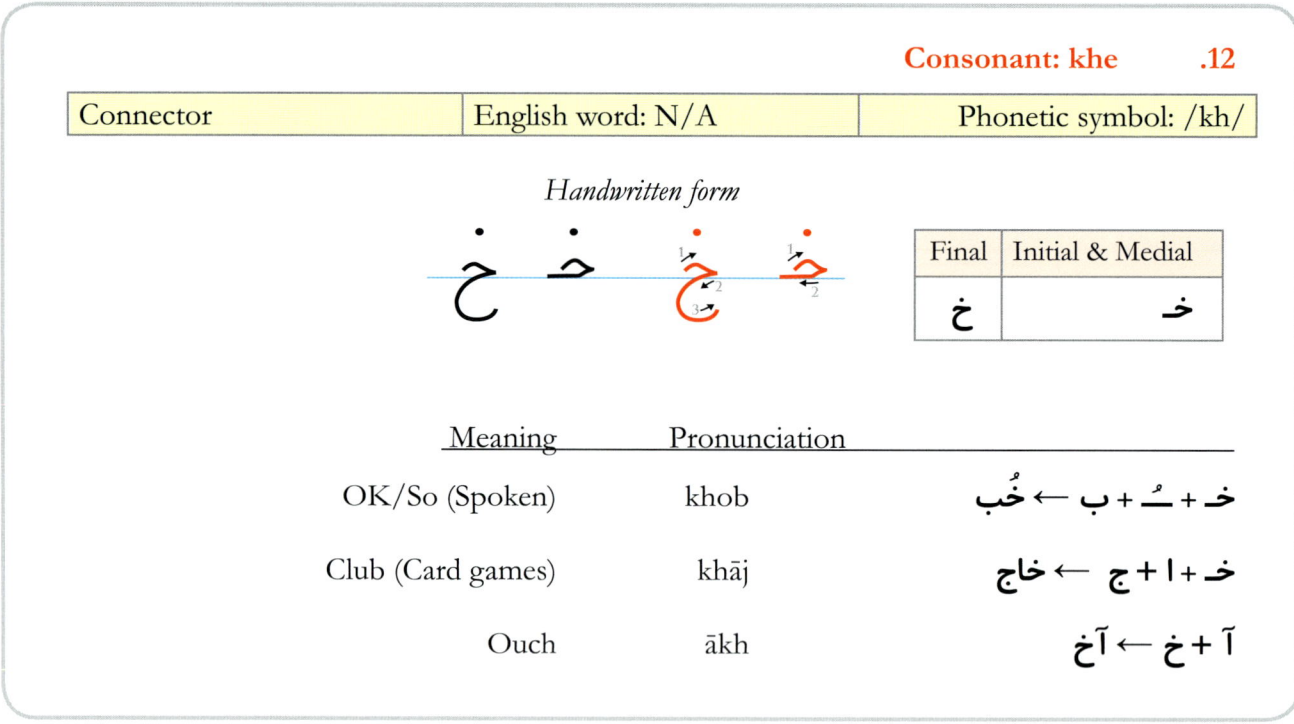

Consonant: khe   12.

Connector	English word: N/A	Phonetic symbol: /kh/

Handwritten form

	Final	Initial & Medial
	خ	خ

Meaning	Pronunciation	
OK/So (Spoken)	khob	خُب ← ب + ـُ + خـ
Club (Card games)	khāj	خاج ← ج + ا + خـ
Ouch	ākh	آخ ← خ + آ

Exercise 15: Listen to the audio file and pronounce each word while looking at its spelling. Then write it several times based on the handwritten form. Follow the direction of the arrows.

Dialogue 2 (Informal)	
A. salām.	*Hello.*
B. salām.	*Hello.*
A. chetowri?	*How are you?*
B. khub, mersi, to chi?	*Good, thanks, what about you?*
A. khubam, mamnun.	*I am fine, thanks.*
B. khodāfez.	*Bye.*
A. khodāfez.	*Bye.*

Group II: خـ خ   حـ ح   چـ چ   جـ ج   ثـ ث   پـ پ   تـ ت

Group III

ژ ز	ز	ر	ذ	د	مـ م	نـ ن	Shape
/zh/	/z/	/r/	/z/	/d/	/m/	/n/	Phonetic symbol

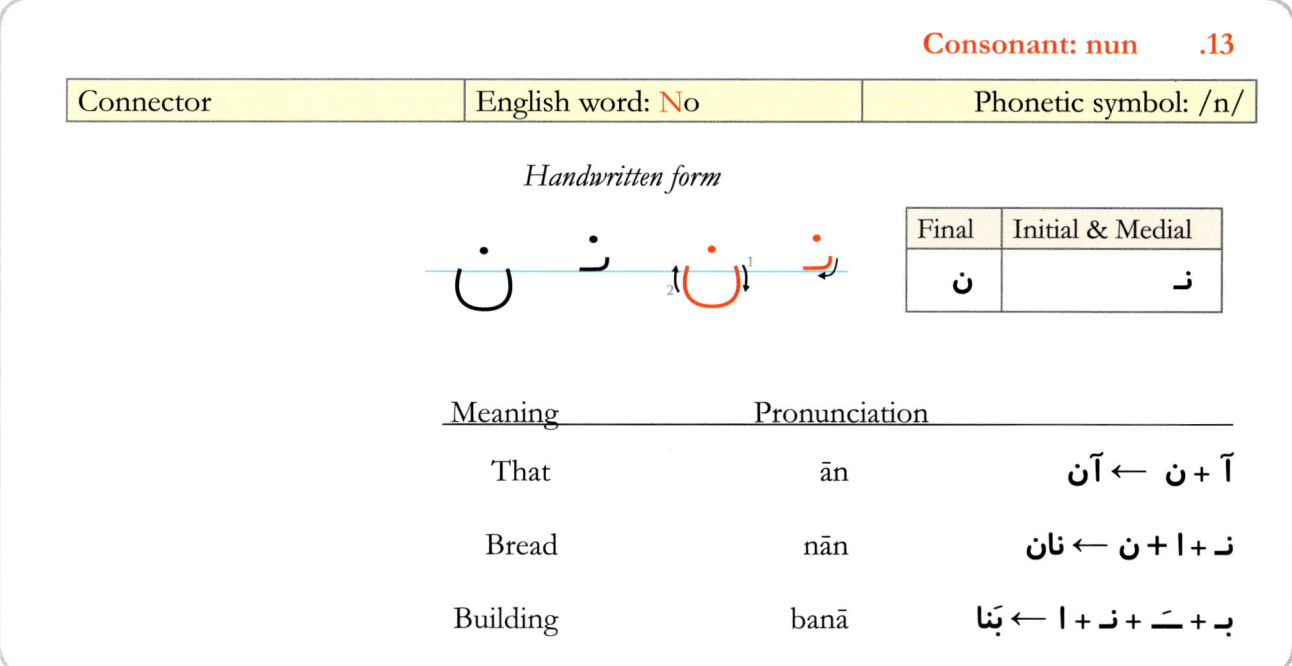

Consonant: nun 13.

Connector	English word: No	Phonetic symbol: /n/

Handwritten form

Final	Initial & Medial
ن	نـ

Meaning	Pronunciation	
That	ān	آ + ن ← آن
Bread	nān	نـ + ا + ن ← نان
Building	banā	بـ + َ + نـ + ا ← بَنا

Exercise 16: Listen to the audio file and pronounce each word while looking at its spelling. Then write it several times based on the handwritten form. Follow the direction of the arrows.

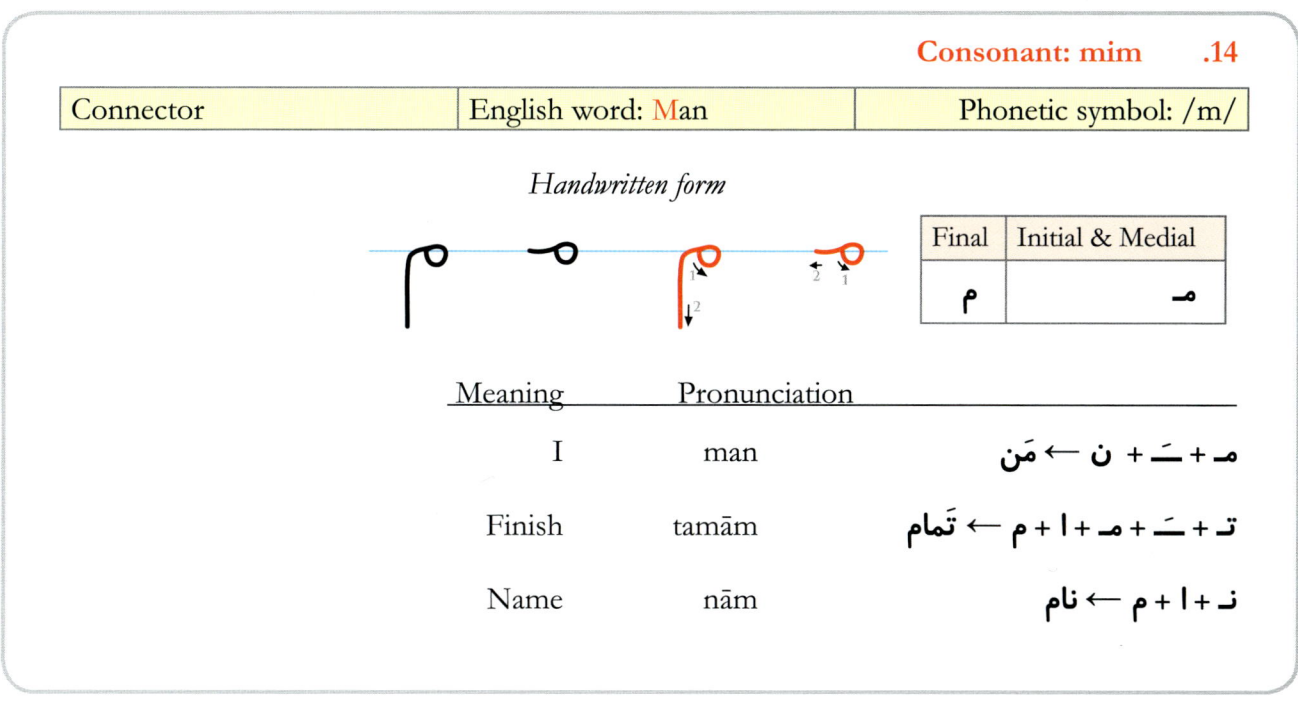

Consonant: mim 14.

Connector	English word: Man	Phonetic symbol: /m/

Handwritten form

Final	Initial & Medial
م	مـ

Meaning	Pronunciation	
I	man	مـ + َ + ن ← مَن
Finish	tamām	تـ + َ + مـ + ا + م ← تَمام
Name	nām	نـ + ا + م ← نام

Group III:	ژ ز	ز	ر	ذ	د	مـ م	نـ ن

Exercise 17: Listen to the audio file and pronounce each word while looking at its spelling. Then write it several times based on the handwritten form. Follow the direction of the arrows.

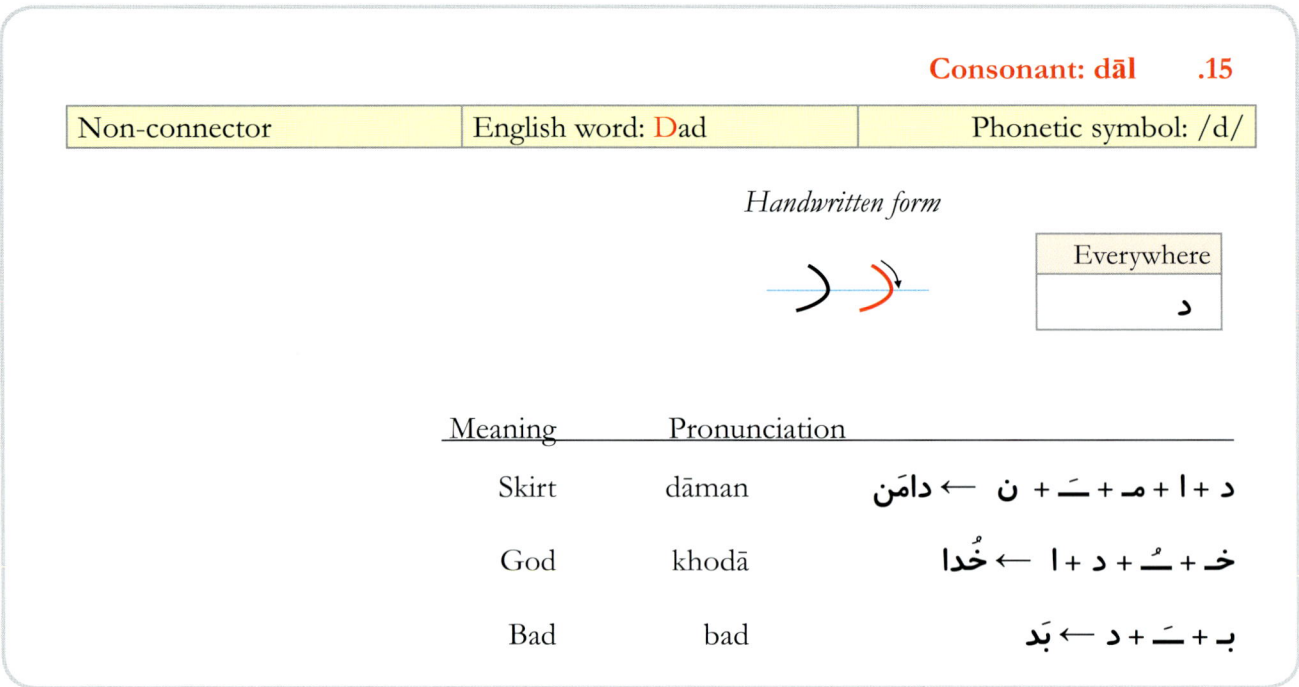

Consonant: dāl .15

Non-connector	English word: Dad	Phonetic symbol: /d/

Handwritten form

Everywhere

د

Meaning	Pronunciation	
Skirt	dāman	د + ا + مــ + ـَـ + ن ← دامَن
God	khodā	خــ + ـُـ + د + ا ← خُدا
Bad	bad	بــ + ـَـ + د ← بَد

Exercise 18: Listen to the audio file and pronounce each word while looking at its spelling. Then write it several times based on the handwritten form. Follow the direction of the arrows.

Consonant: zāl .16

Non-connector	English word: Zoo	Phonetic symbol: /z/

Handwritten form

Everywhere

ذ

Meaning	Pronunciation	
Essence	zāt	ذ + ا + ت ← ذات
	māzā	مــ + ا + ذ + ا ← ماذا
	toz	تــ + ـُـ + ذ ← تُذ

Group III:	ژ	ز	ر	ذ	د	ـم م	نـ ن

Exercise 19: Listen to the audio file and pronounce each word while looking at its spelling. Then write it several times based on the handwritten form. Follow the direction of the arrows.

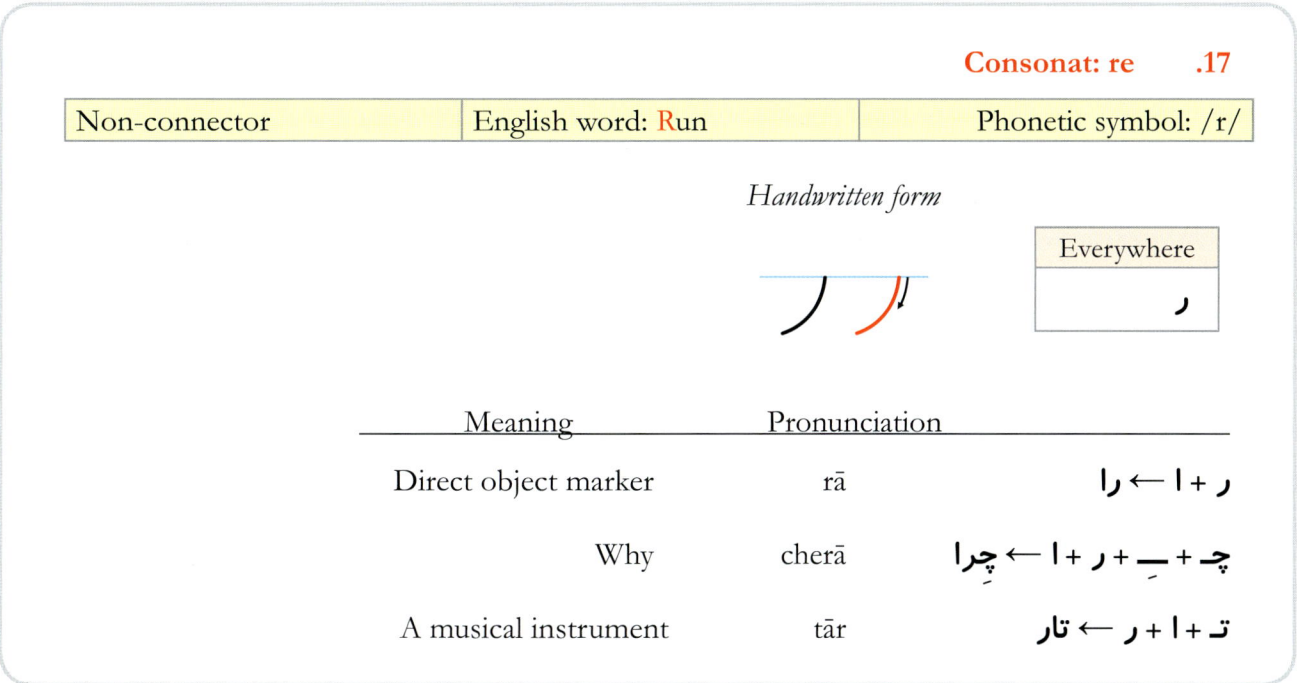

Consonat: re   .17

Non-connector	English word: Run	Phonetic symbol: /r/

Handwritten form

Everywhere

ر

Meaning	Pronunciation	
Direct object marker	rā	را ← ا + ر
Why	cherā	چرا ← ا + ر + ــِ + چـ
A musical instrument	tār	تار ← ر + ا + تـ

Exercise 20: Listen to the audio file and pronounce each word while looking at its spelling. Then write it several times based on the handwritten form. Follow the direction of the arrows.

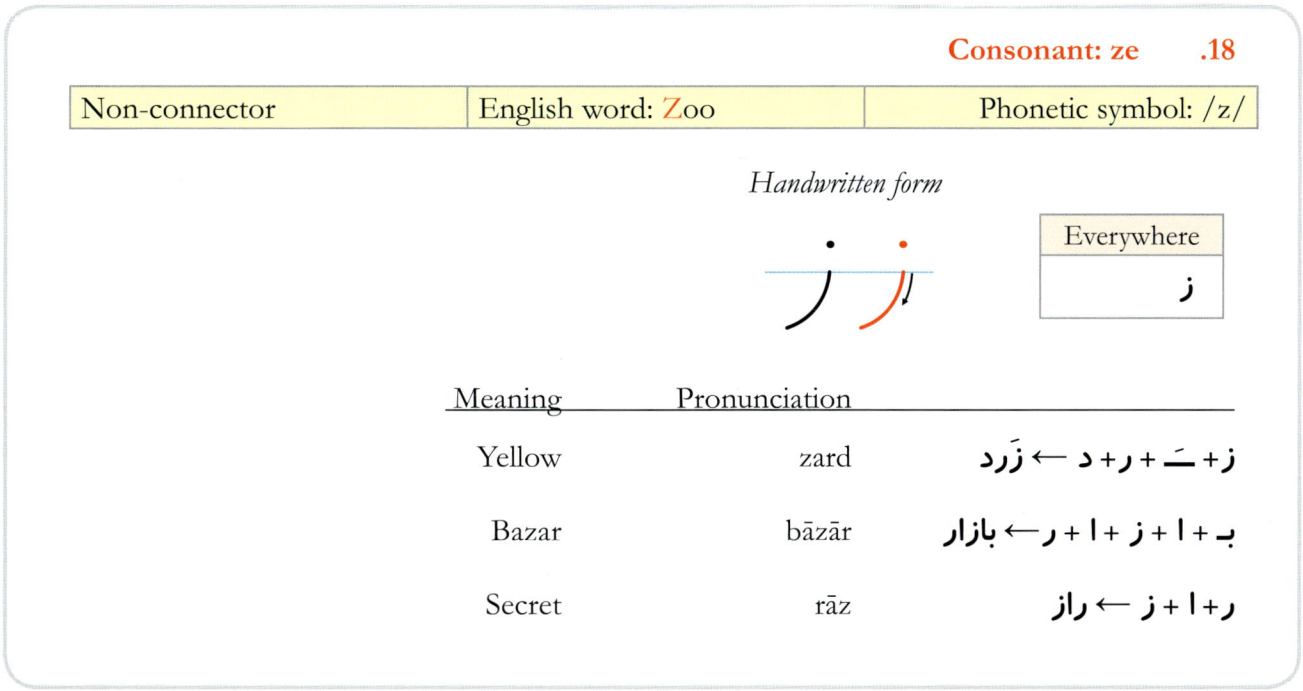

Consonant: ze   .18

Non-connector	English word: Zoo	Phonetic symbol: /z/

Handwritten form

Everywhere

ز

Meaning	Pronunciation	
Yellow	zard	زَرد ← د + ر + ـَ + ز
Bazar	bāzār	بازار ← ر + ا + ز + ا + بـ
Secret	rāz	راز ← ز + ا + ر

Exercise 21: Listen to the audio file and pronounce each word while looking at its spelling. Then write it several times based on the handwritten form. Follow the direction of the arrows.

Group III:	ژ	ز	ر	ذ	د	مـ م	نـ ن

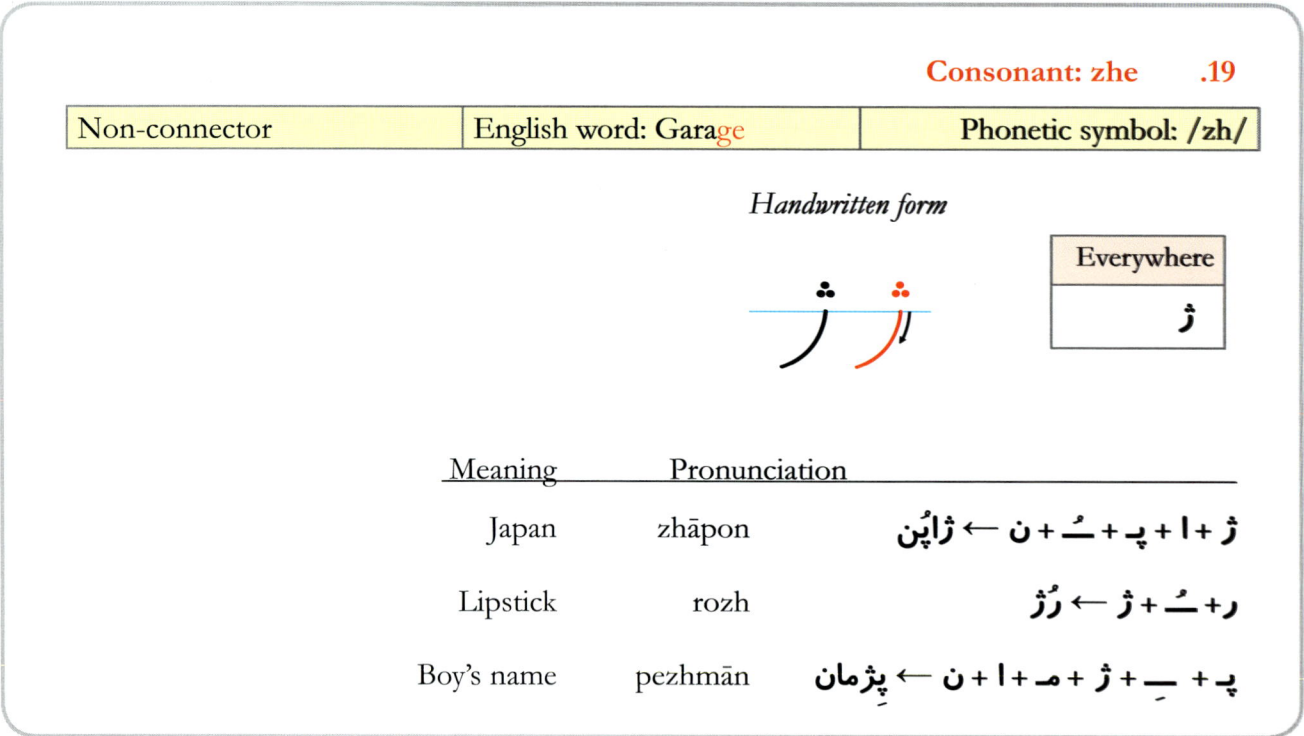

Exercise 22: Listen to the audio file and pronounce each word while looking at its spelling. Then write it several times based on the handwritten form. Follow the direction of the arrows.

Dialogue 3 (Informal)	
A. salām.	*Hello.*
B. sobh be kheir.	*Good morning.*
A. hālet khube?	*Are you doing fine?*
B. āreh, khubam mersi, to chi?	*Yes, I am fine, and you?*
A. bad nistam.	*I'm not bad.*
B. khodāfez.	*Bye.*
A. khodāfez.	*Bye.*

Group III: ژ ز ر ذ د م ـم ن ـن

Group IV

Shape	سـ س	شـ ش	و	او و	ـف ف	ـق ق
Phonetic symbol	/s/	/sh/	/v/	/u/	/f/	/gh/

20. **Consonant: sin**

Connector	English word: Sam	Phonetic symbol: /s/

Handwritten form

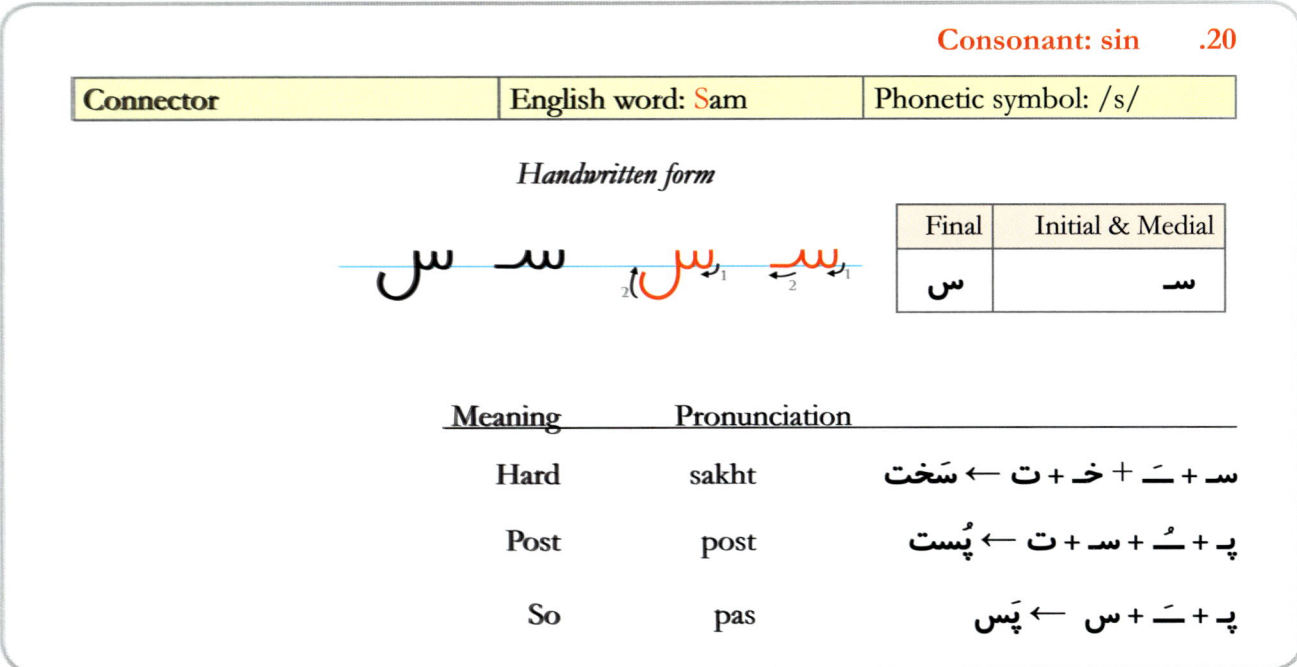

	Final	Initial & Medial
	س	سـ

Meaning	Pronunciation	
Hard	sakht	سَخت ← ت + خـ + ـَ + سـ
Post	post	پُست ← ت + سـ + ُ + پـ
So	pas	پَس ← س + ـَ + پـ

Exercise 23: Listen to the audio file and pronounce each word while looking at its spelling. Then write it several times based on the handwritten form. Follow the direction of the arrows.

21. **Consonat: shin**

Connector	English word: Shut	Phonetic symbol: /sh/

Handwritten form

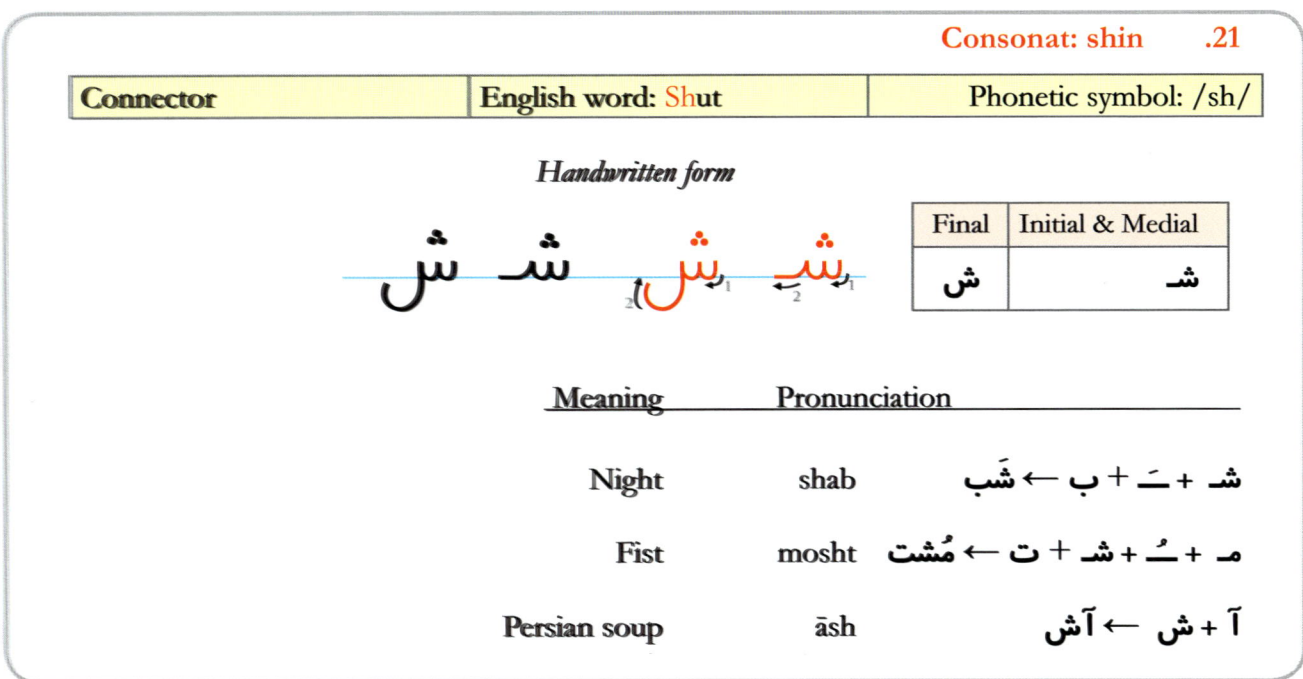

	Final	Initial & Medial
	ش	شـ

Meaning	Pronunciation	
Night	shab	شَب ← ب + ـَ + شـ
Fist	mosht	مُشت ← ت + ش + ُ + مـ
Persian soup	āsh	آش ← ش + آ

Exercise 24: Listen to the audio file and pronounce each word while looking at its spelling. Then write it several times based on the handwritten form. Follow the direction of the arrows.

Group IV:	سـ س	شـ ش	و	او و	ـف ف	ـق ق

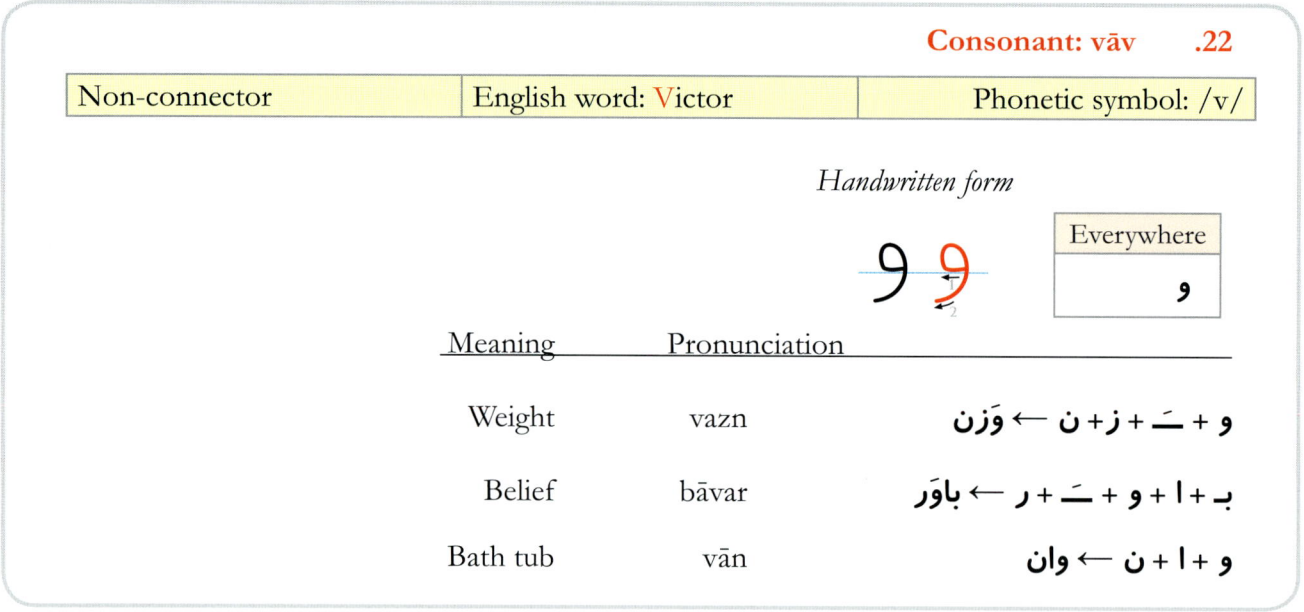

Consonant: vāv .22

Non-connector	English word: Victor	Phonetic symbol: /v/

Handwritten form

	Everywhere
	و

Meaning	Pronunciation	
Weight	vazn	و + ـَ + ز + ن ← وَزن
Belief	bāvar	بـ + ا + و + ـَ + ر ← باوَر
Bath tub	vān	و + ا + ن ← وان

Exercise 25: Listen to the audio file and pronounce each word while looking at its spelling. Then write it several times based on the handwritten form. Follow the direction of the arrows.

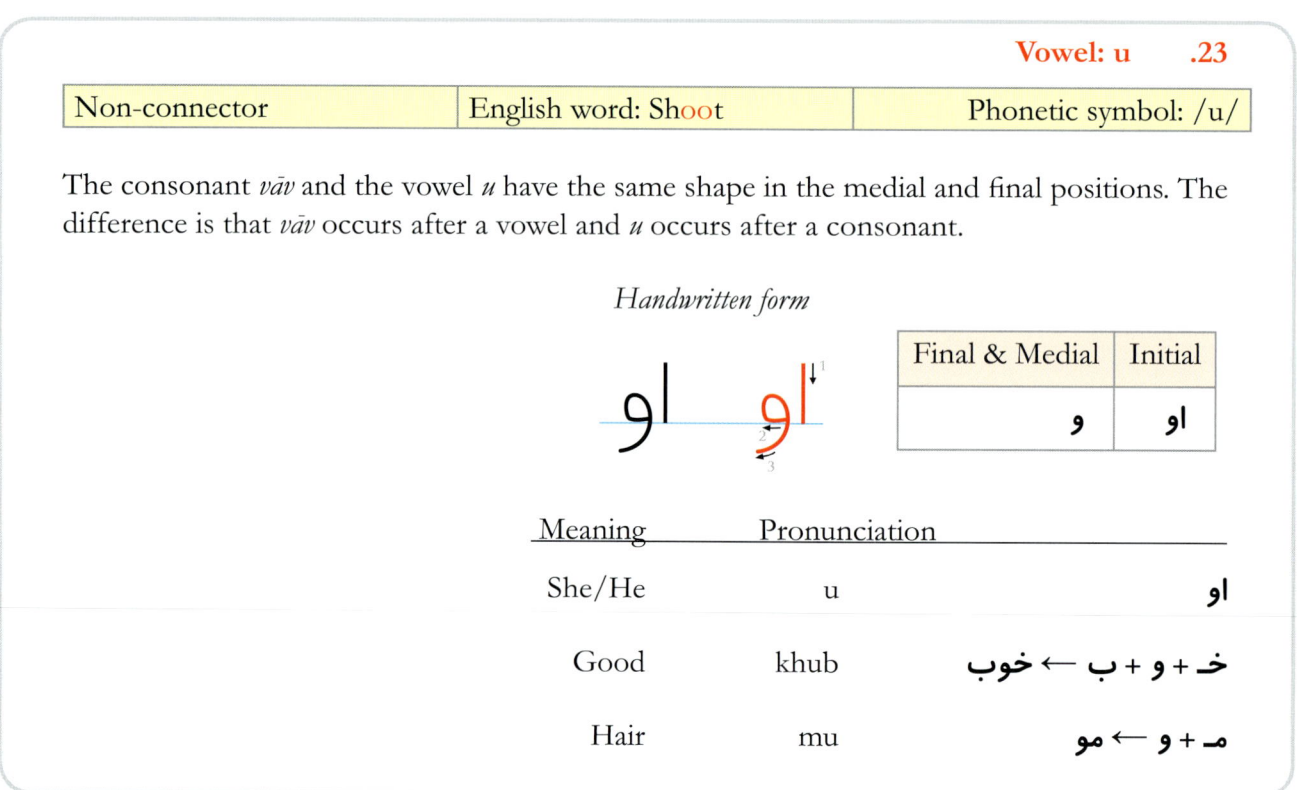

Vowel: u .23

Non-connector	English word: Shoot	Phonetic symbol: /u/

The consonant *vāv* and the vowel *u* have the same shape in the medial and final positions. The difference is that *vāv* occurs after a vowel and *u* occurs after a consonant.

Handwritten form

Final & Medial	Initial
و	او

Meaning	Pronunciation	
She/He	u	او
Good	khub	خـ + و + ب ← خوب
Hair	mu	مـ + و ← مو

Exercise 26: Listen to the audio file and pronounce each word while looking at its spelling. Then write it several times based on the handwritten form. Follow the direction of the arrows.

Exceptions: *vāv* is pronounced as /o/ in تو (*you*) and دو (*two*).

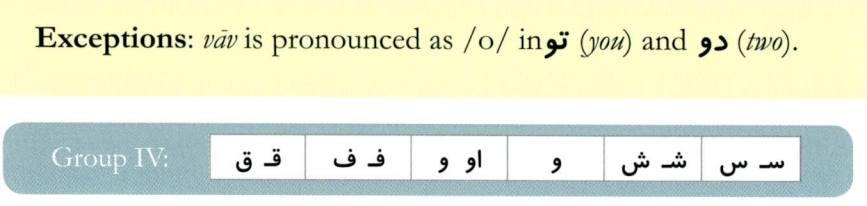

Group IV:	سـ س	شـ ش	و	او و	فـ ف	قـ ق

Consonant: fe   24.

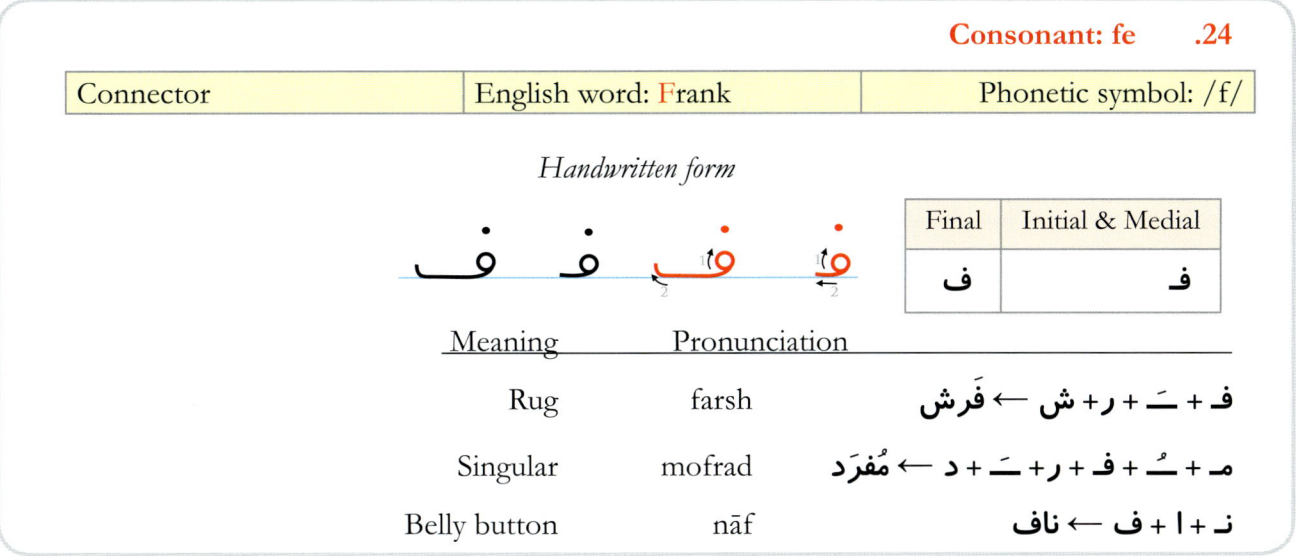

| Connector | English word: **F**rank | Phonetic symbol: /f/ |

Handwritten form

Final	Initial & Medial
ف	ف

Meaning	Pronunciation	
Rug	farsh	ف + ـَ + ر + ش ← فَرش
Singular	mofrad	مـ + ـُ + ف + ـَ + ر + د ← مُفرَد
Belly button	nāf	نـ + ا + ف ← ناف

Exercise 27: Listen to the audio file and pronounce each word while looking at its spelling. Then write it several times based on the handwritten form. Follow the direction of the arrows.

Consonant: ghāf (or qāf)   25.

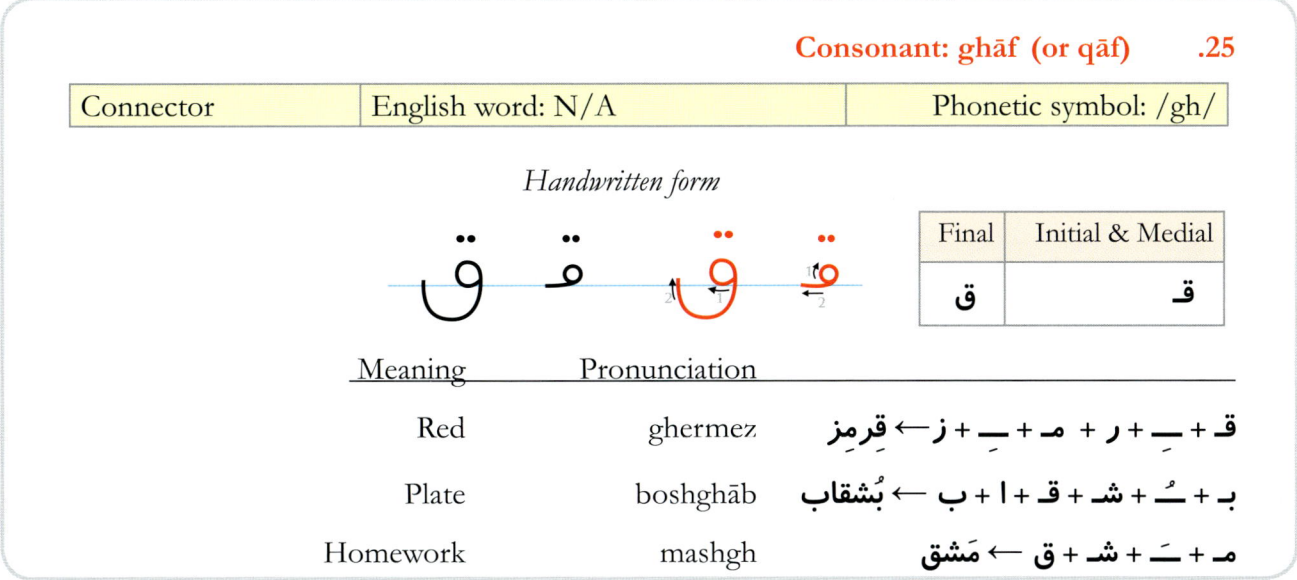

| Connector | English word: N/A | Phonetic symbol: /gh/ |

Handwritten form

Final	Initial & Medial
ق	ق

Meaning	Pronunciation	
Red	ghermez	ق + ـِ + ر + مـ + ـِ + ز ← قِرمِز
Plate	boshghāb	بـ + ـُ + شـ + ق + ا + ب ← بُشقاب
Homework	mashgh	مـ + ـَ + شـ + ق ← مَشق

Exercise 28: Listen to the audio file and pronounce each word while looking at its spelling. Then write it several times based on the handwritten form. Follow the direction of the arrows.

Dialogue 4 (Formal)	
A. salām āghā.	*Hello Sir.*
B. salām khānum.	*Hello Madam.*
A. esm-e man Nushine. esm-e shomā chiye?	*My name is Nushin. What is your name?*
B. esm-e man Johne.	*My name is John.*
A. khoshvaghtam!	*Good to meet you!*
B. khoshvaghtam!	*Good to meet you!*

In the above dialogue, some people use the word "**khoshbakht-am**" instead of "**khoshvaght-am**".

Group IV: س ـس ش ـش و او و ف ـف ق ـق

45

Group V

Shape	صد ص	ض ـض	ط	ظ	یـ ی	ایـ یـ ی
Phonetic symbol	/s/	/z/	/t/	/z/	/y/	/i/

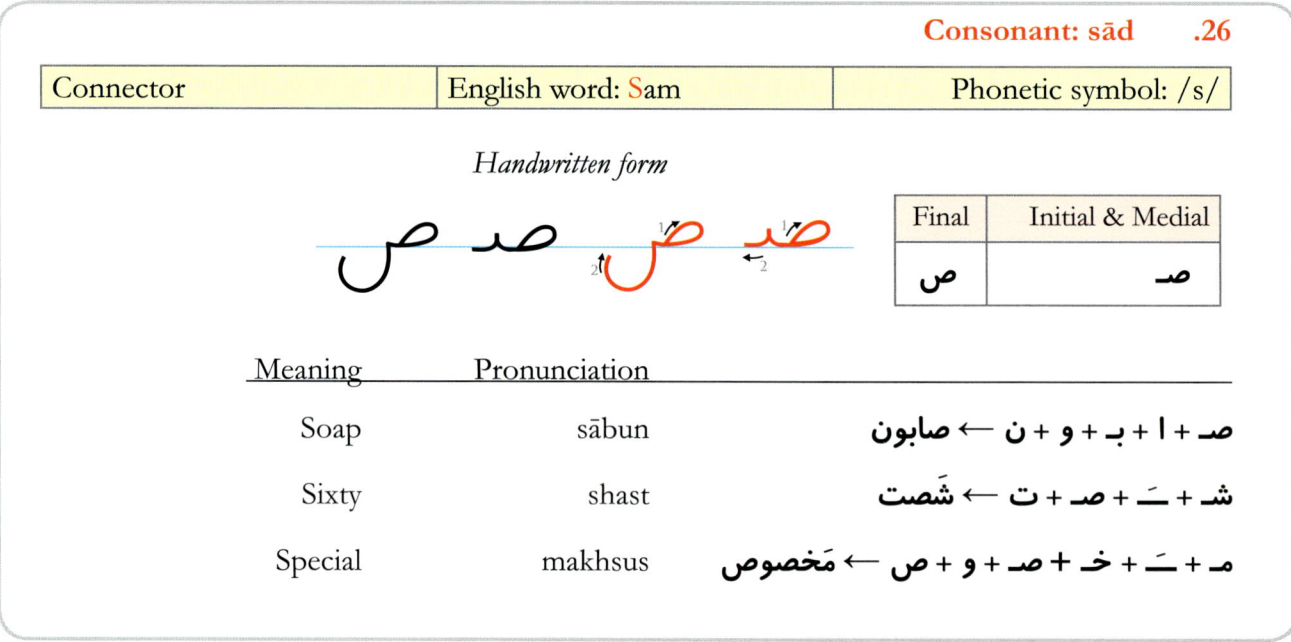

26. **Consonant: sād**

Connector	English word: Sam	Phonetic symbol: /s/

Handwritten form

Final	Initial & Medial
ص	صـ

Meaning	Pronunciation	
Soap	sābun	صـ + ا + بـ + و + ن ← صابون
Sixty	shast	شـ + ◌َ + صـ + ت ← شَصت
Special	makhsus	مـ + ◌َ + خـ + صـ + و + ص ← مَخصوص

Exercise 29: Listen to the audio file and pronounce each word while looking at its spelling. Then write it several times based on the handwritten form. Follow the direction of the arrows.

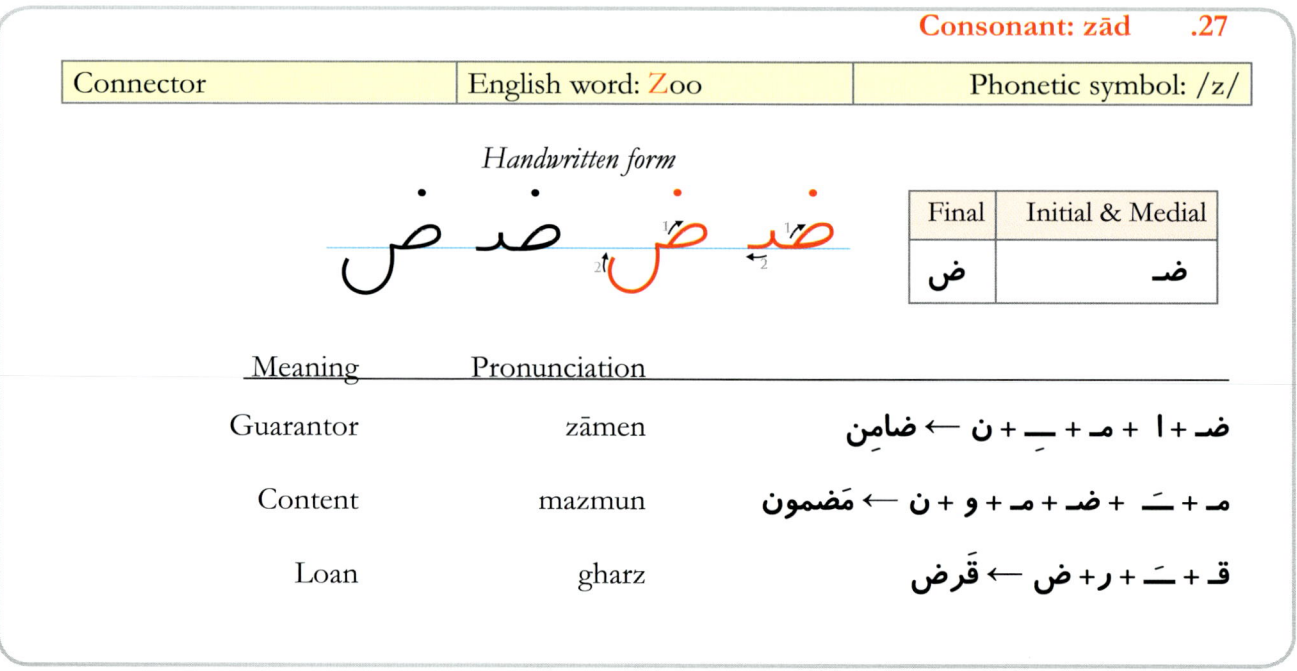

27. **Consonant: zād**

Connector	English word: Zoo	Phonetic symbol: /z/

Handwritten form

Final	Initial & Medial
ض	ضـ

Meaning	Pronunciation	
Guarantor	zāmen	ضـ + ا + مـ + ِ + ن ← ضامِن
Content	mazmun	مـ + ◌َ + ضـ + مـ + و + ن ← مَضمون
Loan	gharz	قـ + ◌َ + ر + ض ← قَرض

Exercise 30: Listen to the audio file and pronounce each word while looking at its spelling. Then write it several times based on the handwritten form. Follow the direction of the arrows.

Group V:	صد ص	ض ـض	ط	ظ	یـ ی	ایـ یـ ی

46

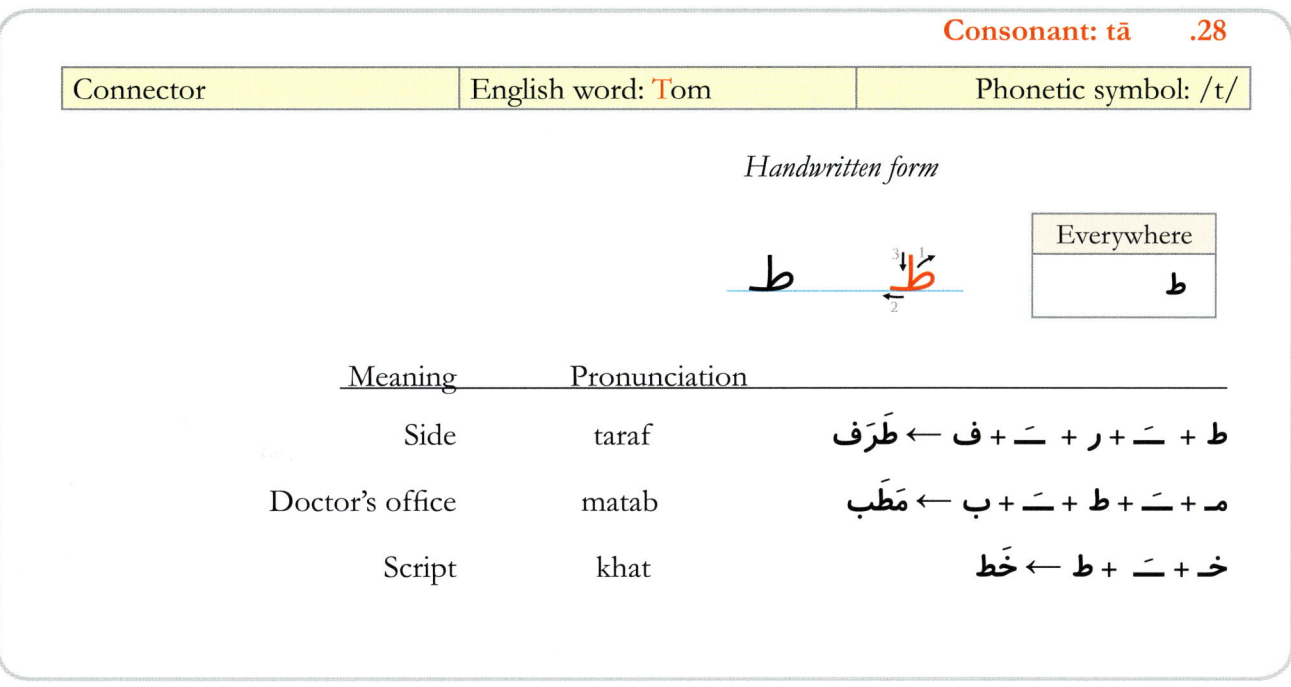

Exercise 31: Listen to the audio file and pronounce each word while looking at its spelling. Then write it several times based on the handwritten form. Follow the direction of the arrows.

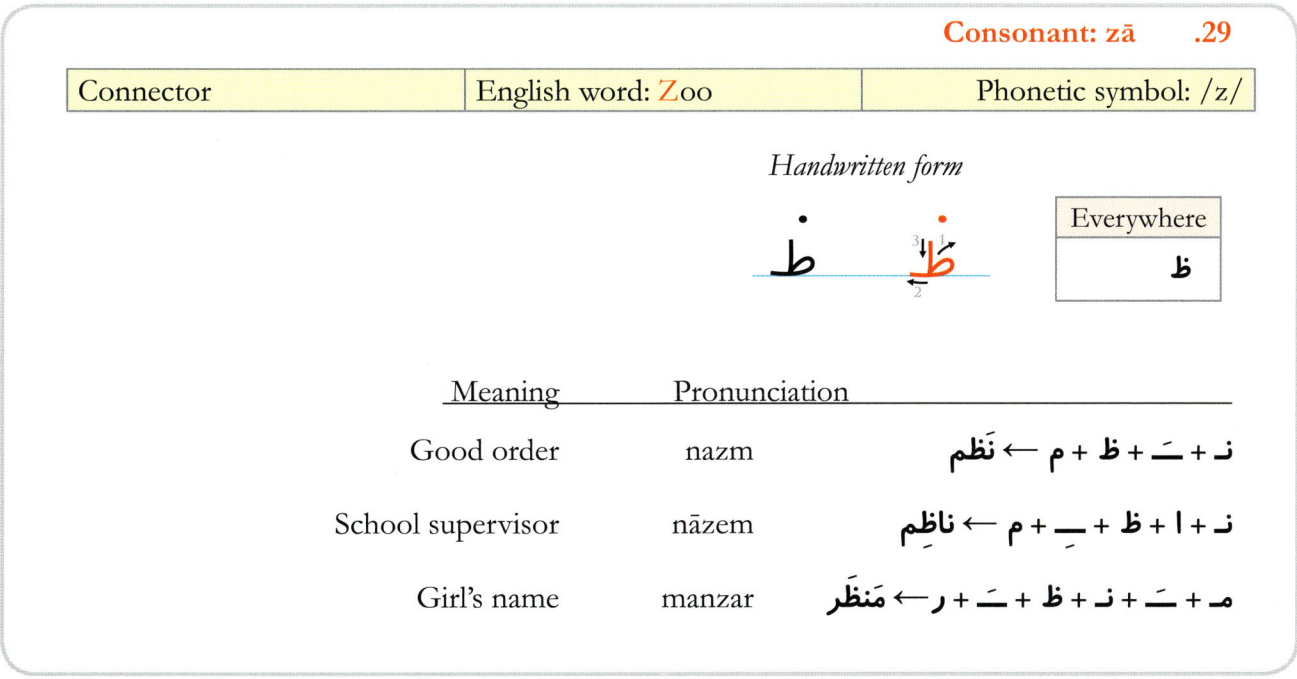

Exercise 32: Listen to the audio file and pronounce each word while looking at its spelling. Then write it several times based on the handwritten form. Follow the direction of the arrows.

Group V: ص ص | ض ض | ط | ظ | ی ی | ایـ یـ ی

47

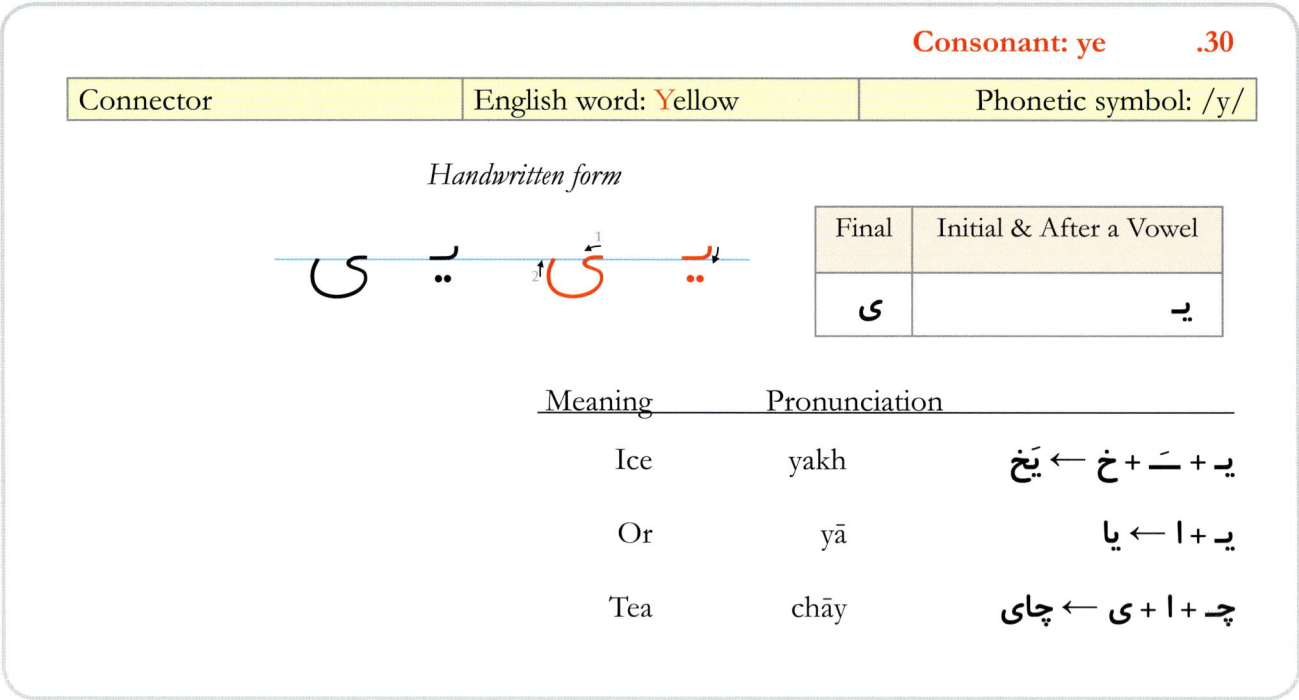

Consonant: ye .30

| Connector | English word: Yellow | Phonetic symbol: /y/ |

Handwritten form

Final	Initial & After a Vowel
ی	یـ

Meaning	Pronunciation	
Ice	yakh	یـ + ـَ + خ ← یَخ
Or	yā	یـ + ا ← یا
Tea	chāy	چـ + ا + ی ← چای

Exercise 33: Listen to the audio file and pronounce each word while looking at its spelling. Then write it several times based on the handwritten form. Follow the direction of the arrows.

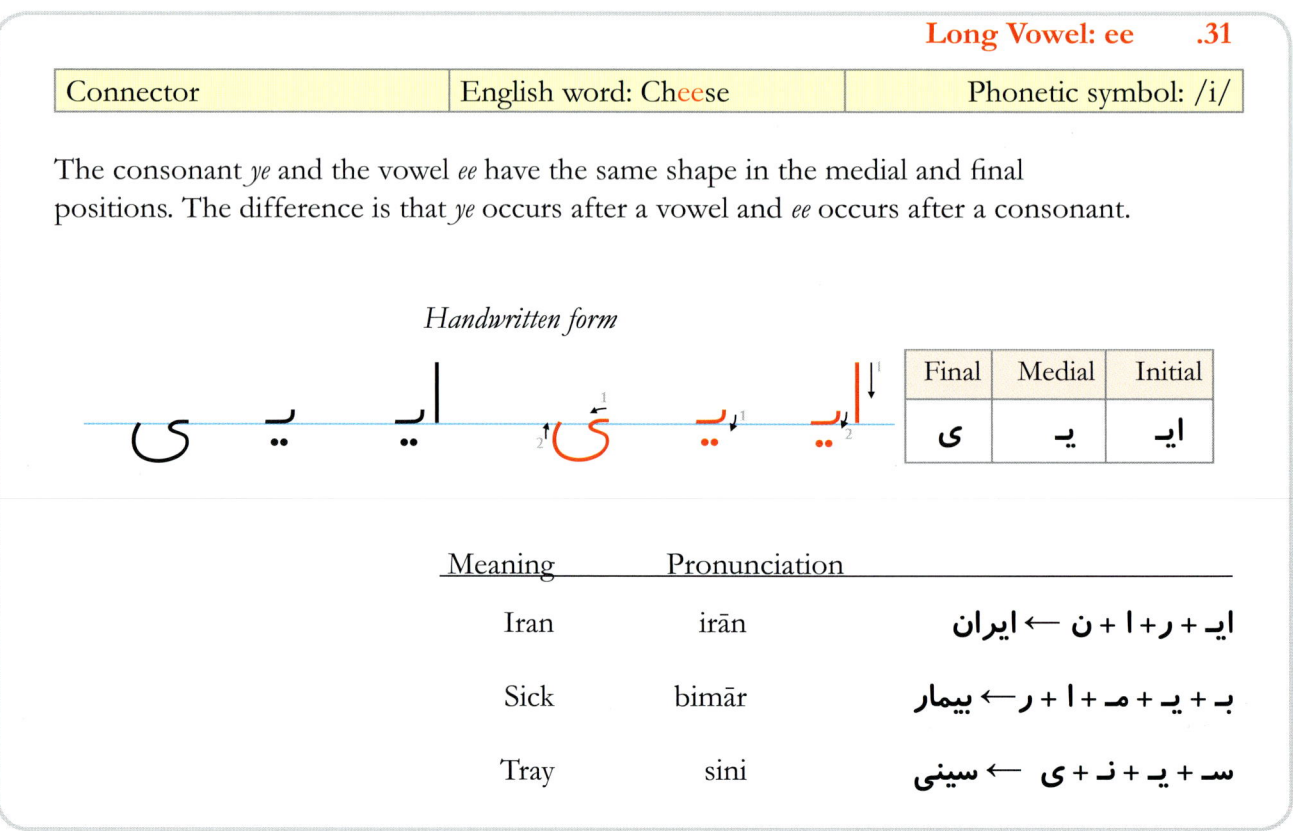

Long Vowel: ee .31

| Connector | English word: Cheese | Phonetic symbol: /i/ |

The consonant *ye* and the vowel *ee* have the same shape in the medial and final positions. The difference is that *ye* occurs after a vowel and *ee* occurs after a consonant.

Handwritten form

Final	Medial	Initial
ی	یـ	ایـ

Meaning	Pronunciation	
Iran	irān	ایـ + ر + ا + ن ← ایران
Sick	bimār	بـ + یـ + مـ + ا + ر ← بیمار
Tray	sini	سـ + یـ + نـ + ی ← سینی

| Group V: | صـ ص | ضـ ض | ط | ظ | یـ ی | ای یـ ی |

48

Exercise 34: Listen to the audio file and pronounce each word while looking at its spelling. Then write it several times based on the handwritten form. Follow the direction of the arrows.

Dialogue 5 (Formal)	
A. sobh be kheir.	*Good morning.*
B. sobh be kheir.	*Good morning.*
A. hāl-e shomā chetowre?	*How are you doing?*
B. khubam, mersi. shomā chetowrin?	*I am fine thanks. How are you?*
A. bad nistam.	*I am not bad.*
B. felan khodāfez.	*Bye for now.*
A. khodāfez.	*Bye.*

Group VI

غ ـغ ـفـ غ	ع ـع ـعـ ع	لـ ل	گ گ	ک ک	Shape
/gh/	/ʔ/	/l/	/g/	/k/	Phonetic symbol

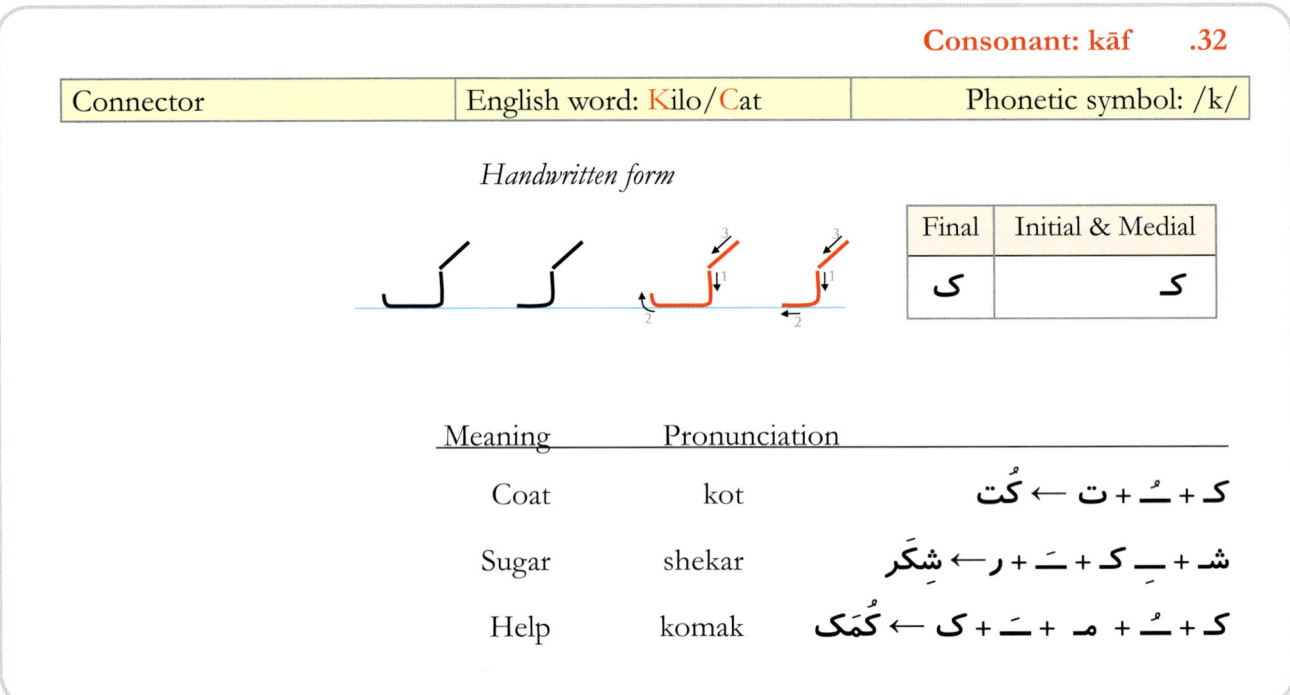

Consonant: kāf   32.

Connector		English word: Kilo/Cat		Phonetic symbol: /k/

Handwritten form

	Final	Initial & Medial
	ک	ک

Meaning	Pronunciation	
Coat	kot	کُت ← ت + ـُ + ک
Sugar	shekar	شِکَر ← ر + ـَ + ک + ـِ + شـ
Help	komak	کُمَک ← ک + ـَ + مـ + ـُ + ک

Exercise 35: Listen to the audio file and pronounce each word while looking at its spelling. Then write it several times based on the handwritten form. Follow the direction of the arrows.

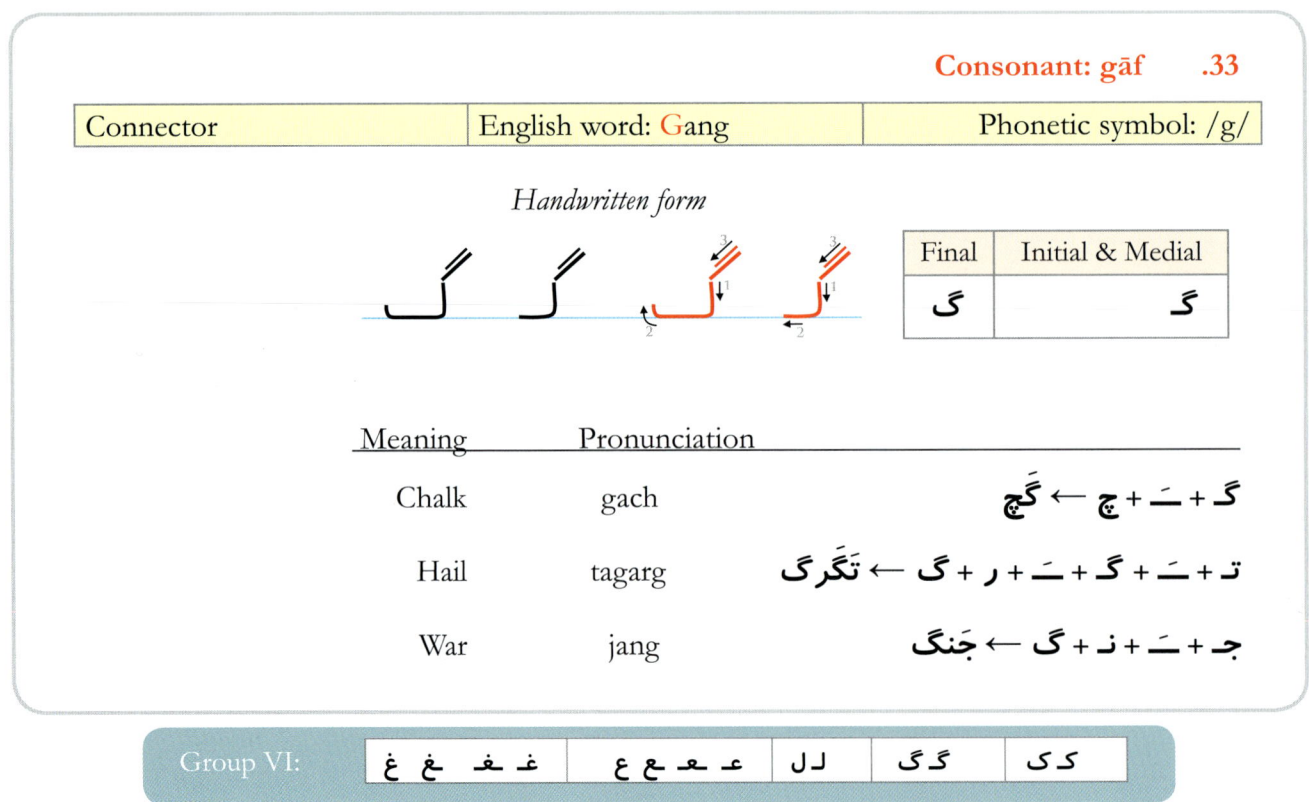

Consonant: gāf   33.

Connector		English word: Gang		Phonetic symbol: /g/

Handwritten form

	Final	Initial & Medial
	گ	گ

Meaning	Pronunciation	
Chalk	gach	گَچ ← چ + ـَ + گ
Hail	tagarg	تَگَرگ ← گ + ـَ + ر + ـَ + گ + ـَ + تـ
War	jang	جَنگ ← گ + ن + ـَ + جـ

Group VI:	غ ـغ ـفـ غ	ع ـع ـعـ ع	لـ ل	گ گ	ک ک

Exercise 36: Listen to the audio file and pronounce each word while looking at its spelling. Then write it several times based on the handwritten form. Follow the direction of the arrows.

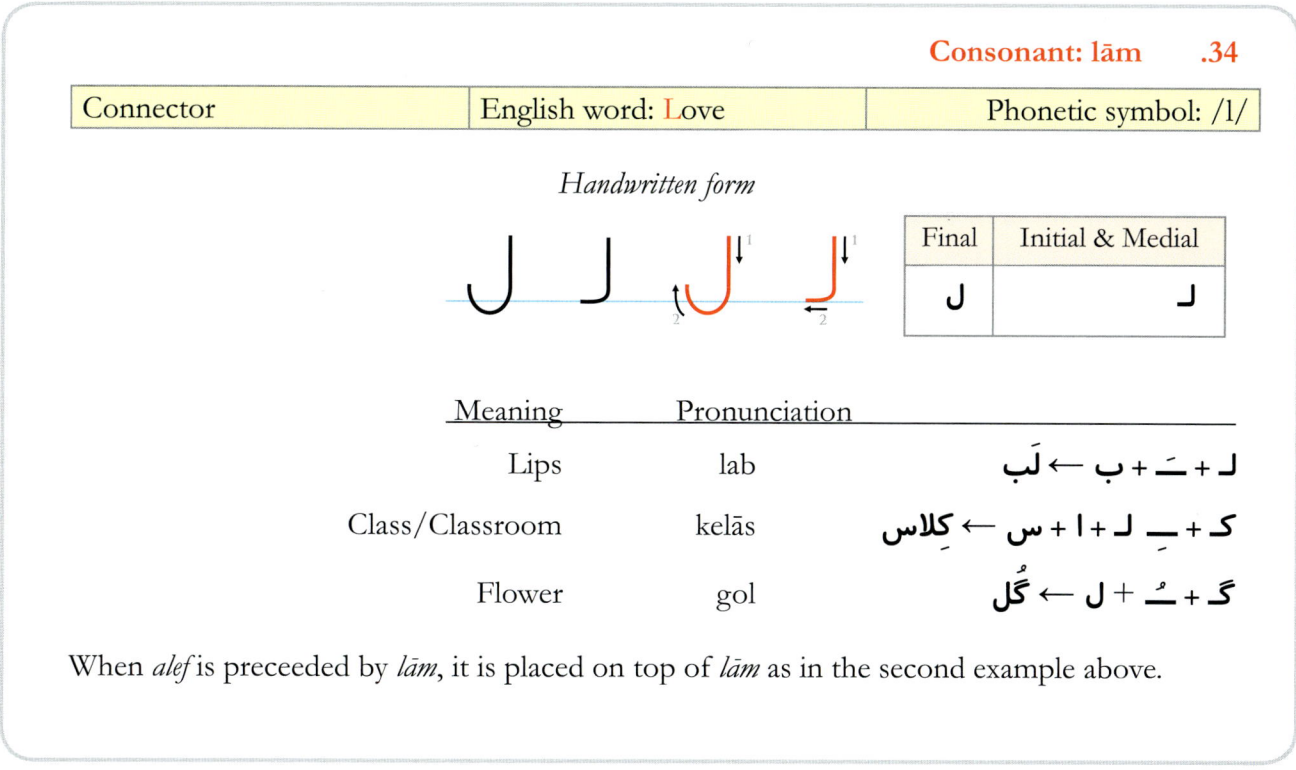

Consonant: lām   .34

| Connector | English word: Love | Phonetic symbol: /l/ |

Handwritten form

Final	Initial & Medial
ل	ـل

Meaning	Pronunciation	
Lips	lab	لـ + ـَ + ب ← لَب
Class/Classroom	kelās	ک + ـِ + لـ + ا + س ← کِلاس
Flower	gol	گ + ـُ + ل ← گُل

When *alef* is preceded by *lām*, it is placed on top of *lām* as in the second example above.

Exercise 37: Listen to the audio file and pronounce each word while looking at its spelling. Then write it several times based on the handwritten form. Follow the direction of the arrows.

Consonant: eyn   .35

| Connector | English word: Uh-oh (Glottal stop) | Phonetic symbol: /ʔ/ |

Final after Non-connector	Final after Connector	Medial	Initial or after Non-connector
ع	ـع	ـعـ	عـ

Handwritten form

Meaning	Pronunciation	
Paternal uncle	ʔamu	عـ + ـَ + مـ + و ← عَمو
Meaning	maʔni	مـ + ـَ + ـعـ + ن + ی ← مَعنی
Candle	shamʔ	شـ + ـَ + مـ + ع ← شَمع
Radius	shoʔāʔ	شـ + ـُ + ـعـ + ا + ع ← شُعاع

| Group VI: | غ ـغ ـغـ غـ | ع ـع ـعـ عـ | ل ـل | گ ـگ | ک ـک |

51

Exercise 38: Listen to the audio file and pronounce each word while looking at its spelling. Then write it several times based on the handwritten form. Follow the direction of the arrows.

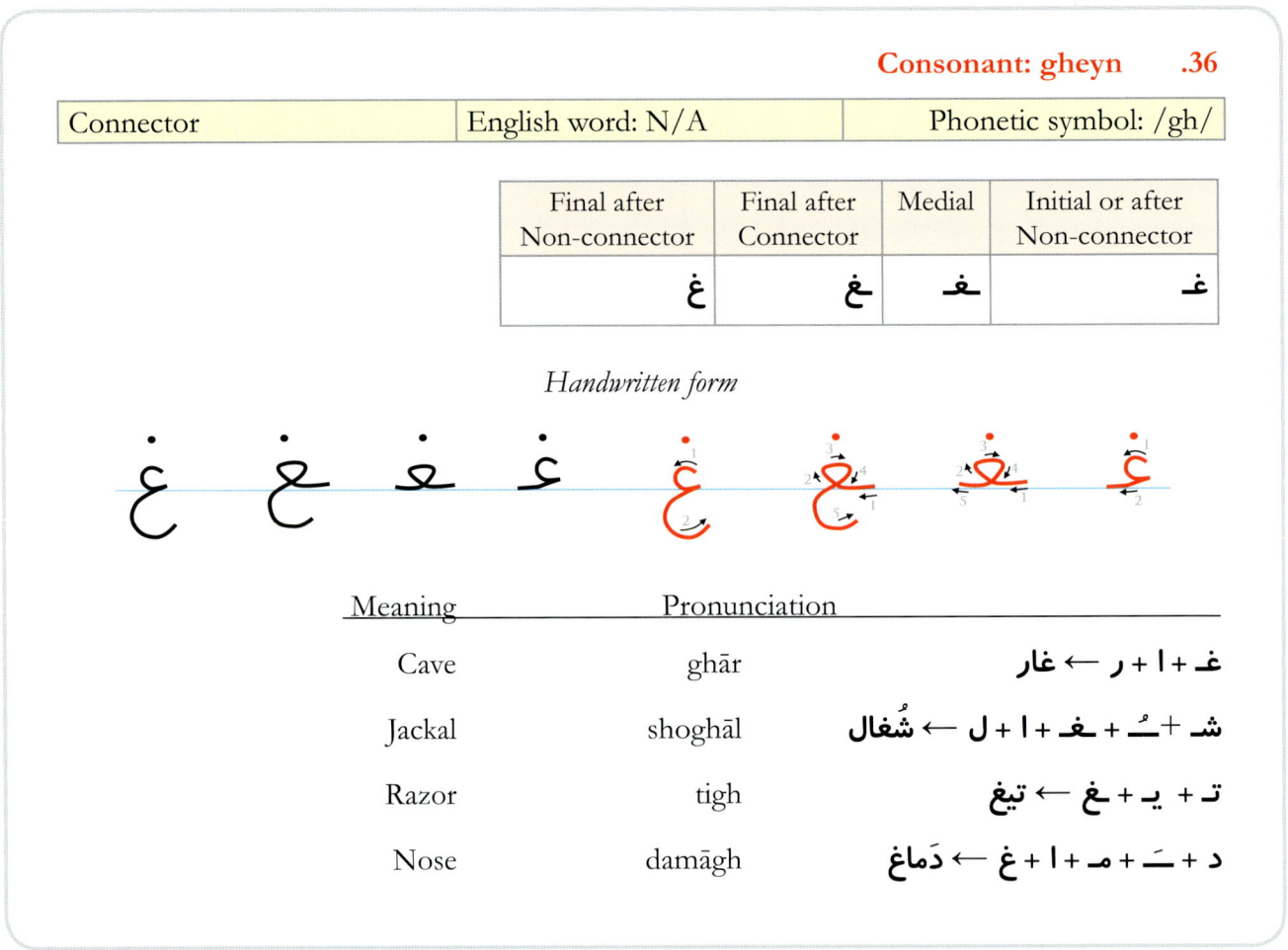

		Consonant: gheyn	.36

Connector	English word: N/A	Phonetic symbol: /gh/

Final after Non-connector	Final after Connector	Medial	Initial or after Non-connector
غ	ـغ	ـغـ	غـ

Handwritten form

Meaning	Pronunciation	
Cave	ghār	غار ← ر + ا + غـ
Jackal	shoghāl	شُغال ← ل + ا + ـغـ + ـُ + شـ
Razor	tigh	تیغ ← غ + یـ + تـ
Nose	damāgh	دَماغ ← غ + ا + ـمـ + ـَ + د

Exercise 39: Listen to the audio file and pronounce each word while looking at its spelling. Then write it several times based on the handwritten form. Follow the direction of the arrows.

Dialogue 6 (Formal)	
A. asr be kheir.	*Good afternoon.*
B. asr be kheir.	*Good afternoon.*
A. hāl-e shomā chetowre?	*How are you doing?*
B. khubam mersi, shomā chetowr?	*I'm fine thanks, how about you?*
A. kheili khub, mersi.	*Very well, thanks.*
B. shomā irāni hastin?	*Are you Iranian?*
A. na, man āmrikāyiam.	*No, I am American.*

Group VI:	غ ـغ ـغـ غـ	ع ـع ـعـ عـ	ل ل	گ گ	ک ک

Group VII

							Shape
ء ئ ؤ أ	ـً	ـّ	و	ه ـه	ه ـه	ه ـه ـهـ	
/ʔ/	/an/	-	-	/e/	/h/		Phonetic symbol

Consonant: he (do cheshm) **.37**

Connector	English word: Ham	Phonetic symbol: /h/

Final after Non-connector	Final after Connector	Medial	Initial or after Non-connector
ه	ـه	ـهـ	هـ

Handwritten form

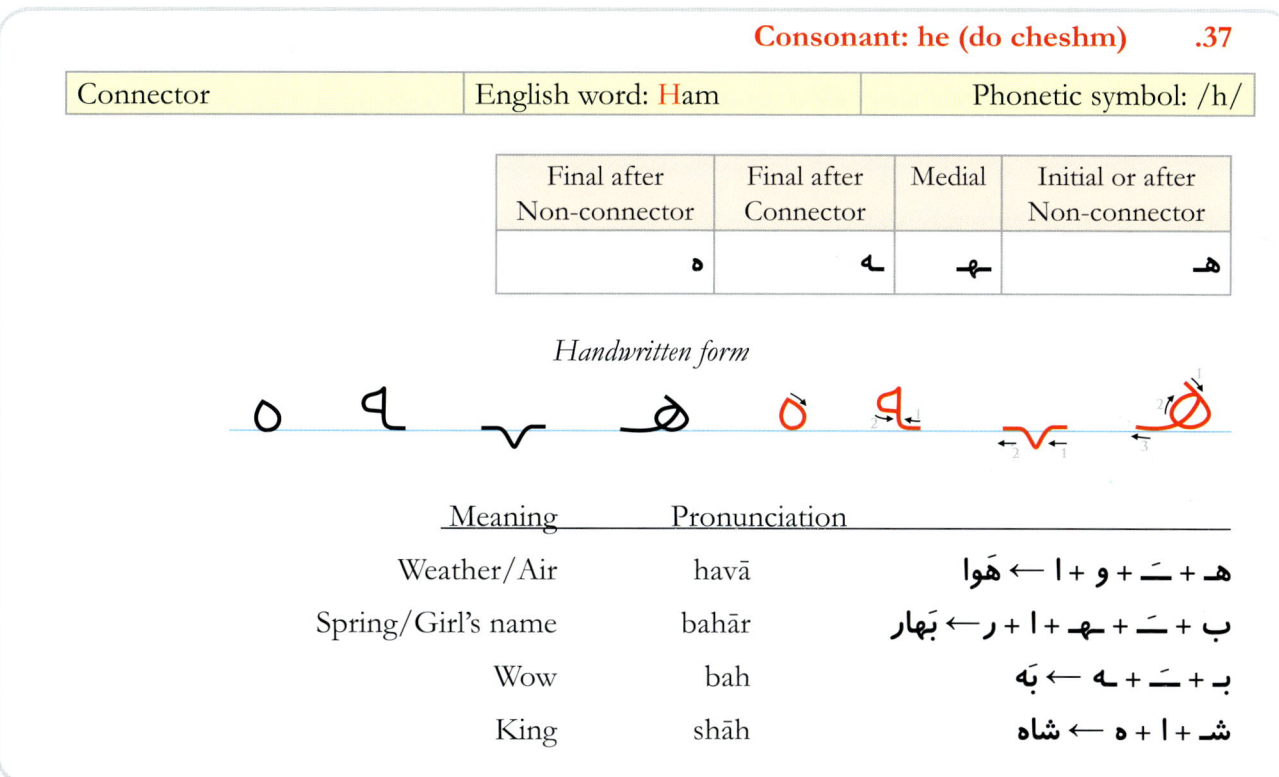

Meaning	Pronunciation	
Weather/Air	havā	هـ + ـَ + و + ا ← هَوا
Spring/Girl's name	bahār	ب + ـَ + ـهـ + ـَ + ا + ر ← بَهار
Wow	bah	بـ + ـَ + ـه ← بَه
King	shāh	شـ + ا + ه ← شاه

Exercise 40: Listen to the audio file and pronounce each word while looking at its spelling. Then write it several times based on the handwritten form. Follow the direction of the arrows.

Vowel: Unpronounced he **.38**

Non-connector	English/French word: Fiance	Phonetic symbol: /e/

The consonant *he* and the vowel (unpronounced *he*) have the same shape in the final positions. The difference is that the consonant *he* occurs after a vowel and the vowel (unpronounced *he*) occurs after a consonant.

Handwritten form

Final after Non-connector	Final after Connector
ه	ـه

Meaning	Pronunciation	
House	khāne	خـ + ا + نـ + ـه ← خانه
Three	se	سـ + ـه ← سه
Butter	kare	کـ + ـَ + ر + ه ← کَره

Group VI:	غ ـغ ـغـ غـ	غ ـغ ـغـ غـ	ع ـع ـعـ عـ	ل لـ	گ گـ	ک کـ

Exercise 41: Listen to the audio file and pronounce each word while looking at its spelling. Then write it several times based on the handwritten form. Follow the direction of the arrows.

> **Note:** When ـه / ه appears at the end of a word:
> a) If it is preceded by a vowel, it functions as the consonant *he*. Example: ماه
>
> b) If it is preceded by a consonant, it functions as the vowel /e/. Example: خانه
>
> **Exception:**
> نَه (*no*) is an exception to this rule.

Exercise 42: Read the words below. Determine whether the letter *he* represents an /h/ sound (consonant) or an /e/ sound (vowel).

(King) شاه	(Shadow) سایه	(Bottom) تَه
(Quince) بِه	(To) به	(Mountain) کوه

Silent *vāv* .39

Silent *vāv* is spelled but not pronounced. This is similar to the "k" in the English word "know". Silent *vāv* only occurs after *kh* and before /ā/ or /i/.

Handwritten form

و

Everywhere
و

Meaning	Pronunciation	
Sister	khāhar	خـ + و + ا + هـ + ـَ + ر ← خواهَر
Self	khish	خـ + و + یـ + ش ← خویش
To want	khāstan	خـ + و + ا + سـ + تـ + ـَ + ن ← خواستَن

Exercise 43: Listen to the audio file and pronounce each word while looking at its spelling. Then write it several times based on the handwritten form. Follow the direction of the arrows.

Group VI:	غ ـغ ـغـ غـ	ع ـع ـعـ عـ	لل	گگ	کک

ADDITIONAL SYMBOLS

When two identical consonants occur in a row, one is removed and *tashdid* is inserted on top of the remaining consonant. *tashdid* looks like a rounded "w".

Handwritten form

Everywhere
ّ

ﺵ   ﺭﺵ

Meaning	Pronunciation	
First	avval	اَ + و + و + َ + ل ← اَوَّل
Painter	naghghāsh	نـ + َ + ق + ق + ا + ش ← نَقّاش
Baby/Kid/Child	bachche	بـ + َ + چـ + چـ + ه ← بَچّه

Exercise 44: Listen to the audio file and pronounce each word while looking at its spelling. Then write it several times based on the handwritten form. Follow the direction of the arrows.

tanvin comes from Arabic. It produces the sound /an/ and is always placed on top of *alef*. The words that have *tanvin* are mainly adverbs of quality or frequency.

Handwritten form

Everywhere
ـً

Meaning	Pronunciation	
Certainly	hatman	حـ + َ + ت + مـ + اً ← حَتماً
Usually	maʔmulan	مـ + َ + عـ + مـ + و + لـ + اً ← مَعمولاً
Approximately	taghriban	تـ + َ + ق + ر + یـ + بـ + اً ← تَقریباً

Exercise 45: Listen to the audio file and pronounce each word while looking at its spelling. Then write it several times based on the handwritten form. Follow the direction of the arrows.

hamzeh **.42**

It comes from Arabic.   English word: Uh-oh (Glottal stop)   Phonetic symbol: /ʔ/

Final	Medial	On *vāv*	On *alef*
ء	ئـ	ؤ	أ

Handwritten form

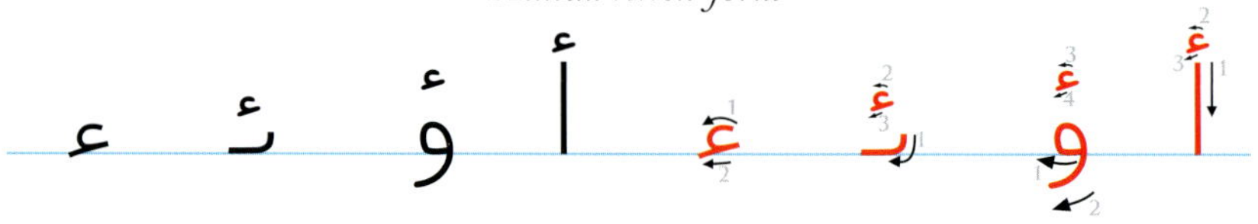

ء   ئ   ؤ   أ   ءِ   ؤِ   وِ   أ

Meaning	Pronunciation	
Vote	raʔi	ر + ـَ + أ + ى ← رَأى
Question	soʔāl	سـ + ـُ + ؤ + ا + ل ← سُؤال
Committee	heyʔat	هـ + ـِ + یـ + ئـ + ـَ + ت ← هِیئَت
Signature	emzaʔ	اِ + مـ + ضـ + ا + ء ← اِمضاء

Exercise 46: Listen to the audio file and pronounce each word while looking at its spelling. Then write it several times based on the handwritten form. Follow the direction of the arrows.

Dialogue 7 (Formal)	
A. salām, āghā.	*Hello Sir.*
B. salām, khānum.	*Hello Madam.*
A. esm-e man Maryame. esm-e shomā chiye?	*My name is Maryam. What is your name?*
B. man Afshinam.	*I am Afshin.*
A. khoshvaghtam!	*Good to meet you!*
B. manam khoshvaghtam!	*Good to meet you too!*
A. shomā irāni hastin?	*Are you Iranian?*
B. bale man irāniam, shomā chi?	*Yes, I am Iranian, and you?*
A. man irāni āmrikāyiam.	*I am Iranian American.*
B. che khub!	*How nice!*

REVIEW OF ALPHABET & SOUNDS

Vowels:

o	اُ ـُ	e	اِ ـِ	a	اَ ـَ	Short
u	او و	i	اـ یـ ی	ā	آ ا	Long

Diphthongs

/ow/	نو
/ey/	کِی

Non-connectors

و	ژ	ز	ر	ذ	د	ا

Similar Shapes

نـ ن	ثـ ث	پـ پ	تـ ت	بـ ب
خـ خ	حـ ح	چـ چ	جـ ج	
	ژ	ز	ر	
	ذ	د		
	شـ ش	سـ س		
	قـ ق	فـ ف		
	گـ گ	کـ ک		
	ضـ ض	صـ ص		
	ظ	ط		
غـ ـغـ غـ غ	عـ ـعـ عـ ع			

Multiple Letters: One Sound

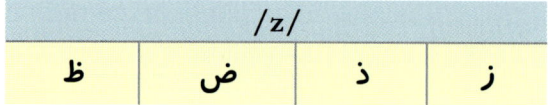

/z/			
ظ	ض	ذ	ز

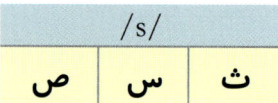

/s/		
ث	س	ص

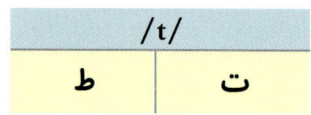

/t/	
ط	ت

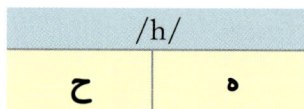

/h/	
ح	ه

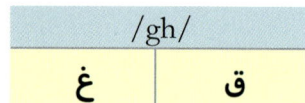

/gh/	
غ	ق

/ʔ/	
ء	ع

One Letter: Multiple Sounds

و			
/ow/	/o/	/u/	/v/
دولَت	دو	روز	وام

ه	
/e/	/h/
خانه	هَوا

ی		
/ey/	/i/	/y/
یِک	میز نِی	نِی

REVIEW EXERCISES

Exercise 47: Connect the following letters and sounds. Decide which shape of each letter to use:

۱. آ + م + ر + ی + ک ← ا + ا

۲. س + ا + ک + ِ + ت ←

۳. ک + ِ + ت + ا + ب ←

۴. س + َ + ل + ا + م ←

۵. ک + ا + ن + ا + د + ا ←

۶. ص + ُ + ب + ح ←

۷. ا + ی + ر + ا + ن + ی ←

۸. اَ + ف + غ + ا + ن + ِ + س + ت + ا + ن ←

Exercise 48: Write the corresponding Persian letter(s) in the box:

/b/	/p/	/t/	/s/
/ch/	/n/	/gh/	/a/
/i/	/z/	/l/	/k/
/sh/	/v/	/r/	/m/

Exercise 49: Circle the following letters in the text on the next page:

ش – ق – د – ا – ن – ه – ک

دوست،

بزرگ بود.

و از اهالی امروز بود.

و باتمام افق های باز نسبت داشت.

و لحن آب و زمین را چه خوب می فهمید.

صداش، به شکل حزن پریشان واقعیّت بود.

و پلک هاش، مسیر نبض عناصر را به ما نشان داد...

سهراب سپهری

BASIC NUMBERS

16	۱۶ - 16	شانزدَه	1	۱	یِک
17	۱۷	هِفدَه	2	۲	دو
18	۱۸	هِجدَه	3	۳	سه
19	۱۹	نوزدَه	4	٤ – ۴	چهار
20	۲۰	بیست	5	٥ - ۵	پَنج
21	۲۱	بیست و یِک	6	٦ - ۶	شِش
22	۲۲	بیست و دو	7	۷	هَفت
23	۲۳	بیست و سه	8	۸	هَشت
24	۲٤ - 24	بیست و چهار	9	۹	نُه
25	۲۵ – 25	بیست و پَنج	10	۱۰	دَه
26	۲٦ – 26	بیست و شِش	11	۱۱	یازدَه
27	۲۷	بیست و هَفت	12	۱۲	دَوازدَه
28	۲۸	بیست و هَشت	13	۱۳	سیزدَه
29	۲۹	بیست و نُه	14	۱٤ - 14	چهاردَه
30	۳۰	سی	15	۱٥ - 15	پانزدَه

PARTS OF SPEECH

How well do you know your native language? ☺

1. What is a noun?

2. What is a verb?

3. What is an adjective?

4. What is an adverb?

5. What is a subject?

6. What is an object?

7. What is a preposition?

8. What is the difference between a direct object and an indirect object?

9. What are the following words?

a. Book

b. Hardly

c. Sad

d. Goes

e. John

f. Against

g. Fast

h. Worse

i. Walking

j. Asleep

USEFUL WORDS & PHRASES

salām	*Hello*
chetowri?	*How are you?*
chetowrid?	*How are you? (Formal)*
man ………… hastam, va shomā?	*I am ……………, and you?*
khodāfez	*Good bye*
mersi	*Thanks*
sobh be kheir	*Good morning*
shab be kheir	*Goodnight*
bále	*Yes*
na	*No*
bebakhshid	*Excuse me*
āghā	*Sir/Mr*
khānom	*Mam/Mrs*
soāl dāram	*I have a question*
………… yani chi?	*………… means what?*
chetor migin ………?	*How do you say ………..?*
gush kon/id!	*Listen! (singular/plural)*
tekrār kon/id!	*Repeat! (singular/plural)*
bekhun/id!	*Read! (to singular/plural)*
fahmidi?	*Did you understand?*
nafahmidam	*I did not understand*
sāket!	*Quiet!*
bāshe	*OK*
chashm	*OK*
khaste	*Tired*
ne-midunam	*I don't know*
chi?	*What?*
lotfan	*Please*
taklif chi dārim?	*What is the home work?*
āfarin!	*Good job!*

احوال‌پرسی و آشنایی
Greetings & Introductions

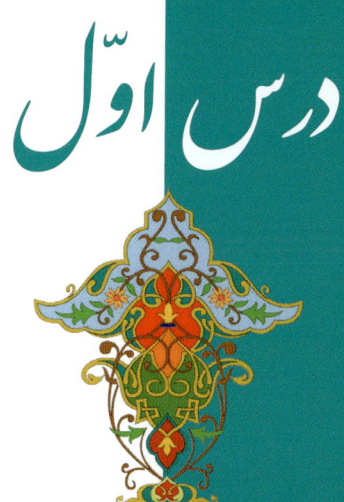

Communication Objectives

Greetings and Farewells
Introducing Yourself
Using Written and Spoken Forms
Using Formal and Informal Forms
Asking Yes/No Questions
Talking about Your Nationality, Hometown, and Profession
Describing People and Things

Contents

WRITTEN & SPOKEN FORMS

The challenging part of learning Persian is the difference between the "written" and "spoken" forms. The written form is mainly used in writing and broadcast news. It can also be used in giving speeches. Dictionaries provide the written form of words.

The spoken form is the way native speakers converse. It can also be used in personal letters, emails, modern poetry, and plays. Unless you are royalty or a very high rank official, never speak in the written form!

In the vocabulary lists, the written form is introduced first and the spoken form is provided after the / symbol. The dialogues are in spoken form and the following box provides the written form. You are expected to learn both forms. Use the spoken form when speaking and use the written form when writing. We will learn more about these two forms later.

واژگان ۱

Yes (Informal)	آره (āré)	Thanks	مِرسی
Good bye	خُداحافظ / خُدافِظ	You (Singular)	تو
For now	فِعلاً	How are you? (Informal)	چِطوری؟
Thanks	مَمنون	I am fine	خوبَم
I	مَن	Yes	بَله (bále)
Are you well? (Informal)	خوبی؟	Hello	سَلام

Informal Greeting & Farewell

Close your book and listen to the dialogue. Then fill in the blanks using the new words.

An interrogative sentence that requires a YES/NO answer ends with a rising tone. The word order does not change.

گفتگو ۱

بیتا: سَلام.

مَریَم: ــــــــــــ .

بیتا: چِطوری؟

مَریَم: مَن خوبَم، مِرسی. ــــــــــــ خوبی؟

بیتا: ــــــــــــ ، مَمنون.

مَریَم: فِعلاً خُدافِظ.

بیتا: خُدافِظ.

Written Form

گفتگو ۱

بیتا: سلام.

مریم: سلام.

بیتا: ـــــــــــ؟

مریم: من خوبم، مرسی. تو خوبی؟

بیتا: بله، ممنون.

مریم: فعلاً خداحافِظ.

بیتا: ـــــــــــ .

بَله can be used in both written and spoken forms.

آره is only used in the spoken form.

تَمرین ۱

Walk around in class. Greet each of your classmates; ask how she/he is doing; and say good bye.

واژگان ۲

How is...?	چِطور اَست/ چِطوره؟	Mr. Parsa	آقای پارسا
Ms./Mrs./Lady	خانُم / خانوم	How are you? (Plural & Formal)	چِطورید/ چِطورین؟
Good bye	خُدانگَهدار	You (Plural & Formal)	شُما
Positive reply to a request	چَشم	Your condition/state (Plural & Formal)	حالِ شُما
Definitely/For sure	حَتماً	Good morning	صُبح به خِیر
I am not bad	بَد نیستَم	Say hello (Plural & Formal)	سَلام بِرسانید/ سَلام بِرسونین

Formal Greeting & Farewell

Close your book and listen to the dialogue. Then fill in the blanks using the new words.

گفتگو ۲

مینا: صُبح به خِیر ـــــــــــ .

آقای پارسا: صُبح به خِیر مینا خانوم.

مینا: حال ـــــــــــ چِطوره؟

آقای پارسا: خوبَم، مرسی. شُما چِطورین؟

مینا: بَد نیستَم، مَمنون.

آقای پارسا: سَلام بِرسونین!

مینا: چَشم، حَتماً! ـــــــــــ .

آقای پارسا: خدافِظ.

65

خانم is used after the first name: مینا خانم

آقا is used before or after the first name: آقا بابک ــ بابک آقا

آقا and خانم are used before the last name:

خانمِ پارسا ــ آقای پارسا

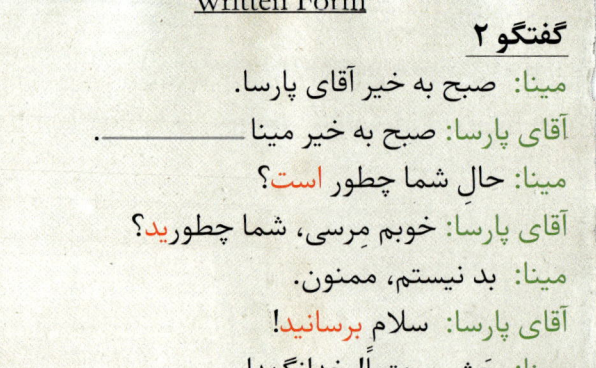

Written Form

گفتگو ۲

مینا: صبح به خیر آقای پارسا.

آقای پارسا: صبح به خیر مینا ــــــــــ .

مینا: حالِ شما چطور است؟

آقای پارسا: خوبم مِرسی، شما چطورید؟

مینا: بد نیستم، ممنون.

آقای پارسا: سلامِ برسانید!

مینا: چَشم، حتماً! خدانگهدار.

آقای پارسا: ــــــــــ .

تَمرین ۲

With a classmate, role-play Dialogue 2, using your own name.

FORMAL & INFORMAL FORMS

The formal form (also known as the "polite" form) is used to show respect and distance. It is used to address people older than you or people you are not very close to (including teachers, clerks, etc.). The informal form is used for familiar people. Although you are very close to your father, you may address him in the formal form to show respect.

In the formal form, the plural pronoun (شُما) is used instead of the singular pronoun (تو) to show respect and distance.

In Dialogue 1, the two classmates are talking in the informal form because they are peers. In Dialogue 2, Mina and Mr. Parsa are talking in the formal form because they are not very close to each other. Examples:

Informal	Formal	
تو چِطوری؟	← شُما چِطورید؟	Written
تو چِطوری؟	← شُما چِطورین؟	Spoken

It is imporant not to confuse the **written/spoken** forms with the **formal/informal** forms.

COMMON MISTAKE

There are two ways to say how you are. Can you tell the difference?

a) "I am fine" → مَن خوب هستم

b) "My condition/state is good" → حالِ من خوب است

Common mistake: It is very common for new learners to confuse the two forms and mix them. Be mindful of not making this mistake!

*حالِ من خوب هستم.

واژگان ۳

Professor	اُستاد	What is?	چیست؟ / چیه؟
University student	دانِشجو	Good day	روز به خِیر
No	نَه	Name	اِسم
You are (Plural & Formal)	هَستید / هَستین	Good to meet you	خوشوَقتَم / خوشبَختَم

Close your book and listen to the dialogue. Then fill in the blanks using the new words.

Formal Introduction

گفتگو ۳

بابَک: روز به‌خِیر.

نِگین: سَلام.

بابَک: من بابَکِ اَفشار هَستم. اِسمِ شُما _____؟

نِگین: مَن نِگینِ کَریمی هَستَم.

بابَک: خوشبَختَم!

نِگین: شُما _____ هَستین؟

بابَک: _____، مَن دانِشجواَم.

Usually, first names and last names are connected with a vowel /e/ except when the first name ends with the long vowels /ā/ or /u/.
Example: سارا کَریمی

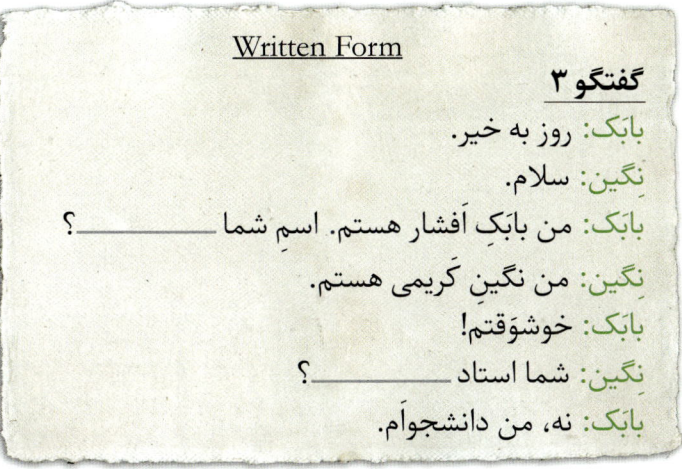

<u>Written Form</u>

گفتگو ۳

بابَک: روز به خِیر.

نِگین: سلام.

بابَک: من بابَکِ اَفشار هستم. اسمِ شما _____؟

نِگین: من نِگینِ کَریمی هستم.

بابَک: خوشوَقتم!

نِگین: شما استاد _____؟

بابَک: نه، من دانِشجواَم.

COMMON MISTAKE

There are two ways to introduce yourself. Can you tell the difference?

a) "I <u>am</u> Maria" → من ماریا هستم

b) "My name <u>is</u> Maria" → اِسمِ من ماریا است

Common mistake: It is very common for new learners to confuse the two forms and mix them. Be mindful of not making this mistake!   *اسمِ من ماریا هستم.

تَمرین ۳

With a classmate, role-play Dialogue 3, using your own name. Write down the name of your classmate in Persian.

واژگان ۴

Where from	کُجایی (kójāyi)	American	آمریکایی
Good Afternoon	عَصر به خِیر	Iranian	ایرانی
Thanks	مُتشَکَّرم	How nice!	چه خوب!
		How are you? (Plural & Formal)	چطورید؟ / چطورین؟

Close your book and listen to the dialogue. Then fill in the blanks using the new words.

Formal Introduction

گفتگو ۴

کامران: ـــــــــ خانوم. حالِ شُما چطوره؟

آلیس: خوبَم، مِرسی. شُما چطورین؟

کامران: بَد نیستَم، مُتشَکَّرم. شُما آمریکایی هَستین؟

آلیس: بَله، مَن آمریکایی‌اَم. اسمِ مَن آلیسِه. اسمِ شُما چیه؟

کامران: ـــــــــ مَن کامرانه.

آلیس: شُما کُجایی هَستین؟

کامران: مَن ـــــــــ اَم.

آلیس: چه خوب!

Written Form

گفتگو ۴

کامران: عصر به خیر خانم. حالِ شما چطور ـــــــــ؟

آلیس: خوبم، مرسی. شما چطورید؟

کامران: بد نیستم، متشکّرم. شما آمریکایی ـــــــــ؟

آلیس: بله، من آمریکایی‌اَم. اسمِ من آلیس است. اسمِ شما چیست؟

کامران: اسمِ من کامران است.

آلیس: شما کُجایی ـــــــــ؟

کامران: من ایرانی‌اَم.

آلیس: چه خوب!

تَمرین ۴

With a classmate, role-play Dialogue 4 (using your own name and nationality). For additional vocabulary look at the list at the end of the lesson.

تَمرین ۵

Find six words in Dialogues 1-4 that are different in written and spoken forms and write them below. Pronounce the words as you write.

Spoken	← Written	Spoken	← Written

خواندن

اِسمِ مَن کامران اَست

اِسمِ مَن کامران اَست. مَن دانِشجو هَستَم. مَن تِهرانی هَستَم. تِهران دَر ایران اَست. تِهران بُزُرگ اَست. دَر تِهران چَند دانِشگاه هَست. دانِشگاهِ تِهران زیبا اَست.

From Tehran	تِهرانی	Big/Large	بُزُرگ
University	دانِشگاه	Several	چَند
Is	اَست	Beautiful	زیبا
In/Inside/At	دَر	(There) is/exists	هَست

تَمرین ۶

Listen to the audio file and follow along in your text. Repeat each sentence several times.

تَمرین ۷

Task: Write an email to a pen pal to introduce yourself. Include your name and your nationality, write that you are a student, and mention the name of your university. Use the above text as a model. For additional vocabulary look at the list at the end of the lesson.

 دستور زبان ۱

PRESENT TENSE OF "TO BE" بودَن

ما خوب هَستیم We are fine	من خوب هَستَم I am fine
شما خوب هَستید You (pl.) are fine	تو خوب هَستی You are fine
آنها (ایشان) خوب هَستَند They are fine	او خوب اَست (هَست) S/he is fine

Verb "To Be" is the only verb that has a **long form** and a **short form** in the present tense. The long form (conjugated above) receives stress on the initial syllable (ex: hástam).

هَست is only used for existential readings. Example:

در تهران چند دانشگاه هست. There are several universities in Tehran.

ایشان can be used instead of او to show respect or distance.

SHORT FORM OF "TO BE" بودَن

ما خوبیم We are fine	من خوبَم I am fine
شما خوبید You (pl.) are fine	تو خوبی You are fine
آنها خوبَند They are fine	او خوب است S/he is fine

The short form of "بودن" does not receive stress. Compare the long and short forms and find out what the difference between them is. What about the third person singular forms?

Writing and Pronunciation

If the short form of "To Be" is connected to words ending in /e/ or /i/, an *alef* is inserted in between. Examples:

من آمریکاییاَم.

If the short form of "To Be" is connected to words ending in /u/, a /y/ is inserted in between to ease the pronunciation (except for third person singular, which remains the same). Examples:

من دانشجویَم ــ تو دانشجویی

او دانشجو است (او دانشجوست)

تَمرین ۸

With a classmate, practice reading the conjugations of the long and short forms of "To Be". Take turns and listen to each other's reading.

PRONOUNS

Unlike English, Persian does not have different sets of pronouns to refer to the subject (*I*), object (*me*), or the possessive pronoun (*mine*). Suffixes or prepositions are added to change the function of pronouns. We will learn more about this in the next lesson. There is **no gender distinction** in Persian.

تَمرین ۹

Based on the conjugation of "To Be", write the pronouns in the following table and read them aloud. Try to memorize the pronouns if you can.

Pronouns			
1st person plural		1st person singular	
2nd person plural		2nd person singular	
3rd person plural		3rd person singular	

VERB ENDINGS

You have probably noticed by now that in Persian the verb ending agrees with the subject in **Person** and **Number**. The verb ending does not carry stress.

تَمرین ۱۰

Based on the conjugation to "To Be", write the verb endings in the following table.

Verb Endings			
1st person plural		1st person singular	
2nd person plural		2nd person singular	
3rd person plural		3rd person singular	

Fill in the blanks with the long form of "To Be" or a pronoun. Pronounce the words aloud.

تَمرین ۱۱

۱. من کامران ————————

> Unlike English, the sentence "*They are students*" contains a singular noun "student" in Persian. We will learn more about it in Lesson 3.
>
> آنها دانشجو هستند.

۲. اسمِ من کامران ————————

۳. آنها چطور ————————؟

۴. ———————— آمریکایی هستیم.

۵. من خوب ————————

۶. حالِ من خوب ————————

۷. تو ایرانی ————————؟

NEGATION

To conjugate the present form of بودَن in negative form, replace هست/است with نیست. Stress falls on the initial syllable (ex: nístam).

Negative form of "To Be" بودن

ما دانِشجو نیستیم We are not students	من دانِشجو نیستَم I am not a student
شما دانِشجو نیستید You are not students	تو دانِشجو نیستی You are not a student
آنها دانِشجو نیستَند They are not students	او دانِشجو نیست S/he is not a student

Short form of "To Be" does not have a negative form.

تَمرین ۱۲

Change the verbs to the short form and pronounce them aloud.

۱. من خوب هستم.

۲. شما دانِشجو هستید؟

۳. آقای پارسا تهرانی است؟

تَمرین ۱۳

Change the verbs to the negative form and pronounce them aloud.

۱. شما استاد هستید؟

۲. آنها ایرانی آمریکایی هستند.

۳. اسمِ من مینا است.

تَمرین ۱۴

Change the verbs to the long form and pronounce them aloud.

۱. ما آمریکایی‌ایم.

۲. تو چطوری؟

۳. آنها استادند؟

بیشتر بدانیم

MORE ON WRITTEN & SPOKEN FORMS

We have already seen many instances of written and spoken forms in Dialogues 1-4. The difference between the written and spoken forms is mainly phonological. For instance words contract in the spoken form. This is similar to the contrast of "*I am going to*" and "*I'm gonna*" in English. Examples:

Spoken ← Written	Spoken ← Written
هَستید ← هَستین	او ← اون
هَستند ← هَستَن	آنها ← اونها ← اونا
خانُم ← خانوم	ایشان ← ایشون
	است ← ه

In some cases, the word order changes or prepositions are dropped in spoken form. Some words, such as آره are not used in **written** form. آره and بله are both used in **spoken** form.

Writing and Pronunciation:

If a word ends in the short vowel /e/, it can only be followed by the written form of *ast*. The spoken form of *ast* which is /e/ cannot follow that word. Example:

او «تَرانه» است ← اون تَرانه‌ست ــ * اون تَرانه‌ه.

If a word ends in the long vowel /i/, a /y/ will be inserted before the short form of *ast* in spoken form. Example:

او ایرانی است ← اون ایرانیه.

تَمرین ۱۵

a) Change to spoken form:

۱. آنها ایرانی هستند.

۲. شما کُجایی هستید؟

۳. آلیس ایرانی است؟

b) Change to written form:

۱. اون آمریکاییه؟

۲. ایشون آقای پارسا هستن؟

۳. اسمِ شما چیه؟

 **دستور زبان ۲**

SENTENCE STRUCTURE (I)

A sentence in Persian begins with the **subject** and ends with the **verb**. Everything else comes in between[1]. Example: من خوب هستم.

Verb – {Everything else} – Subject

In Persian, a sentence does not need to have a "subject pronoun". Example: خوب هستم.

Question: When the subject is omitted, how do you think we can recognize what/who the subject is?

STRESS & INTONATION

In affirmative sentences, stress falls on the predicate (in both declarative and interrogative forms):

آنها دانشجو هستند. ــ آنها دانشجو هستند؟

In negative sentences, stress falls on the verb (in both declarative and interrogative forms):

آنها دانشجو نیستند. ــ آنها دانشجو نیستند؟

In Dialogue 1, we learned that interrogative sentences that require a YES/NO answer have a rising tone.

تَمرین ۱۶

Listen to the audio file to hear the intonation difference between declarative, interrogative, negative, and negative interrogative sentences. Repeat each sentence several times.

---

1 .The word order may change to show emphasis. We will learn more about it later.

تَمرین ۱۷

Change to formal form:

۱. او استاد است.

۲. تو ایرانی هستی؟

تَمرین ۱۸

Decide if each situation is formal or informal and write an appropriate greeting/farewell for it. Use the dialogues at the beginning of the lesson as a model. Read your sentences aloud.

۲.
_____
_____
_____

۱.
_____
_____
_____

۴.
_____
_____
_____

۳.
_____
_____
_____

تَمرین ۱۹

Put the following words in the right order to form a sentence. Read your sentences aloud.

۱. دانشگاهِ تهران – است – بزرگ

۲. هستند – آنها – خوب

۳. چیست – اسم ــ تو – ؟

۴. ایرانی – ما – نیستیم.

۵. خانم ــ پارسا – است – زیبا

۶. هستند ــ خوب – ایشان ــ ؟

بیشتر بدانیم

شما اَهلِ کُجا هستید؟ / شما کُجایی هستید؟

The answer to "*Where are you from?*" can be either your nationality (ex: ایرانی) or the town that you are from (ex: شیرازی). Stress is on the final syllable (ex: irānī).

German	آلمانی	Germany	آلمان
American	آمریکایی	America	آمریکا
Afghan	اَفغانی	Afghanistan	اَفغانِستان
English	اِنگِلیسی	England	اِنگِلیس
Iranian	ایرانی	Iran	ایران
Tajik	تاجیکی	Tajikistan	تاجیکِستان
Turkish	تُرک	Turkey	تُرکیه
From Tehran	تهرانی	Tehran	تهران
Chinese	چینی	China	چین
Japanese	ژاپُنی	Japan	ژاپُن
From Shiraz	شیرازی	Shiraz	شیراز
French	فَرانسَوی	France	فَرانسه
Canadian	کانادایی	Canada	کانادا

Which suffix is added to make the word for nationality? Are there any exceptions?

تَمرین ۲۰

Answer in complete sentences. Read your answer aloud.

۱. نانسی اهلِ کجاست؟

۲. شما اهلِ کجا هستید؟

۳. تو کجایی هستی؟

_____

_____

_____

۴. آنها کجایی هستند؟

۵. آلیس اهلِ کجاست؟

۶. آقای یانگ کجایی هستند؟

_____

_____

_____

تَمرین ۲۱

Listen to the audio file and fill in the blanks:

۱. _____ _____ تاجیکی _____ ؟

۲. آنها _____ هستند.

۳. _____ من _____ نیست.

۴. شما _____ هستید؟

۵. شما اهلِ _____ _____ ؟

۶. اسمِ من _____ . اسمِ شما _____ ؟

77

دستور زبان ۳

THE EZĀFE CONNECTOR

Ezāfe is a vowel /e/ that connects any two or more related words in Persian[2]. Ezāfe appears between the following combinations:

Noun + Adjective	Good university	۱. دانشگاهِ خوب
Noun + Noun/Pronoun/Proper noun	Her university - Mina's university	۲. دانشگاهِ او ــ دانشگاهِ مینا
Preposition + Noun	Behind the university	۳. پُشتِ دانشگاه
Mr./Mrs + Last name	Mrs. Dabiri	۴. خانمِ دَبیری
First name + Last name	Maryam Dabiri	۵. مریَمِ دَبیری
Adjective + Adjective	Good good (Very good)	۶. خوبِ خوب
Noun + Numbers	Example one	۷. تَمرینِ یک

Since Ezāfe is a short vowel, it is usually not indicated in writing as native speakers are able to add it in pronunciation. For foreign language learners it is rather challenging to know where Ezāfe is added, but through time it gets easier.

> *Common Mistake:* Be mindful not to confuse Ezāfe with the short form of "To Be" in the third person singular form. Examples:
>
> تَمرینِ یک
>
> * تَمرینهٔ یک

Writing and Pronunciation:

1) When Ezāfe is added to words that end in /u/, /ā/, or the unpronounced *he*, a /y/ is inserted. Examples:

۱. دانِشجو + ـِ + خوب ← دانشجوی خوب

۲. آقا + ـِ + پارسا ← آقای پارسا

۳. خانه + ـِ + خوب ← خانهی خوب Good house (خانهٔ خوب Older form)

2) When Ezāfe is added to a word that ends in /i/, a /y/ is inserted in pronunciation. The spelling remains the same.

۴. صَندَلی + ـِ + استاد ← صَندَلیِ استاد Professor's chair

3) In spoken form, Ezāfe is sometimes dropped.

دانشگاهِ تهران ← دانشگاه تهران

---

2. The Ezāfe can be viewed as the equivalent of the English "of" in the following combinations: beautiful girl (*girl of beauty*), Mina's mother (*mother of Mina*), and country of Iran.

 بیشتر بدانیم

Adjectives صِفَت‌ها

Old	پیر	Beautiful	زیبا
Polite	با اَدَب	Beautiful/Pretty	قَشَنگ
Quiet	ساکِت	Beautiful/Pretty	خوشگِل
Small	کوچَک / کوچیک	Big/Large	بُزُرگ
Smart	زِرَنگ	Delicious	خوشمَزه
Middle aged	میانسال	Happy	خوشحال
Tired	خَسته	Impolite	بی‌اَدَب
Upset/Sad	ناراحَت	Intelligent	باهوش
Young	جَوان / جَوون	Lazy	تَنبَل
Kind	مِهرَبان / مِهرَبون	Strong (physical)	قَوی
Bad	بَد	Good/Fine	خوب
Married	مُتاَهِّل	Single	مُجَرَّد

Stress falls on the final syllable (ex: ghasháng).

Order of the Adjectives and Adverbs:

Adjectives follow nouns and are connected with Ezāfe. If there is more than one adjective, they are all connected with Ezāfe. Examples:

خانمِ زیبا

خانمِ جَوانِ زیبای مهربان

Adverbs preceed adjectives with no Ezāfe in between. Example:

Very pretty = خیلی قشنگ

 تَمرین ۲۲

Write the following combinations with Ezāfe and read them aloud.

1. Our professor   2. Polite student

3. Beautiful Mina   4. Very tired (tired tired)

5. Young German lady   6. Mr. professor

> While "My professor" requires Ezāfe, "Professor Karimi" does NOT require Ezāfe.
>
> استادِ کریمی * — استاد کریمی

تَمرین ۲۳

Write the corresponding adjective for each image. Read your sentences aloud.

۲. آقای کَریمی ــــــــــ است.   ۱. او ــــــــــ است.

۴. شَهلا ــــــــــ است.   ۳. پیتزا ــــــــــ است.

۶. مینا خیلی ــــــــــ است.   ۵. گُل ــــــــــ است.

۸. او ــــــــــ است.   ۷. نِگین ــــــــــ است.

تَمرین ۲۴

Answer in Persian using a complete sentence. Use the written form. Read your answers aloud.

۱. اسمِ شما چیست؟

۲. حالِ شما چطور است؟

۳. شما اَهلِ کجا هستید؟

۴. شما افغانی نیستید؟

۵. دانشگاهِ شما در تهران است؟

۶. شما مُجَرّد هستید؟

شُغل‌ها Professions

Sales person	فُروشَنده	Professor	اُستاد
Employee (office)	کارمَند	University student	دانِشجو
Artist	هُنَرمَند	Teacher	مُعَلّم
Police officer	پُلیس	Elementary-high school student	دانِش‌آموز
Soldier	سَرباز	Engineer	مُهَندِس
Secretary	مُنشی	Painter	نَقّاش
Nurse	پَرَستار	Cook	آشپَز
Manager/Principal	مُدیر	Doctor	دُکتُر
Singer	خوانَنده	Writer/Author	نویسَنده
Poet	شاعِر	Worker	کارگَر

Stress is on the final syllable (ex: dāneshjú).

تَمرین ۲۵

Listen to the audio file and mark the corresponding adjectives for the following words:

نقّاش	آلمانی	ناراحت	مهربان	باهوش	زیبا	متأهل	
							آقای پارسا
							آلیس
							بابَک
							دانشگاهِ تهران
							مینا
							شما
							استادِ ما

 تَمرین ۲۶

Complete the following sentences. Read your answers aloud.

۱. مَریَم خانم  ‎_____‎ . ‎   ۲. شما ‎_____‎ ؟

۳. آنها  ‎_____‎ . ‎   ۴. من ‎_____‎ نیستم.

۵. تو  ‎_____‎ ؟ ‎   ۶. ما ‎_____‎ .

تَمرین ۲۷ : واژگان

In each line, circle the word that does not match the rest:

۱. شیرازی	تهران	فرانسوی	چینی
۲. آره	چَشم	در	بله
۳. نقّاش	نیستند	فروشنده	نویسنده
۴. قشنگ	خوشحال	خوشگل	خوشمزه
۵. خدانگهدار	صبح به خیر	سلام برسانید	خداحافظ
۶. هنرمند	کارگر	ساکت	خواننده
۷. خیلی	چند	حتماً	ایشان

تَمرین ۲۸

Use the adjectives, professions, and nationalities you have learned and describe the following people. Write at least three complete sentences and read them aloud.

۱. دالای لاما ـــــــــــــــــــ است.

۲. دالای لاما ـــــــــــــــــــ است.

۳. دالای لاما ـــــــــــــــــــ است.

۴. مادرِ تِریسا ـــــــــــــــــــ است.

۵. مادرِ تِریسا ـــــــــــــــــــ است.

۶. مادرِ تِریسا ـــــــــــــــــــ است.

۷. کریستیان آمانپور ـــــــــــــــــــ است.

۸. کریستیان آمانپور ـــــــــــــــــــ است.

۹. کریستیان آمانپور ـــــــــــــــــــ است.

تَمرین ۲۹

Task: You meet someone at school who is almost your age. Say the following in Persian. Use the spoken form:

1. Greet him/her.

2. Ask how s/he is.

3. Introduce yourself.

4. Ask if s/he is Iranian.

5. Tell him/her you are American and married (in two sentences).

6. Ask if s/he is a student.

7. Say "how nice!".

8. Say "good bye".

REVIEW CORNER	
Points that remain unclear about Lesson 1:	
How I plan to work on these points:	

شعر

Read the following poem by Sohrab Sepehri and find five instances of the verb "To Be". You will not be evaluated on the content but you can use it for cultural enrichment.

در گُلِستانه

زندگی خالی نیست.

مهربانی هست.

سیب هست.

ایمان هست.

آری،

تا شقایق هست، زندگی باید کرد.

شاعر: سهراب سپهری (۱۹۸۰ ـ ۱۹۲۸)

نکته‌ی فرهنگی

First Interactions:

It is customary for familiar people and relatives to kiss on the cheek at least twice when greeting. Men also kiss each other when greeting each other. The concept of "personal space" is not practiced in Iran. Iranians hold hands, kiss, pinch cheeks, and sit very close to each other. In formal settings, shaking hands is customary. A man usually waits for a woman to initiate hand shaking. Different regions may have their own customs for greeting. Based on the current Islamic laws, men and women are not allowed to kiss or shake hands in public. Contrary to the western culture, it is not unusual for people to ask about one's marital status or age during the first interactions.

How to Address People Properly:

In everyday interactions, people address each other with their last name unless they are very familiar or relatives. The titles خانم and آقا can be added to both first and last names. Titles are dropped between close friends and acquaintances. The word خان may sometimes be used instead of آقا. The word خان is used only after the first name.

As we learned earlier, plural pronouns شما and ایشان are used instead of singular pronouns تو and او to show respect or distance. You must be very cautious about this distinction and NEVER address someone older or unfamiliar, including your professor, with the pronoun "تو"!

ضرب المثل

شُتر دیدی؟ نَدیدی!

Literal translation: *Did you see the camel? You did not!*

This proverb is used when you want to ask someone to forget about what they just saw or heard, or to ignore the situation that has just happened.

Thematic Review of New Vocabulary

Saying Hello	
Good day	روز به خِیر
Hello	سَلام
Good morning	صُبح به خِیر
Good afternoon	عَصر به خِیر

Saying Good Bye	
Good bye	خُدا نِگَهدار
Good bye	خُداحافِظ
Say hello	سَلام بِرسانید
Bye for now	فِعلاً خُداحافِظ

Saying "Thank you"	
Thanks	مُتَشَکِّرَم
Thanks	مِرسی
Thanks	مَمنون

Saying/Responding to "How are you?"	
I am not bad	بَد نیسَتم
How are you?	چِطوری؟
How are you? (Plural & Formal)	چِطورید؟
How are you? (Plural & Formal)	حال شما چِطور اَست؟
I am well	خوبم
Are you well?	خوبی؟
Are you well? (Plural & Formal)	خوبید؟

Response to question/request	
Yes (Informal)	آره
Yes	بَله
Positive response to a request	چَشم
Definitely/For sure	حَتماً
No	نَه

Adjectives			
Delicious	خوشمَزه	Polite	با اَدَب
Smart	زَرَنگ	Intelligent	باهوش
Beautiful	زیبا	Bad	بَد
Quiet	ساکِت	Big/Large	بُزُرگ
Beautiful/Pretty	قَشَنگ	Impolite	بی اَدَب
Strong (physical)	قَوی	Old	پیر
Small	کوچَک	Lazy	تَنبَل
Married	مُتَاَهِل	Young	جَوان
Single	مُجَرَّد	Tired	خَسته
Kind	مِهرَبان	Good/Fine	خوب
Middle aged	میانسال	Happy	خوشحال
Upset/Sad	ناراحَت	Beautiful/Pretty	خوشگِل

Where Are You From?	
German	آلمانی
American	آمریکایی
Afghan	اَفغانی
English	اِنگِلیسی
Iranian	ایرانی
Tajik	تاجیکی
Turkish	تُرک
From Tehran	تهرانی
Chinese	چینی
Japanese	ژاپُنی
From Shiraz	شیرازی
French	فَرانسَوی
Canadian	کانادایی

Professions			
Sales person	فُروشَنده	Professor	اُستاد
Worker	کارگِر	Cook	آشپَز
Employee (office)	کارمَند	Nurse	پَرستار
Manager/Principal	مُدیر	Police officer	پُلیس
Teacher	مُعَلِّم	Singer	خوانَنده
Secretary	مُنشی	K-12 student	دانِش آموز
Engineer	مُهَندِس	University student	دانِشجو
Painter	نَقّاش	Doctor	دُکتُر
Writer/Author	نِویسَنده	Soldier	سَرباز
Artist	هُنَرمَند	Poet	شاعِر

Pronouns	
They	آنها
S/he	او
They (Plural & Formal)	ایشان
You	تو
You (Plural & Formal)	شُما
We	ما
I	مَن

Nouns	
Name	اِسم
Mr./Sr.	آقا
Exercise	تَمرین
Tehran	تِهران
Mrs./Ms./Lady	خانُم
University	دانِشگاه

Verbs	
Is	اَست
I am not	نیستَم
(There) is/exists	هَست
I am	هَستَم
You are	هَستی
You are (Plural & Formal)	هَستید

Words & Expressions	
Where from	اَهلِ کُجا
Several	چَند
How nice!	چه خوب!
What is…?	چیست؟
Good to meet you	خوشوَقتَم
A lot/Very	خِیلی
In/Inside/At	دَر
How about you?	شما چطور؟
For now	فعلاً
Where from	کُجایی (kójāyi)

Countries	
Germany	آلمان
America	آمریکا
Afghanistan	اَفغانِستان
England	اِنگلیس
Iran	ایران
Tajikistan	تاجیکِستان
Turkey	تُرکیه
Tehran	تهران
China	چین
Japan	ژاپُن
Shiraz	شیراز
France	فَرانسه
Canada	کانادا

درس دوّم

دربارهی تو

About You

🎧 واژگان ۱

The written form is introduced first. The spoken form is provided after the / symbol.

You (singular) have	داری	Baby/Child/Kid	بَچّه
Six	شِش/شیش	Brother	بَرادَر
So	پَس	Very	خِیلی
Sister	خواهَر	Boy/Son	پِسَر
Two	دو	How many	چَند (تا)
Three	سه	Girl/Daughter	دُختَر
Parents (Father & Mother)	پِدَر وَ مادَر	One	یِک/یه
And	وَ/و (o)	Woman/Wife	زَن
I do not have	ندارَم	I have	دارَم
		They have	دارَند/دارَن

Close your book and listen to the dialogue. Then fill in the blanks using the new words.

🎧 گفتگو ۱

سینا : تو چند تا برادر ـــــــــ ؟

رابرت: من سه تا خواهر و دو تا برادر دارم.

سینا: پس پدرِ و مادرِ تو شیش تا بچه دارن؟ خیلی خوبه!

رابرت: آره! تو چند ـــــــــ بچّه داری؟

سینا: من دو تا بچّه دارم، یه دختر و یه ـــــــــ .

رابرت: من زن و بچّه ندارم.

In spoken form, تا is added to a noun to show counting.

تا does not come after number **one**.

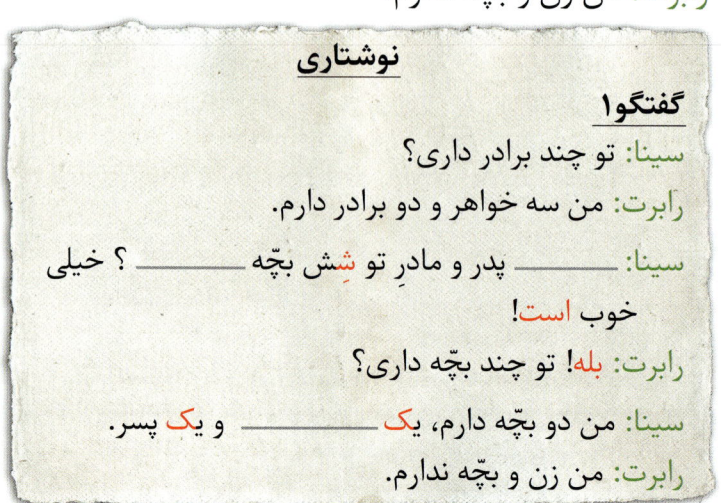

نوشتاری

گفتگو۱

سینا: تو چند برادر داری؟

رابرت: من سه خواهر و دو برادر دارم.

سینا: ـــــــــ پدر و مادرِ تو شِش بچّه ـــــــــ ؟ خیلی خوب **است**!

رابرت: **بله!** تو چند بچّه داری؟

سینا: من دو بچّه دارم، یک ـــــــــ و **یک** پسر.

رابرت: من زن و بچّه ندارم.

تمرین ۱

Talk with your classmate about how many siblings and children you have. For additional vocabulary look at the list at the end of the lesson.

واژگان ۲

Term (academic)	تِرم	English	اِنگِلیسی/اینگِلیسی
Physics	فیزیک	Easy	آسان/آسون
Four	چهار	I like (I have a liking)	دوست دارَم
History - Date	تاریخ	Chemistry	شیمی
This	این	How excellent!	چه عالی!
Persian	فارسی	Class - Classroom	کِلاس
What	چه/چی	Direct object marker	را/رو
		Friend	دوست

Close your book and listen to the dialogue. Then fill in the blanks using the new words.

گفتگو ۲

لورا: تو این _____ _____ چند تا کلاس داری؟

مینا: چهار تا کلاس، شیمی، فیزیک، تاریخ و اینگلیسی. تو چی؟

لورا: سه تا، فارسی، شیمی و اینگلیسی.

مینا: فارسی آسونه؟

لورا: آره! من خیلی کلاسِ _____ رو دوست دارم!

مینا: چه _____!

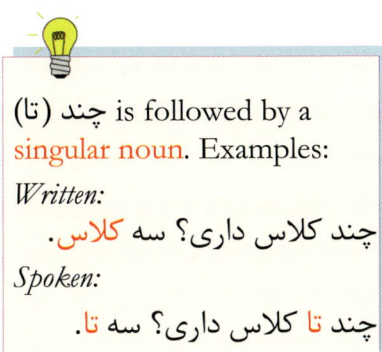

چند (تا) is followed by a
singular noun. Examples:
Written:
چند کلاس داری؟ سه کلاس.
Spoken:
چند تا کلاس داری؟ سه تا.

نوشتاری

گفتگو۲

لورا: تو این ترم چند کلاس داری؟

مینا: چهار کلاس، شیمی، فیزیک، _____ و
انگلیسی. تو چطور؟[1]

لورا: سه کلاس، فارسی، _____ و انگلیسی.

مینا: فارسی آسان است؟

لورا: بله! من خیلی کلاسِ فارسی _____ دوست دارم.

مینا: چه عالی!

---

1. Although the written form of چی is چه, in the above context چی changes to چطور.

Talk with your classmate about what courses you have, if your classes are easy, and if you like your classes. For additional vocabulary look at the list at the end of the lesson.

🎧 واژگان ۳

Book	کِتاب	In/Inside/At (Spoken)	تو (tu)
Affectionately (Informal)	قُربانَت/قُربونِت [2]	Why	چِرا
Have you got time?	وَقت داری؟	Good for you/Lucky you	خوش به حالَت/خوش به حالِت
I need	لازِم دارَم	Library	کِتابخانه/کِتابخونه
		Dear	جان/جون

Close your book and listen to the dialogue. Then fill in the blanks using the new words.

🎧 گفتگو ۳

نگین: سلام نرگس جون. _____ ؟

نرگِس: نه نگین جون. من تو کتابخونه‌ام.

نگین: _____ تو کتابخونه‌ای؟

نرگِس: کتابِ شیمی رو لازم دارم.

نگین: من کتابِ شیمی رو دارم.

نرگِس: _____ به حالِت!

نگین: پس فعلاً خدافِظ.

نرگِس: قُربونِت!

نوشتاری

گفتگو۳

نگین: سلام نرگس _____ وقت داری؟

نرگِس: نه نگین جان. من در کتابخانه‌ام.

نگین: چِرا در _____ ؟

نرگِس: کتابِ شیمی را لازم دارم.

نگین: من کتابِ شیمی را دارم.

نرگِس: خوش به حالَت!

نگین: پس فعلاً خداحافِظ.

نرگِس: _____ !

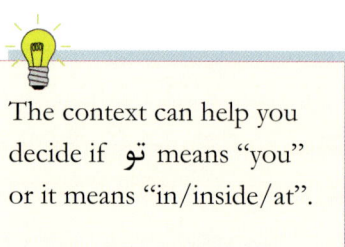

The context can help you decide if تو means "you" or it means "in/inside/at".

---

2. Literally means: "May I be your sacrifice".

تمرین ۳

Practice a phone conversation with your classmate. Ask each other where you are and if you have got time. For additional vocabulary look at the list at the end of the lesson.

تمرین ۴

Find six words in Dialogues 1-3 that are different in written and spoken forms and write them below. Pronounce the words as you write.

Spoken	Written →	Spoken	Written →

خواندن

خانواده‌ی پارسا

نامِ من «بیژَن» است. نامِ خانوادگیِ من «پارسا» است. من پدرِ خانواده هستم. نامِ همسرِ من «هُما» است. ما دو دختر و دو پسر داریم. نامِ دخترِ بزرگِ من «پَریسا» و نامِ دخترِ کوچکِ من «بیتا» است. نامِ پسرِ بزرگِ من «آرش» و نامِ پسرِ کوچکِ من «کامران» است.

Spouse	هَمسَر
Family	خانواده
Name	نام
Last/Family name	نامِ خانوادگی

تمرین ۵

a) Listen to the audio file and read along in your text. Repeat each sentence several times.

b) Answer in complete sentences. Use the written form.

۱. نامِ خانوادگیِ بیژَن چیست؟

۲. **آیا** بیژَن همسر دارد؟

93

۳. بیژَن و هُما چند دختر و چند پسر دارند؟

۴. نامِ دخترِ بزرگِ آنها چیست؟

۵. نامِ پسرِ کوچکِ آنها چیست؟

In written form آیا is added to the begining of an interrogative sentence that requires a YES/NO answer.

Antonyms	Synonyms		
زَن ≠ شوهَر	نامِ خانوادگی = فامیلی (fámili)	دَر = تو (Spoken)	نام = اِسم
	مادَر = مامان	پِدَر = بابا	

تمرین ۶

Use the reading text as a model and write a paragraph about your family. Indicate how many siblings you have and how many children they have. Indicate if you have a spouse. Use the written form.

تمرین ۷: واژگان

Fill in the blanks using the appropriate vocabulary from the list below.

آیا ـ همسر ـ حالت ـ دختر ـ خوبه ـ چند ـ پدر و مادر ـ نام ـ فعلاً ـ دوست دارم ـ خانوادگی ـ لازم

۱. خوش به _____ ! من کتابِ شیمی را ندارم.

۲. من دو بچه دارم. یک پسر و یک _____ .

۳. _____ تو شش بچه دارند؟ خیلی _____ .

۴. فارسی آسان است؟ بله. من خیلی کلاسِ فارسی را _____ .

۵. _____ تو کتابِ فیزیک را _____ داری؟

۶. _____ من میشِل است. نامِ _____ من جانسون است.

۷. پس _____ خداحافِظ.

۸. کلاسِ شما _____ دانشجو دارد؟

دستور زبان ۱

PRESENT TENSE OF "TO HAVE" داشتن

We have	داریم	ما	I have	دارَم	من
you (pl) have	دارید/دارین	شما	You have	داری	تو
They have	دارَند/دارَن	آنها	S/he has	دارَد/داره	او

Stress falls on the initial syllable (ex: dáram). Unlike the verb "To Be", the present tense of all other verbs takes the suffix/-ad/ on the third person singular of the written form.

NEGATION

To make the negative form of "To Have", add the negative prefix نَ to the beginning of the verb. The negative prefix carries stress (ex: nádāram).

We do not have	نَداریم	ما	I do not have	نَدارَم	من
You (pl) do not have	نَدارید/نَدارین	شما	You do not have	نَداری	تو
They do not have	نَدارَند/نَدارَن	آنها	S/he does not have	نَدارَد/نَداره	او

تمرین ۸

Based on the conjugation of "To Have", write the personal endings in the following table.

	1st Person Plural		1st Person Singular
	2nd Person Plural		2nd Person Singular
	3rd Person plural		3rd Person Singular

Compare the above personal endings with the personal endings of the verb "To Be" that you

learned in Lesson 1.

تمرین ۹

Fill in the blanks with the appropriate form of "To Have" or a pronoun. Use the written form.

۱. من کتاب لازم ——————— . (Negative)

۲. آیا استاد وقت ——————— ؟

۳. او کلاسِ فارسی ——————— .

۴. ——————— شیمی داریم.

۵. من این ترم شیمی ——————— . (Negative)

۶. ——————— کتابخانه دارند.

۷. آنها فعلاً بچه ——————— . (Negative)

۸. من سه خواهر ——————— .

Look at the following compound verbs:

To like/have a liking   دوست داشتن

To need/have a need   لازم داشتن

To have time (for...)   وقت داشتن

The part that is conjugated is داشتن.

We will learn more about compound verbs in Lesson 3.

تمرین ۱۰

Conjugate the following verbs.

۱. ما ایرانی ——————— . (بودن) (Negative)

۲. شما زن ——————— ؟(داشتن)

۳. مینا کتابِ انگلیسی را لازم ——————— . (داشتن) (Negative)

۴. آنها فعلاً وقت ——————— . (داشتن) (Negative)

۵. تو ایران را دوست ——————— ؟ (داشتن)

۶. شوهرِ من کانادایی ——————— . (بودن) (Negative)

دستور زبان ۲

THE CONJUNCTION   وَ

وَ is the coordinating conjunction and functions in the same way as "*and*". In the spoken form, وَ is pronounced as ُ /o/ and is added to the first element of coordination.

من یک برادر دارم + من یک خواهر دارم. ← من یک برادر وَ یک خواهر دارم.

برادرِ من باهوش است + برادرِ من با ادب است. ← برادرِ من باهوش وَ با ادب است.

تمرین ۱۱

Connect with وَ and make the necessary changes to the verb:

۱. ما دانشجو هستیم. ما این ترم سه کلاس داریم.

۲. آقای کریمی شیرازی است. نگین شیرازی است.

۳. مادرِ من معلّم است. پدرِ من نویسنده است.

۴. دانشگاهِ تهران زیبا است. دانشگاهِ تهران بزرگ است.

۵. من دو خواهر دارم. من چهار برادر دارم.

بیشتر بدانیم

FIELDS OF STUDY

Psychology	رَوان شِناسی	Literature	اَدَبیات
Persian	فارسی	English	انگلیسی / اینگیلیسی
Biology	زیست شِناسی	Mathematics	ریاضی
Sociology	جامِعه شِناسی	History	تاریخ
Chemistry	شیمی	Physics	فیزیک
Art	هُنَر	Geography	جُغرافی

تمرین ۱۲

Look at the above list. Find some courses that you have taken within the last year and write them below. Pronounce each word as you write.

تمرین ۱۳

On a separate paper, draw a chart with two columns titled "Humanities" and "Science" in English. Under each column, write as many of the above Persian words as you see fit.

در کِلاس

🗣 🎧 DEMONSTRATIVE PRONOUNS

	Answer			Question	
	Book	کِتاب	این		این This
	Computer	کامپیوتر ـ رایانه			
	Pencil	مِداد		چیست؟/ چیه؟	
	Pen	خودکار			
است / ـه Is	Notebook	دَفتَر		What is?	
	Table/Desk	میز			
	Chalk	گَچ	آن/اون		آن/اون That
	Board	تَخته			
	Wall	دیوار			
	Chair	صَندَلی			
	Door	دَر			
	My bag	کیفِ من			

Sentences with demonstrative pronouns do not require an article (a/the) in Persian.

این and آن precede the noun and carry stress.

👄 🎧 WHO IS SHE/HE?

Answer			Question	
است / ـه	بابَک	او / اون	کیست؟ / کی است؟ او / اون کیه؟ Who is?	او / اون
	اَلِکس			
	خانمِ / آقای کَریمی			
	نِگین خانم			
	دُکترِ من			
	دوستِ خواهرِ من			

Practice the new words and come to class prepared for a Q & A session identifying your classmates and classroom objects.

تمرین ۱۴ 👄 ✏

Translate and pronounce aloud:

1. What is this? This is my pencil.

2. What is that? That is her computer.

3. Who is she? She is our teacher.

4. What is this? This is (a) bag.

5. Who are they? They are my parents.

تمرین ۱۵ : واژگان

In each line, circle the word that does not match the rest:

جغرافی	فامیلی	هنر	۱. ریاضی
گچ	خانواده	رایانه	۲. کامپیوتر
جامعه شناسی	روان شناسی	ادبیات	۳. زیست شناسی
دختر	مادر	خواهر	۴. شوهر
وقت دارید	لازم داری	هستند	۵. دوست دارم
خودکار	مداد	دفتر	۶. چه عالی
قربانت	تخته	میز	۷. صندلی

دستور زبان ۳

SPECIFIC, NON-SPECIFIC, AND GENERIC NOUNS

There is no definite article "the" or indefinite article "a" in Persian. Persian nouns exist in three states: "specific", "non-specific", and "generic". The specific noun is known by both listener and speaker.

The non-specific noun is not known by the listener. The word کتاب can either mean '*the book*' (about which we already know something) or '*books*' (in general). Examples:

Specific noun	I have (this/that) book.	۱. من (این ـ آن) کتاب را دارم.
	I have the book.	۲. من کتاب را دارم.
	Where is the book? (*Spoken*)	۳. کتابه کجاست؟
Non-specific noun	I have (a/any/some/one) book.	۴. من یک کتاب دارم.
	I have (a/any/some/one) book. (*Literary*)	۵. من کتابی دارم.
Generic noun	I like books.	۶. من کتاب دوست دارم.

In Example 1, این/آن are demonstrative adjectives.

Example 2 has a suffix را and we will learn about it on the next page.

Example 3 has a specific suffix ه /e/ which is only used in spoken form.

Example 5 has a non-specific suffix ی /i/ which is mainly used in literary writing.

> ## Review
> A "specific" noun needs: …….. or ….… or …….… or ….….
> A "non-specific" noun needs: …….. or …….…
> A "generic" noun needs: …….…

> *Common Mistake:* Be mindful not to confuse the specific suffix ه /e/ with Ezāfe.

تمرین ۱۶

Determine if the underlined nouns are "specific", "non-specific", or "generic":

۱. این مداد است.

۲. سارا و نگین دانشجو هستند.

۳. من یک کامپیوتر لازم دارم.

۴. کامپیوتر خوب است.

۵. آن زن خواهرِ من است.

۶. دانشگاهِ تهران زیبا است.

۷. کتابه خوبه؟

۸. دخترِ من خیلی روان شناسی را دوست دارد.

دستور زبان ۴

SPECIFIC DIRECT OBJECT MARKER را

را is an unstressed suffix that is added after a specific direct object (or the word that modifies it). In spoken form, را is pronounced as either /ro/ or /o/. را should be written separately. Non-specific and generic direct objects do not need را. Examples:

Specific Direct Object: Needs را	I have this/that book.	۱. من (این ـ آن) کتاب را دارم.
	I have the book.	۲. من کتاب را دارم.
	I have the book. (Spoken)	۳. من کتابه رو دارم.
	I have your book.	۴. من کتابِ تو را دارم.
Non-specific Direct Object: Does NOT need را	I have (a/any/some/one) book.	۵. من یک کتاب دارم.
	I have (a/any/some) book. (Literary)	۶. من کتابی دارم.
Generic Direct Object: Does NOT need را	I like books.	۷. من کتاب دوست دارم.

Verbs are divided into three categories:

Intransitive verbs (*To be, To walk*) do not require a direct object so they do not need را.

Transitive verbs (*To read, To see*) require a direct object. If the direct object is specific, it needs را.

Di-transitive verbs (*To send, To give*) require both a direct object and an indirect object. While the specific direct object needs را, the indirect object needs a preposition. Example:

I gave the book to Mina.　من کتاب را به مینا دادم.

تمرین ۱۷

Insert را where needed:

۱. سلام ـــــــ برسانید.

۲. او ایرانی ـــــــ است.

۳. من دانشگاه تهران ـــــــ دوست دارم.

۴. آقای پارسا خواهر ـــــــ ندارند.

۵. شما آن رایانه ـــــــ لازم دارید؟

۶. آنها این ترم سه کلاس ـــــــ دارند.

تمرین ۱۸

Replace the non-specific suffix with یک and vice versa. Note that the non-specific suffix ی can be added to a **noun** or an **adjective**. Determine if the ی is added to a noun or an adjective.

۱. آن نویسنده یک کتاب دارد.

۲. او دختری زیباست.

۳. آقای مهندس کامپیوترِ قشنگی دارد.

۴. خانمِ پرستار یک کیفِ کوچک دارد.

۵. دانشگاهِ تهران، دانشگاهِ بزرگی است.

تمرین ۱۹

Pronounce the following sets of words aloud and explain the difference between the two in each set. Note that the green letters are inserted to ease the pronunciation.

کتابی	کتابِ
کتابخانه‌ای	کتابخانه‌ی
دانشجویی	دانشجوی
بچّه‌ای	بچّه‌ی
آقایی	آقای
صندلیی	صندلیِ

تمرین ۲۰

Listen to the audio file and complete the following dialogue:

نسرین: سلام رابرت.

رابرت : ـــــــ ـــــــ ـــــــ .

نسرین: ـــــــ نیستم ـــــــ چطوری؟

رابرت: ـــــــ ـــــــ مرسی.

نسرین: تو ـــــــ ترم ـــــــ داری؟

رابرت: ـــــــ ـــــــ ـــــــ ـــــــ .

نسرین: من ـــــــ ـــــــ رو لازم ـــــــ .

رابرت: ـــــــ لازم ندارم ـــــــ تو!

نسرین: ـــــــ ! ـــــــ !

دستور زبان ۵

POSSESSION WITH مال

Persian does not have a specific set of possessive pronouns that correspond to the English words *mine, yours, his/hers. etc.* Instead, these pronouns are expressed through the word مال. مال literally means "property" and when followed by Ezāfe and a personal pronoun, it functions in the same way as the English possessive pronouns. مال is always in singular form and carries stress.

Plural		Singular		
Ours	مالِ ما	Mine	مالِ من	1st person
Yours	مالِ شما	Yours	مالِ تو	2nd person
Their	مالِ آنها	His/Hers	مالِ او	3rd person

مال can also be followed by Ezāfe and a noun/proper noun as in مالِ کلاس (the class's or that of class) or مالِ مینا (Mina's or that of Mina).

مال can refer to notions beyond possession. For instance, مالِ ایران can mean "Made in Iran" or "a person from Iran". Also, مالِ دانشگاه means "university's" or "used for the university".

Common Mistake: Be mindful not to confuse the following three forms:

This is MINE.	این مالِ من است.
This is MY book.	این کتابِ من است
This book is MINE.	این کتاب مالِ من است.

تمرین ۲۱

Translate the following sentences and read them aloud. Use the written form and آیا where needed:

1. This book is not yours.

2. Is this the university's/for the university?

3. Is that computer yours?

4. This chair is not made in France.

5. That bag does not belong to my friend.

6. This is the baby's.

 بیشتر بدانیم

Expressing Needs & Wants

 Short Dialogues (Spoken Form)

دوست داشتن To Like	لازم داشتن To Need
۲. خواهرِ تو چی دوست داره؟ خواهرِ من کیف دوست داره.	۱. تو چی لازم داری؟ من یه دفتر لازم دارم.
۴. شما چی دوست دارین؟ من پیتزا دوست دارم.	۳. تو این کتابَه رو لازم داری؟ نه لازم ندارم.

چی carries stress (chí). In Example 3, due to a vowel harmony rule, the specific suffix /e/ changes to /a/ before /ro/. Hence "ketāb-e ro" changes to "ketāb-a ro".

 تمرین ۲۲

Practice the above phrases with your classmates and write a similar dialogue of at least 6 lines. For additional vocabulary look at the list at the end of the lesson.

 تمرین ۲۳

Arrange the following words to make a sentence. Read your sentences aloud:

۱. را – من – خودکار – آن – لازم دارم

۲. چند تا – این ترم – کلاس – داری – تو – ؟

۳. برادر ـ علی ـ خواهر ـ ندارد ـ و

۴. است – آن – صندلی – مال – من

۵. هستی – دانشگاه – تو – در ـ؟

۶. کتاب ـ دوست ندارند – جامعه شناسی – آنها – را

عددها ۰–۱۰۰

							صِفر	۰
Numericals are written from left to right.

۴۰	چِهِل	۲۱	بیست و یِک	۱۱	یازدَه	۲	یِک	۱
۵۰	پَنجاه	۲۲	بیست و دو	۱۲	دَوازدَه	۲	دو	۲
۶۰	شَصت	۲۳	بیست و سه	۱۳	سیزدَه	۳	سه	۳
۷۰	هَفتاد	۲۴	بیست و چهار	۱۴	چهاردَه	۴	چهار	۴
۸۰	هَشتاد	۲۵	بیست و پَنج	۱۵	پانزدَه/پونزده	۵	پَنج	۵
۹۰	نَوَد	۲۶	بیست و شِش/ بیست و شیش	۱۶	شانزدَه/شونزده	۶	شِش/شیش	۶
۱۰۰	صَد	۲۷	بیست و هَفت	۱۷	هِفدَه/هیفده	۷	هَفت	۷
		۲۸	بیست و هَشت	۱۸	هِجدَه/هیژده	۸	هَشت	۸
		۲۹	بیست و نُه	۱۹	نوزدَه	۹	نُه	۹
		۳۰	سی	۲۰	بیست	۱۰	دَه	۱۰

When saying numbers, /va/ is pronounced as /o/ in spoken (and sometimes in written) form.

Nouns remain singular after numbers. Example: چهار کلاس

تمرین ۲۴

Write the following numbers using the Persian alphabet and pronounce them aloud:

۵۲	۹۳
۸۸	۶۶
۲۷	۱۴
۶۱	۷۹

تمرین ۲۵ 👄

Phone numbers are read in 2-digit or 3-digit groups in Persian. Look at Maryam's phone book and read the phone numbers aloud with your classmate. Example:

تِلِفُن	نام خانوادگی	نام
۸۸۳۶۹۷۰۹	کامیاب	پَری
۷۱۹۸۲۰۴۹	پارسا	کوروش
۲۰۶۴۸۱۷۳	کیوانی	مینا
۸۰۷۳۲۶۱۵	آفشار	هومَن

Student 1: پَری کامیاب
Student 2: ۸۸۳۶۹۷۰۹

تو چند سال داری؟ ـ تو چند ساله‌ای؟   How Old Are You? 🎧 👄

Option 2	Option 1
۲. تو چند ساله‌ای؟ من بیست ساله‌ام.	۱. تو چند سال داری؟ من سی سال دارم.
۴. علی چند ساله‌ست؟ علی بیست و یک ساله‌ست.	۳. دخترِ تو چند سال دارد؟ دخترِ من پنج سال دارد.

چند ساله constitutes one word. Stress falls on the final syllable: (chand sālé).
What do you think is the difference between Options 1 and 2 above?

تمرین ۲۶ 👥 ✏️

Talk with your classmates about the age of their parents, siblings, and children. Write your findings in the form of a short report. Example:

مادرِ لورا پنجاه و هفت سال دارد. پدرِ لورا شصت و دو سال است....

چهار عَمَلِ اَصلی BASIC ARITHMETIC

Addition	جَمع	۱ + ۲ = ۳	یک به اِضافه‌ی دو مُساوی است با سه.
Subtraction	مِنها	۳ − ۲ = ۱	سه مِنهای دو مُساوی است با یک.
Multiplication	ضَرب	۲ × ۲ = ۴	دو ضَرب دَر دو مُساوی است با چهار.
Division	تَقسیم	۴ ÷ ۲ = ۲	چهار تَقسیم بر دو مُساوی است با دو.

It is common for the digit to follow the verb.

تمرین ۲۷

Write the following calculations using the Persian alphabet and read them aloud. Use the above chart as a model.

۱۶ ÷ ۲ =   _____ .۱

۳۸ − ۲۵ =   _____ .۲

۱۲ × ۴ =   _____ .۳

۹۸ + ۲ =   _____ .۴

۴۳ − ۲۷ =   _____ .۵

تمرین ۲۸

The following information is written on a building sign. Underline familiar words. What is this sign about?

> نشر و پخش کتاب دانش
> کتاب‌های دانشگاهی
> زبان‌های خارجه
> ادبیات انگلیس و فرانسه

تمرین ۲۹

Answer in Persian using complete sentences. Use the written form.

۱. آیا تو بچّه داری؟

۲. دانشگاهِ شما بزرگ است؟

۳. اسمِ کتابِ فارسیِ شما چیست؟

۴. آیا این کامپیوتر مالِ تو است؟

۵. تو چند سال داری؟

۶. پدرِ تو چند ساله است؟

تمرین ۳۰

Listen to the audio file and fill out the following chart:

مادر آقای نوری	همسر نیلوفر	دخترکاوه	کاوه	نیلوفر	خانمِ نوری	آقای نوری	
							پنجاه و نه سال
							سی و یک ساله
							هفده سال
							بیست و نه ساله
							نویسنده
							مدیر
							پرستار

تمرین ۳۱

Work with a classmate and find the following words in the advertisement below:

- A phone number

- An address

- The names of three countries

- What do you think this flyer is about?

> **تابستان به یادماندنی با ایران سفر**
> **تورهای اروپایی**
> **تور کانادا و آمریکا**
> **تورهای داخل کشور**
> **آدرس: خیابان کارگر ــ پلاک ۸۲۱**
> **تلفن: ۲۰۶۱۳۱۷۶**

Now that you have learned the verb "To Have" you can say *"What is the homework?"* in Persian:

تَکلیف چی داریم؟

تمرین ۳۲

Task: You meet a guy, almost your age, at school. Say the following in Persian. Use the informal spoken form:

1. Greet him.

2. Ask him if he has got time.

3. Ask him his last name.

4. Ask him if he is Iranian.

5. Tell him "How nice! I have Persian this term".

6. Ask how many classes he has this term

7. Tell him how many classes you have and what they are.

8. Tell him that you don't like the chemistry class.

9. Ask him if his parents are in Tehran.

10. Tell him that your brother is in Tehran and that you like Iran a lot.

11. Say good bye.

REVIEW CORNER	
Points that remain unclear about Lesson 2:	
How I plan to work on these points:	

شعر

Read the following poem by Abbas Yamini-Sharif and find two instances of the Ezāfe construction. Find six instances of the short form of "To Be". You will not be evaluated on the content but you can use it for cultural enrichment.

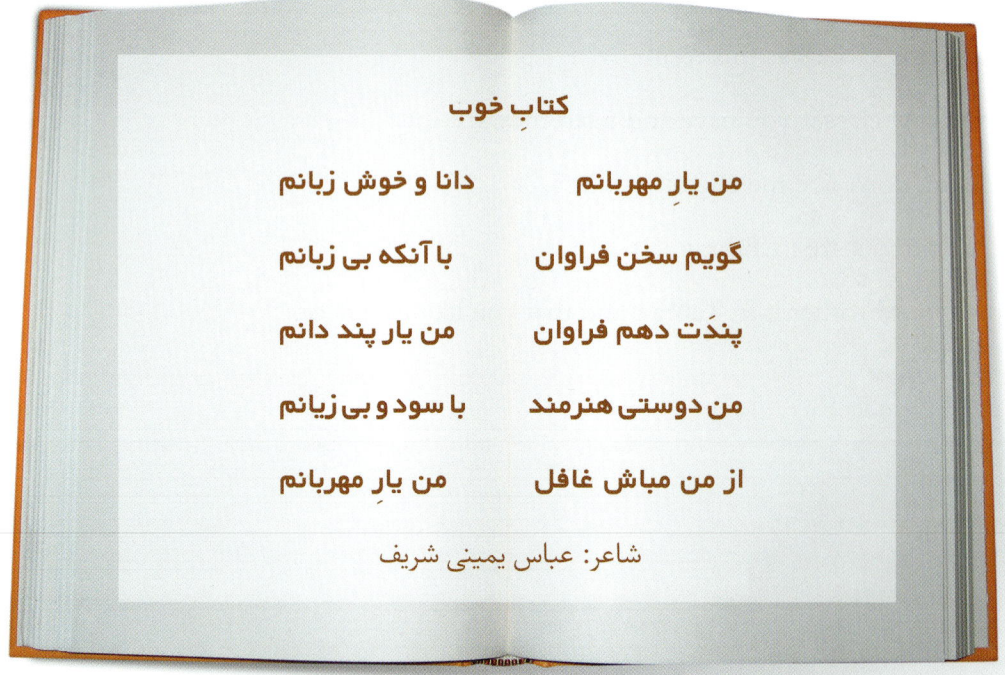

کتابِ خوب

دانا و خوش زبانم   من یارِ مهربانم

با آنکه بی زبانم   گویم سخن فراوان

من یار پند دانم   پندَت دهم فراوان

با سود و بی زیانم   من دوستی هنرمند

من یارِ مهربانم   از من مباش غافل

شاعر: عباس یمینی شریف

نکته‌ی فرهنگی

Diverse Iran

Iran is a diverse country that consists of many different ethnic groups including Azaris, Turks, Turkmans, Kurds, Lors, Baluchis, Gilakis, Bakhtiaris, Ghashghayis, etc. These ethnic groups have lived in Iran for several thousand years. They are often regionally located and have their own traditions and rituals. They often speak their own dialect or language. Despite Iran's linguistic diversity, Persian remains the official language of the nation. Persian may be spoken with different accents regionally. This textbook introduces the standard form of Persian which is used in broadcasts and the media. The spoken forms are in the Tehrani accent. In order to become familiar with some of the regional accents, Dialogue 1 at the beginning of the lesson is repeated here with Mashhadi, Gilaki, and Esfahani accents.

The Persian-speaking World

In addition to Iran, Persian is widely spoken in Afghanistan and Tajikistan and other Central Asian countries such as Uzbekistan. While the name of the Persian language has been changed to Dari and Tajiki for political reasons, Dari and Tajiki are in fact variants of Persian. This is similar to the difference between the French spoken in France and the French spoken in Quebec, Canada. Speakers can understand each other but there are variations in terms of accent and terminology. So the languages spoken in Afghanistan and Tajikistan are in fact Dari Persian and Tajiki Persian.

Persian vs. Farsi

Farsi is the native name of the Persian language (similar to Deutsch/German, Français/French, and Español/Spanish). The Academy of the Persian Language & Literature (Farhangestān) indicates that "Persian" rather than "Farsi" is the preferred term to be used in western languages. So when speaking in English, we should use the term "Persian" and when speaking in Persian, we should use the term "Farsi".

ضرب المثل

Literal translation: *"I used to have, I used to have"* does *not count. "I have, I have"* is what counts.

داشتَم داشتَم حِساب نیست. دارم دارم حسابه!

This proverb states that one should not dwell on the past but should focus on the present.

Thematic Review of New Vocabulary

Family	
Dad	بابا
Baby/Child/Kid	بَچّه
Brother	بَرادَر
Father	پِدَر
Parents	پِدَر وَ مادَر
Boy/Son	پِسَر
Family	خانواده
Sister	خواهَر
Girl/Daughter	دُختَر
Woman/Wife	زَن
Husband	شوهَر
Mother	مادَر
Mom	مامان
Spouse	هَمسَر

Fields of Study	
Literature	اَدَبیات
English	اِنگلیسی
History - Date	تاریخ
Sociology	جامِعه شِناسی
Geography	جُغرافی
Psychology	رَوان شِناسی
Mathematics	ریاضی
Biology	زیست شِناسی
Chemistry	شیمی
Persian	فارسی
Physics	فیزیک
Arts	هُنَر

Prepositions & Suffixes	
In/Inside/At (Spoken)	تو (tu)
Specific direct object suffix	را
Specific suffix	ه
Non-specific suffix	ی

Class Objects	
Board	تَخته
Pen	خودکار
Door	دَر
Notebook	دَفتَر
Wall	دیوار
Chair	صَندَلی
Computer	کامپیوتر - رایانه
Book	کِتاب
My bag	کیفِ من
Chalk	گَچ
Pencil	مِداد
Table/Desk	میز

Nouns & Adjectives	
Easy	آسان
Term	تِرم
Homework	تَکلیف
Friend	دوست
Year	سال
Last/Family Name	فامیلی (fámili)
Library	کتابخانه
Class/Classroom	کِلاس
Name	نام
Last/Family Name	نامِ خانِوادِگی

Words & Expressions	
This	این
That	آن
So	پَس
Dear	جان
Why	چرا
How many	چَند (تا)
How old...?	چند ساله...؟
What	چه
How excellent!	چه عالی!
Good for you	خوش به حالَت
Affectionately	قُربانَت
Who	کی
Who is?	کیست؟
And	وَ

Calculations	
Plus	به اِضافه(ی)
Division	تَقسیم
Divided (by)	تَقسیم (بَر)
Addition	جَمع
Multiplication	ضَرب
Multiplied (by)	ضَرب (دَر)
Equal (to)	مُساوی (با)
Subtraction	مِنها
Minus	مِنها(ی)

Verbs & Phrases	
I have	دارم
They have	دارَند
You have	داری
I like (I have a liking)	دوست دارم
I need	لازم دارم
I do not have	نَدارم
Have you got time?	وَقت داری؟

Numbers							
						٠	صِفر
٤٠	چِهِل	٢١	بیست و یِک	١١	یازدَه	١	یِک
٥٠	پَنجاه	٢٢	بیست و دو	١٢	دَوازدَه	٢	دو
٦٠	شَصت	٢٣	بیست و سه	١٣	سیزدَه	٣	سِه
٧٠	هَفتاد	٢٤	بیست و چهار	١٤	چهاردَه	٤	چهار
٨٠	هَشتاد	٢٥	بیست و پَنج	١٥	پانزدَه	٥	پَنج
٩٠	نَود	٢٦	بیست و شِش	١٦	شانزدَه	٦	شِش
١٠٠	صَد	٢٧	بیست و هَفت	١٧	هِفدَه	٧	هَفت
		٢٨	بیست و هَشت	١٨	هِجدَه	٨	هَشت
		٢٩	بیست و نُه	١٩	نوزدَه	٩	نُه
		٣٠	سی	٢٠	بیست	١٠	دَه

فعّالیّت‌های روزانه
Daily Activities

Communication Objectives

Talking about Daily Activities and the Weekly Schedule
Talking about Means of Transportation
Talking about Actions Taking Place in the Near Future
Talking about Knowing Someone vs. Something
Using Common Courtesies
Saying Where Things Are

Contents

Thematic Review of New Vocabulary

واژگان ۱

In the vocabulary lists, the parentheses contain the **Present Stem** of the verbal element.

I do not work	کار نمی‌کُنَم (کُن)	Tonight	اِمشَب
Kabab	کَباب	Wow!/Yum Yum!	بَه بَه!
I sleep	می‌خوابَم (خواب)	What do you do?	چه کار می‌کُنی؟/چی کار می‌کُنی؟ (کُن)
I eat	می‌خورَم (خور)	House/Home	خانه/خونه
I go	می‌رَوَم/می‌رَم (رَو)	Dinner	شام
You do	می‌کُنی (کُن)	Food	غَذا
Bread	نان/نون	Tomorrow	فَردا
		Work/Job	کار

Close your book and listen to the dialogue. Then fill in the blanks using the new words.

گفتگو ۱

نرگس: امشب چی کار می‌کنی؟

سینا: می‌رم خونه. غذا می‌خورم و می‌خوابم.

نرگس: ——— ——— چی می‌خوری؟

سینا: نون و کباب می‌خورم .

نرگس: به به! من خیلی کباب دوست دارم.

سینا: فردا چی کار می‌کنی؟

نرگس: فردا کار می‌کنم. تو چی؟

سینا: من فردا ——— ——— .

کارکَردَن

In line 6 "*what do you do?*" refers to an activity.

In line 7 "*I work*" refers to a job.

نوشتاری

گفتگو ۱

نرگس: امشب چه کار می‌کنی؟

سینا: ——— خانه. غذا می‌خورم و می‌خوابم.

نرگس: شام چه می‌خوری؟

سینا: ——— و کباب می‌خورم .

نرگس: به به! من خیلی کباب دوست دارم.

سینا: فردا ——— کار می‌کنی؟

نرگس: فردا کار می‌کنم. تو چطور؟

سینا: من فردا کار نمی‌کنم .

تمرین ۱

Talk with your classmates about what you will do today, what you will eat tonight, and what you will do tomorrow. Use Dialogue 1 as a model. For additional vocabulary look at the list at the end of the lesson.

واژگان ۲

North	شُمال	Bus	اُتوبوس
City	شَهر	With/By	با
Far	دور	To	به
You come	می‌آیی / می‌آی (آ)	Dormitory	خوابگاه
Usually	مَعمولاً	You live	زِندِگی می‌کُنی (کُن)
But/Though	وَلی	I live	زِندِگی می‌کنم (کُن)
I come	می‌آییم / می‌آم (آ)	Busy/Crowded	شُلوغ

Close your book and listen to the dialogue. Then fill in the blanks using the new words.

گفتگو ۲

نرگس: تو تو خوابگاه زندگی می‌کنی؟

سینا: نه، من با پدر و مادرم زندگی می‌کنم. تو چی؟

نرگس: من تو خوابگاه زندگی می‌کنم.

سینا: ــــــــــ چطوره؟

نرگس: بد نیست ولی شلوغه.

سینا: خونه‌ی ما بزرگ و خوبه، ــــــــــ دوره.

نرگس: خونه‌ی شما کجای شهره؟

سینا: شمالِ شهره.

نرگس: آره، خیلی دوره! با چی می‌آی دانشگاه؟

سینا: ــــــــــ با اتوبوس می‌آم دانشگاه.

The م at the end of پدر و مادرم is a suffix pronoun (my parents). We will learn more about it in Lesson 4.

117

نوشتاری

گفتگو ۲

نرگس: تو در خوابگاه ــــــــــــ ؟

سینا: نه، من با پدر و مادرم زندگی می‌کنم. تو چطور؟

نرگس: من دَر خوابگاه زندگی می‌کنم.

سینا: خوابگاه چطوراست؟

نرگس: بد نیست ولی ــــــــــــ است.

سینا: خانه‌ی ما بزرگ و خوب است، ولی دور است.

نرگس: خانه‌ی شما کجای شهر است؟

سینا: شمالِ ــــــــــــ است.

نرگس: بله، خیلی دوراست. با چه به دانشگاه می‌آیی؟

سینا: معمولاً با اتوبوس به دانشگاه می‌آیم.

In spoken form, verbs of motion such as *"To Come"* آمَدَن and *"To Go"* رَفتَن are not placed at the end of the sentence. They are used before the destination. The preposition به is also dropped:

به خانه می‌رَوَم. *Written*

می‌رَم خونه. *Spoken*

با اتوبوس به دانشگاه می‌آیم. *Written*

با اتوبوس می‌آم دانشگاه. *Spoken*

 تمرین ۲

Talk with your classmates about where you live, who you live with, and how you come to school. Use Dialogue 2 as a model. For additional vocabulary look at the list at the end of the lesson.

واژگان ۳

Arabic	عَرَبی	Spanish (language)	اِسپانیایی
You know (skill/language)	بَلَدی	With each other	باهَم
You know (someone)	می‌شِناسی / می‌شناسی (شِناس)	We study	دَرس می‌خوانیم / دَرس می‌خونیم (خوان)
You know (something)	می‌دانی / می‌دونی (دان)	Because	چون
Always	هَمیشه	Tongue/Language	زَبان / زَبون
From	اَز	French (language)	فَرانسَوی ـ فَرانسه

Close your book and listen to the next dialogue. Then fill in the blanks using the new words.

گفتگو ۳

مریم: تو اونو _____؟

بیتا: آره، اون پیتره. دوستِ منه. خیلی باهوشه!

مریم: از کجا می‌دونی؟

بیتا: چون اون پنج تا زبون می‌دونه، اینگلیسی، فارسی، فرانسه، اسپانیایی و _____!

مریم: چه عالی! تو چند تا زبون بلدی؟

بیتا: دو تا، اینگلیسی و فارسی.

مریم: شما _____ درس می‌خونین؟

بیتا: آره، همیشه تو کتابخونه درس می‌خونیم.

نوشتاری

گفتگو ۳

بیتا: تو او را می‌شناسی؟

مریم: بله، او پیتر است. دوستِ من است. خیلی باهوش است!

بیتا: از کجا می دانی؟

مریم: چون او پنج _____ می‌داند، انگلیسی، فارسی، فرانسوی، اسپانیایی و عربی!

بیتا: چه عالی! تو چند زبان بلدی؟

مریم: دو زبان، انگلیسی و فارسی.

بیتا: شما با هم درس می‌خوانید؟

مریم: بله، _____ در کتابخانه درس می‌خوانیم.

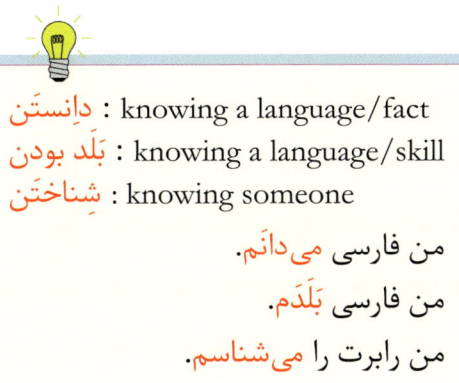

knowing a language/fact : دانِستَن

knowing a language/skill : بَلَد بودن

knowing someone : شِناخَتَن

من فارسی می‌دانَم.

من فارسی بَلَدَم.

من رابرت را می‌شناسم.

تمرین ۳

Role-play the above dialogue with your classmates. For additional vocabulary look at the list at the end of the lesson.

تمرین ۴

Find six words in Dialogues 1-3 that are different in written and spoken forms and write them below. Pronounce the words as you write.

Spoken	← Written	Spoken	← Written

119

خواندن

برنامه‌ی روزانه‌ی کامران

کامران در تهران زندگی می‌کند. او فارسی و انگلیسی می‌داند. او مهندسیِ کامپیوتر می‌خواند. کامران هر روز صبح بیدارمی‌شود، صبحانه می‌خورد و با اتوبوس به دانشگاه می‌رود. کلاسِ او بعد از ظهر تمام می‌شود. کامران به خانه می‌آید، شام می‌خورد، کمی درس می‌خواند و می‌خوابد. کامران معمولاً در دانشگاه ناهار می‌خورد.

S/he wakes up	بیدار می‌شَوَد (شَو)
Program/Plan/Schedule	بَرنامه
Daily	روزانه
Finishes (something)	تَمام می‌شَوَد (شَو)
Breakfast	صُبحانه
Computer engineering	مُهَندِسیِ کامپیوتر
S/he reads	می‌خوانَد (خوان)

Each/Every	هَر	Lunch	ناهار
Academic field	رِشته	A little	کَمی

خواندن vs. درس خواندن
درس خواندن means to **study** (in general); خواندن means to **read** or to **study a specific topic/field**. Examples:
من درس می‌خوانم
من فیزیک می‌خوانم
*من فیزیک درس می‌خوانم   *Common Mistake:*

تمرین ۵

a) Listen to the audio file and follow along in your text. Repeat each sentence several times.

b) Answer in complete sentences. Use the written form.

۱. کامران در کجا زندگی می‌کند؟

۲. آیا کامران فارسی و انگلیسی می‌داند؟

۳. کامران چه رشته‌ای می‌خواند؟

۴. برنامه‌ی روزانه‌ی کامران چیست؟

۵. کامران معمولاً در کجا ناهار می‌خورد؟

بیشتر بدانیم

Times of the Day			
Later afternoon/Evening	عَصر	Morning	صُبح
Night	شَب	Noon	ظُهر
Midnight	نیمه شب	Afternoon	بَعد از ظهر

تمرین ۶

Write a paragraph about your daily routines. Use the reading text as a model.

تمرین ۷: واژگان

Fill in the blanks using the appropriate vocabulary from the list below.

اتوبوس ــ امشب ــ می‌شناسی ــ معمولاً ــ کجا ــ خوابگاه ــ به به ــ بلدی ــ شمال ــ دوست

۱. ‏ـــــــــــ من خیلی کباب دوست دارم.

۲. تو در ‏ـــــــــــ کار می‌کنی؟

۳. من در ‏ـــــــــــ زندگی می‌کنم.

۴. با چی می‌آی دانشگاه؟ با ‏ـــــــــــ. (Spoken)

۵. شما کجای شهر زندگی می‌کنید؟ ‏ـــــــــــ شهر.

۶. کامران ‏ـــــــــــ در دانشگاه ناهار می‌خورد.

۷. تو مینا را ‏ـــــــــــ؟ بله. مینا ‏ـــــــــــ من است.

۸. تو چند تا زبان ‏ـــــــــــ؟ سه تا، انگلیسی، فارسی و اسپانیایی.

 دستور زبان ۱

SIMPLE PRESENT TENSE حالِ ساده

The simple present tense performs a number of functions in Persian:

1. A current fact or state of being: من کَباب دوست دارم. I like kabab.

2. An action that takes place habitually or routinely:

علی هر روز در دانشگاه ناهار می‌خورد.   Ali eats lunch at the university everyday.

3. An action that takes place in the near future:

من فردا کار می‌کنم.   I will work tomorrow.

In order to form the present tense, you need the "**Present Stem**" of the verb. The present stem of a verb cannot usually be predictably derived from the infinitive and must be memorized as each is introduced[1]. Examples:

Present Stem	← Infinitive	
خَند	خَندیدن ←	To Laugh
رَو	رَفتن ←	To Go
کُن	کَردَن ←	To Do

The list of verbs and their present stems is included in Appendix A.

To form the Present Tense:

1) Add the prefix می before the present stem: خَند + می

2) Add the appropriate verb ending: م + خَند + می

The /mí/ prefix is stressed and should be written separately. In older writings, you may see it connected to the verb.

Present Tense (To Laugh) خندیدن

ما می‌خندیم	من می‌خندَم
We laugh	I laugh
شما می‌خندید	تو می‌خندی
You(pl) laugh	You laugh
آنها می‌خندَند	او می‌خندَد
They laugh	He/She laughs

Common Mistake: Be mindful not to use the **past stem** instead of the **present stem**! We will learn more about the past stem in Lesson 6.

---

1. The present stem of some of the verbs can be derived through rules but it is easier for students to memorize them.

COMPOUND VERBS فِعل‌های تَرکیبی

The majority of Persian verbs are "compound verbs" and consist of more than one element. This is similar to the English verb "*To take a trip*" (compound verb) as opposed to "*To travel*" (simple verb). Compound verbs consist of a verbal component (ex: *to take*) and a non-verbal component *(ex: a trip)*. The verbal component of a compound verb provides the present stem. Examples:

Present Stem	← Infinitive
دَرس‌خوان	دَرس خوانَدن ←
کار‌کُن	کار کردن ←

In the infinitive form, stress falls on the final syllable of compound verbs (dars khāndán).

Important: The می prefix is inserted between the verbal and non-verbal components.

Present Tense (To Study)   درس خواندن

درس می‌خوانیم	ما	درس می‌خوانَم	من
درس می‌خوانید	شما	درس می‌خوانی	تو
درس می‌خوانَند	آنها	درس می‌خوانَد	او

Stress falls on the final syllable of the non-verbal component (dárs mikhānam).

Writing and Pronunciation:

If the present stem ends with a vowel, a /y/ is inserted after the present stem:

Translation	Conjugated	Present Stem	Infinitive
I come	می‌آیَم	آ	آمَدن
I say	می‌گویَم	گو	گُفتَن

NEGATION

To negate the simple present tense insert the نِ prefix before the می prefix. The negative prefix takes primary stress in both simple and compound verbs (némikhandam) and (dàrs némikhānam). In (dàrs némikhānam), the final syllable of the non-verbal component takes secondary stress.

درس خواندن

درس نِمی‌خوانیم	ما	درس نِمی‌خوانم	من
درس نِمی‌خوانید	شما	درس نِمی‌خوانی	تو
درس نِمی‌خواند	آنها	درس نِمی‌خواند	او

خندیدن

نِمی‌خندیم	ما	نِمی‌خندم	من
نِمی‌خندید	شما	نِمی‌خندی	تو
نِمی‌خندند	آنها	نِمی‌خندد	او

تمرین ۸

With a classmate, practice reading the present tense of "*To Laugh*" and "*To Study*" (affirmative and negative forms). Take turns and listen to each other's reading.

123

تمرین ۹

Use Appendix A and conjugate the following verbs in the simple present tense.

۱. آنها فردا شب به ایران ———————— . (رفتَن)

۲. تو فارسی ———————— ؟ (دانِستَن)

۳. آنها آمریکایی ———————— . (بودن) (Negative)

۴. دخترِ من معمولاً بعد از ظهر ———————— . (درس خواندَن)

۵. من در ایران ———————— . (زندگی کردن) (Negative)

۶. آیا شما مینا را ———————— ؟ (شِناختَن)

۷. پدر و مادرِ من ———————— .(درس خواندَن) (Negative)

۸. آیا شما به آمریکا ———————— ؟ (آمَدَن)

۹. تو هَمیشه در دانشگاه ناهار ———————— ؟ (خوردَن)

۱۰. آنها آمریکایی ———————— . (بودن)

۱۱. کلاسِ من بعد از ظهر ———————— . (تمام شُدَن)

۱۲. من اِمروز ———————— . (کار کردَن) (Negative)

تمرین ۱۰

Describe each picture using a verb from Appendix A.

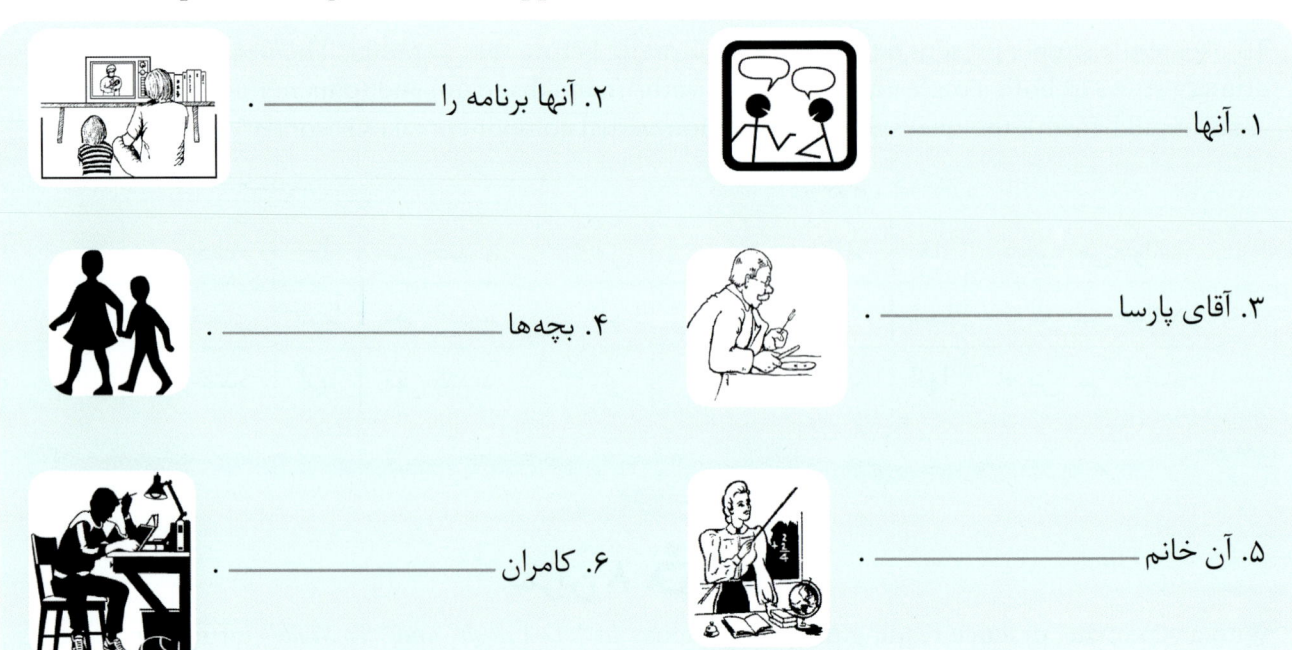

۲. آنها برنامه را ———————— .

۱. آنها ———————— .

۴. بچه‌ها ———————— .

۳. آقای پارسا ———————— .

۶. کامران ———————— .

۵. آن خانم ———————— .

بیشتر بدانیم

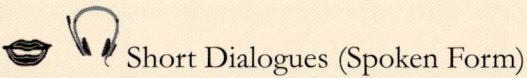

Means of Transportation

Car	ماشین	Bus	اُتوبوس
Airplane	هَواپیما	Bicycle	دوچَرخه
Taxi	تاکسی	On foot	پیاده

Short Dialogues (Spoken Form)

Option 2	Option 1
۲. a: مامانِ تو با چی می‌ره شیراز؟ b: با هواپیما.	۱. a: چطوری می‌آی دانشگاه؟ b: پیاده.
۴. a: شما با چی مسافرت می‌کنین؟ b: با ماشین.	۳. a: پدر و مادرِ تو چطوری می‌رن خونه؟ b: با تاکسی.

Stress falls on the final syllable of چطوری (chetorí).

 تمرین ۱۱

Task A: Interview your classmate and ask about his or her daily schedule. Begin with the first thing they do in the morning and continue in chronological order. Ask them what type of transportation they use to go to different places. Examples:

۲. چطوری می‌آی دانشگاه؟	۱. تو هر روز صبح چی کار می‌کنی؟
۴. تو هر شب چی کار می‌کنی؟	۳. تو هر روز بعد از ظهر چی کار می‌کنی؟

Task B: Write down your findings about your classmate's daily routine in the form of a short report.

 درس سوم

زبان‌ها Languages

Arabic	عَرَبی	Pashto	پَشتو	Spanish	اِسپانیایی
Persian	فارسی	Turkish	تُرکی	English	اِنگِلیسی
French	فَرانسَوی – فَرانسه	Chinese	چینی	Italian	ایتالیایی
Hindi	هِندی	Japanese	ژاپُنی	German	آلمانی

Short Dialogues (Spoken Form)

Option 2	Option 1
۲. a: خواهرِ تو آلمانی می‌دونه؟	۱. a: تو چند تا زبون بلدی؟
b: نه، مینا آلمانی نمی‌دونه.	b: دو تا، انگلیسی و فارسی.
۴. a: شما تو دانشگاه چی می‌خونین؟	۳. a: شما فارسی بلدین؟
b: ما تو دانشگاه هندی و عربی می‌خونیم.	b: بله، من کمی فارسی بلدم.

تمرین ۱۲

Make sentences using the following words. The verbs are in the infinitive form and need to be conjugated. Make negative sentences for 1 and 3. Use the written form.

۱. پشتو - دانستن :

۲. فارسی - بلد بودن:

۳. ژاپنی - خواندن:

۴. فارسی و چینی - دانستن:

دستور زبان ۲

PLURALS

The plural suffix that can be used for all nouns is ها. The plural suffix ان is used only for animates. Both plural suffixes carry stress. In Persian, all nouns, including the uncountable nouns such as "water" (آب), can be in plural form. Examples:

Plural ← Singular	Plural ← Singular	Plural ← Singular
کتاب ← کتاب‌ها	ترم ← ترم‌ها	آب ← آب‌ها
پدر و مادر ← پدر و مادرها ـ پدر و مادران	دختر ← دخترها ـ دختران	مَرد ← مَردها ـ مَردان

Not all animate nouns can take ان. For instance, بابا does not take ان. Some plants and body parts are considered animates and take ان (ex: Trees درَختان and Hands دَستان). Compound nouns take only one plural suffix at the end (ex: پدر و مادران).

There are other less common plural suffixes that we will learn later.

Writing and Pronunciation:

ها may be written connected or separately (older texts write it connected to the word). ان is always written connected.

- If a word ends in the long vowels /ā/, /u/, or /i/, a /y/ is inserted before ان. Examples:

آقا + ان ← آقایان

دانشجو + ان ← دانشجویان

- If a noun that ends in ها is followed by an adjective, a /y/ is inserted between the noun and the adjective. Example:

کتاب‌های خوب   The good books

Inanimate Plural Subjects:

Inanimate plural subjects can have a singular or a plural verb. Examples:

کتاب‌ها در کلاس است. (or) کتاب‌ها در کلاسَند.   The books are in the classroom.

Generic nouns are in singular form:

In English, generic (countable) nouns are in plural form (ex: *I like books*). In Persian, generic nouns are always in **singular** form. Examples:

من کتاب دوست دارم.   I like books.

کتاب خوب است.   Books are good.

> *Common Mistake:* Be mindful not to follow the English pattern!
>
> *من کتاب‌ها دوست دارم.
>
> *کتاب‌ها خوب است.
>
> *من چهار کتاب‌ها دارم.

The Non-Specific Plural:

In Persian, a plural noun is considered "specific" unless it has the non-specific suffix /i/. Examples:
کتاب‌ها (Specific) The books ــ کتاب‌هایی Some/any books (Non-specific)

In the second example, a /y/ (in blue) is inserted before the non-specific suffix /i/ to ease the pronunciation.

Adjectives: If a noun has an adjective, the non-specific suffix /i/ can be added to either part. Examples 1 and 2 mean the same. The only difference is that Example 1 is used in the written form and Example 2 is used in both written and spoken forms.

Non-specific Plural	Some/any good books	ketāb-ha-**y-i** khub	۱. کتاب‌هایی خوب
Non-specific Plural	Some/any good books	ketāb-hā-**y-e** khub-**i**	۲. کتاب‌های خوبی

In Example 1, the non-specific suffix /i/ is in red and a /y/ is inserted to ease the pronunciation (in blue). In example 2, there is an Ezāfe between the two words (in green) and a /y/ is inserted to ease the pronunciation. It is important to learn the pronunciation difference between 1 and 2.

> *Common Mistake:* Be mindful not to prounuce Examples1 and 2 the same!

تمرین ۱۳

1. Write the plural form(s) of the following words. Use a dictionary to find the new words.

۴. _____ ۳. _____ ۲. _____ ۱. _____

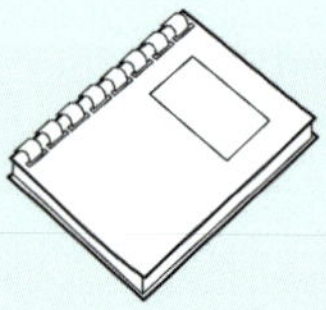

۸. _____ ۷. _____ ۶. _____ ۵. _____

۱۲. _____ ۱۱. _____ ۱۰. _____ ۹. _____

تمرین ۱۴

Choose the appropriate suffix. Note that there may be more than one appropriate suffix or no need for a suffix at all.

۱. تهرانِ شهر (ها ـ ان ـ ی) بزرگ است.

۲. تو امروز چند کلاس (ها ـ ان ـ Ø) داری؟

۳. مادرِ من کامپیوتر (ها ـ ان ـ Ø) لازم دارد.

۴. آن دختر (ها ـ ان ـ ی) با هواپیما به ایران می‌روند.

۵. من اتوبوس (ها ـ هایی ـ هایِ) بزرگ را دوست ندارم.

۶. این گل (ها ـ ان ـ ی) مالِ مادرِ من است.

تمرین ۱۵

Pronounce the following sets of words and indicate the difference between the two in each set:

برنامه‌هایی خوب	۴. برنامه‌های خوبی	ماشین‌هایی قشنگ	۱. ماشین‌های قشنگی
شهرهایی دور	۵. شهرهای دوری	کارهایی زیاد	۲. کارهای زیادی
دانشجوهایی باهوش	۶. دانشجوهای باهوشی	خوابگاه‌هایی بزرگ	۳. خوابگاه‌های بزرگی

> 💡 We have already learned that a specific direct object needs را. Therefore, any plural noun in the direct object position requires را, unless it has the non-specific suffix /i/.

تمرین ۱۶

Insert را where needed:

۱. من آن کتاب‌ها _____ لازم ندارم.

۲. آنها کارهای زیادی _____ دارند.

۳. مینا به کتابخانه‌های زیادی _____ می‌رود.

۴. تو امشب کباب‌ها _____ می‌خوری؟

۵. آن دانشجویان در خوابگاه‌های بزرگی _____ زندگی می‌کنند.

بیشتر بدانیم

🎧 PREPOSITIONS OF LOCATION

Under/Underneath	زیر	In/Inside/At	دَر	Behind/Back	پُشت	Above	بالا
Next to/Beside	کِنار	On top	رو	In/Inside/At	تو	Between	بین
In the middle of	وَسَط	Facing	رو بِرو	In front of	جُلو	Below	پایین

The above prepositions preceed the noun and are connected with Ezāfe. Examples:

زیرِ میز - رویِ کتاب - جلویِ کلاس - پشتِ من

Exceptions: تو may or may not take Ezāfe.

دَر does not take Ezāfe.

تمرین ۱۷

Answer the following question based on each image. Pronounce each sentence as you write it. Use the written form.

موش کجاست؟

۱. _____

۲. _____

۳. _____

۴. _____

۵. _____

۶. _____

۷. _____

تمرین ۱۸

Listen to the audio file and complete the following chart.

	زیرِ	رویِ	رو بروی	درِ	پشتِ	
						خانه‌ی ما
						شهرِ تهران
						کتابِ تاریخ
						کیفِ تو
						صبحانه

COMMON COURTESIES

Here you are/go Come in/Response to hello on the phone	بِفَرمایید / بِفَرمایین	Excuse me	بِبَخشید / بِبَخشین
Kind of you	لُطف دارید / لُطف دارین	You are welcome/ Please	خواهِش می‌کنم
I am sorry	مُتِأَسّفَم	Affectionately	قُربانِ شُما / قُربونِ شُما
May you not be tired	خَسته نَباشید / خَسته نَباشین	Please	لُطفاً
Thank you	دَستِتان دَرد نَکُنَد / دَستِتون دَرد نَکُنه	Sorry to bother you	بِبَخشید مُزاحِم شُدَم / بِبَخشین مُزاحِم شُدَم
		Be safe!	به سَلامَت!

The above phrases are in **formal** form. You can practice their **informal** form with your teacher. بفرمایید is a versatile word with many usages. It can mean "*here you go*", or be used as a polite expression asking someone to do something such as "*come in*", "*eat*", "*sit*", etc. It is also used as the response to a phone call.

Body-gestures that accompany common courtesies may include bowing your head and upper body slightly forward, holding one hand on the chest, and shaking your head downwards. Body gestures are practiced by men more than women. Common courtesies are further explained in the cultural note at the end of the lesson.

131

تمرین ۱۹

What is the appropriate courtesy phrase for each image? Read your sentences aloud.

.۲

.۱

a: _____

a: _____

b: _____

b: _____

.۴

.۳

a: _____

a: _____

b: _____

b: _____

تمرین ۲۰

With a classmate, prepare a conversation to perform in front of the class. Use at least five courtesy phrases. Add the appropriate body gestures.

DAYS OF THE WEEK روزهای هَفته

In Iran, the first day of the week is **Saturday**. There is only one official day off, which is **Friday**. Most offices work a half day on Thursdays.

Can you tell how the days of the week are formed in Persian?

Saturday	شَنبه
Sunday	یِکشَنبه
Monday	دوشَنبه
Tuesday	سه شَنبه
Wednesday	چهارشَنبه
Thursday	پنجشَنبه
Friday	جُمعه

Stress falls on the final syllable (ex: shanbé).

تمرین ۲۱

Listen to the audio file and fill out Mina's schedule:

			شنبه
			یکشنبه
			دوشنبه
			سه شنبه
			چهارشنبه
			پنجشنبه
			جمعه

What courses does Mina have on Thursdays? When does she have Biology? Does she have English on Saturdays? Which word means "history"?

133

تمرین ۲۲

Answer in Persian using complete sentences. Read your answers aloud.

۱. امروز چند شنبه است؟

۲. فردا چند شنبه است؟

۳. کلاسِ فارسیِ تو چند شنبه است؟

۴. تو چه روزی کلاسِ شیمی داری؟

۵. تو معمولاً چه روزهایی کار نمی کنی؟

۶. یک هفته چند روز دارد؟

تمرین ۲۳

Write down your weekly schedule and compare it with your classmate's. Find out when you are both free.

	۸- ۱۰	۱۲- ۱۰	۲ - ۱۲	۲-٤
شنبه				
یکشنبه				
دوشنبه				
سه شنبه				
چهارشنبه				
پنج شنبه				
جمعه				

دستور زبان ۳

SENTENCE STRUCTURE (II)

Verb – Indirect Object – Adverb of Place – Direct Object – Adverb of Time - Subject

من فردا کتابِ فارسی را در کتابخانه به تو می‌دهم.

Sentence structure is rather flexible in Persian. Different parts of the sentence can be moved around to show emphasis. This quality has made Persian an excellent language for rhyming and versification. Persian poetry, thus, is one of the world's greatest literatures. The sentences below show how elements of a sentence can be scrambled in Persian.

فردا من کتابِ فارسی را در کتابخانه به تو می‌دهم.

کتابِ فارسی را من فردا در کتابخانه به تو می‌دهم.

در کتابخانه من فردا کتابِ فارسی را به تو می‌دهم.

به تو من فردا کتابِ فارسی را در کتابخانه می‌دهم.

تمرین۲۴

Answer in Persian using complete sentences. Use the written form.

۱. آیا تو امشب درس می‌خوانی؟

۲. آیا تو فردا بعد از ظهر فیزیک می‌خوانی؟

۳. آیا پدر و مادرِ تو همیشه در خانه غذا می‌خورند؟

۴. آیا برادرِ تو در انگلیس زندگی می‌کند؟

۵. تو خواهرِ من، مینا را می‌شناسی؟

۶. تو ژاپنی بلدی؟

۷. استادِ شما چند زبان می‌داند؟

۸. آیا تو هر روز صبحانه می‌خوری؟

تمرین ۲۵

Describe the location of the objects in the following picture in Persian. Use at least four prepositions.

_____

_____

_____

_____

_____

تمرین ۲۶: واژگان

In each line, circle the word that does not match the rest:

ماشین	هواپیما	پیاده	۱. هندی
شناختن	دانستن	تمام شدن	۲. بلد بودن
باهم	وسط	رو برو	۳. پشت
ببخشید	خواهش می‌کنم	برنامه‌ی روزانه	۴. بفرمایید
خداحافظ	سلام برسانید	صبح به خیر	۵. خدانگهدار
با	ولی	به	۶. بعد از
معمولاً	ناهار	همیشه	۷. امشب
پایین	ظهر	عصر	۸. نیمه شب
خسته نباشید	بفرمایید	لطفاً	۹. لطف دارید
مهندسی	روبرو	برنامه	۱۰. رشته

تمرین ۲۷

a) Change into written form:

۱. تو با چی می‌آی خوابگاه؟

۲. کلاسِ ما شنبه تموم می‌شه.

b) Change into spoken form:

۱. مینا پیاده به خانه می‌رود.

۲. من فارسی نمی‌دانم.

تمرین ۲۸

Fill in the blanks with the appropriate preposition:

۱. کامپیوترِ من ـــــــــــ ـــــــــــ میز نیست. (با – به –روی)

۲. من ـــــــــــ ـــــــــــ پدر و مادرم زندگی می‌کنم. (با – به – از)

۳. رابرت ـــــــــــ ـــــــــــ کلاس کار می کند. (زیر – به –بعد از)

۴. ـــــــــــ ـــــــــــ کجا می‌دانی؟ (با – پشت – از)

۵. کامران معمولاً ـــــــــــ دانشگاه ناهار می‌خورد. (در – به – از)

۶. آنها ـــــــــــ ـــــــــــ هواپیما مسافرت می‌کنند؟ (در – با – از)

تمرین ۲۹

Task: You meet an old classmate and catch up with her/him. Ask the following questions. Use the spoken form.

1. Greet her.

2. Ask her what classes she has this term.

3. Ask her if Biology and French are easy.

4. Tell her that you study/do not study engineering.

5. Tell her that your classes are not easy.

6. Ask her where she lives.

7. Ask her if the dormitory is busy and if she likes the dorm.

8. Tell her that your house is far (away) and you come to school by bus.

9. Say bye for now.

REVIEW CORNER	
Points that remain unclear about Lesson 3:	
How I plan to work on these points:	

شعر

The following poem by Sa'di is posted at the entrance to the United Nations' *"Hall of Nations"* building in New York. Find the short forms of the verb "To Be" in this poem. You will not be evaluated on the content but you can use it for cultural enrichment.

که در آفرینش ز یک گوهرند	بنی آدم اعضای یک پیکرند
دگر عضوها را نماند قرار	چو عضوی به درد آورد روزگار
نشاید که نامت نهند آدمی	تو کز محنت دیگران بی غمی

سَعدی (۱۲۹۱–۱۲۱۰)

Sa'di is welcomed to a forum in Bukhara, 1547 AD.

ترانه

Listen to the following song by Simin Ghanem on YouTube and try to find the familiar words. Is this song in the written form or spoken form? Underline the verbs in the present tense. You will not be evaluated on the content but you can use it for cultural enrichment.

سیب

من از اون آسمونِ آبی می‌خوام

من از اون شب‌های مهتابی می‌خوام

دلم از خاطره‌های بد جداست

من از اون وقت‌های بی‌تابی می‌خوام

من می‌خوام یه دسته‌گل به آب بدم

آرزوهامو به یک حباب بدم

سیبی از شاخه‌ی حسرت بچینم

بندازم رو آسمون و تاب بدم

گل ایوونِ بهاره دل من

یه بیابون لاله زاره دل من

من از اون آسمون آبی می‌خوام

من از اون شب های مهتابی می‌خوام

دلم از خاطره‌های بد جدا

من از اون وقت‌های بی‌تابی می‌خوام

مث یک دسته‌گل اقاقیا

دلم آواز می‌کنه بیا بیا

تو می‌ری پشت علف‌ها گم می‌شی

من می‌مونم و گل اقاقیا

گل ایوونِ بهاره دل من

یه بیابون لاله زاره دل من

گل ایوونِ بهاره دل من

یه بیابون لاله زاره دل من

خواننده: سیمین غانم

139

 نکته‌ی فرهنگی

Ta'ārof

Ta'ārof or Tārof (تعارُف کردن) is a set of polite behaviors practiced by Iranians. According to the concept of Ta'ārof, social etiquette obligates one to behave "politely" towards others (including unfamiliar and familiar people). Ta'ārof may cause people to give up their true wants and needs. This concept covers a wide range of behaviors. For instance, if you compliment someone on a belonging of theirs, they will offer it to you and insist on you having it. They will say (*It is not valuable* قابلی نداره). The appropriate response is (*You are the valuble one* صاحِبِش قابِل داره).

When eating out, Iranians insist on paying for each other's meals. This may or may not be their true intention, but based on Ta'ā'rof both parties insist on paying. Another instance of Ta'ārof happens between guests and hosts: based on Ta'ā'rof, guests do not accept food or a beverage even if they are extremely hungry or thirsty. The host will then insist on offering the food despite the guest's rejection.

The concept of Ta'ārof should not be confused with Iranians' hospitality. Iranians offer their guests the best possible treatment even if they cannot afford the same treatment for themselves. It is important for foreigners to be aware of the concept of Ta'ā'rof and to be able to respond to it in a culturally appropriate manner.

Exercise:

With a classmate, prepare a scenario which involves Ta'ārof and perform it in front of the class. Your instructor will provide feedback as to whether or not your scenario can be considered Ta'ārof.

 ضرب المثل

Literal translation: *It doesn't become spring with one flower!*
(One swallow does not make a spring!)

با یه گل بهار نمی‌شه!

This Persian proverb states that a small, positive action is not enough to bring about change.

140

Thematic Review of New Vocabulary

Adverbs of Time	
Today	اِمروز
Tonight	اِمشب
Tomorrow	فَردا
Usually	مَعمولاً
Every day	هَر روز
Always	هَمیشه

Places	
House/Home	خانه
Dormitory	خوابگاه
City	شَهر

About Eating	
Dinner	شام
Breakfast	صُبحانه
Food	غَذا
Kabab	کَباب
Bread	نان
Lunch	ناهار

Means of Transportation	
Bus	اُتوبوس
Bicycle	دوچَرخه
On foot	پیاده
Taxi	تاکسی
Car	ماشین
Airplane	هَواپیما

Prepositions	
From	اَز
With/By	با
After	بعد از
To	به

Words & Expressions	
With each other	با هَم
Wow!/Yum Yum!	به بَه!
Because	چون
What do you do?	چه کاری می کُنی؟
Daily	روزانه
A little	کَمی
But/Though	وَلی

Days of the Week	
Saturday	شَنبه
Sunday	یکشَنبه
Monday	دوشَنبه
Tuesday	سه شَنبه
Wednesday	چهارشَنبه
Thursday	پنج شَنبه
Friday	جُمعه

Times of the day	
Morning	صُبح
Noon	ظُهر
Afternoon	بَعد از ظهر
Later afternoon/ Evening	عَصر
Night	شَب
Midnight	نیمه شب

Languages	
Spanish	اِسپانیایی
English	اِنگِلیسی
Italian	ایتالیایی
German	آلمانی
Pashto	پَشتو
Turkish	تُرکی
Chinese	چینی
Japanese	ژاپُنی
Arabic	عَرَبی
Persian	فارسی
French	فَرانسَوی
Hindi	هِندی

141

Nouns & Adjectives	
Water	آب
Program/Plan/Schedule	بَرنامه
Tree	دِرَخت
Hand/Arm	دَست
Far	دور
Academic field	رشته
Tongue/Language	زَبان
Busy/Crowded	شُلوغ
North	شُمال
Work/Job	کار
Flower	گُل
Man	مَرد
Mouse	موش
Week	هَفته

Common Courtesies (Formal)	
Excuse me	بِبَخشید
Sorry to bother you	بِبَخشید مُزاحم شُدَم
Here you go/are Come in/Response to hello on the phone	بِفَرمایید
Be safe	به سَلامَت
May you not be tired	خَسته نَباشید
You are welcome/Please	خواهِش می کُنَم
Thank you	دَستِتان دَرد نَکُنَد
You are the valuable one	صاحِبش قابل دارد
This is not valuable	قابلی نَدارَد
Affectionately	قُربان شُما
Kind of you	لُطف دارید
Please	لُطفاً
I am sorry	مُتِاَسِفَم

Prepositions of Location	
Above	بالا
Between	بین
Below	پایین
Behind/Back	پُشت
In/Inside (Informal)	تو
Front	جُلو
In/Inside/At	دَر
On top	رو
Facing	روبِرو
Under/Underneath	زیر
Next to/Beside	کنار
Middle	وَسَط

Verbs & Phrases	
You know (skill/language)	بَلَدی (بودَن: هَست)
S/he wakes up	بیدار می شَوَد (شُدَن: شَو)
Finishes (something)	تَمام می شَوَد (شُدَن: شَو)
We study	دَرس می خوانیم (خواندن: خوان)
You live	زِندِگی می کُنی (کَردَن: کُن)
I do not work	کار نمی کُنَم (کَردَن: کُن)
You come	می آیی (آمَدَن: آ)
I sleep	می خوابَم (خوابیدَن: خواب)
S/he reads	می خوانَد (خواندَن: خوان)
I eat	می خورَم (خوردَن: خور)
You know (something)	می دانی (دانِستَن: دان)
I go	می رَوَم (رَفتَن: رو)
You know (someone)	می شناسی (شِناختَن: شِناس)
You do	می کُنی (کَردَن: کُن)

خانه و زندگی

Housing & Living

درس چهارم

Communication Objectives

Talking about Your House and Belongings

Inquiring about a Rental Apartment

Talking about Time and Being Late

Requesting Information on the Phone

Asking Questions Using Question Words

Contents

Interactive Dialogue 1: You are Not Ready Yet?

Interactive Dialogue 2: I'm Looking for a Two-Bedroom Apartment

In-class Reading: Parsa Family's House

Grammar 1: Suffix Pronouns

Difference between Suffix Pronouns &

Full Pronouns

Let's Learn More: Numbers (100-1,000,000,000)

Ordinal Numbers

Grammar 2: Question Words

Let's Learn More: What Time is It?

Colors

Body Parts

Pets

Review Corner

Poem: پرنده مُردنی است by Forough Farrokhzad

Song: گلِ سنگم (Singer: Hayedeh)

Cultural Note: Using Body Parts in Expressions

Proverb

Thematic Review of New Vocabulary

واژگان ۱

No problem	عِیب نَدارد/ عِیب نَداره	Now	اَلان
I am late	دیر کَردَم	It means	یَعنی
Come in (Informal)	بَفَرما	I get ready	حاضِر می‌شَوَم/ حاضِر می‌شَم (شَو)
Are you not ready?	حاضِر نیستی؟	Welcome! (Informal)	خوش آمَدی!/ خوش اومَدی!
Quarter/15 minutes	رُبع	It gets late	دیر می‌شَوَد/ دیر می‌شه (شَو)
Hour/Clock/Watch	ساعَت	Restaurant	رِستوران
Your sofa/Love seat	مُبلِتان/ مُبلِتون	We arrive	می‌رِسیم (رِس)
Close by/Near	نَزدیک	There (over)	آنجا/ اونجا
All	هَمه	We have got time	وَقت داریم
Fast/Quickly/Soon	زود	Still/Yet	هَنوز

Close your book and listen to the dialogue. Then fill in the blanks using the new words.

گفتگو ۱

نگین: سلام. ـــــــــــ اومدی!

کامران: مرسی. ببخشین دیر کردم.

نگین: عیب نداره. وقت داریم. می‌رسیم. ـــــــــــ تو.

کامران: نه، دیر می‌شه. چه مبلِتون قشنگه!

نگین: ممنون. ساعت چند شام می‌خوریم؟ رستوران دوره؟

کامران: نه، نزدیکه. همه‌ی بچّه‌ها الان اونجان. ساعت هشت شام می‌خوریم.

نگین: الان ساعت یه ربع به هشته! ـــــــــــ حاضر می‌شم.

کامران: یعنی هنوز حاضر نیستی؟!

نوشتاری

گفتگو ۱

نگین: سلام. خوش ـــــــــــ!

کامران: مرسی. ببخشید دیر کردم.

نگین: عیب نداردد. وقت داریم. می‌رسیم. بفرما تو.

کامران: نه دیر می‌شَوَد. چه مبلِتان قشنگ است!

نگین: ممنون. ساعتِ چند شام می‌خوریم؟ رستوران دور است؟

کامران: نه نزدیک است. همه‌ی بچّه‌ها الان آنجا هستند. ساعتِ هشت شام می‌خوریم.

نگین: الان ساعت یک ربع به هشت است! زود حاضر ـــــــــــ.

کامران: ـــــــــــ هنوز حاضر نیستی؟!

خوش آمدی and بفرما are informal forms. Can you tell what their formal forms are? When do we use the formal forms?

تمرین ۱

Role-play the above dialogue with a classmate. Invite them into your house, apologize for being late, ask them if they are ready, etc.

واژگان ۲

Half	نیم	Are present (Polite verb)	تَشریف دارند/ تَشیف دارَن (دار)
For	بَرای	Real estate agency	بُنگاه
First word on the phone	اَلو	To you	به شما/ بِهتان/ بِهتون
Garage/Parking space	پارکینگ	Until/Till	تا
Apartment	آپارتمان	One million	یِک میلیون/ یه میلیون
When	کِی	Email address	آدرسِ اِلکترونیکی
We email	ایمیل می‌کنیم (کُن)	Your budget	بودجه‌تان/ بودجه‌تون
How much	چقَدر/ چِقَد	You look (for)...	دُنبالِ ... می‌گردید/ می‌گردین (گَرد)
Two-bedroom	دو خوابه	Rent (Noun)	اِجاره
No (Formal/Emphatic)	نه‌خِیر	List	لیست

Close your book and listen to the dialogue. Then fill in the blanks using the new words.

گفتگو ۲

نگین: ــــــــــــ ؟

مُنشی: بنگاهِ زمانی، بفرمایین.

نگین: سلام. من نگینِ کریمی هستم. ببخشین آقای زمانی تشیف دارن؟

مُنشی: نه‌خیر، تشریف ندارن. دنبالِ آپارتمان می‌گردین؟

نگین: بله. دنبالِ یه آپارتمانِ دو خوابه با پارکینگ می‌گردم.

مُنشی: برای ــــــــــــ ؟ بودجه‌تون چقده؟

نگین: بله، اجاره. بینِ یه میلیون تا یه میلیون و ــــــــــــ .

مُنشی: آقای زمانی آدرس الکترونیکی‌تونو دارن؟

نگین: بله دارن. ایشون کِی می‌آن؟

مُنشی: ساعتِ دو. یه لیست از آپارتمان‌هامون بِهتون ایمیل می‌کنیم.

نگین: متشکّر. خدانگهدار.

مُنشی: خدانگهدار.

نه‌خیر is used in formal settings. It can also be used in informal settings to show emphasis or sarcasm.

The verb ایمیل می‌کُنم includes the loan word "email".
Other examples are: تِلِفُن می‌کُنم and چَت می‌کُنم.
Some of these loan words have a Persian equivalent. For example "email" means:
پُستِ اِلِکترونیکی

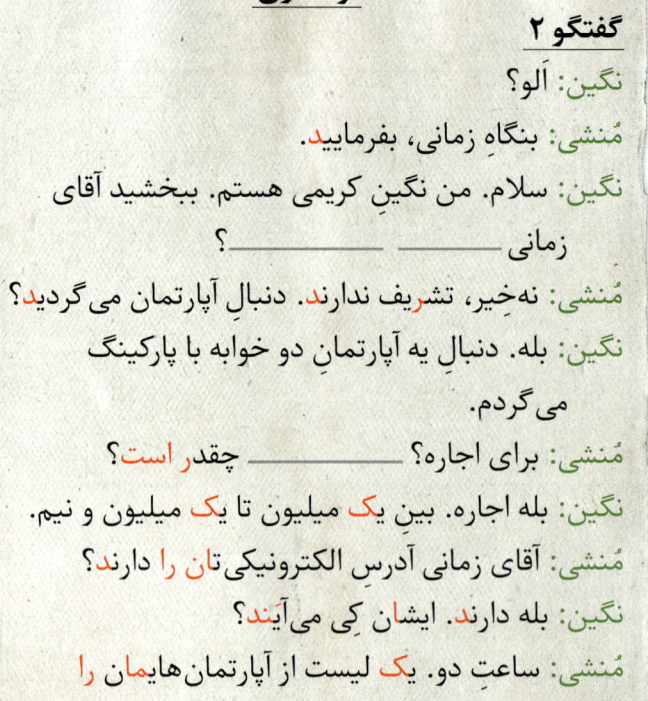

نوشتاری

گفتگو ۲

نگین: اَلو؟

مُنشی: بنگاهِ زمانی، بفرمایید.

نگین: سلام. من نگینِ کریمی هستم. ببخشید آقای زمانی ـــــــ ـــــــ ـــــــ؟

مُنشی: نه‌خیر، تشریف ندارند. دنبالِ آپارتمان می‌گردید؟

نگین: بله. دنبالِ یه آپارتمانِ دو خوابه با پارکینگ می‌گردم.

مُنشی: ـــــــ برای اجاره؟ ـــــــ چقدر است؟

نگین: بله اجاره. بینِ یک میلیون تا یک میلیون و نیم.

مُنشی: آقای زمانی آدرسِ الکترونیکی‌تان را دارند؟

نگین: بله دارند. ایشان کِی می‌آیَند؟

مُنشی: ساعتِ دو. یک لیست از آپارتمان‌هایمان را به شما ایمیل می‌کنیم.

نگین: متشکّر. خدانگهدار.

مُنشی: خدانگهدار.

تمرین ۲

Role-play the above dialogue. Provide the specifications of the apartment you are looking for (bedrooms, parking, etc.). For additional vocabulary look at the list at the end of the lesson.

تمرین ۳

Find six words that are different in written and spoken forms and write them below. Pronounce the words as you write.

Spoken	← Written	Spoken	← Written

خواندن

منزلِ خانواده‌ی پارسا

منزلِ خانواده‌ی پارسا دو طبقه است. طبقه‌ی اوّل یک آشپزخانه، یک اتاقِ نشیمن، یک اتاقِ ناهارخوری، و یک دستشویی دارد. در طبقه‌ی دوّم سه اتاقِ خواب و یک حمّام و دستشویی هست. منزلِ خانواده‌ی پارسا یک حیاطِ بزرگ و یک گاراژ دارد. منزلِ خانواده‌ی پارسا به ایستگاهِ اتوبوس نزدیک است.

Dining room	اُتاقِ ناهارخوری/اُتاق ناهارخوری	Story/Floor	طَبقه
Kitchen	آشپزخانه/آشپزخونه	First	اوّل
Bath	حمّام/حَموم	House/Home	مَنزِل
Washroom	دَستشویی/دَسشویی	Garage	گاراژ
Yard	حَیاط	Second	دوّم
Living room	اُتاقِ نِشیمَن/اُتاق نِشیمَن	Third	سوّم
Bedroom	اُتاقِ خواب/اُتاق خواب	Bus stop/Station	ایستگاه

تمرین ۴

a) Listen to the audio file and follow along in your text. Repeat each sentence several times.

b) Answer in complete sentences. Use the written form.

۱. منزلِ خانواده‌ی پارسا چند طبقه است؟

۲. در طبقه‌ی اوّل چیست؟

۳. در طبقه‌ی دوّم چیست؟

۴. خانه‌ی شما چند طبقه است؟

۵. خانه‌ی شما چند اتاق خواب و چند دستشویی دارد؟

۶. آیا خانه‌ی شما به ایستگاهِ اتوبوس نزدیک است؟

147

Antonyms		Synonyms	
دیر ≠ زود	آنجا ≠ اینجا	مَنزِل = خانه	تَشریف داشتَن = بودن
	دور ≠ نَزدیک	نَه خِیر = نَه	

تمرین ۵

Draw a basic map of the Parsa family's house. Next, prepare some questions for the next session to ask your classmate about his/her house.

تمرین ۶

Use the reading text as a model and write a paragraph to describe your house. Use the written form.

تمرین ۷ واژگان

Fill in the blanks using the appropriate vocabulary from the list below.

ایشان ــ قشنگه ــ ببخشید ــ ایمیل ــ یعنی ــ منزلِ ما ــ طبقه ــ آشپزخانه ــ تشریف دارند ــ بفرمایید

۱. _____ یک حیاطِ بزرگ و یک گاراژ دارد.

۲. _____ دیر کردم!

۳. مینا: اَلو؟

منشی: _____

۴. _____ آدرسِ الکترونیکی شما را دارند؟

۵. به به! چه خونه تون _____ !

۶. پس _____ هنوز حاضر نیستی؟

۷. من هر روز صبح در _____ صبحانه می‌خورم.

۸. خانم کریمی _____ ؟ نه خیر، نیستند.

درس چهارم

دستور زبان ۱

SUFFIX PRONOUNS

Persian has suffix pronouns that are connected to the end of a word. They do not carry stress and cannot appear alone. Suffix pronouns can be added to a **noun** to express possession (ex: **his** book); they can be added to a **preposition** (ex: for **him**); or they can be added to a **verb** to indicate the direct object (ex: I see **him**). Examples:

Noun + Suffix pronoun	His book	کتابَش / کتابِش	۱. کتابِ او ←
Preposition + Suffix pronoun	For him	بَرایَش / بَراش	۲. بَرای او ←
Verb + Suffix pronoun	I see him.	می‌بینَمَش / می‌بینِمش	۳. او را می‌بینم ←

In Examples 1 and 2, the suffix pronoun is added to a **noun** and a **preposition**. In Example 3, the suffix pronoun is added to a **verb** and indicates the **direct object**. The full pronoun and را are dropped when the suffix pronoun is used in Example 3.

Suffix Pronouns

Plural	Singular	
ـِ مان / ـِ مون	ـَ م	1st person
ـِ تان / ـِ تون	ـَ ت / ـِ ت	2nd person
ـِ شان / ـِ شون	ـَ ش / ـِ ش	3rd person

If a noun has an adjective, the suffix pronoun is attached to the adjective.   ۱. دخترِ قشنگَم

Writing and pronunciation:

1) If a word ends in /ā/, /o/, or /u/:

    a. In written form, a /y/ is inserted before the suffix pronoun. Examples: ۲. غذا + ش ← غذایَش

                                             ۳. جلو + ت ← جلویَت

    b. In spoken form, the vowel before the suffix pronoun is dropped. Examples:

                     ۴. غذا + ش ← غذاش and جلو + ت ← جلوت

2) If a word ends in an unpronounced *he*, an *alef* is inserted before the singular form of the suffix pronouns in both written and spoken forms. Examples:

                             ۵. خانه + م ← خانه‌اَم / خونه‌اَم

                           ۶. خانه + مان ← خانه‌مان / خونه‌مون

In the spoken forms of Examples 5 and 6, the unpronounced *he* will change to /a/ due to a vowel harmony rule (khune + mun → khun-a-mun).

3) If a word ends in the vowel /i/:

    a. In written form, an *alef* is inserted before the **singular** form of a suffix pronoun. Examples:

                             ۷. صندلی + م ← صندلی‌اَم

                             ۸. صندلی + مان ← صندلی‌مان

In spoken form, the vowel before the suffix pronoun is dropped. Examples:

۹. صندلی + م ← صندلیم

۱۰. صندلی + مان ← صندلیمون

Common Mistake: Be mindful not to confuse **suffix pronouns** with **verb endings**. Examples:

من خوبم (I am fine) ــ کتاب خوبم (My good book)

Difference Between Suffix Pronouns & Full Pronouns

Most of the time, full pronouns can be replaced by suffix pronouns except in the following situations:

1) Full pronouns are used for emphasis: "This is MY book (not yours)"

این کتابِ **من** است.

2) Full pronouns cannot be used in a sentence in which they are also the subject (even if the subject is dropped):

(من) کتابَم را می‌خوانم.

(من) کتابِ من را می‌خوانم.

3) Suffix pronouns cannot be added to some prepositions in written form. Examples: از ــ با ــ به

In spoken form, suffix pronouns can be added to all prepositions. Examples:

اَزم (from me) ــ باهام (with me) ــ بِهِم (to me)

4) Suffix pronouns cannot be used with مال.

این کتاب مالِ من است. / این کتاب مالم است.

تمرین ۸

Write the following in Persian using suffix pronouns. Provide both written and spoken forms.

1. Our Persian professor

2. Your beautiful house

3. I read them.

4. With us (Spoken)

5. My tomorrow's class

6. From you (Spoken, Singular)

7. They do not eat it.

8. I see you.

تمرین ۹

Make sentences using the following words. The odd numbers are in spoken form.

۱. روبروم:

۲. کتاب‌هایش:

۳. باهات:

۴. خانه‌ام:

تمرین ۱۰

Replace the underlined words with suffix pronouns.

۱. به آنها:

۲. آن را می‌خورم:

۳. کامپیوترِ پدر و مادرِ مینا:

۴. من تو را دوست دارم:

۵. از کتاب:

۶. با اون:

> When a suffix pronoun is added to a compound verb, it attaches to the non-verbal part.
> دوستَش دارم / دوسِش دارم.
> I like her/him/it.

تمرین ۱۱

Choose the correct form.

۱. من معمولاً در اتاقِ خواب ———— درس می‌خوانم. (من ــ م)

۲. شما با دوستِ ایرانی ———— زندگی می کنید؟ (شما ــ تان)

۳. آقای زمانی و منشی ———— تشریف دارند؟ (آنها ــ شان)

۴. این کتاب مالِ ———— است؟ (تو ــ ت)

۵. ماشین ———— را لازم داری؟ (تو ــ ت)

۶. طبقه‌ی اوّل خانه‌ی شما نیست، خانه‌ی ———— ———— است. (ما ــ مان)

۷. خانمِ پارسا با دانشجوها ———— در کلاس است. (او ــ یش)

تمرین ۱۲ 👥

How much is the rent for the following apartment? What are the apartment's specifications?

اجاره آپارتمان مسکونی

آپارتمان ۱۲۰ متری ــ سه خوابه

واقع در میدان نفت ــ مجتمع قدس

طبقه اول ــ پارکینگ و انباری

۸۵۰٬۰۰۰ تومان اجاره

۲۰٬۰۰۰٬۰۰۰ تومان پیش پرداخت

تلفن: ۶۶۴۳۹۸۰۷

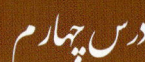

بیشتر بدانیم

 NUMBERS   عددها ۱۰۰ - ۱٬۰۰۰٬۰۰۰٬۰۰۰

1000	۱۰۰۰	هِزار	100	۱۰۰	صَد/ (یکصد)
1001	۱۰۰۱	هِزار و یک	200	۲۰۰	دِویست
2000	۲۰۰۰	دوهزار	300	۳۰۰	سیصد
100,000	۱۰۰٬۰۰۰	صدهزار	400	۴۰۰	چهارصد
100,001	۱۰۰٬۰۰۱	صدهزار و یک	500	۵۰۰	پانصد/پونصد
1,000,000	۱٬۰۰۰٬۰۰۰	یک میلیون	600	۶۰۰	شِشصد/شیشصد
1,000,001	۱٬۰۰۰٬۰۰۱	یک میلیون و یک	700	۷۰۰	هفتصد
2,000,000	۲٬۰۰۰٬۰۰۰	دو میلیون	800	۸۰۰	هشتصد
1,000,000,000	۱٬۰۰۰٬۰۰۰٬۰۰۰	یک میلیارد	900	۹۰۰	نُهصد

 ORDINAL NUMBERS   عددهای تَرتیبی

Ordinal numbers are formed by adding /om/ or /omin/ to cardinal numbers. The suffix /om/ follows the noun and is connected by an Ezāfe (Example 1). The suffix /omin/ precedes the noun with no Ezāfe in between (Example 2).

۱. طبقه‌ی دوّم	Second floor	
۲. دوّمین طبقه	Second floor	
۳. دو طبقه	Two-story	

Ordinal	Ordinal	Cardinal
یِکُمین ـ اَوّلین ـ نُخستین	یِکُم ـ اَوّل ـ نُخست	یک
دوّمین	دوّم	دو
سوّمین	سوّم	سه
چهارُمین	چهارُم	چهار
پنجُمین	پنجُم	پنج
شِشُمین/شیشُمین	شِشُم/شیشُم	شش/شیش
هفتُمین	هفتُم	هفت
هشتُمین	هشتُم	هشت
نُهُمین	نُهُم	نه
دهُمین	دهُم	ده

یازدهُمین	یازدهُم	یازده
دوازدهُمین	دوازدهُم	دوازده
بیستُمین	بیستُم	بیست
بیست و یکُمین	بیست و یکُم	بیست و یک
بیست و دوُّمین	بیست و دوُّم	بیست و دو
سی‌اُمین	سی‌اُم	سی
چهلُمین	چهلُم	چهل
صدُمین	صدُم	صد
صد و یکُمین	صد و یکُم	صد و یک
دویست و دوُّمین	دویست و دوُّم	دویست و دو
هزارُمین	هزارُم	هزار
صد هزارُمین	صد هزارُم	صد هزار
یک میلیونُمین	یک میلیونُم	یک میلیون

/om/ and /omin/ can also be added to چند as in چندُم and چندُمین. There is no English equivalant for such words but basically they mean "in which order". Examples:

Option 2	*Option 1*
تو در چندمین طبقه زندگی می‌کنی؟ سوّمین طبقه	تو در طبقه‌ی چندم زندگی می‌کنی؟ طبقه‌ی سوّم
تو چندمین بچّه‌ی خانواده هستی؟ اوّلین بچّه	تو بچّه‌ی چندمِ خانواده هستی؟ بچّه‌ی اوّل

تمرین ۱۳

Translate into Persian. Use the written form.

1. My house has three stories.

2. I am the third child.

3. Do you live in a four-bedroom apartment?

4. She does not live on the tenth floor.

5. The third door is the washroom.

6. In which house do you live? (use چندمین)

دستور زبان ۲

درس چهارم

QUESTION WORDS

In Persian interrogative sentences, the question word replaces the information that is being asked. All question words carry stress.

When	کِی	Who	کی
How	چِگونه	Who	چه کَسی
How/How come	چطور	Where	کُجا
How much	چِقَدر	What	چه / چی
How many	چند (تا)	Which	کُدام / کُدوم
Which	چه ...... ی	Why	چرا
N/A	چندُم – چندُمین	Whose	مالِ کی – مالِ چه کَسی

The Persian words for "who" and "when" differ only in a vowel (ki & key). Since short vowels are often omitted in Persian, it is only the context that helps you decide which one is used in the sentence. Examples:

مرجان امروز سه کتاب از دانشگاه می‌خرد.	
مرجان امروز چه کتابی (را) از دانشگاه می‌خرد؟	کی امروز سه کتاب از دانشگاه می‌خرد؟
مرجان امروز کدام کتاب را از دانشگاه می‌خرد؟	مرجان کِی سه کتاب از دانشگاه می‌خرد؟
مرجان امروز چند کتاب از دانشگاه می‌خرد؟	مرجان امروز سه کتاب از کجا می‌خرد؟
چرا مرجان امروز سه کتاب از دانشگاه می‌خرد؟	مرجان امروز چه از دانشگاه می‌خرد؟

Exceptions:

1) چرا comes at the beginning of the sentence.

2) A noun that follows چه requires the non-specific suffix /-i/.

چه کتابی؟/چه کتابهایی؟[1]   Which book/books

3) A noun that follows کُدام does not require the non-specific suffix /-i/.

کدام کتاب؟/ کدام کتابها؟[2]   Which book/books

4) چند can be followed by other words to make other question words such as:

چند وَقت   How long

چند بار   How many times

چند نَفَر   How many people

---

1. If the noun is the direct object, را may or may not appear afterwards.
2. If the noun is the direct object را must appear afterwards.

تمرین ۱۴

Form questions using the given question words.

۱. من با مادرم از ایران می‌آییم. (کجا)

۲. آنها فردا بعد از ظهر به ایران می‌روند. (کِی)

۳. سارا دنبالِ یک مبلِ خوب است. (چرا)

۴. خانه‌ی ما سه طبقه است. (کی)

۵. او خیلی این آپارتمان را دوست دارد. (چی)

۶. من با پدر و مادرم زندگی می‌کنم. (کی)

۷. نگین در اتاقِ نشیمن درس می‌خواند. (چرا)

۸. ما سه تا برادر داریم. (چند)

۹. شما با ماشین به دانشگاه می‌روید. (چطور)

۱۰. من آن کتاب را دوست دارم. (کدام)

تمرین ۱۵

Read the answers to the following questions and fill in the blanks with the appropriate vocabulary.

۱. تو امروز ———— کلاسی داری؟ کلاسِ فارسی.

۲. ———— در این خانه زندگی می‌کند؟ من و مادرم.

۳. شما ———— به تهران می‌روید؟ فردا صبح.

۴. خانمت برای ———— به ایران می‌رود؟ برای سه هفته.

۵. ———— این آپارتمان را دوست نداری؟ چون به دانشگاه دور است.

۶. دخترت ———— می‌خواند؟ ادبیاتِ انگلیسی می‌خواند.

۷. تو در طبقه‌ی ———— زندگی می‌کنی؟ در طبقه‌ی بیستُم.

تمرین ۱۶

Answer the following questions. Work in pairs, groups, or as a class. Example:

Student 1: (*book open*) خانه‌ی شما چند طبقه است؟

Student 2: (*book closed*) خانه‌ی ما یک طبقه است.

Group 2	Group 1
۱. تو در طبقه‌ی چندم زندگی می‌کنی؟	۱.تو چهار شنبه‌ها ساعتِ چند به خانه می‌روی؟
۲. آیا شما معمولاً در آشپزخانه غذا می‌خورید؟	۲. پدر و مادرت در کجا زندگی می‌کنند ؟
۳. این چندمین کلاسِ امروزت است؟	۳. شما آدرسِ الکترونیکیِ من را دارید؟
۴. تو چندمین بچّه‌ی خانواده هستی؟	۴. دنبالِ آپارتمانِ چند خوابه می‌گردی؟
۵. تو همیشه در کجای خانه‌تان درس می‌خوانی؟	۵. در دانشگاهِ شما چند تا رستوران هست؟

تمرین ۱۷

Find an ordinal number in the following advertisement. How much discount do they offer? Underline any familar words. What are some of the listed housing items? What do you think the word کالا means?

بیشتر بدانیم

What time is it? ساعَت چند است؟/ساعَت چنده؟

	ساعت هفت است./ ساعت هفته.
	ساعت ده و ده دقیقه است./ ساعت ده و ده دقیقهس.
	ساعت دوازده و پانزده دقیقه است./ ساعت دوازده و پونزده دقیقهس. ساعت دوازده و رُبع است./ ساعت دوازده و رُبعه.
	ساعت هشت و بیست دقیقه است./ ساعت هشت و بیست دقیقهس.
	ساعت نُه و سی دقیقه است./ ساعت نُه و سی دقیقهس. ساعت نُه و نیم است./ ساعت نُه و نیمه.
	ساعت هفت و چهل دقیقه است./ ساعت هفت و چهل دقیقهس.
	ساعت نه و چهل و پنج دقیقه است./ ساعت نه و چهل و پنج دقیقهس. ساعت یک ربع به ده است./ ساعت یه ربع به دهه.
	ساعت دوازده و پنجاه دقیقه است./ ساعت دوازده و پنجاه دقیقهس. ساعت ده دقیقه به یک است./ ساعت ده دقیقه به یکه.

The word ساعت means both *Hour* and *O'clock* (to tell time). When ساعت means *Hour*, it follows a number in singular form with no Ezāfe (Example 1). When ساعت means O'clock (to tell time), it precedes numbers with no Ezāfe (Example 2). When ساعت means o'clock and is used as an adverbial, it precedes numbers and requires an Ezāfe (Example 3).

Five hours	پنج ساعت	۱.
It is five o'clock.	ساعت پنج است.	۲.
(at) Five o'clock	ساعتِ پنج	۳.

In spoken form the Ezāfe is omitted ساعت پنج می‌آم. The word ساعت may also be omitted in spoken form (ex: پنج می‌آم).

تمرین ۱۸

Answer in complete sentences. Use the written form. Next, read your answers aloud in spoken form.

۱. ساعت چند است؟ _____

۲. ساعت چند است؟ _____

۳. ساعت چند است؟ _____

۴. ساعت چند است؟ _____

۵. ساعت چند است؟ _____

۶. ساعت چند است؟ _____

تمرین ۱۹

Answer in Persian using complete sentences. Use the written form.

۱. تو هر روز صبح ساعتِ چند از خواب بیدار می‌شوی؟

۲. الان ساعت چند است؟

۳. کلاسِ فارسیِ تو چند ساعت در هفته است ؟

۴. یک روز چند ساعت دارد؟

۵. تو معمولاً روزی چند ساعت درس می‌خوانی؟

۶. کلاسِ فارسیِ تو ساعتِ چند شروع می‌شود و ساعتِ چند تمام می‌شود؟

رَنگ ها Colors

	سیاه ـ مِشکی	زَرد	
	سِفید	آبی	
	بَنَفش	سُرمه‌ای	
	قِرمِز	سَبز	
	نارِنجی	قَهوه‌ای	
	صورَتی	کِرم	

تمرین ۲۰

Translate into Persian. Pronounce your sentences aloud.

1. My chemistry book is brown.

2. The rainbow (رنگین کَمان) has seven colors.

3. I do not like orange and purple.

4. Our classroom is green.

5. Where is the black cat?

6. Why don't you like yellow?

		اعضای بدن Body Parts			
Face		صورَت	Arm/Hand		دَست
Lip		لَب	Ear		گوش
Nose		بینی ـ دَماغ	Eye		چَشم / چِشم
Tooth		دَندان / دَندون	Finger/Toe		انگُشت
Eyebrow		اَبرو	Hair		مو
Eyelash		مُژه	Leg/Foot		پا

تمرین ۲۱

Arrange the following words to make a sentence. Read your sentence aloud:

۱. رنگِ زرد ـ دوست ندارم ـ را ـ من

۲. دلار ـ داریم ـ ما ـ پنجاه و ـ پنج هزار ـ لازم

۳. چشم‌های ـ است ـ ما ـ دخترِ ـ سبز

۴. سفید ـ پدرم ـ موهای ـ است ـ رنگِ

۵. دارد ـ او ـ دندان‌های ـ خیلی سفیدی

۶. دست ـ انگشت ـ تا ـ پنج ـ دارد ـ یک

159

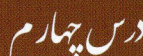

تمرین ۲۲

Underline the body parts that are indicated in the following advertisement. What do you think the advertisement is about?

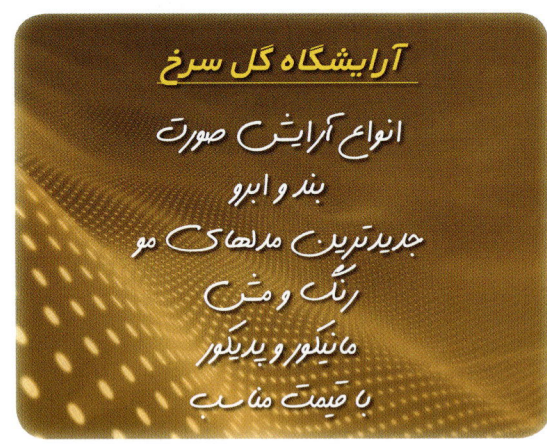

تمرین ۲۳

Use the Persian alphabet to write the following numbers.

۴۵	_____	۱۰۱۲	_____
۱۳۶	_____	۱۱۰	_____
۱۰۰۲	_____	۳۲۰	_____
۸۹	_____	۹۹۹	_____
۷۶	_____	۱۰۹۰۰	_____
۱۴۴	_____	۱۰۰۰۲	_____
۸۴۷	_____	۷۸۳	_____

تمرین ۲۴

a) Change into written form:

۱. خونه‌ی شما چند تا حموم داره؟

۲. چرا فردا می‌ریم خونه‌شون؟

b) Change into spoken form:

۱. آقای زمانی آدرسِ الکترونیکیِ شما را دارند؟

۲. آقای جانسون یک لیست از آپارتمان‌هایمان را به شما ایمیل می‌کنند.

تمرین ۲۵

Connect each phrase to the appropriate verb:

می‌خورد	۱. آنها در طبقه‌ی اوّل
است؟	۲. ما در اتاق ناهارخوری
نمی‌خوابیم	۳. ماشینِ شما سفید
درس می‌خوانی؟	۴. او درآشپزخانه غذا
دارم	۵. تو در اتاقِ خوابت
زندگی می‌کنند	۶. من کامپیوترِ خیلی خوبی

تمرین ۲۶

The following advertisement is for a local veterinary clinic.

Find the names of four animals. What is the word for "etc." in Persian? Can you find a word that is similar to the color "white"? What is the difference between the two words? Find two words in the text that are similar to the English word.

In English, puppy has a sweet meaning but in Persian توله سَگ means "Little brat" or can be used as a light swear word. Among other light swear words are: خَر (Donkey), کُرّه خَر (Donkey foal), گاو (Cow/Cattle), and گوساله (Heifer/Calf).

تمرین ۲۷: واژگان

In each line, circle the word that does not match the rest:

نخست	سه هزار	اوّلین	۱. دوّم
کدام	چقدر	چگونه	۲. همه
سفید	سیاه	قهوه ای	۳. انگشتان
ساعت	هنوز	ربع	۴. دقیقه
صورتی	لب	گوش	۵. دماغ
اتاقِ نشیمن	آشپزخانه	دوخوابه	۶. دستشویی
هنوز	تقسیم	بعد از	۷. پس

 تمرین ۲۸

Task: You want to learn more about your pen pal who lives in Iran. Use the spoken Persian form to ask the following questions. Then write his/her answers in the form of a report using the written form. See the example below:

1. How old are you?

2. Where do you live?

3. Who do you live with?

4. How many floors does your house have?

5. Is your house crowded?

6. How many bedrooms and bathrooms does your house have?

7. What color is your bedroom?

8. Does your house have a big yard?

9. Does your house have parking?

10. Do you like your house?

> دوستِ من، سپیده، ۲۴ سال دارد. او با خانواده‌اش در تهران زندگی می‌کند. خانه‌ی آنها ....

REVIEW CORNER	
Points that remain unclear about Lesson 4:	
How I plan to work on these points:	

شعر

Read the following poem by Forough Farrokhzad and find a body part. Underline the familiar words. You will not be evaluated on the content but you can use it for cultural enrichment.

پرنده مردنی است

دلم گرفته است

دلم گرفته است

به ایوان می روم و انگشتانم را بر پوست کشیده‌ی شب می‌کشم

چراغهای رابطه تاریکند

چراغهای رابطه تاریکند

کسی مرا به آفتاب

معرفی نخواهد کرد

کسی مرا به میهمانِ گنجشکها نخواهد برد

پرواز را به خاطر بسپار

پرنده مردنی‌ست

شاعر: فروغ فرخزاد (۱۹۶۷ ـ ۱۹۳۴)

163

ترانه

Listen to the following song by Hayedeh on YouTube and try to find the familiar words. Is this song in the written form or spoken form? Underline the verbs in the present tense. You will not be evaluated on the content but you can use it for cultural enrichment.

گلِ سنگَم

گلِ سنگم، گلِ سنگم

چی بگم از دل تنگم

مثل آفتاب اگه بر من نتابی

سردم و بی رنگم

همه آهم، همه دردم

مثل طوفان پرِ گردم

همه آهم، همه دردم

مثل طوفان پرِ گردم

باد مستم که تو صحرا

می‌پیچم دورِ تو، می‌گردم

گل سنگم، گل سنگم

چی بگم از، دل تنگم

مثل آفتاب، اگه بر من نتابی

سردم و بی رنگم

مثل بارون اگه نباری

خبر از حال من نداری

بی تو پرپر می‌شم دو روزه

دل سنگت، برام می سوزه

گل سنگم، گل سنگم

چی بگم از، دل تنگم

خواننده: هایِده (۱۹۹۰ـ۱۹۴۲)

نکته‌ی فرهنگی

Using Body Parts in Expressions

Persian culture relates many body parts to emotions. For instance, the word معده (stomach) is the physical organ, دل (stomach/heart) is used metaphorically to convey many emotions. Examples:

Translation	Persian
Sympathetic	دلسوز
Favorite	دلخواه
Sad	دلگیر
Sweetheart	دلبَر

Usage Translation	Literal Translation	Persian
I feel pity (for) …	My heart burns	دِلَم می‌سوزد
I want/desire …	My heart wants	دِلَم می‌خواهد
I feel sad/blue	My heart gets/tightens	دِلَم می‌گیرد
S/he steals my heart	S/he takes my heart	او دِلَم را می بَرد

Also جِگَر, which literally means (liver), is used in many expressions of emotion.

Usage Translation	Literal Translation	Persian
A beloved child	Corner of liver	جِگَر گوشه
Heartbreaking	Liver burning	جِگَر سوز
Cutie/Hottie (Slang)	Golden liver	جِگَر طَلا / جیگَر طَلا
You are a cutie/hottie! (Slang)	I may/want to eat your liver!	جِگَرَت را بُخورم! / جیگَرِتو بُخورم!

Another body part is پُشت (back)[3], which is used similarly to in English:

Usage Translation	Literal Translation	Persian
To turn your back (on someone)	To turn (your) back	پُشت کردن (به)
To back stab (someone)	To kick (backward)	پُشتِ پا زدن (به)
To be someone's rock	To be back and refuge	پُشت و پَناه … بودن
I was devastated	My back broke	پُشتَم شکست

The above information is only for cultural enrichment and is not part of the content on which students are evaluated.

ضرب المثل

Literal translation: *The one with a bigger roof will get more snow.*

(Much coin, much care.)

This proverb states that the more material belongings you own, the more stress and responsibility you endure.

هرکه بامَش بیش، برفش بیشتَر.

---

3. Although پُشت means back, the word کَمَر (waist) is also used to refer to back pain: کَمَر دَرد

Thematic Review of New Vocabulary

Housing	
Bedroom	اُتاقِ خواب
Dining room	اُتاقِ ناهارخوری
Living room	اُتاقِ نشیمَن
Rent (noun)	اِجاره
Apartment	آپارتمان
Kitchen	آشپزخانه
Real estate agency	بُنگاه
Garage/Parking space	پارکینگ
Bath	حَمّام
Yard	حَیاط
Washroom	دَستشویی
Two-bedroom	دوخوابه
Storey/Floor	طَبَقه
Garage	گاراژ
Sofa/Love seat	مُبل
House/Home	مَنزِل

About Animals	
Puppy	توله سَگ
Donkey	خَر
Rabbit	خَرگوش
Veterinary	دامپزِشکی
Dog	سَگ
Parrot	طوطی
Baby donkey	کُرّه خَر
Cow/Cattle	گاو
Cat	گُربه
Heifer/Calf	گوساله

Colors	
Blue	آبی
Purple	بَنَفش
Yellow	زَرد
Green	سَبز
Navy	سُرمهای
White	سِفید
Black	سیاه ـ مِشکی
Pink	صورَتی
Red	قِرمِز
Brown	قَهوهای
Cream	کِرِم
Orange	نارِنجی

Nouns & Adjectives	
Bus stop/Station	ایستگاه
Email address	آدرسِ اِلِکترونیکی
Budget	بودجه
Far	دور
Late	دیر
Restaurant	رستوران
Rainbow	رَنگین کَمان
Quickly/Early/Fast	زود
List	لیست
Close by/Near	نَزدیک

Prepositions	
For	بَرای
Until/Till	تا

Body Parts	
Eyebrow	أبرو
Finger/Toe	انگُشت
Nose	بینی
Leg/Foot	پا
Eye	چِشم
Arm/Hand	دَست
Nose	دَماغ
Tooth	دَندان
Face	صورَت
Ear	گوش
Lip	لَب
Eyelash	مُژه
Hair	مو

166

Question Words	
Why	چِرا
How/How come	چِطور
How much	چقَدر
How	چِگونه
How many	چَند (تا)
How many times	چَندبار
N/A	چَندُم – چَندُمین
How many people	چَندنَفَر
How long	چَندوقت
Which	چه ...... ی
Who	چه کسی
What	چه
Where	کُجا
Which	کُدام
Who	کی
When	کِی
Whose	مالِ چه کسی – مالِ کی

Words & Expressions	
Now	اَلان
Word to answer phone	اَلو
Here	اینجا
There	آنجا
Come in/Here you go (Informal)	بِفَرما
Are you not ready?	حاضِر نیستی؟
Welcome! (Informal)	خوش آمدی!
No problem	عیب نَدارد
No (Formal/Emphatic)	نهخیر
All	هَمه
Still/Yet	هَنوز
It means	یَعنی

Suffix Pronouns		
Plural	*Singular*	
ـِ مان/ ـِ مون	ــَ م	1st person
ـِ تان / ـِ تون	ــَ ت/ ـِ ت	2nd person
ـِ شان/ ـِ شون	ــَ ش / ـِ ش	3rd person

About Time	
Five hours	پنج ساعت
Minute	دَقیقه
Quarter/15 minutes	رُبع
Hour/Time/Clock/Watch	ساعَت
Five o'clock	ساعتِ پنج
It is five o'clock.	ساعت پنج است
Half	نیم

Verbs & Phrases	
We email	ایمیل می کنیم (کردن: کُن)
Are present (Polite verb)	تَشریف دارند (داشتن: دار)
I get ready	حاضِر میشَوَم (شدن: شَو)
You look (for)...	دُنبالِ ... می گردید (گشتن: گَرد)
I am late	دیر کَردَم (کردن: کُن)
It gets late	دیرمیشَوَد (شدن: شَو)
We arrive	می رسیم (رسیدن: رِس)
We have got time	وَقت داریم (داشتن: دار)

167

— درس چهارم

Numbers	
100	صد ـ یکصد
200	دویست
300	سیصد
400	چهارصد
500	پانصد
600	ششصد
700	هفتصد
800	هشتصد
900	نُهصد
1000	هزار
1001	هزار و یک
2000	دو هزار
100,000	صد هزار
100,001	صد هزار و یک
1,000,000	یک میلیون
1,000,001	یک میلیون و یک
2,000,000	دو میلیون
1,000,000,000	یک میلیارد

Ordinal Numbers		
First	یکمین ـ اَوّلین ـ نُخستین	یِکُم ـ اَوّل ـ نُخست
Second	دوّمین	دوم
Third	سوّمین	سِوّم
Fourth	چهارُمین	چهارُم
Fifth	پَنجُمین	پَنجُم
Sixth	شِشُمین	شِشُم
Seventh	هَفتُمین	هَفتُم
Eighth	هَشتُمین	هَشتُم
Ninth	نُهُمین	نُهُم
Tenth	دَهُمین	دَهُم
Eleventh	یازدهُمین	یازدهُم
Twelfth	دَوازدهُمین	دَوازدهُم
Twentieth	بیستُمین	بیستُم
Twenty first	بیست و یکُمین	بیست و یکُم
Twenty second	بیست و دوّمین	بیست و دوّم
Thirtieth	سی‌اُمین	سی‌اُم
Fortieth	چهلُمین	چهلُم
Hundredth	صَدُمین	صَدُم
Hundred first	صد و یکُمین	صد و یکُم
Hundred second	دویست و دوّمین	دویست و دوُم
Thousandth	هزارُمین	هِزارُم
Hundred thousandth	صد هزارُمین	صد هِزارُم
One millionth	یک میلیونُمین	یک میلیونُم

خرید
Shopping

درس پنجم

واژگان ۱

Sir	جَناب [1]	Must/Should	بایَد
Wait! (Plural & Formal)	صَبر کُنید / صَبر کُنین (کُن)	I should/may ask	بِپُرسَم (پُرس)
Price	قیمَت	I should/may buy	بِخَرَم (خَر)
Co-worker	هَمکار	Go! (Plural & Formal)	بِرَوید / بِرین (رَو)
Bookstore	کتاب‌فُروشی	Student discount	تَخفیفِ دانشجویی
I should/may find it	پیدایَش کُنَم / پیداش کُنَم	I can/I am able to	می‌تَوانَم / می‌تونَم (تَوان)
Moment	لَحظه	Client/Customer	مُشتَری
Ask! (Plural & Formal)	بِپُرسید / بِپُرسین (پُرس)	I want	می‌خواهم / می‌خوام (خواه)

Close your book and listen to the dialogue. Then fill in the blanks using the new words.

گفتگو ۱

در کتاب‌فُروشیِ دانشگاه

کامران: سلام، خسته نباشین. من می‌خوام کتابِ شیمیِ سالِ اوّل
رو بخرم. می‌دونین کجا می‌تونم پیداش کنم؟

فروشنده: لطفاً یه لحظه صبر کنین. ‫‬———— از همکارم بپرسم.

کامران: بفرمایین، بپرسین.

فروشنده: لطفاً برین طبقه‌ی سوّم. کتابِ شیمیِ سالِ اوّل رو
می‌تونین اونجا پیدا کنین.

کامران: خیلی ممنونم. می‌تونم ———— قیمتش چنده؟

فروشنده: باید ببخشین. نمی‌دونم. از طبقه‌ی سوّم بپرسین.

کامران: شما اینجا تخفیف دانشجویی دارین؟

فروشنده: نه ———— ! مشتری‌های ما همه دانشجوان!

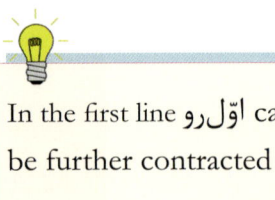

In the first line اوّل‌رو can
be further contracted to
اوّلو

---

1. جَناب literally means "your excellency".

نوشتاری

گفتگو ۱

کامران: سلام، خسته ——————. من می‌خواهم کتابِ شیمیِ سالِ اوّل را بخرم. می‌دانید کجا می‌توانم پیدایش کنم؟

فروشنده: لطفاً یک لحظه صبر کنید. باید از همکارم بپرسم.

کامران: بفرمایید، ——————.

فروشنده: لطفاً به طبقه‌ی سوّم بروید. کتابِ شیمیِ سالِ اوّل را می‌توانید در آنجا پیدا کنید.

کامران: خیلی ممنونم. ——————. بپرسم قیمتش چند است؟

فروشنده: باید ببخشید. نمی‌دانم. از طبقه‌ی سوّم بپرسید.

کامران: شما اینجا تخفیفِ دانشجویی دارید؟

فروشنده: نه جناب! مشتری‌های ما همه دانشجو هستند!

Unlike English, in which "can" is a modal and cannot be conjugated, تَوانِستَن is a main verb and can be conjugated. Examples:

You can. .شما می‌تَوانید

S/he can. .او می‌تَواند

They can. .آنها می‌تَوانند

تمرین ۱

Role-play the above dialogue with your classmates and pretend that you are in a bookstore. Ask for a specific book. Ask if they have a student discount.

واژگان ۲

Expensive	گِران / گِرون	Store	فُروشگاه
It should/may not be	نَباشَد / نَباشه	All kinds	هَمه نوع
I should/may take it	بِبَرَمَش / بِبَرِمش	Qilim	گِلیم
Silk	اَبریشَم	Gabbeh	گَبّه
Light (weight)	سَبُک	Rug	فَرش
Taste	سَلیقه	I buy it	می‌خَرَمَش / می‌خَرِمش
Ok/Well	خُب	Heavy	سَنگین
That/Which/Who/When/Where/Whose/Whom	که	Sell it for less so that we become customers	اَرزان بِدهید مُشتَری بشویم / اَرزون بِدین مُشتَری شیم
Toman (Iranian currency)	تومان / تومَن	I should/may count	حساب کُنَم
OK (response)	باشَد / باشه	Congratulations!	مُبارَک است! / مُبارَکه!
May it bring you luck	خِیرَش را بِبینید / خِیرشو بِبینین	For example	مَثَلاً

Close your book and listen to the dialogue. Then fill in the blanks using the new words.

گفتگو ۲

پریسا: روزتون به خیر. چه ———— قشنگی!

فروشنده: ممنون. ما همه نوع فرش، گلیم، و گبه داریم.

پریسا: من یه فرشِ خوبِ ———— می‌خوام که ببرم آمریکا.

فروشنده: فرشِ ابریشم سنگین نیست ولی قیمتش بالاس.

پریسا: مثلاً این فرشه چنده؟

فروشنده: این ———— تبریزه. چه سلیقه‌تون خوبه!

پریسا: مرسی. خُب، این با تخفیف چنده؟

فروشنده: قابِلی نداره. برای شما ده میلیون تومن.

پریسا: نه آقا! ده میلیون خیلی گرونه! ارزون بدین مشتری شیم!

فروشنده: خب، با تخفیف می‌تونم براتون نه میلیون و هشتصد تومن حساب کنم.

پریسا: باشه، می‌خرمش.

فروشنده: مبارکه! خیرِشو ببینین!

نوشتاری

گفتگو ۲

پریسا: روزتان به خیر. چه فروشگاهِ قشنگی!

فروشنده: ممنون. ما همه نوع فرش، گلیم، و گبه داریم.

پریسا: من یک فرشِ خوبِ سبک ———— که به آمریکا ببرم.

فروشنده: فرش ابریشم سنگین نیست ولی قیمتش بالاست.

پریسا: مثلاً این فرش چند است؟

فروشنده: این فرشِ تبریز است. چه سلیقه‌تان خوب است!

پریسا: مرسی. خُب، این با تخفیف چند است؟

فروشنده: قابِلی ندارد. برای شما ده میلیون تومان.

پریسا: نه آقا! ده میلیون خیلی گران است! ارزان بدهید مشتری شَویم!

فروشنده: خب، با تخفیف ———— برایتان نه میلیون و هشتصد تومان حساب کنم.

پریسا: باشد، ————.

فروشنده: مبارک است! خیرَش را ببینید!

💡 که has other usages that we will learn in Lesson 10.

تمرین ۲ 👥

Role-play the above dialogue. Provide the specifications for the rug/gabbeh/qilim you want to buy. Make sure you haggle for a price!

تمرین ۳ 👄 ✏️

Find six words that are different in written and spoken forms and write them below. Pronounce the words as you write.

Spoken	← Written	Spoken	← Written

خواندن 👤 🎧

آقای شریفی بیمار است

مدیر مدرسه‌ی ما، آقای شریفی، بیمار است. او باید برای مداوا به بیمارستان برود. آقای شریفی میانسال است. او متاهل است و سه بچّه دارد. آقای شریفی مردِ مهربانی است. ما خیلی برای آقای شریفی ناراحت هستیم و امیدواریم او به زودی خوب شَوَد. معلّم ما، خانم افشار، می‌گوید ما باید امسال خیلی درس بخوانیم و آقای شریفی را خوشحال کنیم. ما می‌خواهیم برای آقای شریفی یک کامپیوترِ خوب بخریم و به او هدیه بدهیم.

This year	اِمسال
We hope	اُمیدواریم
We should/may give	بِدَهیم (دَه)
S/he should/may go	بِرَوَد (رَو)
Quickly/Soon	به زودی
Sick/Ill	بیمار
Hospital	بیمارِستان
Present/Gift	هدیه
We should/may study	دَرس بخوانیم (خوان)
We should/may make... happy	خوشحال کُنیم (کُن)
School	مَدرسه
Medical treatment	مُداوا

We want	می‌خواهیم (خواه)
We may/should buy	بخریم (خَر)
S/he says	می‌گوید (گو)

173

تمرین ۴

a) Listen to the audio file and follow along in your text. Repeat each sentence several times.

b) Answer in complete sentences. Use the written form.

۱. نامِ مدیرِ مدرسه چیست؟

۲. چرا او باید به بیمارستان برود؟

۳. درباره‌ی آقای شریفی چه می‌دانید؟

۴. خانم افشار به دانش‌آموزان چه می‌گوید؟

۵. دانش‌آموزان می‌خواهند برای آقای شریفی چه بخرند؟

۶. «مداوا» به انگلیسی یعنی چه؟

Antonyms
گِران/ گِرون ≠ اَرزان/ ارزون
سَبُک ≠ سَنگین

Synonyms	
فَرش = قالی	فُروشگاه = مَغازه
بیمار = مَریض	باشد/ باشه = چشم

تمرین ۵ واژگان

Fill in the blanks using the appropriate vocabulary from the list below.

بفرمایین ـ نه جناب ـ مداوا ـ قیمت ـ چند تا ـ مریض ـ مشتری شیم ـ قابلی نداره ـ ابریشم

۱. ببخشید، می‌توانم بپرسم ＿＿＿＿＿＿ این کامپیوتر چند است؟

۲. این رایانه با تخفیفِ دانشجویی چند است؟ ＿＿＿＿＿＿ .

۳. مینا خانم برای ＿＿＿＿＿＿ باید به آمریکا برود.

۴. باشه، ＿＿＿＿＿＿ بپرسین! (Spoken)

۵. شما اینجا تخفیفِ دانشجویی دارین؟ ＿＿＿＿＿＿ مشتری‌های ما همه دانشجوأن! (Spoken)

۶. تو چه فرشی دوست داری؟ من فرشِ ＿＿＿＿＿＿ دوست دارم.

۷. مادرِ علی ＿＿＿＿＿＿ است و در بیمارستان است.

۸. آرزون بِدین ＿＿＿＿＿＿ ! (Spoken)

 **دستور زبان ۱**

أَمر IMPERATIVE

The imperative form is used to make direct commands and requests, both positive and negative.

The imperative form only applies to the **second person (singular and plural)**. The imperative does not apply to the **first person** and the **third person**.

Formation:

a. The singular imperative is formed by adding the prefix بِ to the present stem of the verb with no verb ending.

b. The plural imperative is formed by adding the second person plural ending /-id/ to the singular imperative. Examples:

خندیدن

	Imperative	
تو	بِ + خَند ← بِخَند!	Laugh! (sing)
شما	بِ + خَند + ید ← بِخَندید!	Laugh! (pl)

The prefix بِ is inserted in between the two components of the compund verbs. Examples:

درس خواندن

	Imperative	
تو	درس بِخوان!	Study! (sing)
شما	درس بِخوانید!	Study! (pl)

In written form, the imperative form of most compound verbs, particularly those whose verbal element is کردن or شدن, is formed without the بِ prefix. The prefix may be present in spoken form.

تو	کار کُن!	Work! (sing)!
شما	کار کُنید!	Work! (pl)

The equivalent of the words "*Please*", لطفاً and خواهش می‌کنم accompany the imperative forms.

Writing and Pronunciation:

1. If the present stem has the vowel /o/, the imperative prefix changes to بُ due to a vowel harmony rule (exception: بِپُرس). Example:

تو	بُخور! (خور)	Eat!
شما	بُخورید! (خور)	Eat! (pl)

2. If the present stem ends in /ow/, in the **plural** form, the /ow/ changes to /av/. Example:

تو	بُرو!	Go!	بیدار شُو!	Wake up	
شما	بَروید!	Go! (pl)	بیدار شَوید!	Wake up! (pl)	

175

3. If the present stem begins with a vowel, a /y/ is inserted to ease the pronunciation. Hence the imperative prefix changes to /bi/[2].

تو	بیا! (آ)	Come!	بیاوَر/ بیار! (آوَر)	Bring!
شما	بیایید! / بیاین! (آ)	Come! (pl)	بیاوَرید/ بیارین! (آوَر)	Bring! (pl)

4. If the present stem has more than one vowel and the first vowel is /e/ or /o/, that vowel is ususally contracted. Look at the transliteration of the examples to understand it better.

تو	بگُذار! ← بُگذار!/ بِذار! (گُذار)	Put/Allow (it)!	be-gozār → bogzār/bezār
تو	بِنشین!← بُنشین!/ بِشین! (نشین)	Sit	be-neshin → benshin/beshin

NEGATION

To form the negative imperative, replace the بـ prefix with prefix نَـ. نَـ carries stress and always remains the same, regardless of the following vowel.

درس خواندن

تو	درس نَخوان!	Do not study!
شما	درس نَخوانید!	Do not study! (pl)

خندیدن

تو	نَخند!	Do not laugh!
شما	نَخندید!	Do not laugh! (pl)

Writing and Pronunciation:

If the present stem begins with a vowel, a /y/ is inserted after the نَـ prefix.

تو	نَیا! (آ)	Do not come!	نَیاوَر/ نَیار! (آوَر)	Do not bring!
شما	نَیایید/ نَیاین (آ)	Do not come! (pl)	نَیاوَرید/ نَیارین! (آوَر)	Do not bring! (pl)

EXCEPTIONS (To Be & To Have)

The imperative forms of the verbs بودن and داشتن are not derived from their present stems. They are derived from the following stems: باش and داشته باش.

تو	ساکِت باش!	Be quiet!	صَبر داشته باش!	Be patient!
تو	ساکِت نَباش!	Do not be quiet!	صَبر نَداشته باش!	Do not be patient!
شما	ساکِت باشید!	Be quiet! (pl)	صَبر داشته باشید!	Be patient! (pl)
شما	ساکِت نَباشید!	Do not be quiet! (pl)	صَبر نَداشته باشید!	Do not be patient! (pl)

---

2. The exception is ایستادَن in both affirmative and negative forms.

تمرین ۶

Use Appendix A and write the following imperative forms and pronounce them aloud:

2nd Person Plural Neg.	2nd Person Singular Neg.	2nd Person Plural	2nd Person Singular	
				پرسیدن
				خوردن
				دوست داشتن
				کار کردن
				گذاشتن
				نشستن

تمرین ۷

Use Appendix A and write the imperative forms (singular & plural) for each image. The odd numbers require a negative verb. Use the polite words لطفاً or خواهش می‌کنم before each verb.

_____ .2   _____ .1

_____ .4   _____ .3

_____ .6   _____ .5

تمرین ۸

Use Appendix A and conjugate the following verbs in the plural imperative form.

۱. بچّه‌ها، کتاب‌هایتان را _____ ! (باز کردن To open)

۲. لطفاً به انگلیسی _____ ! (نوشتن)

۳. خواهش می‌کنم به من _____ !(گوش کردن)

۴. بچّه‌ها، از روی درس _____ ! (خواندن)

۵. بچّه‌ها، ساکت _____ ! (بودن)

 دستور زبان ۲

PRESENT SUBJUNCTIVE حالِ التِزامی

The present subjunctive[3] form is used in a variety of situations in Persian:

۱. It is used with modals (such as باید or شاید) (ex: *I must/may/shall study*).[4]

2. It is used as a second verb after expressions of desire, doubt, hope, possibility, probability, preference, and necessity (ex: *I want to see you*).

3. It is used after conjunctions (such as تا or که) and in conditional sentences. We will learn more about these usages in future lessons. Examples:

I should/may study.	۱. من باید/ شاید درس بخوانم.
I want to see you.	۲. من می‌خواهم تو را ببینم.
I like to study.	۳. من دوست دارم درس بخوانم.
I go to school to/in order to study.	۴. من به مدرسه می‌روم تا درس بخوانم.

To form the Present Subjunctive:

1) Add the prefix بِ to the present stem of the verb: بِخَند ← خَند + بِ

2) Add the personal endings used for the simple present tense.

	درس خواندن				خندیدن	
ما	درس بِخوانیم	من	درس بِخوانم	ما	بِخندیم	من	بِخندم
شما	درس بِخوانید	تو	درس بِخوانی	شما	بِخندید	تو	بِخندی
آنها	درس بِخوانند	او	درس بِخواند	آنها	بِخندند	او	بِخندَد

Writing and Pronunciation:

The writing and pronunciation rules of the imperative apply to the subjunctive form, except in the following verbs:

رفتَن: (رو) ← بِرَوَم/ بِرَم

بیدار شُدَن: (شَو) ← بیدار شَوَم/بیدار شَم

Similar to the imperative form, the prefix بِ may be omitted in the subjunctive form of some verbs such as: شُدَن ـ کردن. The spoken form may not follow this rule.

کار کنیم/ کار بُکنیم.

EXCEPTIONS (To Be & To Have)

Similar to the imperative form, داشتن and بودن are irregular in the subjunctive form and their stems are: باش and داشته باش. Examples: تو باید ساکت باشی!ـ تو باید صبر داشته باشی!

---

3. Persian has both present and past subjunctive forms. In this book, we will learn only the present subjunctive form. Hence the word subjunctive is used instead of present subjunctive.

4. The Persian equivalent of "can" (تَوانستن = *to be able to*) must be conjugated in Persian.

NEGATION

To negate a verb in the subjunctive form, replace the بـ prefix with the stressed prefix نَـ.

درس خواندن

من	درس نَخوانم	ما	درس نَخوانیم
تو	درس نَخوانی	شما	درس نَخوانید
او	درس نَخوانَد	آنها	درس نَخوانند

خندیدن

من	نَخندم	ما	نَخندیم
تو	نَخندی	شما	نَخندید
او	نَخندد	آنها	نَخندند

تمرین ۹

With a classmate, practice reading the imperative and subjunctive forms provided in the grammar sections. Take turns and listen to each other's reading.

تمرین ۱۰

Use Appendix A and conjugate the verbs in the subjunctive form. Read your sentences aloud.

۱. من می‌خواهم به ایران ـــــــــــــــ (رفتن).

۲. آقای شریفی باید ـــــــــــــــ (مداوا شدن).

۳. ما شاید ـــــــــــــــ (توانستن) به شما ـــــــــــــــ (کمک کردن).

۴. آنها شاید فردا فارسی ـــــــــــــــ (داشتن).

۵. من شنبه نمی‌توانم تو را ـــــــــــــــ (دیدن).

۶. او هر روز باید دخترش را به مدرسه ـــــــــــــــ (بردن).

۷. من فکر می‌کنم فردا به او ـــــــــــــــ (گفتن).

۸. تو باید تمرین ها را بهتر ـــــــــــــــ (انجام دادن).

۹. آنها می‌توانند خیلی خوب فارسی ـــــــــــــــ (حرف زدن).

۱۰. مادرِ من هم خیلی دوست دارد ـــــــــــــــ (آمدن).

۱۱. من می‌خواهم یک کتاب به تو ـــــــــــــــ (دادن).

۱۲. او شاید امشب با ما ـــــــــــــــ (بودن).

The Persian equivalent of "can" is: تَوانستن which literally means "To be able to" and must be conjugated.

تمرین ۱۱

Underline the subjunctive and imperative forms in the written version of Dialogues 1, 2, and the reading passage. Explain why you think they are in either the subjunctive or imperative form.

Subjunctive as an Independent Verb

When the subjunctive form is used independently, a modal (may/must/can/should/would) is implied. It can also be used as an interrogative form with a rising tone. Examples:

He must/should go!	برود!
Can/may he go?	برود؟
Let's eat!	بخوریم!
Shall we eat?	بخوریم؟

Subjunctive vs. Imperative

When the subjunctive form is used independently, the second person plural form is identical to the imperative form. While they both have a command tone, the subjunctive form has a stronger tone than the imperative form and can be used for warning. Examples:

Do not talk!	حرف نزن!	Eat!	غذا بخور!	*Imperative*
You must not talk!	حرف نزنی!	You must eat!	غذا بخوری (ها)!	*Subjunctive*

In spoken form, ها may be added for emphasis.

Subjunctive vs. Simple Present

The difference between the present subjunctive and the simple present forms is shown below:

What do I do?	۱. چه کار می‌کنم؟
What would I do?	۲. چه کار کنم؟
Where do they go?	۳. کجا می‌روند؟
Where would they go?	۴. کجا بروند؟
We go to school tomorrow.	۵. فردا به مدرسه می‌رویم.
Should we go to school tomorrow?	۶. فردا به مدرسه برویم؟

تمرین ۱۲

Arrange the following words to make a sentence. Read your sentence aloud:

۱. کتاب‌فروشی ـ لطفاً ـ برای من ـ خودکار ـ بخر ـ از ـ یک

۲. همکارم ـ چند روز ـ باید ـ کار نکند ـ مریض است ـ و

۳. ببینم ـ خیلی ـ را ـ دوست دارم ـ ایران ـ من

۴. یاد بگیرید؟ ـ می‌خواهید ـ فارسی ـ شما ـ چرا

۵. آقای شریفی ـ با ـ صحبت کنم؟ ـ ببخشید ـ می‌توانم

تمرین ۱۳

Form questions about the underlined words.

۱. _____ ؟ من امروز عصر می‌خواهم به خرید بروم.

۲. _____ ؟ او باید خودکارِ قرمز بخرد.

۳. _____ ؟ علی با دوستش باید درس بخوانند.

۴. _____ ؟ چون من باید فردا صبحِ زود کار کنم.

۵. _____ ؟ ببخشید. نمی‌توانم ساعت پنج بیایم.

۶. _____ ؟ من دوست دارم یک فرش ابریشم بخرم.

تمرین ۱۴

Write a paragraph about what you want to do tomorrow night. Use at least five subjunctive forms.
Example:

> من می‌خواهم فردا شب به خانه‌ی دوستم بروم. ما شاید به یک رستوران ایرانی برویم. امیدوارم
> رستورانِ خیلی گرانی نباشد چون من زیاد پول ندارم ....

تمرین ۱۵

Change into written form. Pronounce your answers aloud.

۱. تو چی می‌خوای بخری؟

۲. پسرتون هم باید باهاتون بیاد؟

۳. تو دوست داری بری ایران؟

۴. اونا می‌تونن بیان اینجا؟

۵. می‌تونی از اونجا غذا بخری؟

۶. چرا براش کامپیوتر نمی‌خری؟

بیشتر بدانیم

پوشاک - لِباس 🎧

کُت	شَلوار	پیراهَن / پیرَهن / پیرَن	تیشِرت	بُلوز / بُلیز	دامَن

کاپشَن / کاپِشِن	ژاکَت	کُت و شَلوار / کُت شَلوار	روسَری	چادُر	روپوش - مانتو

کَفش	جوراب	کُلاه

182

تمرین ۱۶

Talk with your classmate about the type and color of the clothes you are wearing. Ask each other what you want to wear tomorrow. Examples:

a: تو این کُلاه رو دوست داری؟	a: شلوارِ من چه رنگیه؟
b: نه من کلاه دوست ندارم.	b: شلوارِت آبیه.
a: جورابِ پیتر چه رنگیه؟	a: تو فردا چی می‌پوشی؟
b: جورابش سفیده.	b: من فردا کت و شلوار می‌پوشم.

تمرین ۱۷

What kind of shoes are advertised in the following ad? What are the advantages of using these shoes? Underline the names of body parts in the text. If you live in a city other than Tehran, how can you get these shoes?

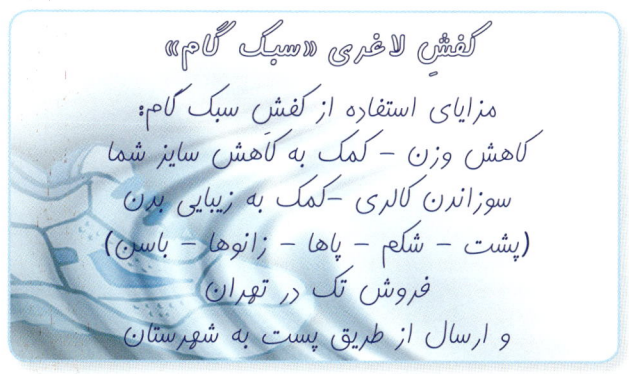

تمرین ۱۸ : واژگان

In each line, circle the word that does not match the rest:

پارچه	ارزان	سبک	۱. سنگین
دامن	بلوز	مشتری	۲. شلوار
لحظه	قابلی نداره	ارزون بدین مشتری شیم	۳. مبارکه
باشه	خب	امیدواریم	۴. مثلاً
روسری	مغازه	بیمار	۵. قالی
نباید	نباش	نروید	۶. نخور
کفش	پول	روپوش	۷. چادر

👄 🎧 More About Shopping

Listen to the audio file and pronounce the following short dialogues.

a: سیب کیلویی/کیلو چنده؟
b: کیلویی پنج هزار تومن

a: ببخشین قیمتِ این مانتو چنده؟
b: هفتاد هزار تومن

a: یه متر از این پارچه چنده؟ /این پارچه متری چنده؟
b: متری دوازده هزار تومن

a: نون دونه‌ای چنده؟
b: دونه‌ای پنج هزار تومن

a: خُرما بَسته‌ای چنده؟
b: بَسته‌ای هفتاد هزار ریال

a: تُخمِ مُرغ شونه‌ای چنده؟
b: شونه‌ای چهار هزار تومن

a: این کَفش آخَرِش چنده؟
b: قابلی نداره!

a: تخفیف نمی‌دین؟
b: نه، قیمت‌ها مقطوعه!

تمرین ۱۹

Read the text below and fill in the blanks with the given words. Next, answer the following questions.

خریدِ شیرین و میترا

«شیرین» دخترِ آقای شریفی با ـــــــــــ «میترا» امروز می‌خواهند به خرید بروند. آنها ـــــــــــ خوشحالند چون امروز مدرسه ندارند. آنها می‌خواهند به مرکزِ خرید ـــــــــــ و تا عصر خرید کنند. شیرین یک ـــــــــــ و یک جُفت کفش لازم ـــــــــــ . میترا هم می‌خواهد یک روسریِ ـــــــــــ بخرد. ـــــــــــ معمولاً مقطوع هستند ولی آنها می‌خواهند چانه بزنند و ـــــــــــ بگیرند.

قیمت‌ها ـ دوست ـ تخفیف ـ سفید ـ بروند ـ خیلی ـ دارد ـ جوراب

> Look at the end of the lesson for the meaning of the new words.

۱.شیرین و میترا امروز می‌خواهند به کجا بروند؟

۲. شیرین و میترا امروز می‌خواهند تا کی خرید کنند؟

۳. شیرین چه چیزی لازم دارد؟

۴. میترا چه چیزی از مرکز خرید می‌خرد؟

تمرین ۲۰

Use the shopping phrases you have learned and prepare a conversation about shopping. Make sure you ask for a bargain and use the appropriate terminology. Role-play your conversation with a classmate in front of the class.

تمرین ۲۱

Listen to the audio file and complete the following chart.

گَتّه‌هاتون	کفش قرمزها	تخمِ مرغ	خرما	سیب	این شلوارِ جین	
						شونه‌ای ۸۰۰۰ تومن
						کیلویی ۱۰,۰۰۰ تومن
						هفتاد هزار تومن
						قابلی نداره!
						قیمت‌ها مقطوعه!
						بسته‌ای ۱۲,۰۰۰تومن

185

🎧 Technology-related Words

Email	پُستِ الکترونیکی	Internet	اینترنت
Text message	پیامَک	Website	تارنَما ـ وِبگاه
Results	یافته‌ها	Main menu	مِنوی اَصلی
Contact us	تَماس با ما	First page	صَفحه نُخست
Fax	دورنگار	Search	بگَرد
Links	پیوَندها	Search	جُستُجو
Enter	وُرود	Password	رَمزِ عبور ـ گُذَر واژه
Cursor	اِشاره‌گر	User name	نامِ کاربَری
Icon	آیکُن ـ نَمادِ تَصویری	Button	دُکمه

تمرین ۲۲ 👥

You have received the following note on your Facebook page. Conjugate the given verbs in the plural imperative form. What is your friend asking you to do?

دوستان عزیزم:

لطفاً این تغییرات را برایم ————— (انجام دادن)

اشاره‌گر ماوس را بر روی اسم من در بالای این پست ————— (گذاشتن).

پنجره‌ای بازمی شود. اشاره‌گر ماوس را بدون اینکه ————— (کلیک کردن) روی

گزینه‌ی Friends ————— (قرار دادن). در لیست ظاهر شده بر روی Setting

————— (کلیک کردن). در این قسمت تیک را از کنار Comments and Likes

————— (برداشتن).

ممنون!

تمرین ۲۳

The following information is provided on a clothing website. Underline any words you recognize. Which word means "cheap"? What is this advertisement about? Note that this authentic advertisement uses a mix of spoken and written forms. Can you identify them?

تبلیغ رایگان

اگه شوی لباس دارید و اجناستون رو
می‌خواهید ارزون بفروشید و یا اگه
کالای تولید ایران دارید
(فقط در زمینه‌ی لباس و آرایش)
تو قسمت نظرات بصورت خصوصی
یادداشت بگذارید،
تا در اسرع وقت اقدام به تبلیغ نماییم.

تمرین ۲۴

You receive the following email. What is this email about? What is the email address <u>pooya@qmail.com</u> for?

شما مشترک گروه «پویا» هستید. اعضای این گروه هفته‌ای یک بار ایمیل دریافت می‌کنند.

برای مشترک شدن نامه بفرستید به: برای قطع اشتراک نامه بفرستید به:

ba-pooya@yahoogroups.com   bi-pooya@yahoogroups.com

برای ارسال نامه به مدیر:

pooya@qmail.com

تمرین ۲۵

Decide if each phrase is in formal or informal form and change it to the other form:

۱. قربونِ شما:

۲. دستت درد نکنه:

۳. بفرما تو:

۴. ببخشین مزاحم شدم:

۵. سلام برسونین:

تمرین ۲۶

Listen to the audio file and fill in the blanks:

کورش: امشب می خوای ـــــــــــــ ؟

پروین: کاری ـــــــــــــ چطور؟

کورش: ـــــــــــــ بریم سینما؟

پروین: آره. تو چه فیلمی ـــــــــــــ ببینی؟

کورش: من ـــــــــــ دوست دارم یه فیلم ـــــــــــ ببینم ـــــــــ چی؟

پروین: چه خوب! من هم ـــــــــ ساعت چند ـــــــــــ ـــــــــ ؟

کورش: ساعت ـــــــــ چطوره؟

پروین: بد ـــــــ . تو چی ـــــــــ ـــــــــــ ؟

کورش: ـــــــــــ تو چی؟

پروین: من ـــــــــ و ـــــــــ می‌پوشم.

کورش: باشه، پس منم ـــــــــــ ـــــــــ می‌پوشم.

تمرین ۲۷

Choose the correct form:

۱. دوستِ من، ناهید، شش ـــــــــــ دارد. (خواهر ـ خواهران)

۲. چند تا از ـــــــــــ من در ایران زندگی می‌کنند. (دوست ـ دوستان)

۳. تو این ترم چند تا ـــــــــــ داری؟ (کلاس ـ کلاس‌ها)

۴. تو این ترم چه ـــــــــــ داری؟ (کلاس‌ها ـ کلاس‌هایی)

۵. ببخشید آقا، این نان‌ها ـــــــــــ چند است؟ (دانه ـ دانه‌ای)

۶. در دانشگاه، هر ـــــــــــ یک نامِ کاربری دارد. (دانشجو ـ دانشجویان)

۷. مشتری‌های ما همه ـــــــــــ هستند. (استاد ـ استادها)

۸. همه‌ی ـــــــــــ در کلاس هستند. (دانش‌آموز ـ دانش‌آموزان)

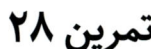

تمرین ۲۸

Arrange the words in parenthesis in the right order and fill in the blanks:

۱. من باید ــــــــــــ او را ببینم. (ساعت ــ شش)

۲. چه ــــــــــــ داری! (قشنگی ــ کفش‌های)

۳. ــــــــــــ باید آسان نباشد. (آدرسِ الکترونیکی ــ رمزِ عبور)

۴. ــــــــــــ ما به مدرسه نمی آید. (بیمار ــ مدیر)

۵. ببخشید، این ــــــــــــ چند است؟ (پارچه ــ متری)

۶. مادرِ من ــــــــــــ دارد و همیشه برای من لباس می خرد. (خوبی ــ سلیقه‌ی)

۷. این ــــــــــــ من است. (ماشین ــ اوّلین)

۸. خانواده‌ی پارسا در ــــــــــــ زندگی می کنند. (چهارمین ــ طبقه)

تمرین ۲۹

Task: Your friend wants to buy a rug. You want to convince your friend to take you along. Say the following in Persian. Use the spoken form:

1. Do you want to buy a rug?

2. Where do you want to buy the rug from?

3. Can I come with you?

4. We can go in my car.

5. I have good taste!

6. Maybe they have a student discount.

7. I can ask the seller about a student discount.

8. Do not buy (an) expensive rug because you are a student.

9. I really like to see the rugs.

REVIEW CORNER	
Points that remain unclear about Lesson 5:	
How I plan to work on these points:	

شعر

The following poem by Ferdowsi is from شاهنامه, the national epic of the Persian-speaking world. Find the familiar words. Find three instances of imperative and two instances of subjunctive forms. You will not be evaluated on the content but you can use it for cultural enrichment.

از شاهنامه

بهمهر اندرین کشور افسون کنید	ز دلها همه کینه بیرون کنید
ز خون ریختن گرد کشور گلست	که از ما چنین دردشان در دلست
بران گنج دادن سپاهی نهم	همه گنج توران شما را دهم
چو دیدید سرما بهار آورید	بکوشید و خوبی بکار آورید
کنم یکسر از گنج دینار سیر	من ایرانیان را یکایک نه دیر
سر بیگناهان نباید برید	زخون ریختن دل بباید کشید

شاعر: فِردوسی (۱۰۲۰ ـ ۹۴۰)

Ferdowsi's tomb in Tus, near Mashhad

ترانه

Listen to the following song by Mohammad Nouri on YouTube and find the familiar words. This song is in a regional accent. Find the suffix pronouns and indicate how they are pronounced differently from the Tehrani spoken form. Underline the verbs in the imperative form. You will not be evaluated on the content but you can use it for cultural enrichment.

جانِ مریم

آی گل سرخ و سفیدُم کی می‌آیی؟

بنفشه برگ بیدُم کی می‌آیی؟

تو گفتی گل درآید من می‌آیم

وای گل عالم تموم شد کی می‌آیی؟

جانِ مریم چشماتو واکن، منو صدا کن!

شد هوا سپید، در اومد خورشید

وقت اون رسید که بریم به صحرا

آی نازنینِ مریم

جانِ مریم چشماتو واکن، منو صدا کن!

بشیم رَوونه، بریم از خونه، شونه به شونه، به یاد اون روزا

آی نازنین مریم

باز دوباره صبح شد، من هنوز بیدارم

کاش می‌خوابیدم، تو رو خواب می‌دیدم

خوشه‌ی غم توی دلم زده جوونه دونه به دونه

دل نمی دونه چه کنه با این غم

آی نازنینِ مریم

بیا رسید وقت درو، مال منی از پیشم نرو

بیا سر کارمون بریم، درو کنیم گندما رو

بیا بیا نازنینِ مریم، نازنینِ مریم

آی مریم مریم، ای نازنینِ مریم

خواننده: محمّد نوری (۲۰۱۰ـ۱۹۲۹)

191

نکته‌ی فرهنگی

Bargaining Brings Prosperity!

Bargaining is a customary practice in Iran. Not only is it culturally accepted, it is said that giving a discount will bring prosperity for both parties. Specific terminology (introduced throughout the lesson) is utilized during bargaining. In some cases, prices can be reduced by two-thirds or even cut in half. Unlike western countries where most stores are franchised and run by big corporations, most of the stores in Iran are privately owned so the seller/owner has the authority to offer a discount. In smaller stores, products may not have a price tag, so foreigners may end up purchasing overpriced products. Bargaining can be a source of amusement for some people. When sellers respond positively to bargaining, customers return to the store for more purchases.

Traditional Bazaars

Traditional Bazaara are the equivalent of modern malls and shopping centers. A traditional Bazaar is a long roofed area with shops on both sides. Traditional Bazaars have beautiful architectural details and designs. Bazaars have sunroofs to let the light in. A wide variety of products, from spices and nuts (such as Saffron and Pistachios) to rugs, china, and jewelry, can be found under one roof.

بازارِ تهران

ضرب المثل

از آن نترس که های و هوی دارد. از آن بترس که سر به تو دارد!

Literal translation: *Do not be afraid of the loud one! Be afraid of the quiet one!*
(Barking dogs seldom bite!)

This proverb states that, generally, the true nature of an extroverted person is easier to read and is revealed more readily than that of an introverted person.

Thematic Review of New Vocabulary

About Shopping	
What is the final price?	آخَرِش چند؟
Sell it for less so that we become customers	اَرزان بِدهید مُشتَری بِشَویم
Cheap	اَرزان
Per box	بَستهای
Money	پول
Discount	تَخفیف
Student discount	تَخفیفِ دانشجویی
Toman (Iranian currency)	تومان
May it bring you luck	خِیرش را ببینید
Each	دانهای
Taste	سَلیقه
Egg crates	شانه
Seller	فروشنده
Price	قیمَت
Per Kilogram	کیلویی
Expensive	گِران
Congratulations	مُبارَک است!
Per meter	مِتری
Client	مُشتَری
Firm/fixed price	مَقطوع

Places for Shopping	
Small grocery store	بَقّالی
Boutique	بوتیک
Fabric store	پارچهفروشی
Supermarket	سوپرمارکت
Store	فُروشگاه
Bookstore	کتابفروشی
Shoe store	کَفّاشی
Spice & herb store	عَطّاری
Shop	مَغازه
Shopping center	مرکزِ خرید
Fruit store	میوهفروشی
Bakery	نانوایی

Nouns & Adjectives	
Silk	اَبریشَم
Fabric	پارچه
Egg	تُخم مُرغ
Dates	خُرما
Light (weight)	سَبک
Heavy	سَنگین
Apple	سیب
Rug	فَرش
Rug	قالی
Gabbeh	گَبّه
Qilim	گِلیم
Moment	لَحظه
School	مَدرسه
Present/Gift	هِدیه
Co-worker	هَمکار

193

Technology-related words	
Cursor	اِشاره‌گر
Icon	آیکُن – نَماد تَصویری
Internet	اینترنِت
Search	بِگَرد
Email	پُستِ اِلِکترونیکی
Text message	پَیامَک
Links	پیوَندها
Website	تارنَما – وِبگاه
Contact us	تَماس با ما
Search	جُستُجو
Button	دُکمه
Fax	دورنِگار
Password	رَمزِ عبور – گُذَر واژه
First page	صَفحهِ نُخُست
Main menu	منوی اَصلی
User name	نام کارَبری
Enter	وُرود
Results	یافته‌ها

Clothing & More	
Blouse	بلوز
Clothes	پوشاک
Dress	پیراهَن
T-shirt	تی‌شِرت
Sock	جوراب
Denim/Jeans	جین
Chador	چادُر
Skirt	دامَن
Ladies' long coat	روپوش – مانتو
Scarf	روسَری
Cardigan	ژاکَت
Pants	شَلوار
Winter coat	کاپِشَن
Coat	کُت
Suit	کُت و شَلوار
Shoe	کَفش
Hat	کُلاه
Clothes	لِباس

Health & Sickness	
Sick/Ill	بیمار
Hospital	بیمارِستان
To get well	خوب شُدن
Medical Treatment	مُداوا
Sick/Ill	مَریض

Modals	
Must/Should	بایَد
May	شایَد

Words & Expressions	
A lot/Many	زیاد
OK (Spoken)	باشه
Must	بایَد
Quickly/Soon	به زودی
So that/Until	تا
Pair	جُفت
Sir/Excellency	جِناب
OK/Well	خُب
About/Concerning	درباره(ی)
That/Which/Who/When/Where/Whose/Whom	که
For example	مَثَلاً
All kinds	هَمه نوع

Verbs & Phrases	
We hope	اُمیدواریم (بودن)
I should/may ask	بِپُرسَم (پُرسیدَن: پُرس)
I should/must buy	بخَرَم (خَریدَن: خَر)
We should/may give	بِدَهیم (دادَن: دَه)
S/he should/may go	بِرَوَد (رَفتَن: رَو)
Go! (Plural & Formal)	بِروید (رَفتَن: رَو)
I should/may find it	پیدایَش کُنَم (کردن: کُن)
They should/may haggle	چانه بزنند (زَدن: زَن)
I should/may count	حساب کُنَم (کردن: کُن)
We should/may study	دَرس بخوانیم (خواندَن: خوان)
Wait! (Plural & Formal)	صَبرکُنید (کردن: کُن)
You wear	می‌پوشی (پوشیدَن: پوش)
I can/I am able to	می‌تَوانم (تَوانِستَن: تَوان)
I want	می‌خواهم (خواستَن: خواه)
We want	می‌خواهیم (خواستَن: خواه)
It should/may not be	نَباشَد (بودن: هست)
Don't you give…?	نِمی‌دَهید؟ (دادَن: دَه)

درس ششم

جغرافی و آب‌وهوا

Geography & Weather

واژگان ۱ 🎧

You liked	دوست داشتی (دار)	Tomb	آرامگاه
I saw	دیدَم (بین)	Man/Dude (Slang)	بابا
You saw	دیدی (بین)	Tell me so that I see	بگو ببینم
Famous Persian poet	سَعدی	In my opinion	به نَظرِ من
I fell in love with …	عاشِقِ .... شُدَم (شَو)	More	بیشتَر
Month/Moon	ماه	Summer	تابِستان/ تابِستون
I used to think	فکر می‌کردم (کُن)	Entire/All	تَمام/ تَموم
More beautiful	قَشَنگ‌تر	What's up?	چه خَبَر؟
The most beautiful	قَشَنگ‌ترین	What did you do?	چه کار کردی/چی کار کردی؟
You stayed	ماندی/ موندی (مان)	Famous Persian poet	حافظ
You were missed	جایَت خالی/ جات خالی	Had a good time	خوش گُذَشت (گُذَر)

Close your book and listen to the dialogue. Then fill in the blanks using the new words.

گفتگو ۱ 🎧

بیتا: چه خبر؟ بگو ببینم ———— ———— چی کار کردی؟

مریم: جات خالی، تابِستون رفتم ایران. خیلی عالی بود!

بیتا: خوش به حالت! چند وقت ایران موندی؟

مریم: سه ماه. خیلی بِهِم خوش گذشت. تهران[1] و اصفهان و شیراز رو دیدم.

بیتا: کدوم شهر رو بیشتر دوست داشتی؟

مریم: عاشقِ شیراز شدم. به نظرِ من ———— ———— شهرِ ایرانه!

بیتا: آرامگاهِ «سعدی» و «حافظ» رو هم ———— ؟

مریم: آره، تمومِ شهر رو دیدم!

بیتا: پس به نظرِ تو شیراز از تهران قشنگ‌تره؟ من فکر می‌کردم تهران قشنگ‌تره!

مریم: نه بابا!

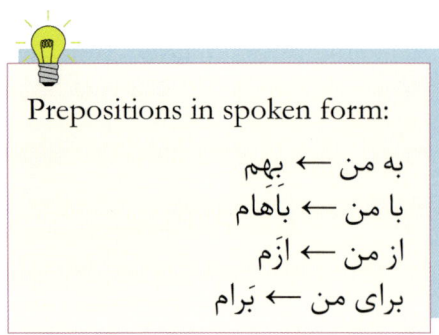

Prepositions in spoken form:

به من ← بِهِم
با من ← باهام
از من ← ازَم
برای من ← بَرام

---

1 . تهران is sometimes changed to تهرون in spoken form.

نوشتاری

گفتگو ۱

بیتا: ــــــــــ؟ بگو ببینم تابستان چه کار کردی؟

مریم: جایت خالی، به ایران رفتم. خیلی عالی بود!

بیتا: خوش به حالَت! چند وقت در ایران ــــــــــ ؟

مریم: سه ماه. خیلی به من خوش گذشت. تهران و اصفهان و شیراز را دیدم.

بیتا: کدام شهر را بیشتر دوست داشتی؟

مریم: عاشقِ شیراز شدم. به نظر من قشنگ‌ترین شهر ایران است!

بیتا: آرامگاهِ «سعدی» و «حافظ» را هم دیدی؟

مریم: بله، ــــــــــ شهر را دیدم!

بیتا: پس به نظرِ تو شیراز از تهران قشنگ‌تر است؟ من فکر می‌کردم تهران قشنگ‌تر است!

مریم: نه خیر!

تمرین ۱

Talk with your classmate about what you did last summer. Express your opinion by using : به نظرِ من or فکر می‌کنم . Take some notes about your conversation so that you can report it to the class.

واژگان ۲

Paternal uncle	عَمو	Those times/days	آن وَقت‌ها/ اون وَقتا
Paternal aunt	عَمّه	I was	بودم
Extended family	فامیل	You were	بودی
Grandmother	مادر بُزُرگ	The day before yesterday	پَریروز
We used to laugh	می‌خَندیدیم (خَند)	Maternal aunt's son	پسرخاله
We used to say/talk	می‌گُفتیم (گو)	Paternal aunt's son	پسرعَمّه
Near each other	نَزدیکِ هَم	Lonely	تَنها
Really	واقِعاً	Now	حالا
When (in declarative sentence)	وَقتی	Maternal aunt	خاله
Each one/Anyone	هَر کَسی/ هَر کِسی	Maternal uncle	دایی
Good old days	یادَش به خِیر/ یادِش به خِیر	Maternal aunt's daughter	دخترخاله
		We used to get together	دورِ هَم جَمع می‌شُدیم (شو)

Close your book and listen to the dialogue. Then fill in the blanks using the new words.

گفتگو ۲

کامران: سلام! پریروز کجا بودی؟

آرش: شمال بودم. خونه‌ی ——————— بودم.

کامران: چه خوب! چطور بودن؟

آرش: خوب، ولی خیلی تنها هستن.

کامران: وقتی بچّه بودیم، هر جمعه خونه‌ی مادربزرگ جمع می‌شدیم.

آرش: آره، عمّه، عمو، خاله، دایی، پسرعمو، دخترعمو، پسرخاله، دخترخاله، تمومِ فامیل بودن!

کامران: آره، همیشه دورهم جمع می‌شدیم، می‌گفتیم و ———————.

آرش: ولی حالا هر کسی تو یه شهری زندگی می‌کنه.

کامران: آره، اون وقتا همه نزدیکِ هم زندگی می‌کردیم.

آرش: واقعاً ———————!

نوشتاری

گفتگو ۲

کامران: سلام! ——————— کجا بودی؟

آرش: شمال بودم. خانه‌ی مادر بزرگ بودم.

کامران: چه خوب! چطور بودند؟

آرش: خوب ولی خیلی ——————— هستند.

کامران: وقتی بچه بودیم، هر جمعه خانه‌ی مادربزرگ جمع می‌شدیم.

آرش: بله، عمّه، عمو، خاله، دایی، پسرعمو، دخترعمو، پسرخاله، دخترخاله، تمامِ ——————— بودند.

کامران: بله، همیشه دورهم جمع می‌شدیم، می‌گفتیم و می‌خندیدیم.

آرش: ولی حالا هر کسی در یک شهری زندگی می‌کند.

کامران: بله، آن وقت‌ها همه نزدیکِ هم زندگی می‌کردیم.

آرش: واقعاً یادَش به خیر!

تمرین ۲

Role-play the above dialogue with your classmate.

تمرین ۳

Find six words that are different in written and spoken forms and write them below.

Spoken	← Written	Spoken	← Written

خواندن

رامسر

مسافرتِ خانواده‌ی پارسا

ماهِ گذشته خانواده‌ی پارسا سه هفته تعطیل بودند. آنها دو هفته به مسافرت رفتند. دخترانِشان بیتا و پریسا با آنها به مسافرت نرفتند چون آنها در آمریکا زندگی می‌کنند. خانواده‌ی پارسا اوّل به شهرِ «رامسَر» رفتند. خانم پارسا برای اوّلین بار «دَریای خَزَر» را می‌دید. بعد به شهرِ «رَشت» رفتند. آقای پارسا قبلاً در آنجا زندگی می‌کرد. بعد به شهرِ «تَبریز» رفتند. خانمِ پارسا تَبریز را خیلی دوست دارد چون وقتی بچّه بود با خانواده‌اش در آن شهر زندگی می‌کردند. پدربزرگ و مادربزرگِ خانمِ پارسا هنوز هم در تبریز زندگی می‌کنند.

Previously	قَبلاً	Suffix to count how-many times	بار
Past/Previous	گُذَشته	They were	بودند
Travel/Trip	مُسافِرَت	Next/Afterwards/Then	بَعد
S/he used to/would see	می‌دید	Off/Not working	تعطیل
They did not go	نَرَفتند	Caspian Sea	دَریای خَزَر
They went	رفتند	S/he used to live	زندگی می‌کرد

Synonyms		
حالا = اَلان	مُسافِرَت = سَفَر	مادربزرگ = مامان بزرگ
	گُذَشته = پیش	پدربزرگ = بابا بزرگ

تمرین ۴

a) Listen to the audio file and follow along in your text. Repeat each sentence several times.

b) Answer in complete sentences. Use the written form.

۱. خانواده‌ی پارسا به چه شهرهایی مسافرت کردند؟

۲. آقای پارسا قبلاً در کجا زندگی می‌کرد؟

۳. خانمِ پارسا چه شهری را دوست دارد و چرا؟

۴. وقتی شما بچه بودید، در کجا زندگی می‌کردید؟

۵. آیا آن شهر را دوست دارید؟ چرا؟

تمرین ۵ واژگان

Fill in the blanks using the appropriate vocabulary from the list below.

آرامگاه ـ گذشته ـ دیشب ـ زندگی می‌کرد ـ تعطیل ـ اوّلین ـ جایتان خالی ـ عمّه ـ عاشق

۱. ماه ــــــــــــــ رفتم ایران. خیلی عالی بود!

۲. ــــــــــــــ سعدی و حافظ را هم دیدی؟

۳. من در ایران ــــــــــــــ شیراز شدم.

۴. ــــــــــــــ تابستان رفتم ایران. خیلی عالی بود.

۵. چه خبر؟ ــــــــــــــ کجا بودی؟

۶. هما برای ــــــــــــــ بار دریای خَزر را می دید.

۷. ماهِ پیش هما و همسرش سه هفته ــــــــــــــ بودند.

۸. وقتی هما بچه بود، با خانواده‌اش در آنجا ــــــــــــــ .

بیشتر بدانیم

🎧 Adverbs of Time

Two nights before last	پَس پَریشَب	Two days before yesterday	پَس پَریروز
The night before last	پَریشَب	The day before yesterday	پَریروز
Last night	دیشَب	Yesterday	دیروز
Tonight	اِمشَب	Today	اِمروز
Tomorrow night	فَردا شَب	Tomorrow	فَردا
The night after tomorrow night	پَس فَردا شَب	The day after tomorrow	پَس فَردا

تمرین ۶

Fill in the blanks using adverbs of time:

۱. امروز شنبه است. ــــــــــــــ چهارشنبه بود.

۲. فردا شب چهارشنبه است. پس فردا شب ــــــــــــــ است.

۳. پریروز جمعه بود. فردا ــــــــــــــ است.

۴. پس فردا یک شنبه است. ــــــــــــــ پنج شنبه بود.

 دستور زبان ۱

SIMPLE PAST TENSE گُذَشتهی ساده

The usage of the simple past tense in English and Persian is almost the same. It indicates an action or state that occurred once and was completed in the past:

I saw Mina yesterday.	من دیروز مینا را دیدم.
I was in Tehran yesterday.	من دیروز در تهران بودم.

To form the Simple Past Tense:

1) Drop /-an/ from the end of the infinitive to obtain the past stem. The past stem is always regular with no exceptions. Examples:

Past Stem	Infinitive
خندید	خندیدن ←
درس‌خواند	درس‌خواندن ←

2) Add the appropriate verb ending of the past tense as shown below. **The third person singular form takes no personal ending in the past tense.**

خندیدن

خندیدیم	ما	خندیدَم	من
خندیدید	شما	خندیدی	تو
خندیدَند	آنها	خندید	او

Stress remains constant on the final syllable of the past stem (khandídam).

درس خواندن

درس خواندیم	ما	درس خواندَم	من
درس خواندید	شما	درس خواندی	تو
درس خواندَند	آنها	درس خواند	او

In compound verbs, the final syllable of the non-verbal component carries stress (dárs khāndam).

NEGATION

To negate the simple past tense, add the stressed /na/ نَ prefix to the beginning of the verb (ná khandid-am).

خندیدن

نَخندیدیم	ما	نَخندیدم	من
نَخندیدید	شما	نَخندیدی	تو
نَخندیدند	آنها	نَخندید	او

203

For compound verbs, add the stressed /na/ نَ prefix to the last component of the compound verb.

درس خواندن

من	درس نَخواندم	ما	درس نَخواندیم
تو	درس نَخواندی	شما	درس نَخواندید
او	درس نَخواند	آنها	درس نَخواندند

Writing and Pronunciation

1) If the past stem begins with any vowel other than /i/, a /y/ is inserted. In Examples 2 and 3 the initial *alef* is dropped:

S/he/it did not come	۱. آمَد ← نَیامَد
S/he/it did not drop	۲. اَنداخت ← نَیَنداخت
S/he/it did not fall	۳. اُفتاد ← نَیُفتاد

OTHER USAGE OF THE SIMPLE PAST TENSE

In Persian, the simple past tense can be used for actions that are about to occur but have not occurred yet:

I am gone/I am out of here. رفتم

I am coming/Be there in a sec. آمدم/اومدم

 تمرین۷

With a classmate, practice reading the conjugations of the simple past tense. Take turns and listen to each other's reading.

 تمرین ۸

Write the personal endings of the past tense in the following table.

	1ˢᵗ Person Plural		1ˢᵗ Person Singular
	2ⁿᵈ Person Plural		2ⁿᵈ Person Singular
	3ʳᵈ Person Plural		3ʳᵈ Person Singular

تمرین ۹

Conjugate in the simple past tense:

۱. من پنج سال در ایران ————— (زندگی کردن)

۲. پس پریروز پسر عمویم خیلی دیر به خانه‌ی ما ————— (آمدن)

۳. دیشب تمام فامیل دورِ هم ————— (جمع شدن)

۴. دختر خاله‌ام سه ساعت در سوپرمارکت ————— (ماندن)

۵. ماهِ گذشته ما سه هفته تعطیل ————— (بودن)

۶. ببخشید، کارم خیلی ————— (طول کشیدن)

۷. دیروز کلاسِ تو ساعت سه ————— ؟ (تمام شدن)

۸. پس پریروز چند تا کلاس ————— ؟ (داشتن)

تمرین ۱۰

Change the verbs into the simple past tense. Change the adverbs of time to match the tense of the verb. Work in pairs, groups, or as a class. Example:

Student 1 (*book open*): هما امروز چطور است؟

Student 2: (*book closed*): هما دیروز چطور بود؟

Group 2	Group 1
۱. تو کی به مسافرت می‌روی؟	۱. کدام شهر را بیشتر دوست دارید؟
۲. شما چند روز تعطیلید؟	۲. به چند شهر مسافرت می‌کنی؟
۳. امروز چند تا کلاس داری؟	۳. من فردا تعطیلم.
۴. فردا برنامه‌ات چیست؟	۴. مینا پس فردا شب کار می‌کند؟
۵. ما شنبه شب دورِ هم جمع می‌شویم.	۵. فردا تمامِ روز درس می‌خوانم!

تمرین ۱۱

Write a paragraph about what you did yesterday based on the following images. Use the written form.

دیروز چه کار کردی؟

206

دستور زبان ۲

گُذَشته‌ی اِستِمراری PAST CONTINUOUS TENSE

The past continuous (or habitual past tense) is used in the following situations:

1) For actions that took place habitually or repeatedly in the past.

وقتی بچّه بودم، هر هفته به خانه‌ی پدربزرگ و مادر بزرگم می رفتم.

When I was a child, I used to go to my grandparents' house every week.

2) For actions that took place at a certain time or a period of time:

I was writing a letter yesterday at ten o'clock. ‌دیروز ساعتِ ده نامه می‌نوشتم.

I was working in the bookstore last year. ‌پارسال در کتابفروشی کار می‌کردم.

To form the Past Continuous Tense:

1) Conjugate the verb in the simple past tense.

2) Add the می prefix. The می prefix carries stress (mí-khandid-am).

خندیدن

می‌خندیدیم	ما	می‌خندیدم	من
می‌خندیدید	شما	می‌خندیدی	تو
می‌خندیدند	آنها	می‌خندید	او

In compound verbs, the می prefix is inserted between the two parts of the compound verb.

درس خواندن

درس می‌خواندیم	ما	درس می‌خواندم	من
درس می‌خواندید	شما	درس می‌خواندی	تو
درس می‌خواندند	آنها	درس می‌خواند	او

In compound verbs, the final syllable of the non-verbal component carries primary stress (dárs mikhānd-am).

NEGATION

To negate the past continuous tense, add the stressed نـ prefix to the beginning of the continuous prefix (ex: némikhandidam).

خندیدن

ما	نِمی‌خندیدیم	من	نِمی‌خندیدم
شما	نِمی‌خندیدید	تو	نِمی‌خندیدی
آنها	نِمی‌خندیدند	او	نِمی‌خندید

In compound verbs, the negative prefix takes primary stress and secondary stress falls on the non-verbal component (ex: dàrs némikhāndam).

درس خواندن

ما	درس نِمی‌خواندیم	من	درس نِمی‌خواندم
شما	درس نِمی‌خواندید	تو	درس نِمی‌خواندی
آنها	درس نِمی‌خواندند	او	درس نِمی‌خواند

Exceptions:

The verbs بودن and داشتن do not take می in contemporary usage (in both written and spoken forms). Hence, they have the same form as the simple past tense[2]. Examples:

When I was a child, I used to be there every day.	۱.وقتی بچه بودم، هر روز آنجا بودم.
When I was a child, I used to have three cats.	۲. وقتی بچّه بودم، سه تا گربه داشتم.

In archaic form, the می prefix was added to the above verbs.

OTHER USAGE OF THE PAST CONTINUOUS TENSE

Sometimes the past continuous tense is used to show other tenses (often with stative verbs). Examples:

Excuse me, I want a red bag. (*at the store*)	۱. ببخشید، یه کیفِ قرمز می‌خواستم.
I could see her/him through the window.	۲. از پنجره او را می‌دیدم.

تمرین ۱۲

With a classmate, practice reading the conjugations of the past continuous tense. Take turns and listen to each other's reading.

---

2. Some compound verbs that contain the verb داشتن (like بَرداشتن) are an exception and require the می prefix.

تمرین ۱۳

Conjugate the following verbs in the past continuous tense:

۱. من همیشه بیتا را در مرکزِ خرید ــــــــــــــ (دیدن)

۲. او هر روز بچّه‌ها را برای مدرسه ــــــــــــــ (آماده کردن)

۳. وقتی علی بچّه بود، با پسرعموهایش ــــــــــــــ (دورهم جمع شدن)

۴. ترم پیش رابرت ــــــــــــــ (درس خواندن) Negative

۵. وقتی بچّه بودیم، در تاجیکستان ــــــــــــــ (زندگی کردن)

۶. وقتی دانشجو بودم، زیاد پول ــــــــــــــ (داشتن) Negative

تمرین ۱۴

Translate into Persian. Use the written form.

1. I used to study physics.

2. She did not know Persian.

3. I used to go to the university on Saturdays.

4. My parents watched that film.

5. They did not read Hafez's book.

6. Last night, my cousin returned home late.

7. When I was a child I used to like pizza a lot.

تمرین ۱۵

Write a story for the following image. Use at least seven verbs that are in the simple past or past continuous tense. Use the reading text at the beginning of the lesson as a model.

تمرین ۱۶

Form groups of three. Change the verbs into the simple past tense and then into the past continuous tense. Switch roles after each sentence. Example:

Student 1 (*book open*):   من درس می‌خوانم.

Student 2 (*book closed*):   من درس خواندم.

Student 3 (*book closed*):   من درس می‌خواندم.

۱. پسرخاله‌هایم همیشه با اتوبوس به مسافرت می‌روند.

۲. من یک فرش ابریشم می‌خواهم.

۳. تو امروز چند تا کلاس داری؟

۴. ما در شمالِ دورِ هم جمع می‌شویم.

۵. شیراز قشنگ‌ترین شهرِ ایران است.

۶. تو کجا زندگی می‌کنی؟

بیشتر بدانیم

🎧 Geography-related Words جغرافی

River	رود	Province	اُستان
Peak	قُلّه	Capital city	پایتَخت
Country	کِشوَر	Population	جَمعیَّت
Desert	کَویر	Gulf	خَلیج
Provincial capital	مَرکَزِ اُستان	Sea	دَریا
Map	نَقشه	Lake	دَریاچه
Neighbor(s)	هَمسایه - هَمسایگان	Mountain range	رِشته کوه

🎧 Continents قارّه‌ها

Asia	آسیا
Africa	آفریقا
America	آمریکا
Europe	اُروپا
Australia	اُسترالیا
Antarctica	قُطبِ جُنوب

🎧 Directions جَهَت‌ها

South East	جُنوبِ شَرقی	South	جُنوب
South West	جُنوبِ غَربی	North	شَمال
North East	شَمالِ شَرقی	East	شَرق
North West	شُمالِ غَربی	West	غَرب

کشورِ ایران

کشورِ ایران در غربِ آسیا است. پایتختِ کشورِ ایران تهران است. ایران دو رشته کوهِ بزرگ دارد. رشته کوه‌های ایران «اَلبُرز» و «زاگُرس» هستند. دریای خزر در شمالِ ایران است. در جنوبِ ایران «خَلیجِ فارس» و «دریای عُمان» قرار دارد. رودِ بزرگِ ایران «کارون» است. همسایگانِ شمالیِ ایران اَرمَنِستان، تُرکَمَنِستان و آذربایجان هستند. همسایگانِ شرقیِ ایران اَفغانِستان و پاکِستان هستند. همسایگانِ غربیِ ایران تُرکیه و عَراق هستند.

 تمرین ۱۷

a) Listen to the audio file and follow along in your text. Repeat each sentence several times.

b) Answer in complete sentences. Use the written form.

۱. نام رشته کوه‌های ایران چیست؟

۲. در جنوبِ ایران چه چیزی قرار دارد؟

۳. رودِ بزرگِ ایران چه نام دارد؟

۴. همسایگانِ شرقی و غربیِ ایران را نام ببرید.

تمرین ۱۸

به نقشه‌ی کشورِ ایران نگاه کنید. پایتخت را پیدا کنید. دریای خزر³، دریاچه‌ی اُرومیّه، خلیجِ فارس و دریای عمان را پیدا کنید. همسایگانِ ایران را روی نقشه پیدا کنید:

---

3. دریای خزر is technically not a sea as it is not connected to any oceans. However, since it is the largest lake on earth, it is referred to as a sea.

تمرین ۱۹

Prepare some questions to ask your classmate about Iran's neighboring countries. Example:

۱. اَفغانِستان در کجای ایران قرار دارد؟

۲. نامِ همسایگانِ شمالیِ ایران چیست؟

تمرین ۲۰

Write the names of the continents on the following map. If a continent has two parts, mention them both.

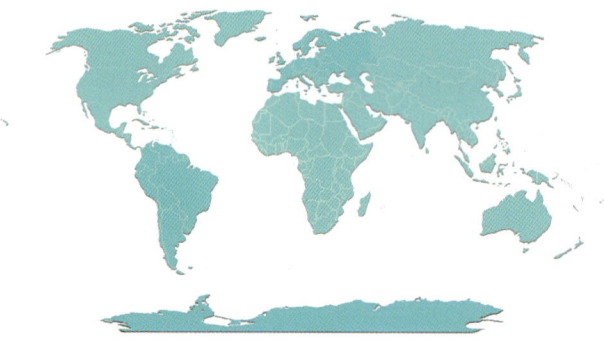

فصل‌ها　Seasons 🎧

تابِستان/تابِستون

بَهار

زِمِستان/زِمِستون

پاییز

آب و هَوا (Weather (Climate 🎧

Answer			Question	
Sunny	آفتابی			
Cloudy	اَبری			
Rainy	بارانی / بارونی	است / ه	هَوا	هَوا چطور است / ه؟
Snowy	بَرفی			
Mild	مُلایِم			
Cold	سَرد			
Warm/Hot	گَرم			

🎧 **Short Dialogues about Weather**

۲. هوای تابستان چطور است؟ هوای تابستان گرم است.

۱. در پاییز هوا چطور است؟ در پاییز هوا ملایم است.

۴. هوای شمال چطور است؟ اینجا هوا بارانی است.

۳. هوای آنجا چطور است؟ هوای اینجا سرد است.

۶. فردا هوا چطوراست؟ فردا هوا برفی است.

۵. هوای شیراز چطور است؟ هوای اینجا خوب و آفتابی است.

تمرین ۲۱

Interview your classmate about what kind of weather s/he likes and dislikes. Write down your findings in the form of a report.

تمرین ۲۲

Look at the following information. What is tomorrow's forecast for Kermanshah? What time are sunrise and sunset today? What are the words for Minimum and Maximum?

فردا	امروز
وضعیت: نیمه ابری	آخرین بروز رسانی: ۱۳۹۱/۱۱/۲۴
کمینه: ۱°-	وضعیت: تمام ابری
بیشینه: ۱۳°-	سرعت باد: کیلومتر در ساعت ۱۱.۲۷
	رطوبت: ۵۰٪
	طلوع آفتاب: ۷:۳۰ بامداد
	غروب آفتاب: ۶:۰۰ بعد از ظهر
	کمینه: ۲°- بیشینه: ۱۵°

وضعیت آب و هوای شهر کرمانشاه (۵:۲۹ بامداد)

تمرین ۲۳

Listen to the audio file and answer using complete sentences:

۱. جَزیره‌ی کیش در کجا قرار دارد؟

۲. آب و هوای جزیره‌ی کیش در زمستان چگونه است؟

۳. جزیره‌ی کیش به چه نامی مشهور است؟

۴. آیا در کشورِ شما جزیره‌ای مثلِ جزیره‌ی کیش هست؟

تمرین ۲۴

With a classmate, check your local forecast for today, tomorrow, and the day after tomorrow. Find the Minimum and Maximum temperatures for each day. Write down your findings in Persian.

تمرین ۲۵

Look at the following information. Which province has the lowest temperature? Which province has the highest temperature? What is the forecast like in Semnān? Which province is divided into three parts? What are they?

بیشینه / کمینه		پیش بینی وضع هوای شنبه	استان
۱۲	۲۲	نیمه ابری – در پاره‌ای نقاط رگبار و رعد و برق	خُراسانِ شمالی
۱۱	۲۶	قسمتی ابری تا نیمه ابری – گاهی افزایش ابر در پاره‌ای نقاط رگبار و رعد و برق یا بارش پراکنده	خُراسانِ مَرکَزی
۸	۲۴	کمی ابری – در پاره‌ای نقاط نیمه ابری و بارش پراکنده	خراسانِ جنوبی
۱۷	۳۲	کمی ابری – گاهی وزش باد	خوزستان
٤	۲۱	کمی ابری تا نیمه ابری همراه با بارش پراکنده	زَنجان
۱۵	۲۱	قسمتی ابری تا نیمه ابری – گاهی افزایش ابر در پاره‌ای نقاط رگبار و رعد و برق	سِمنان
۱۲	۳۰	کمی ابری – در پاره‌ای نقاط نیمه ابری – در بعضی ساعات رگبار و رعد و برق و وزش باد	سیستان و بَلوچِستان
۹	۲۳	قسمتی ابری – در شهرهای شمالی نیمه ابری در بعضی ساعات رگبار و رعد و برق و وزش باد – اوایل شب قسمتی ابری	فارس
۸	۲۴	قسمتی ابری تا نیمه ابری – گاهی افزایش ابر در پاره‌ای نقاط رگبار و رعد و برق یا بارش باران پراکنده	قَزوین

تمرین ۲۶

With a classmate, answer the following questions using the written form. Search online to find the answers.

۱. مرکزِ استانِ گیلان چه نام دارد؟

۲. تهران در کجای ایران قرار دارد؟

۳. همسایگانِ غربیِ ایران چه کشورهایی هستند؟

۴. کشورِ ایران چند استان دارد؟

صِفَتِ بَرتَر COMPARATIVE ADJECTIVES

The comparative adjective is formed by adding the stressed suffix تَر to the adjective. The suffix may be written attached or separate from the adjective.

قشنگ ← قشنگتر	زیبا ← زیباتَر
خسته ← خستهتَر	بد ← بدتَر

Exceptions:

The following two adjectives have a regular and an irregular comparative form. The irregular form is used more often.

	Irregular Comparative	Regular Comparative	Adjective
Better	بِهتَر	خوبتَر	خوب Good ←
More	بیشتَر	زیادتَر	زیاد Much/A lot ←

In a sentence with a comparative adjective, the preposition اَز is used like the English "*than*". Examples:

I am older than my sister.	۱. من از خواهرم بزرگتر هستم.
Is Shiraz more beautiful than Tehran?	۲. شیراز از تهران قشنگتر است؟

The comparative adjective can precede the noun as in Examples 3 and 4:

۳. من بزرگتر از خواهرم هستم.

۴. شیراز قشنگتر از تهران است؟

The comparative adjective is treated as a normal adjective, i.e. it follows the noun (as in 5). The comparative adjective can also follow a noun with Ezāfe and the non-specific suffix /i/ (as in 6), or a possesive pronoun (as in 7).

Ezāfe	I bought the more expensive book.	۵. من کتابِ گرانتر را خریدم.
Non-specific suffix	I bought a more expensive book.	۶. من کتابِ گرانتری خریدم.
Possesive pronoun	My younger sister is sick.	۷. خواهرِ کوچکتَرم مریض است.

تمرین ۲۷

Put the following words in the right order:

۱. دخترخاله‌ی من ــ است ــ باهوش‌تر ــ از ــ من

۲. قارّه‌ی آمریکا - از ــ قارّه‌ی اروپا ــ است ــ شلوغ‌تر

۳. دیروز ــ حالم ــ بد ــ بود ــولی امروز ــ خیلی ــ شدم ــ بهتر

۴. وقتی ــ آنها ــ در آفریقا ــ زندگی می‌کردند ــ بودند ــ خیلی راحت‌تر

۵. است ــ زندگی در آسیا ــ از ــ زندگی در اروپا ــ ارزان‌تر

۶. بزرگ‌تر ــ است ــ تهران ــ رامسر ــ از

۷. زیادتر ــ جمعیّتِ تهران ــ از ــ جمعیّتِ همدان ــاست

تمرین ۲۸

Form comparative sentences by adding the words in parentheses to the sentence. Example:

جنوبِ ایران گرم است. (از شمالِ ایران) ← جنوبِ ایران از شمالِ ایران گرم‌تر است.

۱. هوای اینجا بارانی است. (از هوای آنجا)

۲. جمعیّتِ آمریکا زیاد است. (از جمعیتِ قطبِ جنوب)

۳. شمالِ کشور برفی است. (از جنوبِ کشور)

۴. عموی من جوان نیست. (از پدرم)

۵ مسافرت با هواپیما خوب است. (از مسافرت با ماشین)

۶. من خاله‌ام را کم دوست دارم. (از عمّه‌ام)

تمرین ۲۹

a) Change into written form:

۱. تابستون چی کار کردی؟

۲. آره، تمومِ شهر رو دیدم!

b) Change into spoken form:

۱. آن وقت‌ها همه نزدیکِ هم زندگی می‌کردیم.

۲. هُما تَبریز را خیلی دوست دارد.

دستور زبان ۴

صفتِ بَرتَرین SUPERLATIVE ADJECTIVE

The superlative adjective is formed by adding the stressed suffix تَرین to the adjective. The suffix may be written attached or separate from the adjective. Examples:

قشنگ ← قشنگتَرین	زیبا ← زیباتَرین
بد ← بدتَرین	خسته ← خستهتَرین

Exceptions:

The following two adjectives have a regular and an irregular superlative form. The irregular form is more common.

	Irregular Superlative	Regular Superlative	Adjective
Best	بهتَرین	خوبتَرین	خوب Good ←
Most	بیشتَرین	زیادتَرین	زیاد Much/A lot ←

The word order for the superlative adjectives is the same as in English, i.e. the superlative adjective precedes the noun and does not require Ezāfe:

Esfehan is the most beautiful city in Iran.	اصفهان زیباترین شهرِ ایران است.
This is the easiest lesson.	این آسانترین درس است.

The English phrase "*most of*" is usually translated as بیشترِ. Example:

I work most of the time. من بیشترِ وَقتها کار میکنم.

Another Variant of the Superlative:

SUPERLATIVE ← از همه + COMPARATIVE

Example:

مینا از همه زیباتر است.

مینا زیباتر از همه است.

Mina is more beautiful than all/Mina is the most beautiful.

تمرین ۳۰

Follow the order in the above examples and translate the sentences on the next page into Persian:

1. Tehran is the largest city in Iran.

2. In my opinion, winter is the worst season.

3. She is my youngest paternal aunt.

4. Europe is not the biggest continent.

5. When I was a child, I had the best teacher.

6. I do not want to have the most expensive computer.

تمرین ۳۱

Circle the appropriate adjective:

۱. دریای خزر ــــــــــــــ دریاچه است. (بزرگ‌تر ــ بزرگ‌ترین)

۲. من ــــــــــــــ بچّه‌ی خانواده نیستم. (کوچک‌تر ــ کوچک‌ترین)

۳. زندگی در تهران از زندگی در مشهد ــــــــــــــ است. (گران‌تر ــ گران‌ترین)

۴. جمعه ــــــــــــــ روزِ هفته است. (آخر ــ آخرین)

۵. فصلِ زمستان از فصل پاییز ــــــــــــــ است. (سردتر ــ سردترین)

۶. خانمِ شریفی ــــــــــــــ استادِ ما هستند. (جوان‌تر ــ جوان‌ترین)

۷. ــــــــــــــ شهرِ ایران کدام شهر است؟ (بارانی‌تر ــ بارانی‌ترین)

تمرین ۳۲

Change to a superlative adjective. Work in pairs, groups, or as a class. Example:

Student 1 (*book open*): من در خانه‌ی بزرگی زندگی می‌کردم.

Student 2: (*book closed*): من در بزرگ‌ترین خانه زندگی می‌کردم.

Group 2	Group 1
۱. ما در کشورِ سردی زندگی می‌کنیم.	۱. این درس سخت است.
۲. شهر ما از شهر شما جنوبی‌تر است.	۲. شیراز آب و هوای خوبی دارد.
۳. فرشِ ابریشم گران‌تر است.	۳. من نمره‌ی بدی گرفتم.
۴. مینا دوستِ خوبِ من است.	۴. این شهر از آن شهر شلوغ‌تر است.
۵. تو از خواهرت بزرگ‌تر هستی؟	۵. به نظرِ تو ایران کشورِ خوبی است؟

درس ششم

بیشتر بدانیم

 Extended Family فامیل

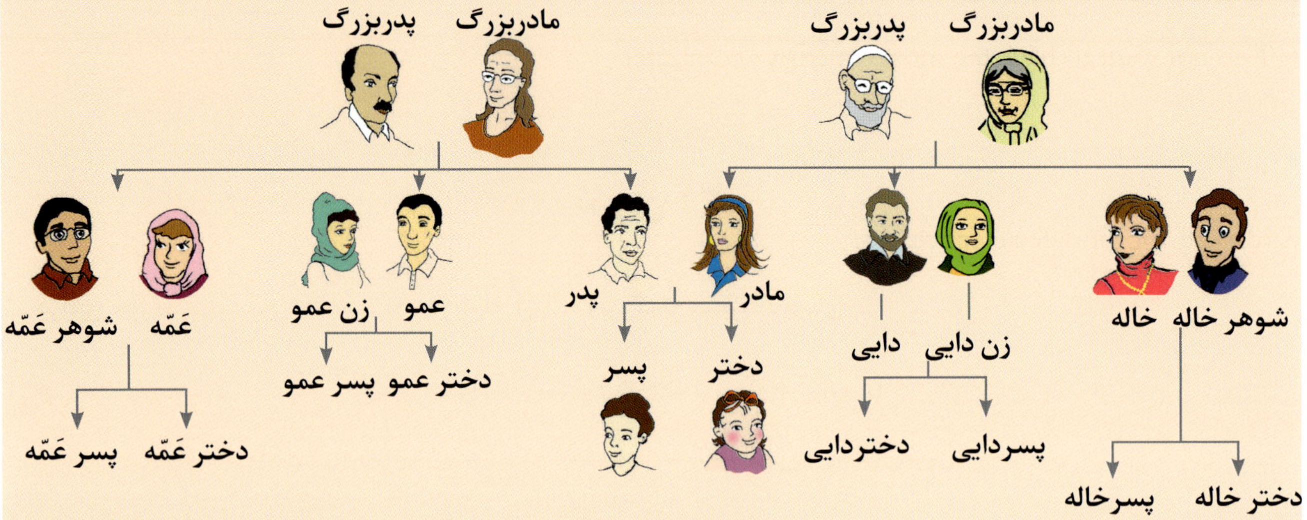

پدربزرگ مادربزرگ   پدربزرگ مادربزرگ

شوهر عَمّه   عَمّه   عمو زن عمو   پدر مادر   دایی زن دایی   شوهر خاله خاله

دختر عَمّه پسر عَمّه   دختر عمو پسر عمو   پسر دختر   دختردایی پسردایی   دختر خاله پسرخاله

Other Family Members

Daughter in law/Bride	عَروس	Brother's child	برادرزاده
Wife's mother	مادرزَن	Husband's father	پدرشوهَر
Husband's mother	مادرشوهَر	Sister's child	خواهرزاده
Grandchild	نَوه	Son in law/Groom	داماد

 تمرین ۳۳

Prepare seven questions about your classmate's family to ask her/him. Write your findings in the form of a report (at home). Examples:

۱. تو چند تا دختر خاله داری؟

۲. نام بزرگ‌ترین عموی تو چیست؟

۳. تو به فامیلِ پدرت نزدیکتری یا به فامیلِ مادرت؟

۴. چند وقت یکبار پدربزرگ و مادر بزرگت را می‌بینی؟

220

تمرین ۳۴

Read the following paragraph from دایی جان ناپلئون, a popular novel by Iraj Pezeshkzad. Find three words that show family relationships. Underline the verbs in the simple past and past continuous forms. Underline the familiar words. Can you tell what this paragraph is about?

دایی جان ناپلئون

من یک روزِ گرمِ تابستان، دقیقاً یک سیزدهِ مُرداد، حدودِ ساعتِ سه و ربع کم بعداز ظهر عاشق شدم. من که پسرِ آقا جان بودم، عاشقِ لیلی دخترِ دایی جان ناپلئون شدم... لیلی دخترِ دایی جان و برادرِ کوچکش نیم ساعتی بود در باغ انتظارِ ما را می‌کشیدند. بینِ خانه‌های ما که در یک باغِ بزرگ ساخته شده بود، دیواری وجود نداشت. مثلِ هر روز زیرِ سایه‌ی درختِ گردوی بزرگ، بدونِ سر و صدا، مشغول بازی و صحبت شدیم. یکوقت نگاهِ من به نگاهِ لیلی افتاد. یک جفت چشمِ سیاهِ درشت به من نگاه می‌کرد...

ایرَج پِزشکزاد

تمرین ۳۵: واژگان

In each line, circle the word that does not match the rest:

شرق	جنوب	قطب	۱. شمال
دریاچه	کوه	خلیج	۲. دریا
بهار	پاییز	تابستان	۳. بارانی
مادرشوهر	پسرخاله	عمو	۴. داماد
بارانی	برفی	آبی	۵. ابری
جنوب غربی	تعطیل	مسافرت	۶. سفر
همسایگان	اروپا	استرالیا	۷. آفریقا
خوش گذشت	پس پریروز	دورهم جمع می‌شدیم	۸. یادش به خیر

REVIEW CORNER	
Points that remain unclear about Lesson 6:	
How I plan to work on these points:	

شعر

Read the following poem by Hamid Mosaddegh and try to find the familiar words. Underline the verbs in the simple past tense and past continuous tense. You will not be evaluated on the content but you can use it for cultural enrichment.

در آمد

تو به من خندیدی

و نمی‌دانستی

من به چه دلهره از باغچه‌ی همسایه

سیب را دزدیدم

باغبان از پیِ من تند دوید

سیب را دستِ تو دید

غضب آلود به من کرد نگاه

سیب دندان زده از دست تو افتاد به خاک

و تو رفتی و هنوز

سال‌هاست که در گوش من آرام آرام

خش خش گامِ تو تکرار کنان

می‌دهد آزارم

و من اندیشه کنان غرق این پندارم

که چرا باغچه‌ی کوچك ما سیب نداشت

شاعر: حمید مُصَدّق (۱۹۴۰-۱۹۹۸)

222

ترانه

Listen to the following song by Googoosh on YouTube and try to find the familiar words. Underline the verbs in the simple past tense and past continuous tense. You will not be evaluated on the content but you can use it for cultural enrichment.

دو ماهی

کوکوش

ما دو تا ماهی بودیم

توی دریای کبود

خالی از اشکای شور

از غم بود و نبود

پولکامون رنگارنگ

روزامون خوب و قشنگ

آسمونمون یکی

خونمون یه قلوه سنگ

خنده‌مون موجارو تا ابرا می‌برد

وقتی دلگیر بودم اون غصه می‌خورد

تورای ماهیگیرا وا نمی شد

عاشقی تو دریا تنها نمی شد

خوابمون مثل صدف

پر مروارید نور

پر شد این قصّه‌ی ما

توی دریاهای دور

همیشه توک می‌زدیم

به حبابای درشت

تا که مرغ ماهی خوار

اومدو جفتمو کشت

دلش آتیش بگیره

دل اون خونه خراب

دیگه نوبت منه

سایه‌ش افتاده رو آب ....

خواننده: گوگوش

223

نکته‌ی فرهنگی

Iran's Ancient Sites:

Iran has one of the world's oldest major civilizations which dates back to 4000 BC. The ruins of many ancient sites still stand around the country. Below are a few examples:

Chogha Zanbil (چُغازَنبیل) is an ancient Elamite complex in the province of Khuzestan (خوزستان). It is considered the best preserved ziggurat in the world. Chogha Zanbil lies 42 km southwest of Dezful (دزفول), 30 km west of Susa (شوش), and 80 km north of Ahvaz (اَهواز). It was built around 1250 BC by King Untash-Napirisha, to honor the great god Inshushinak. Chogha Zanbil is the first Iranian site to be inscribed on the UNESCO World Heritage List.

Persepolis (پرسپولیس) or (تختِ جَمشید) was the ceremonial capital and one of the four capitals of the Achaemenid Empire (امپراطوری هَخامَنِشی). Persepolis is located in the province of Fars (فارس) and lies 70 km northeast of Shiraz (شیراز). The construction of Persepolis was ordered by Cyrus the Great (کوروشِ بزرگ) around 515 BC and it was completed by subsequent kings. The majestic halls, Gate of Nations, monumental stairways, throne rooms (Apadana), reception rooms, and annex buildings were immaculately designed to celebrate especial events and festivals especially the Nowruz (نوروز) about which we will learn more in Lesson 8. Persepolis, the magnificent symbol of the Achaemenid Empire, was looted and burnt by Alexander the Great's troops in 330 BC. UNESCO declared Persepolis a World Heritage Site in 1979.

Bisotun (بیسُتون) is an archeological site located in the province of Kermanshah (کرمانشاه), near the city of Kermanshah (کرمانشاه) in western Iran. Bisotun features remains from prehistoric times to the Median, Achaemenid, Sassanian, and Ilkhanid periods. The main monument is the bas-relief and cuneiform inscription ordered by Darius the Great (داریوشِ بزرگ) around 521 BC. The inscription portrays Darius holding a bow, as a sign of sovereignty, and treading on the chest of a figure who lies on his back before him. Faravahar (فَروَهَر) floats above, giving blessings to the king. Below and around the bas-reliefs, there are approximately 1,200 lines of inscriptions telling the story of Darius's battles in three languages.

ضرب المثل

کوه به کوه نمی رسه. آدم به آدم می رسه!

Literal translation: *Mountains cannot reach one another, but people can!*
(It's a small world!)

This proverb means that a mountain with all its greatness cannot reach another mountain, but people can! So be mindful of your actions to others.

Thematic Review of New Vocabulary

Geography	
Province	اُستان
Capital city	پایتَخت
Caspian	خَزَر
Gulf	خَلیج
Sea	دَریا
Lake	دَریاچه
Mountain range	رِشته کوه
River	رود
Continent	قارّه
Peak	قُلّه
Country	کِشور
Desert	کَویر
Provincial capital	مَرکزِ اُستان
Map	نَقشه
Neighbor(s)	هَمسایه ـ هَمسایگان

Nouns & Adjectives	
Tomb	آرامگاه
Man (slang)	بابا
Previous	پیش
Off/Not working	تَعطیل
Lonely	تَنها
Famous Persian poet	حافِظ
Famous Persian poet	سَعدی
Travel/Trip	سَفَر
Month/Moon	ماه
Travel/Trip	مُسافِرَت

Weather	
Weather/Climate	آب و هوا
Cloudy	اَبری
Sunny	آفتابی
Rainy	بارانی
Snowy	بَرفی
Cold	سَرد
Warm/Hot	گَرم
Mild	مُلایم
Air/Weather forecast	هَوا

Comparative & Superlative Adjectives	
Worse	بَدتر
The worst	بَدترین
More	بیشتَر
The most	بیشتَرین
The oldest	پیرترین
More tired	خَسته‌تر
More beautiful	زیباتَر
The most beautiful	زیباترین
More beautiful	قَشَنگ‌تر
The most beautiful	قَشَنگ‌ترین

About Continents	
Europe	اُروپا
Australia	اُسترالیا
Asia	آسیا
Africa	آفریقا
America	آمریکا
Antarctica	قُطبِ جُنوب

Seasons	
Spring	بَهار
Fall/Autumn	پاییز
Summer	تابِستان
Winter	زِمِستان
Season	فَصل

Prepositions	
Next/Afterwards/Then	بَعد
Or	یا

Words & Expressions	
Those times/days	آن وَقت‌ها
Suffix to count how many times	بار
In my opinion	به نظرِ من
Entire/All	تَمام
You were missed	جایَت خالی
What's up?	چه خبر؟
What did you do?	چه کار کردی؟
Had a good time	خوش گُذَشت
I fell in love with …	عاشِقِ …. شُدَم
Near each other	نَزدیکِ هَم
Really	واقعاً
When (in declarative sentence)	وَقتی
Each one/Anyone	هَرکَسی
Also	هَم
All	هَمه
Good old days	یادَش به خیر

Adverbs of Time	
Today	اِمروز
Tonight	اِمشَب
The day before yesterday	پَریروز
The night before last	پَریشَب
Two days before yesterday	پَس پَریروز
Two nights before last	پَس پَریشَب
The day after tomorrow	پَس فَردا
The night after tomorrow night	پَس فَردا شَب
Now	حالا
Yesterday	دیروز
Last night	دیشَب
Tomorrow	فَردا
Tomorrow night	فَردا شَب
Previously	قَبلاً
Past/Previous	گُذَشته

227

Directions	
South	جُنوب
South East	جنوبِ شرقی
South West	جنوبِ غربی
East	شَرق
North	شُمال
North East	شمالِ شرقی
North West	شمالِ غربی
West	غَرب

Verbs & Phrases	
I was	بودم (بودن: هست)
They were	بودند (بودن: هست)
You were	بودی (بودن: هست)
We used to get together	دورِهم جَمع می‌شُدیم (شُدَن: شو)
You liked	دوست داشتی (داشتن: دار)
I saw	دیدَم (دیدَن: بین)
You saw	دیدی (دیدَن: بین)
They went	رفتند (رَفتن: رَو)
S/he used to live	زندگی می‌کرد (کردن: کُن)
I used to think	فکر می‌کردم (کردن: کُن)
Is located	قرار دارد (داشتن: دار)
You stayed	ماندی (ماندن: مان)
We used to laugh	می‌خَندیدیم (خَندیدن: خَند)
We used to see	می‌دیدیم (دیدَن: بین)
We used to talk/say	می‌گُفتیم (گُفتن: گو)
Name! (Plural)	نام بِبَرید (بُردن: بَر)
They did not go	نَرَفتند (رَفتن: رَو)

Extended Family	
Grandpa	بابا بزرگ
Brother's child	برادرزاده
Grandfather	پدربزرگ
Grandparents	پدربزرگ و مادربزرگ
Husband's father	پدرشوهَر
Maternal aunt's son	پسر خاله
Paternal aunt's son	پسر عَمّه
Maternal uncle's son	پسردایی
Paternal uncle's son	پسرعَمو
Maternal aunt	خاله
Sister's child	خواهرزاده
Son in law/Groom	داماد
Maternal uncle	دایی
Daughter of maternal aunt	دختر خاله
Daughter of paternal aunt	دختر عَمّه
Daughter of maternal uncle	دختردایی
Daughter of paternal uncle	دخترعَمو
Daughter in law/Bride	عَروس
Paternal aunt	عَمّه
Paternal uncle	عَمو
Extended family	فامیل
Grandmother	مادربزرگ
Wife's mother	مادرزَن
Husband's mother	مادرشوهَر
Grandma	مامان بزرگ
Grandchild	نَوه

درس هفتم

غذا و مراسم ویژه

Food & Special Occasions

Communication Objectives

Talking about Different Kinds of Persian Food
Talking about Serving Food
Interacting at a Restaurant: Ordering Food, Asking for the Bill, etc.
Talking about Special Occasions: Birthday, Wedding, Funeral, etc.
Planning for Parties and Responding to Invitations
Expressing Congratulations and Condolences
Expressing Sensations and Feelings

Contents

Interactive Dialogue 1: I am Hungry and Thirsty, Mom!
Interactive Dialogue 2: Welcome to Persepolis Restaurant!
In-class Reading: Ladan's Birthday
Grammar 1: Psychological Verbs
Let's Learn More: Fruits & Vegetables
Dairy & Meat
Pastry & Bread
Tastes & Food Portions
A Restaurant Menu
Grammar 2: Uses of هَم
Recipe for Kuku Sabzi
Let's Learn More: Classic Birthday Song
Special Occasions
Grammar 3: Reflexive Pronouns
Reading from a Short Story: قصّه‌ی آه by Samad Behrangi
Review Corner
Poem: پَریا by Ahmad Shamloo
Song: دست‌های تو (Singer: Dariyush)
Cultural Note: Persian Cuisine - Food Temperament
Proverb
Thematic Review of New Vocabulary

🎧 واژگان ۱

Salad	سالاد	Sister/Sis (Slang)	آبجی
Fresh greens	سَبزی خوردَن	Hooray!/Yay!	آخ جان/آخ جون!
Tablecloth (for eating on the floor)	سُفره	You brought	آوردی/آؤردی (آؤر)
My dear	عَزیزَم	Plate	بُشقاب
Spoon	قاشُق	Cooked rice	پُلو
A Persian stew	قورمه سَبزی	Spread!	پَهن کُن (کُن)
I am hungry	گُرسنه‌ام است/گُرسنَمه	I am thirsty	تِشنه‌ام است/تِشنَمه
Cup/Glass	لیوان	Fork	چَنگال
I bring	می‌آوَرَم/می‌آرَم	Yourself	خودَت/خودِت
You forgot	یادَت رَفت/یادِت رَفت	Stew	خورِش/خورِشت
I remember	یادَم است/یادَمه	I like	خوشَم می‌آید/خوشَم می‌آد
Bravo!/Good job!	آفَرین	Brother/Bro (Slang)	داداش
Call!	صِدا کُن! (کُن)	By the way	راستی

Close your book and listen to the dialogue. Then fill in the blanks using the new words.

🎧 گفتگو ۱

ساسان: مامان جون! من هم گُرسنَمه هم تشنَمه. غذا کِی حاضِر میشه؟

مامان: غذا حاضِره عزیزَم. داداشِت و آبجیتو صدا کُن. خودَم برو سُفره رو پهن کُن.

ساسان: بچّه‌ها! بچّه‌ها! بیاین شام حاضِره! ——— مامان شام چی داریم؟

مامان: خورِشتِ قورمه سبزی با پُلو.

ساسان: آخ جون! من خیلی از ——— ——— ——— خوشَم می‌آد!

مامان: بشقابا و قاشق ـ چنگالا رو آؤردی؟

ساسان: آره، مامان جون. لیوانا کجاست؟

مامان: یادِت رَفت لیوانا کجاست؟

ساسان: نه، نه، یادَمه! سالاد و سبزی خوردنم می‌آرم.

مامان: ——— پسرم، دست دَرد نکنه!

نوشتاری

گفتگو ۱

ساسان: مامان جان! من هم گُرسنه‌اَم است هم _____ . غذا کی حاضر می‌شود؟

مامان: غذا حاضر است عزیزم. برادرت و خواهرَت را صدا کن. خودَت هم برو سفره را پهن کن.

ساسان: بچّه‌ها! بچّه‌ها! بیایید شام حاضر است! راستی مامان شام چه داریم؟

مامان: خورشِ قورمه‌سبزی با پلو.

ساسان: آخ جان! من خیلی از قورمه سبزی خوشم می‌آید!

مامان: بشقاب‌ها و قاشق ـ چنگال‌ها را _____ ؟

ساسان: بله. مامان جان. لیوان‌ها کجاست؟

مامان: یادَت رفت لیوان‌ها کجاست؟

ساسان: نه نه _____ ! سالاد و سبزی خوردن را هم می‌آورم.

مامان: آفرین پسرم، دستَت درد نکند!

تمرین ۱

Role-play the above dialogue. Take turns and switch roles.

واژگان ۲

I got/became full	سیر شُدَم (شَو)	Lima bean, rice & meat dish	باقالی پُلو با گوشت
It is a good idea	فکرِ خوبی است / فکرِ خوبیه	I do not dislike	بَدَم نمی‌آیَد / بَدَم نمی‌آد
Formal form of "tā" used for inanimates	عَدَد	Pepsi	پِپسی
Fillet mignon Kabab	کباب بَرگ	Onion	پیاز
Ground beef Kabab	کباب کوبیده	Tea would be nice!	چای می‌چَسبَد / چایی می‌چَسبه!
Bill/Invoice	صورَت‌حِساب	Soltani rice & Kabab	چلوکبابِ سُلطانی
Server	گارسُن	Chelo Kabab restaurant	چلوکبابی
Me too	من هم هَمین‌طور / منم هَمین‌طور	I am sleepy	خوابَم می‌آیَد / خوابَم می‌آد
Yoghurt & minced cucumber side dish	ماست و خیار / ماست خیار	I do not like	خوشَم نِمی‌آیَد / خوشَم نمی‌آد

We should/may order	سِفارش بِدَهیم/ سِفارِش بِدیم (دَه)	Beverage	نوشیدَنی
You want (Polite verb)	مِیل دارید/ مِیل دارین (دار)	Hello to you	درود بَر شما
Good appetite!/ Eat heartily!	نوشِ جان!	Yoghurt drink	دوغ
		I am cold	سَردَم است/ سَردَمه

Close your book and listen to the dialogue. Then fill in the blanks using the new words.

در چلوکبابِ پرسپولیس

گارسُن: درود بَر شما! به رستورانِ پرسپولیس خوش اومدین. نوشیدنی چی میل دارین؟

کاوه: پریسا جون تو چی می‌خوری؟

پریسا: من یه لیوان دوغ می‌خوام، تو چی؟

کاوه: من از دوغ خوشم نمی‌آد. پپسی می‌خورم.

پریسا: تو چی می‌خوری عزیزم؟

کاوه: نمی‌دونم. بدم نمی‌آد یه باقالی پلو با گوشت بخورم.

پریسا: باشه، منم یه چلوکباب سلطانی می‌گیرم، با هم می‌خوریم.

کاوه: ــــــــــــــ یه کباب برگ داره یه کباب کوبیده؟

پریسا: آره، خوبه یه ماست و خیارَم سفارش بدیم.

کاوه: جناب، من یه باقالی پلو با گوشت و یه پپسی می‌خوام با کمی پیاز.

پریسا: برای منم یه چلوکباب سلطانی بیارین با دوغ و یه ــــــــــــــ.

(گارسُن غذا را می‌آورد)

گارسُن: بفرمایین، ــــــــــــــ !

کاوه: به به! دستتون درد نکنه!

گارسُن: خواهش می‌کنم.

(بعد از غذا)

کاوه: من سیر شدم. خیلی خوشمزه بود!

پریسا: منم همین‌طور. حالا هم سردمه و هم خوابم می‌آد!

کاوه: الان یه چایی می‌چسبه!

پریسا: فکرِ خوبیه!

کاوه: آقا لطفاً دو تا چایی بیارین و صورتحساب.

نوشتاری

گفتگو ۲

گارسُن: درود بر شما! به رستورانِ پرسپولیس خوش آمدید. نوشیدنیٔ چه ـــــــــــــــ ؟

کاوه: پریسا جان تو چه می خوری؟

پریسا: من یک لیوان دوغ می خواهم، تو چه می خواهی؟

کاوه: من از دوغ خوشم نمی‌آید. پپسی می خورم.

پریسا: تو چه می خوری عزیزم؟

کاوه: نمی‌دانم. بدم نمی آید یک ـــــــــــ ـــــــــــ ـــــــــــ بخورم.

پریسا: باشد، من هم یک چلوکبابِ سلطانی می گیرم، با هم می خوریم.

کاوه: چلوکبابِ سلطانی یک کبابِ برگ و یک کبابِ کوبیده دارد؟

پریسا: بله، خوب است یک ماست و خیار هم سفارش بدهیم.

کاوه: جناب، من یک باقالی پلو با گوشت و یک پپسی با کمی ـــــــــــ ـــــــــــ می‌خواهم.

پریسا: برای من هم یک چلوکبابِ سلطانی با دوغ و یک ماست و خیار بیاورید.

(گارسُن غذا را می آورد)

گارسُن: بفرمایید، نوشِ جان!

کاوه: به به! دستتان درد نکند!

گارسُن: خواهش می کنم.

(بعد از غذا)

کاوه: من سیر شدم. خیلی خوشمزه بود!

پریسا: من ـــــــــــ همین‌طور. حالا هم سردم ـــــــــــ و هم خوابم می آید!

کاوه: الان یک چای می چسبد!

پریسا: فکرِ خوبی است!

کاوه: آقا لطفاً دو عدد چای و صورتحساب را بیاورید.

تمرین ۲

Role-play the above dialogue. Take turns and switch roles.

تمرین ۳

Find six words that are different in written and spoken forms and write them below. Pronounce the words as you write.

Spoken	← Written	Spoken	← Written

خواندن

تَوَلُّدِ لادَن

هفته‌ی دیگر تولّدِ لادَن است. او هفته‌ی آینده بیست و شش ساله می‌شود. هم‌کلاسی‌های لادن می‌خواهند برای او جشنِ تولّد بگیرند. بچّه‌ها می‌خواهند بعد از کلاس به رستورانِ ایرانیِ نزدیکِ دانشگاه بروند و تولّدِ لادن را در آنجا جشن بگیرند. لادن خیلی از پاریس خوشش می‌آید و فکر می‌کند پاریس قشنگ‌ترین شهرِ دنیاست. آرَش دوست پسرِ لادن می‌خواهد برای تولّدِ لادن او را به پاریس ببرد. این بهترین هدیه‌ی تولّد برای لادن است. آرش خودش هم عاشقِ پاریس است چون وقتی بچّه بود با خانواده‌اش در نزدیکِ پاریس زندگی می‌کردند. آرش جنوبِ فرانسه را هم خیلی دوست دارد چون فکر می‌کند آب و هوایش از پاریس بهتر است.

Future	آینده
Birthday	تَوَلُّد
Celebration	جَشن
They should/may celeberate	جَشن بگیرند (گیر)
World	دُنیا
Boyfriend	دوست پِسر
Next - Other	دیگر / دیگه
Classmate	هَم‌کلاسی

تمرین ۴

a) Listen to the audio file and follow along in your text. Repeat each sentence several times.

b) Answer in complete sentences. Use the written form.

۱. لادنِ هفته‌ی آینده چند ساله می شود؟

۲. هم‌کلاسی‌های لادن می‌خواهند چه کار کنند؟

۳. آرش کیست؟

۴. هدیه‌ی آرش برای تولّدِ لادن چیست؟

۵. لادن فکر می‌کند چه شهری قشنگ‌ترین شهرِ دنیاست؟

۶. وقتی آرش بچّه بود با خانواده‌اش در کجا زندگی می‌کردند؟

۷. چرا آرش جنوبِ فرانسه را خیلی دوست دارد؟

Synonyms		
پُلو = چُلو	برادر = داداش	خواهر = آبجی
غذا = خوراک	هِدیه = کادو	گُرسنه = گُشنه

Antonyms	
خوشمَزه ≠ بدمَزه	دوست پسر ≠ دوست دختر
خوشَم می‌آید ≠ بَدَم می‌آید	گرسنه -گُشنه ≠ سیر

تمرین ۵ واژگان

Fill in the blanks using the appropriate vocabulary from the list below.

هدیه‌ی ــ عزیزم ــ سیر ــ سفره ــ صورتحساب ــ خوشم می‌آید ــ چلوکباب ــ چنگال ــ جشنِ تولّد

۱. هم‌کلاسی‌های لادن می‌خواهند برای او ــــــــــ ــــــــــ ــــــــــ بگیرند.

۲. آرش بهترین ــــــــــ تولّد را برای لادن خرید.

۳. من خیلی از قورمه سبزی با پلو ــــــــــ.

۴. تو چی می‌خوری ــــــــــ؟ (Spoken)

۵. ناهار حاضر است. لطفاً ــــــــــ را پهن کنید!

۶. برای من یک ــــــــــ بیاورید با دوغ و یک ماست و خیار.

۷. بشقاب‌ها و قاشق ــــــــــ ها را آوردی؟

۸. آقا لطفاً دو تا چایی بیارین و ــــــــــ

Dating is not part of traditional Iranian culture. Usually boys and girls date secretly. Recently, some modern families have allowed dating for their children.

 دستور زبان ۱

PSYCHOLOGICAL VERBS فعل‌های اِحساسی

We have already learned that verbs agree with the subject in Persian. Hence, the verb has an ending that matches the subject in person and number. The new category of verbs, which we call "Psychological verbs" are rather exceptional because the verb does not agree with the subject. No matter what the subject is, the verb ending of these verbs is always third person singular.

These verbs always express a psychological or physiological experience (ex. being cold, feeling sleepy, etc.). In these verbs there is always a noun or adjective that expresses the experience (sleep, cold). This noun or adjective is always followed by a **suffix pronoun** that matches the subject. The verb itself is **always** in the third person singular form. So the structure is as below:

[3sg+Verb] + [Suffix prounoun + Noun/Adjective] + Subject

Here are some examples:

Simple Past Tense (To like)

ما خوشمان آمد We liked	من خوشم آمد I liked
شما خوشتان آمد You (pl.) liked	تو خوشت آمد You liked
آنها خوششان آمد They liked	او خوشش آمد S/he liked

Present Tense (To like)

ما خوشمان می‌آید We like	من خوشم می‌آید I like
شما خوشتان می‌آید You (pl.) like	تو خوشت می‌آید You like
آنها خوششان می‌آید They like	او خوشش می‌آید S/he likes

Simple Past Tense (To feel cold)

ما سردمان بود We were cold	من سردم بود I was cold
شما سردتان بود You (pl.) were cold	تو سردت بود You were cold
آنها سردشان بود They were cold	او سردش بود S/he was cold

Present Tense (To feel cold)

ما سردمان است We are cold	من سردم است I am cold
شما سردتان است You (pl.) are cold	تو سردت است You are cold
آنها سردشان است They are cold	او سردش است S/he is cold

Past Tense (To get sleepy)

ما خوابمان گرفت I got sleepy	من خوابم گرفت I got sleepy
شما خوابتان گرفت You (pl.) got sleepy	تو خوابت گرفت You got sleepy
آنها خوابشان گرفت They got sleepy	او خوابش گرفت S/he got sleepy

Present Tense (To get sleepy)

ما خوابمان می‌گیرد We get sleepy	من خوابم می‌گیرد I get sleepy
شما خوابتان می‌گیرد You (pl.) get sleepy	تو خوابت می‌گیرد You get sleepy
آنها خوابشان می‌گیرد They get sleepy	او خوابش می‌گیرد S/he gets sleepy

Stress falls on the first syllable of the non-verbal component. Example: (khósh-am miāyad).

Only a small number of verbs function as the verbal component of psychological verbs. Examples:

(آمدن ← خوشم آمد) ــ (رفتن ← یادم رفت) ــ (بودن ← تشنه‌ام بود) ــ (گرفتن ← خوابم گرفت)

NEGATION

The negative prefix precedes the verbal component of psychological verbs. Examples:

Past Tense (To like)

ما خوشمان نَیامد	من خوشم نَیامد
We did not like	I did not like
شما خوشتان نَیامد	تو خوشت نَیامد
You (pl.) did not like	You did not like
آنها خوششان نَیامد	او خوشش نَیامد
They did not like	S/he did not like

Present Tense (To like)

ما خوشمان نِمی‌آید	من خوشم نِمی‌آید
We do not like	I do not like
شما خوشتان نِمی‌آید	تو خوشت نِمی‌آید
You (pl.) do not like	You do not like
آنها خوششان نِمی‌آید	او خوشش نِمی‌آید
They do not like	S/he does not like

Past Tense (To feel cold)

ما سردمان نَبود	من سردم نَبود
We were not cold	I was not cold
شما سردتان نَبود	تو سردت نَبود
You (pl.) were not cold	You were not cold
آنها سردشان نَبود	او سردش نَبود
They were not cold	S/he was not cold

Present Tense (To feel cold)

ما سردمان نیست	من سردم نیست
We are not cold	I am not cold
شما سردتان نیست	تو سردت نیست
You (pl.) are not cold	You are not cold
آنها سردشان نیست	او سردش نیست
They are not cold	S/he is not cold

Past Tense (To get sleepy)

ما خوابمان نَگرفت	من خوابم نَگرفت
We did not get sleepy	I did not get sleepy
شما خوابتان نَگرفت	تو خوابت نَگرفت
You (pl.) did not get sleepy	You did not get sleepy
آنها خوابشان نَگرفت	او خوابش نَگرفت
They did not get sleepy	S/he did not get sleepy

Present Tense (To get sleepy)

ما خوابمان نِمی‌گیرد	من خوابم نِمی‌گیرد
We do not get sleepy	I do not get sleepy
شما خوابتان نِمی‌گیرد	تو خوابت نِمی‌گیرد
You (pl.) get sleepy	You do not get sleepy
آنها خوابشان نِمی‌گیرد	او خوابش نِمی‌گیرد
They do not get sleepy	S/he does not get sleepy

The negative prefix takes primary stress. Example: (khosham némiāyad).

Question: While psychological verbs look like compound verbs, what makes them different from compound verbs? (*Hint*: Suffix pronoun, Verb agreement)

Some of the psychological verbs have a regular counterpart which is conjugated regularly. Examples:

	Regular Verb	Psychological Verb
I like.	من دوست دارم.	من خوشم می‌آید.
I forgot.	من فراموش کردم.	من یادم رفت.

Note: The direct object of some of the psychological verbs which normally takes را takes the preposition اَز instead. Examples:

I like winter.	۱. من از زمستان خوشم می‌آید.
I dislike winter.	۲. من از زمستان بدم می‌آید.

تمرین ۶

With a classmate, practice reading the conjugations of psychological verbs provided in the grammar section. Take turns and listen to each other's reading.

تمرین ۷

Find at least eight examples of psychological verbs in Dialogues 1 & 2 and write them below:

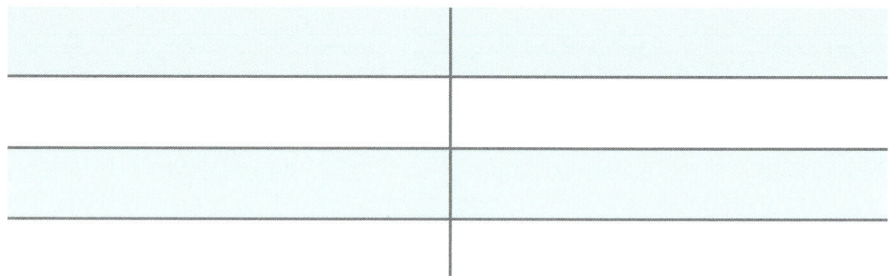

تمرین ۸

Conjugate the following psychological verbs in the given tenses:

۱. من از دانشگاه ـــــــــــــ (بد آمدن) (Present/Negative)

۲. سگِ کوچک من همیشه ـــــــــــــ (خواب آمدن) (Present)

۳. وقتی صبحِ زود از خواب بیدار شدم خیلی ـــــــــــــ (سرد بودن) (Past)

۴. علی از زندگی در تهران ـــــــــــــ (خوش آمدن) (Present/Negative)

۵. تو نباید اسم من از ـــــــــــــ (یادرفتن) (Subjunctive)

۶. شما هم خیلی ـــــــــــــ ؟ (گرسنه بودن) (Past)

۷. تو همیشه بعد از غذا ـــــــــــــ ؟ (خواب گرفتن) (Present)

۸. امیدوارم دوست پسرم بعد از غذا ـــــــــــــ . (خواب گرفتن)(Subjunctive/Negative)

تمرین ۹

Connect the related phrases to make a complete sentence:

عبارات مناسب را به هم وصل کنید:

خیلی خوب فارسی حرف می زنی!	۱. بچّه‌ها می‌خواهند
خوابش می‌آید.	۲. شما
آمد.	۳. داداشم
با هم زندگی می کنید؟	۴. دوست دخترم و خواهرش
خیلی گرسنه شونه.	۵. تو
یک ماست و خیار هم بگیرم.	۶. دیروز باران و برف زیادی
بعد از کلاس به رستوران بروند.	۷. بدم نمی‌آید

بیشتر بدانیم

 Fruits میوه‌ها

پُرتقال	سیب	موز	اَنار
گُلابی	 هِندِوانه / هِندونه	 گِردو	پِسته

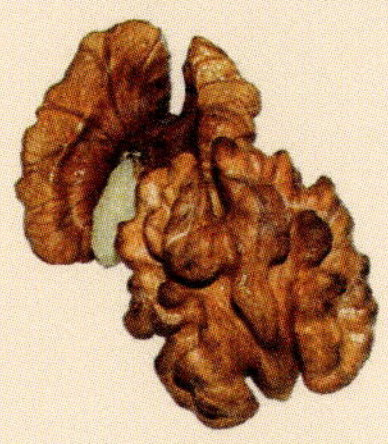

سَبزیجات Vegetables

گوجه فَرَنگی	خیار	هَویج	کاهو

سیر	بادِمجان / بادِمجون	تُربچه	سیب زَمینی

لَبنیّات Dairy

ماست	شیر	پَنیر	کَره

While cucumber is considered a vegetable in western culture, in Persian culture, it is considered a fruit.

240

نان/ نون Bread

| تافتون | بَربَری | لَواش | سَنگَک |

تمرین ۱۰

Find the differences between the above breads. You can search online or ask an Iranian friend.

گوشت Meat

Fish	ماهی	Lamb	گوشتِ بَرّه	Beef	گوشتِ گاو
Baby chicken	جوجه	Chicken	گوشتِ مُرغ	Mutton	گوشتِ گوسفند

مَزّهها Tastes

Salty	شور	Sweet	شیرین
Hot/Spicy	تُند	Sour	تُرش

شیرینی و دِسِر Pastry & Sweets

| بَستَنی | شیرینی | فالوده | حَلوا |

241

تمرین ۱۱

Using the above vocabulary, write a paragraph about what kinds of food you like and dislike. Use at least four psychological verbs. Use the written form. Examples:

من از ــــــــــــــــــ بدم می‌آید.

من از ــــــــــــــــــ خوشم می‌آید.

تمرین ۱۲

Listen to the audio file and fill in the missing information:

۱. ــــــــ ــــــــ از فالوده ــــــــ ست.

۲. نمی دونم چرا از ــــــــ تو غذا بدم می آد.

۳. رستورانِ «نَوید» ــــــــ بهترین ــــــــ تهران را دارد.

۴. لطفاً یه کیلو ــــــــ با نیم کیلو ــــــــ بدین.

۵. ناهار رو نباید ــــــــ بخوری چون ــــــــ می‌شی ــــــــ می‌گیره.

۶. ــــــــ و ــــــــ برای سلامتی بدن لازمند؟

۷. تو سالاد شیرازی بیشتر دوست داری یا سالادِ ــــــــ ؟

۸. در ایران برای ــــــــ چای ــــــــ می‌خورند.

🗣️🎧 **Short Dialogues about Food Portions**

The two most common food units/portions in Persian are given below:

۱) a: چلو کباب پُرسی چنده؟
b: پُرسی بیست هزار تومن.

۲) a: کباب سیخی چنده؟
b: سیخی ده هزار تومن.

تمرین ۱۳ 👄 👄

Answer in Persian and pronounce aloud. Use the spoken form.

به سؤال‌های زیر پاسخ دهید:

۱. تو از غذای تند خوشت می‌آد؟

۲. از هوای ابری بدت می‌آد؟

۳. معمولاً زود خوابت می‌بره یا دیر؟

۴. الان گرمته یا سردته؟

۵. معمولا زودتر گرسنه‌ات می‌شه یا تشنه‌ات می‌شه؟

۶. اسمِ استادِ فارسیِ ترمِ اوّلت یادته؟

تمرین ۱۴

Translate the following sentences into Persian. Use the written form.

1. The night before last, I was hungry and my brother was thirsty.

2. My brother dislikes birthday celebrations.

3. They like to come to the restaurant too.

4. We usually do not study together.

5. I do not feel sleepy.

6. I forgot your phone number.

تمرین ۱۵ 👥

Task: You are going to the Zagros restaurant with two of your classmates. Look at the menu in the next two pages and order an entire meal: appetizer, main course, beverage, and dessert. Ask your questions about the menu from your instructor who is taking your order. Try to stay on a 100,000 toomān total budget for the three of you.

رستوران زاگرس

غذای اصلی

چلوکباب کوبیده .... ۱۰۰,۰۰۰ ریال

چلو کباب برگ .... ۱۵۰,۰۰۰ ریال

چلو کباب بختیاری .... ۱۲۰,۰۰۰ ریال

چلو کباب سلطانی .... ۱۵۰,۰۰۰ ریال

شیشلیک .... ۲۰۰,۰۰۰ ریال

جوجه کباب .... ۱۲۰,۰۰۰ ریال

آلبالو پلو با مرغ .... ۸۰,۰۰۰ ریال

ته چین .... ۸۰,۰۰۰ ریال

سبزی پلو با ماهی .... ۱۰۰,۰۰۰ ریال

خورش قورمه سبزی .... ۵۰,۰۰۰ ریال

خورش قیمه .... ۵۰,۰۰۰ ریال

رستوران زاگرس

نوشیدنی

دوغ ..... ۷,۰۰۰ ریال

آب معدنی ..... ۶,۰۰۰ ریال

نوشابه ..... ۷,۰۰۰ ریال

چای ..... ۶,۰۰۰ ریال

پیش غذا

سالاد فصل ..... ۴۰,۰۰۰ ریال

سالاد شیرازی ..... ۳۰,۰۰۰ ریال

کشک بادمجان ..... ۵۰,۰۰۰ ریال

ماست موسیر ..... ۲۰,۰۰۰ ریال

بورانی اسفناج ..... ۲۰,۰۰۰ ریال

دسر

شُله زرد ۵۰,۰۰۰

بستنی سنتی ۴۰,۰۰۰

بستنی میوه‌ای ..... ۵۰,۰۰۰ ریال

فالوده ..... ۴۰,۰۰۰ ریال

 **دستور زبان ۲**

Uses of هَم

The word هم means "*also*". هم can have several usages. Below are some examples:

Are you a student? I am a student too.	۱. تو دانشجویی؟ من هم دانشجوام.
As for me, I get a Soltani Cholo Kabab	۲. من هم یک چلوکباب سلطانی می‌گیرم.
We eat together.	۳. با هم می‌خوریم.
Me, likewise.	۴. من هم همین‌طور.
I am both hungry and thirsty.	۵. من هم گرسنه‌ام هم تشنه‌ام.

هم carries stress only when it is used to mean *not only... but also...* (as in Example 5).

Common Mistake:

Unlike in English, هم cannot appear at the beginning of a sentence to mean "also":

Also, please bring two yoghurt drinks (dugh).	لطفاً دو تا دوغ هم بیاورین / هم لطفاً دو تا دوغ بیارین

تمرین ۱۶

Insert هم in the following sentences. You may need to omit words or combine sentences.

۱. غذای شما سرد است؟

۲. یادت نرود قاشق‌ها و لیوان‌ها را بیاوری!

۳. ماست و خیار ندارید؟

۴. پسرم خسته است. پسرم خوابش می‌آید.

۵. مادرم چلوکباب می‌خواهد. دوست دخترم چلوکباب می‌خواهد.

۶. علی از تو خوشش نمی‌آید.

تمرین ۱۷

Choose the appropriate phrase for each image and write it below the image.

۲. به به! عجب کبابی! من هم می‌خوام!	۱. ببخشین، می‌دونین ساعت چنده؟
۴. این جوجه کباب پرسی چنده؟	۳. خیلی ممنون. من سیرم. میل ندارم!
۶. لطف دارین. چشماتون قشنگ می‌بینه!	۵. مواظب باشین. چایی داغه!

ب. ＿＿＿＿＿＿＿

الف. ＿＿＿＿＿＿＿

ت. ＿＿＿＿＿＿＿

پ. ＿＿＿＿＿＿＿

تمرین ۱۸

Listen to the audio file and list the names of foods that you hear. Find a new way of saying "*Thank you*". Next, answer the following questions using the written form. Use complete sentences.

۱. آقای زمانی از کی به «کافه نادری» می‌آمد؟

۲. چرا خانم زمانی از «کافه نادری» خوشش می‌آید؟

۳. بچّه‌ها از چه چیزی خوششان نمی‌آید؟ چرا؟

۴. خانواده‌ی زمانی پولِ غذا را مهمانِ کی هستند؟

تمرین ۱۹

Here is the recipe for "Kuku Sabzi" (a herb patty). Underline all the verbs in the simple present tense and change them into the past tense. Look up the unfamiliar words in a dictionary. Try to cook this recipe at home. If you cannot find all the indicated herbs, use as many as you can. *Hint*: به هم زدن means "*To Scramble*".

طرز تهیه کوکو سبزی (برای چهار نفر)

۱. سبزی (تَره ـ جَعفری ـ شِوید ـ گِشنیز ـ پیازچه): یک کیلو

۲. تخم مرغ: ۵ تا ۶ عدد

۳. زِرِشک: یک قاشق غذا خوری

۴. گِردوی خُردشده: یک قاشق غذا خوری

۵. نمک ـ فلفل ـ زرد چوبه: به مقدارِ لازم

۶. روغن: به مقدارِ لازم

سبزی را خُرد کرده و داخل کاسه‌ای می‌ریزیم. تخم مرغ‌ها را به آن اضافه می‌کنیم. نمک و فلفل و زرد چوبه را هم به آن اضافه کرده و خوب هم می‌زنیم. زرشک و گردوی خرد شده را به آن اضافه کرده و باز هم می‌زنیم.

روغن را در یک تابه خوب داغ می‌کنیم و مایه را داخل روغن می‌ریزیم و روی مایه را با پشت قاشق صاف می‌کنیم و درِ آن را می‌گذاریم و حرارت را ملایم می‌کنیم تا مایه کاملاً بسته شود. بعد آن را می‌بُریم و برمی‌گردانیم تا روی دیگر آن هم سرخ شود.

زِرِشک (dried barberry) can be purchased at Middle Eastern supermarkets.

تمرین ۲۰

Listen to the audio file and fill in the blanks:

۱. تو چلوکباب می‌خوری یا _____ _____ کباب؟

۲. تخم مرغ با _____ خیلی _____ !

۳. من عاشقِ _____ ام ولی از فالوده _____ .

۴. _____ _____ معروف دریای _____ ماهی _____ است.

۵. مصرفِ روزانه‌ی _____ و _____ _____ برای بدن لازم است.

۶. _____ _____ معمولاً با چلوکباب _____ می‌خورند.

بیشتر بدانیم

🎧 Happy Birthday Song

تولّدت مبارک

مبارک مبارک تولّدت مبارک	تولّد تولّد تولّدت مبارک
که صد سال زنده باشی	بیا شمع ها رو فوت کن
تولّد تولّد تولّدت مبارک	مبارک مبارک تولّدت مبارک
چو گل پرخنده باشی	لبت شاد و دلت خوش
مبارک مبارک تولّدت مبارک	تولّد تولّد تولّدت مبارک

Translation:

Birthday, birthday, happy birthday
Congratulations, congratulations, happy birthday
Come blow out the candles
So that you will live hundred years
Congratulations, congratulations, happy birthday
Birthday, birthday, happy birthday
May your lips be smiling and your heart pleased
Like a flower/rose may you be full of laughter
Birthday, birthday, happy birthday
Congratulations, congratulations, happy birthday

Learn the following words about special occasions and work on Exercises 21-24:

🎧 Special Occasions مَراسمِ ویژه

Wedding	عَروسی	To get married	اِزدِواج کردن (کُن)
Religious ceremony of marriage	عَقد	To be born	بهدُنیا آمدن (آ)
To pass away	فُوت کردن (کُن) fowt	To congratulate	تَبریک گفتن (گو)
Formal party	مَجلِس	To offer condolences	تَسلیَّت گفتن (گو)
Ceremony	مَراسِم	Funeral	خَتم
Congratulations!	مُبارَک باشد! / مُبارَک باشه!	Passing away (noun)	دَرگُذَشت
Congratulations!	تَبریک!	To invite	دَعوَت کردن (کُن)
Party	مِهمانی / مِهمونی	To attend	شِرکَت کردن (کُن)

249

تمرین ۲۱

Read the following text and find out what it is about. Underline any familiar words.

ای چراغ زندگانی مادرم یادت به خیر

یاد و نامت تا ابد در قلبمان محفوظ باد

چهل روز گذشت

چهلمین روز درگذشت شادروان «فرزانه خلیلی» را به اطّلاع می‌رسانیم. به همین مناسبت مجلسِ یادبودی روز شنبه ۹۰/۱۰/۲۱ از ساعت ۱۶ الی ۱۸ بعداز ظهر در مسجد «امام علی» برگزار می‌شود.

فرزندان: آرام و اشکان والایی

همسر: محمود والایی

و بقیه‌ی فامیل های وابسته

تمرین ۲۲

Read the following letter that has been mailed to you. Find out what it is about and write a paragraph to respond to it. Use the following words (مُتَأَسِّفَم – نمی‌توانم – اُمیدوارم).

به نام ایزد یکتا

رویا   و   منوچهر

زیباترین شب زندگی خود را

به سپیده ی زیباترین روز زندگی خود پیوند می‌دهند

و خانواده‌های

کامیاب   زرتاش

حضور شما را در این جشنِ عشق مایهٔ شادی خود می‌دانند.

تاریخ: ۹۲/۶/۱۰   ساعت: ۲۳ – ۱۸

به صرف: شیرینی و شام

نشانی: تالار گل – خیابان پونک – پلاک ۱۴

تمرین ۲۳

Read the following text and find out what it is about. Fill in the blanks with your best guess. Next, write a paragraph to respond to this letter. Use the following words (دوست دارم – خوشحال می‌شوم – مرسی).

سلام دوست عزیزم

می‌دونستی پنجشنبه ۱۳ بهمن تولّدمه؟

مامانم می‌خواد ساعت ۳ تا ۶ واسم ———— تولّد بگیره. من هم

به مامانم گفتم دوست دارم حتماً تو دوستِ خوبم تو تولّدم باشی.

خیلی ———— می‌شم اگه دعوتم رو قبول کنی.

راستی، هدیهٔ من به به ———— در روز جشن یه عکس آتلیهٔ خوشگل

از خودته!

———— : خیابان سعادت آباد- خیابان یکم- پلاک ۲۶ - ———— دوّم

———— : ۸۸۰۷۰۹۲۴

نیلوفر امیری

تمرین ۲۴

Here is the brochure of a wedding planning company. Find out what services they provide and in which province they are located.

ازدواج آسان

برگزاری ازدواج آسان در تمامی استان گیلان

با ارائه خدمات زیر:

تالار عروسی به دلخواه عروس و داماد

سفره عقد و گل آرایی

شام برای ۳۰۰ نفر با سالاد فصل و نوشابه

فیلمبرداری و موزیک

۳۰ کیلو شیرینی عالی و ۳۰ کیلو کیک با کیفیت

تمام این مجموعه تنها با مبلغ

دومیلیون و هفتصد هزار تومان

با ما تماس بگیرید ۰۹۳۱-۱۳۶-۸۱۴۱

دستور زبان ۳

ضمایرِ انعکاسی REFLEXIVE PRONOUNS

Can you find the rule for making reflexive pronouns?

خودِمان/خودِمون Ourselves	خودَم Myself
خودِتان/خودِتون Yourselves	خودَت/خودِت Yourself
خودِشان/خودِشون Themselves	خودَش/خودِش Herself/Himself

Similar to English, reflexive pronouns can also be used in the emphatic form. The only difference is that the emphatic form carries stress and the reflexive form does not. Examples:

Reflexive Pronoun	I saw myself in the mirror.	(khod-am)	۱. من خودم را در آینه دیدم.
Emphatic Pronoun	I saw him, myself.	(khód-am)	۲. من خودم او را دیدم.

Question: Can you tell if the following sentence from Dialogue 1 contains a reflexive pronoun or an emphatic pronoun?

خودتم برو سفره رو پهن کن.

In literary writings, خود by itself can be used as a reflexive or emphatic pronoun. Examples:

Reflexive Pronoun	They saw themselves in the mirror.	۳. آنها خود را در آینه دیدند.
Emphatic Pronoun	They knew themselves.	۴. آنها خود می‌دانستند.

تمرین ۲۵

Write the appropriate reflexive pronoun:

۱. تو نباید ــــــــــ را ناراحت کنی.

۲. بچه‌ها هنوز ــــــــــ را به خوبی نمی‌شناسند.

۳. شما خانه‌ی ــــــــــ را دارید یا با پدر و مادرتان زندگی می‌کنید؟

۴. ما ــــــــــ شامِ امشب را پختیم.

۵. شما می‌خواهید با ماشینِ ــــــــــ بیایید یا با ماشینِ ما؟

۶. آن دختر در کلاس با ــــــــــ حرف می‌زد.

تمرین ۲۶

Work in pairs, groups, or as a class and answer the following questions. Example:

Student 1 (*book open*): تو امروز ناهار چی خوردی؟

Student 2: (*book closed*): من امروز ناهار ساندِویچِ مرغ خوردم.

Group 2	Group 1
۱. اسمِ رستورانِ موردِ علاقه‌ی تو چیست؟	۱. شما خودتان این غذا را درست کردید؟
۲. در خانه‌ی خودتان غذا می‌خوریم یا در رستوران؟	۲. تو دیروز خورش قورمه سبزی خوردی؟
۳. تو روزِ تولّدت چه کار کردی؟	۳. خانواده‌ی شما بیشتر چه نوع غذایی دوست دارند؟
۴. در دانشگاهِ شما چه رستوران‌هایی هست؟	۴. تو همیشه خودت غذا می‌پزی؟
۵. امروز دوست داری چه غذایی بخوری؟	۵. تو از مهمانیِ کوچک خوشت می‌آید یا از جشنِ بزرگ؟

تمرین ۲۷

Read the following paragraph from the folk tale "Story of Sigh" by Samad Behrangi. Underline the familiar words. Look up the unfamiliar words in a dictionary. What is the gist of the story? *Hint*: The word تاجر means "*Merchant*".

قصّه‌ی آه

یکی بود یکی نبود. تاجری بود سه تا دختر داشت. روزی می‌خواست برای خرید و فروش به شهر دیگری برود. به دخترهایش گفت: هرچه دلتان می‌خواهد بگویید برایتان بخرم.

یکی گفت: پیراهن. یکی گفت: جوراب. دختر کوچکتر هم گفت: گل می‌خواهم به موی سرم بزنم.

تاجر رفت خرید و فروشش را کرد، اما گل یادش رفت. توی خانه نشسته بودند که یک دفعه یادش افتاد و آه کشید. در این موقع درِ خانه را زدند. تاجر پاشد رفت دید کسی ایستاده دمِ در، یک قوطی در دستش.

تاجر گفت: تو کیستی؟

آن یک نفر گفت: من آه هستم. گل آوردم برای موهای دختر کوچکترت...

نویسنده: صَمَد بهرَنگی (۱۹۶۷ ـ ۱۹۳۹)
از کتابِ افسانه‌های آذربایجان

- Find three psychological verbs.

- Underline the instances of the non-specific suffix /i/.

- Underline all the verbs in the text and identify in which tense they are.

253

 تمرین ۲۸

Here is the brochure of a company that produces herbal extracts. Find the instruction for the use of each of these products. Which one of these products is helpful to people who have back pain? Which one is helpful for people with a heart condition? Which one helps with headaches?

گاوزبان
Gav zaban — طبیعت گرم

با یک لیوان آب سرد صبح و شب میل شود

آرام بخش، تصفیه کننده خون

شوید
Dill fruit water — طبیعت گرم

بعد از هر غذا یک لیوان میل شود

تسکین درد کمر و کلیه و مثانه، زیاد کننده شیر مادران

کاسنی
Cichorium intybus — طبیعت سرد

قبل از هر غذا یک لیوان میل شود

تب بر، تقویت پوست و کلیه و کبد، دارای ویتامین ث

گلاب
Rose water — طبیعت گرم

قبل از هر غذا یک لیوان میل شود

مقوی قلب و اعصاب، خوشبو کننده و معطر، روشن کننده پوست

نعناء
Mint water — طبیعت گرم

بعد از هر غذا یک لیوان میل شود

اشتها آور، رفع دل درد، رفع گرمازدگی کودکان

هل
Cardamom water — طبیعت گرم

با شربت، چای، یا شیرینی میل شود

معطر و خوشبو کننده، رفع سردرد و بوی بد دهان

تمرین ۲۹

a) Change into written form:

۱. چرا ازَش خوشت نیومد؟

۲.درگذشتِ پدرتونو تسلیت می‌گم.

b) Change into spoken form:

۱. نگین دلَش می‌خواهد به تولّدِ دوستَش برود.

۲. جشنِ عروسیِ آنها در کجای شهر است؟

درس هفتم

تمرین ۳۰: واژگان

In each line, circle the word that does not match the rest:

چنگال	بشقاب	قاشق	۱. صورتحساب
گوسفند	ماهی	گوشت	۲. لبنیّات
بربری	مهمانی	جشن	۳. تولّد
گرسنه	خسته	تشنه	۴. هندوانه
بستنی	آبجی	فالوده	۵. حلوا
گلابی	کاهو	پیاز	۶. سیب زمینی
آخ جان	جوجه	من هم همینطور	۷. نوش جان

تمرین ۳۱

Task: Ask the following questions of your classmate using the spoken form. Write your findings in the form of a report using the written form:

1. What do you eat for breakfast every day?

2. What do you usually eat for lunch?

3. Do you eat dinner too?

4. What do you usually eat for dinner?

5. Do you cook your dinner yourself?

6. What kind of (چه نوع) food do you like?

7. Do you like pastries? What kind?

8. Do you like ice cream more than cake?

9. When you were a child, did you like onions?

10. Do you like onions now?

11. What vegetables don't you like?

12. Are you a vegetarian (گیاه خوار)?

13. Why are you/not a vegetarian?

> In Sentence 7, the Persian word for "pastry" is in singular form.

REVIEW CORNER	
Points that remain unclear about Lesson 7:	
How I plan to work on these points:	

شعر

Read the following poem by Ahmad Shamloo and try to find the familiar words. Underline the verbs in the simple past tense and in the past continuous tense. Find two psychological verbs. You will not be evaluated on the content but you can use it for cultural enrichment.

پَریا

یکی بود یکی نبود

زیرِ گنبدِ کبود

لخت و عور تنگ غروب سه تا پری نشسته بود.

زار و زار گریه می کردن پریا

مثِ ابرای باهار گریه می کردن پریا

***

پریا! گشنه تونه؟

پریا! تشنه تونه؟

پریا! خسته شدین؟

مرغ پر بسّه شدین؟

چیه این های های تون

گریه تون وای وای تون؟

پریا هیچی نگفتن، زار و زار گریه میکردن پریا

مثِ ابرای بهار گریه می کردن پریا

شاعر: احمد شاملو (۲۰۰۰-۱۹۲۵)

256

ترانه

Listen to the following song by Dariush on YouTube and find the familiar words. Underline the verbs in the simple past tense and past continuous tense. Find a psychological verb. You will not be evaluated on the content but you can use it for cultural enrichment.

دستهای تو

ای که بی تو خودمو تک و تنها می‌بینم

هر جا که پا می‌ذارم، تو رو اونجا می‌بینم

یادمه چشمای تو، پُر درد و غصه بود

قصه‌ی غربت تو، قدِ صد تا قصه بود

یاد تو هر جا که هستم با منه

داره عمر منو آتیش می‌زنه

تو برام خورشید بودی، توی این دنیای سرد

گونه‌های خیسمو، دستای تو پاک می‌کرد

حالا اون دستا کجاست؟ اون دو تا دستای خوب

چرا بی صدا شده، لب قصّه‌های خوب

من که باور ندارم، اون همه خاطره مُرد

عاشق آسمونا، پشت یک پنجره مُرد

آسمون سنگی شده، خدا انگار خوابیده

انگار از اون بالاها، گریه هامو ندیده

یاد تو هر جا که هستم با منه

داره عمر منو آتیش می‌زنه

خواننده: داریوش اِقبالی

257

نکته‌ی فرهنگی

درس هفتم

Persian Cuisine

The rich Iranian cuisine reflects the regional diversity and the long history of civilization in this country. Rice is an important part of every meal except breakfast. Bread is served with each meal. Persian cuisine includes a diverse variety of vegetable/herb stews flavored with lamb, beef, or chicken (accompanied by plain steamed rice). Another popular variety of food is flavored rice dishes containing varieties of herbs, vegetables and meat. Kabab کباب, the most popular national dish of Iran, is marinated, charbroiled meat (lamb, beef, chicken, and fish). It is served either with steamed, saffroned rice چلو or with Persian bread نان.

Saffron زَعفران is the most important spice in Persian cuisine, giving it a sophisticated taste and aroma. Other frequently used spices are turmeric and cumin. Pomegranate sauce, eggplant, garlic, walnut, and dill are commonly used in Persian dishes. Different regions and ethnicities have their own specialty dishes which add to the diversity and exoticness of the Persian cuisine.

A very popular dish is آش which is a thick soup with Persian noodles, herbs, and different types of beans and grains. Another traditional food is آبگوشت or دیزی which is a broth with lamb, potatoes, chickpeas, white beans, onion, tomatoes, turmeric, and dried black lime.

آبگوشت

آش

A typical meal (lunch or dinner) includes rice (or rice mixed with vegetables), stew, chicken or beef, plain yoghurt, salad, and fresh herbs. Pickled fruits and vegetables (تُرشی) are also very popular. Dessert is not a usual part of the meal in Iran. Iranians eat sweets usually at tea time.

The most common beverage is tea چای which is brewed and steamed over boiling water in a Samāvar سَماوَر (or its modified version that works on a stove).

Traditionally, food was eaten on the floor on سُفره. Modern families eat at the table nowadays.

سَماوَر

A winter tradition is for families to sit around a short square table called کُرسی covered with a blanket and put a metal case with coal underneath it so that the entire family can sit around it to socialize and use its surface as a table (image below).

کرسی

Food Temperament

In Exercise 28 we saw that each herbal remedy was labeled as طَبیعَتِ گرم or طَبیعَتِ سرد. This classification extends to different types of food. The concepts of *warm* گرمی and *cold* سردی come from ancient Persian medicinal practice that views food as a kind of medicine. This concept has nothing to do with the actual temperature of the food but describes its nature and its effect on the balance of health. For instance, yogurt and plums are considered *cold* and walnuts and honey are considered *warm*. Cheese and tea are considered neutral. A well balanced meal contains both *warm* and *cold* ingredients. Some illnesses are also classified as *warm* or *cold* for each of which there are remedies/foods to help cure them. Hence, cold remedies are recommended for an illness labeled *warm* and *warm* remedies are recommended for an illness that is labeled *cold*.

ضرب المثل

Literal translation: *One's mouth does not sweeten by saying "halvā halvā"!*

با خَلوا خَلوا دَهَن شیرین نمی‌شه!

This proverb means that talk is cheap and it does not have the same effect as action.

Thematic Review of New Vocabulary

Food & Beverage	
Lima bean, rice & meat	باقالی پُلو با گوشت
Pepsi	پپسی
Per portion	پُرسی
Steamed rice	پُلو
Thirsty	تِشنه
Tea	چای
Tea would be nice!	چای می چَسبَد!
Steamed rice with …	چُلو
Soltāni rice and Kabab	چُلوکَبابِ سُلطانی
Cholo Kabab specialty restaurant	چُلوکَبابی
Food	خوراک
Stew	خورش
Yoghurt drink	دوغ
Salad	سالاد
Fresh greens	سَبزی خوردَن
Per skewer	سیخی
Full (not hungry)	سیر
Bill/Invoice	صورَتِحِساب
Herbs, beans, and meat stew	قورمِه سَبزی
Fillet mignon Kabab	کباب بَرگ
Ground beef Kabab	کباب کوبیده
Server	گارسُن
Hungry	گُرسنه
Hungry (Informal)	گُشنه
Vegetarian	گیاه خوار
Yoghurt and (minced) cucumber side dish	ماست و خیار
Beverage	نوشیدَنی
Good appetite!/Eat heartily!	نوشِ جان!

Serving Food	
Plate	بُشقاب
Fork	چَنگال
Tablecloth (for eating on the floor)	سُفره
Spoon	قاشُق
Cup/Glass	لیوان

Fruits	
Pomegranate	اَنار
Orange	پُرتِقال
Pistachio	پِسته
Apple	سیب
Walnut	گِردو
Pear	گُلابی
Banana	موز
Fruit	میوه
Watermelon	هِندِوانه

Vegetables	
Eggplant	بادِمجان
Onion	پیاز
Radish	تُربچه
Cucumber	خیار
Vegetables	سَبزیجات
Potato	سیب زَمینی
Garlic	سیر
Lettuce	کاهو
Tomato	گوجه فَرَنگی
Carrot	هَویج

Dairy	
Cheese	پَنیر
Milk	شیر
Butter	کَره
Dairy	لَبَنیّات
Yoghurt	ماست

Persian Bread	
Kind of bread	بَربَری
Kind of bread	تافتون
Kind of bread	سَنگَک
Kind of bread	لَواش

Meat	
Baby chicken	جوجه
Lamb	بَرّه
Beef	گاو
Mutton	گوسفَند
Meat	گوشت
Fish	ماهی
Chicken	مُرغ

Sweets	
Ice cream	بَستَنی
Sweet roasted flour & butter	حَلوا
Pastry	شیرینی
Dessert	دِسِر
Sweet noodles with rose water	فالوده

Special Occasions	
To get married	اِزدِواج کردن
To be born	به دُنیا آمدن
Congratulations	تَبریک
To congratulate	تَبریک گفتن
To offer condolences	تَسلیَت گفتن
Birthday	تَوَلُّد
Celebration	جَشن
Funeral	خَتم
Passing (away)	دَرگُذَشت
To invite	دعوت کردن
To attend	شِرکَت کردن
Wedding	عَروسی
Religious ceremony of marriage	عَقد
To pass away	فُوت کردن (fowt)
Congratulations	مُبارَک باشد
Formal party	مَجلِس
Ceremony	مَراسِم
Party	مِهمانی

Nouns & Adjectives	
Sister/Sis (Slang)	آبجی
Future	آیَنده
Brother/Bro (Slang)	داداش
World	دُنیا
Boyfriend	دوست پِسر
Girlfriend	دوست دختر
Gift/Present	کادو
Guest	مِهمان
Classmate	هَم‌کلاسی

Words & Expressions	
Hooray!/Yay!	آخ جان!
Bravo!/Good job!l	آفَرین
What kind	چه نوع
Yourself	خودَت
Hello to you	دُرود بَر شما
Next - Other	دیگر
By the way	راستی
Formal word used after numbers (For inanimates)	عَدَد
My dear	عَزیزَم
Me too	من هم هَمینطور

Tastes	
Not delicious	بدمَزه
Sour	تُرش
Hot/Spicy	تُند
Salty	شور
Sweet	شیرین

Psychological Verbs	
I dislike	بَدَم می‌آید (آمدن: آ)
I do not dislike	بَدَم نمی‌آید (آمدن: آ)
I am thirsty	تِشنه‌اَم است (بودن: هست)
I am sleepy	خوابَم می‌آید (آمدن: آ)
I like	خوشَم می‌آید (آمدن: آ)
I do not like	خوشَم نمی‌آید (آمدن: آ)
I am cold	سَردَم است (بودن: هست)
I am hungry	گُشنه‌اَم است (بودن: هست)
I am hungry	گُرسنه‌اَم است (بودن: هست)
You forgot	یادَت رَفت (رفتن: رو)
I remember	یادَم است (بودن: هست)

Verbs & Phrases	
You brought	آوَردی (آوَردن: آوَر)
Spread!	پَهن کُن! (کردن: کُن)
They should/may celebrate	جَشن بِگیرند (گیر)
We should/may order	سِفارش بِدَهیم (دادن: دَه)
I got/became full	سیر شُدَم (شُدَن: شو)
Call!	صِدا کُن! (کردن: کُن)
You drink	می‌نوشی (نوشیدن: نوش)
I bring	می‌آوَرَم (آوَردن: آوَر)
You want (Polite verb)	مِیل دارید (داشتن: دار)

تحصیلات و تعطیلات

Schooling & Holidays

درس هشتم

Communication Objectives
Talking about the Education System in Iran
Talking about Traditional Celebrations and Festivals
Talking about Recent Events and Events in Progress
Requesting and Giving Information about the Date
Filling Out an Application
Reporting an Incident
Talking about the Persian Calendar and Months
Using Idiomatic Expressions and Street Talk

Contents

واژگان ۱

I was cooking	داشتم ... می‌پُختم	Nationwide final exam	اِمتِحانِ نَهایی/ اِمتِحان نَهایی
Vocational school	هُنَرِستان	I am making ...	دارم ... دُرُست می‌کنم
S/he phoned	زَنگ زَد (زَن)	I am setting...	دارم ... می‌چینم
haft-seen spread (for Persian new year)	سفره‌ی هفت سین	I am coming	دارم می‌آیم/ دارم می‌آم
Celebration of 13th day of the new year	سیزده به در	They are/someone is knocking	دارند دَر می‌زَنند/ دارن دَر می‌زَنن
Nowruz celebration	عِید[1]	S/he is studying	دارد درس می‌خواند/ داره درس می‌خونه
I see you/See you	می‌بینَمَت/ می‌بینَمِت	What are you doing?	داری چه‌کار می‌کنی/ داری چی کار می‌کنی؟
Is ready	آماده است/ آماده‌س	I was studying	داشتم درس می‌خواندم/ داشتم درس می‌خوندم

کتاب را ببندید و به گفتگو گوش کنید. سپس جاهای خالی را پر کنید.

گفتگو ۱

ناهید: الو، سلام.

سیما: سلام خواهر جون.

ناهید: داری چی کار می‌کنی؟

سیما: دارم سفره‌ی هفت سین رو می‌چینم. تو چی؟

ناهید: صبح رفتم با بچّه‌ها لباس ــــــــــــــ خریدیم. الانم داشتم شام می‌پختم که سُروش زنگ زد.

سیما: خوب بود؟ چی گفت؟ امتحان نهاییش چطور شد؟

ناهید: هنوز داره درس می‌خونه. امتحان نهاییش فرداس. راستی، زنگ زدم بگم بیا اینجا. شامِ ما آماده‌س.

سیما: چه عالی! من از صبح تا حالا داشتم درس می‌خوندم.

ناهید: هنرستانِ شما از پس فردا تا بعد از ــــــــــــــ تعطیله. نه؟

سیما: آره، خیلی خوشحالم!

ناهید: دارن در می‌زنن. حتماً سروشه.

سیما: باشه، پس منم دارم می‌آم.

ناهید: پس می‌بینِمِت.

> You can find the Persian words for the instructions of the exercises at the end of this lesson.

---

1. عِید can also refer to a religious celebration.

درس هشتم

نوشتاری

گفتگو ۱

ناهید: الو، سلام.

سیما: سلام خواهر جان.

ناهید: چه‌کار می‌کنی؟

سیما: سفره‌ی هفت سین را می‌چینم. تو چطور؟

ناهید: صبح رفتم با بچّه‌ها لباسِ عید خریدیم. الان هم شام می‌پختم که سُروش ـــــــــــ .

سیما: خوب بود؟ چه گفت؟ امتحان نهایی‌اش چطور شد؟

ناهید: هنوز درس می‌خواند. امتحان نهایی‌اش فرداست. راستی، زنگ زدم بگویم بیا اینجا.
شامِ ما آماده است.

سیما: چه عالی! من از صبح تا حالا درس می‌خواندم.

ناهید: ـــــــــــ شما از پس فردا تا بعد از «سیزده به در» تعطیل است. نه؟

سیما: بله، خیلی خوشحالم.

ناهید: در می‌زنند. حتماً سروش است.

سیما: باشد، پس من هم می‌آیم.

ناهید: پس ـــــــــــ .

> In the written forms, the verbs are not provided in the *progressive* form as the *progressive* is not used in writing.

تمرین ۱

Role-play the above dialogue. Take turns and switch roles.

واژگان ۲ 🎧

Exact	دَقیق	Catch them! (Plural & Formal)	بِگیریدشان! / بگیرینِشون!
Shape	شِکل	Towards...	به سَمتِ.....
What has happened?	چه شده است؟ / چی شده؟	Miserable	بیچاره
Person	نَفَر	Street	خیابان / خیابون
Laptop	لَپ‌تاپ	I was going	داشتم می‌رَفتَم
Right now	هَمین اَلان	I was talking	داشتم حَرف می‌زَدَم
Article - Paper	مَقاله	For God's sake	تو را به خدا / تو رو خدا
Help!	کُمَک!	Thief	دُزد
Mobile - Cellphone	موبایل	S/he stole my bag	کیفَم را زَد / کیفَمو زَد

درس هشتم

کتاب را ببندید و به گفتگو گوش کنید. سپس جاهای خالی را پر کنید.

🎧 گفتگو ۲

کامران: دزد! دزد! ــــــــــــ ! بگیرینشون! بگیرینشون!

پلیس: بله، آقا. چی شده؟

کامران: ــــــــــــ کیفَمو زد آقای پلیس! تو رو خدا کمکم کنین!

پلیس: کِی؟ همین الان؟ تو این خیابون؟

کامران: بله! داشتم می‌رفتم به سَمتِ دانشگامون که دو نفر با موتور رسیدن و کیفمو زدن!

پلیس: دقیق اونا رو دیدین؟ چه شِکلی بودن؟

کامران: نه، نتونستم ــــــــــــ ببینمشون. داشتم با موبایلم حرف می‌زدم. از پشت اومدن.

پلیس: پیر بودن یا جَوون؟ موتورشون چی بود؟

کامران: مرد بودن و میانسال. نفهمیدم موتورشون چی بود. آقای پلیس بیچاره شدم! لپ‌تاپَم با تمامِ مقاله‌های امتحانام تو کیفم بود!

نوشتاری

گفتگو ۲

کامران: دزد! دزد! کمک! ــــــــــــ ! بگیریدشان!

پلیس: بله، آقا. چه شده است؟

کامران: دزد کیف را زد آقای پلیس! تو را به خدا کمکم کنید!

پلیس: کِی؟ همین الان؟ در این ــــــــــــ ؟

کامران: بله! می‌رفتم به سمتِ دانشگاهمان که دو نفر با موتور رسیدند و کیفم را زدند.

پلیس: دقیق آنها را دیدید؟ چه شکلی بودند؟

کامران: نه. نتوانستم دقیق ببینمشان. با موبایلم حرف می‌زدم. از پشت آمدند.

پلیس: پیر بودند یا جوان؟ موتورشان چه بود؟

کامران: مرد بودند و میانسال. نفهمیدم موتورشان چه بود. آقای پلیس بیچاره شدم! لپ‌تاپَم با تمامِ ــــــــــــ های امتحان‌هایم در کیفم بود!

تمرین ۲ 👥

Role-play the above dialogue. Take turns and switch roles.

خواندن

نامه‌ای از ایران

برادرِ عزیزم سلام! عیدِت مبارک! امیدوارم که حالت خوب باشه. الان که دارم این نامه رو می‌نویسم ساعت یکِ نیمه شبه و همه خوابن. مدّتِ زیادیه که از هم خبر نداریم. من الان دارم برای کنکور درس می‌خونم. آخرین باری که با هم حرف زدیم من داشتم سالِ چهارمِ دبیرستان رو تموم می‌کردم. خیلی دوست دارم بعد از دوره‌ی لیسانسم به اونجا بیام. مامان و بابا خوبن و سلام می‌رسونن. خواهرِ کوچیکمون «نوشین» هم خوبه و امسال سوّمِ راهنمایی رو تموم می‌کنه. برادرِ عزیزم، دوره‌ی فوقِ لیسانسِ تو کی تموم می‌شه؟ برام از خودت و رشته‌ات و تحصیلاتِ دانشگاهیت بنویس. دلم خیلی برات تنگ شده. جات اینجا خیلی خالیه. این نامه رو با کمی پسته برات می‌فرستم. نوشِ جونت! امیدوارم همیشه خوش و سلامت باشی. مواظبِ خودت باش و به امیدِ دیدار!

برادرِ کوچکت اَفشین

Middle school	راهنُمایی	Last time	آخِرین بار
I have missed you	دلَم بَرایَت تَنگ شُده است / دلَم بَرات تَنگ شُده	From each other	از هَم
May you be healthy	سلامت باشی	Hope to see you!	به امیدِ دیدار!
Master's	فوقِ لیسانس	High-school	دَبیرِستان
University entrance exam	کُنکور	Education	تَحصیلات
Duration	مُدَّت	News	خَبَر
Take care of yourself	مواظبِ خودَت باش! / مواظبِ خودِت باش!	Bachelor's	لیسانس
Letter (Mail)	نامه	Period (of time)	دوره

تمرین ۳

a) Listen to the audio file and follow along in your text. Repeat each sentence several times.

b) Answer in complete sentences. Use the written form.

۱. افشین الان چه درسی می‌خواند؟

۲. درباره‌ی برادرِ افشین چه می‌دانید؟

۳. آخرین باری که افشین با برادرش حرف زد چه می‌خواند؟

۴. نوشین کیست؟

۵. افشین از برادرش می‌خواهد که از چه برایش بنویسد؟

269

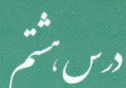

بیشتر بدانیم

Educational Levels مَقطَع‌های تَحصیلی

Pre-school	Age: 5-6	پیش دَبِستانی
Primary-school	Age: 6-11	دَبِستان
Middle-school	Age: 11-14	راهنَمایی
High-school - Vocational-school	Age: 14-18	دَبیرستان – هُنَرستان
University	Age: 18+	دانشگاه

Academic Degrees مَدرَک‌های تَحصیلی

High-school diploma	دیپلُم
Associate degree	کاردانی – فوقِ دیپلُم
Bachelor's	کارشِناسی – لیسانس
Master's	کارشِناسیِ اَرشَد – فوقِ لیسانس
Doctorate	دُکتُری

تمرین ۴ واژگان

جاهای خالی را با واژگان جدید پر کنید.

هنرستان – دبستان – تَحصیلات – خبر – پیش دبستانی – کارشناسیِ ارشد – استاد – کنکور – سیزده به در

۱. من سالِ بعد دوره‌ی ‌‌‌‌‌‌‌‌‌‌‌‌‌‌‌‌‌‌‌‌‌‌‌‌‌‌‌‌‌‌‌ را تمام می‌کنم.

۲. ‌‌‌‌‌‌‌‌‌‌‌‌‌‌‌‌‌‌‌‌‌‌‌‌‌‌‌‌‌‌‌ دانشگاهیِ تو کی تمام می‌شود؟

۳. دبیرستانِ ما از فردا تا بعداز ‌‌‌‌‌‌‌‌‌‌‌‌‌‌‌‌‌‌‌‌‌‌‌ تعطیل است!

۴. خواهرِ من دو سالِ دیگر به راهنمایی می‌رود. الان او به ‌‌‌‌‌‌‌‌‌‌‌‌‌‌‌‌‌‌‌ می‌رود.

۵. برادرِ من به دبیرستان نمی‌رود. او هنرمند است و به ‌‌‌‌‌‌‌‌‌‌‌‌‌‌‌‌‌ می‌رود.

۶. دوره‌ی ‌‌‌‌‌‌‌‌‌‌‌‌‌‌‌‌‌ قبل از دبستان است.

۷. ‌‌‌‌‌‌‌‌‌‌‌‌‌‌‌‌‌ فیزیکِ ما دکترایِ فیزیک دارد.

۸. در ایران، بعد از دیپلم باید امتحانِ ‌‌‌‌‌‌‌‌‌‌‌‌‌‌‌‌‌ بدهی.

تمرین ۵

The following questionnaire is given to students to fill out at the Bayan language institute. Fill out your information in the questionnaire. Look up the unfamiliar words in a dictionary.

به نام خدا

آموزشگاه بیان

شماره : _____

تاریخ : _____

فرم درخواست نام نویسی

تاریخ نام نویسی: _____

ترم : بهار ☐   تابستان ☐   پاییز ☐   زمستان ☐

بدین‌وسیله اینجانب با مشخصات زیر:

نام و نام خانوادگی : _____   نام پدر : _____   شماره شناسنامه : _____

تاریخ تولد : روز _____ ماه _____ سال _____   دانش‌آموز کلاس : _____

رشته تحصیلی : _____   میانگین آخرین سال تحصیلی : _____

نشانی محل سکونت : _____

نام محل تحصیل : _____   شغل پدر : _____   شغل مادر : _____

تلفن منزل : _____   تلفن محل کار : _____   تلفن همراه : _____

با آگاهیِ کامل از قوانینِ این آموزشگاه درخواست ثبت نام در درس زبانِ _____ را دارم.

نام و امضاء _____

تمرین ۶

The following advertisement is for tutorial classes. What classes are taught? at which levels? How much are the math classes? What do you know about the instructor?

تدریس خصوصی زبان و ریاضی توسط خانم

برای بانوان توسط خانم تدریس خصوصی دروس زبان انگلیسی و ریاضی

با تضمینِ قبولی در تمام مقاطع تحصیلی دبستان، راهنمایی و دبیرستان

با تضمینِ قبولی و کیفیت مناسب. تدریس بصورت فردی و یا کلاس

قیمت: انگلیسی از ساعتی چهل هزار تومان

ریاضی از ساعتی چهل و دو هزار تومان

271

PRESENT PROGRESSIVE TENSE حالِ مَلموس

The present progressive tense describes an action that is in progress and is taking place right now. It corresponds to the "*ing*" form in English. Example:

من دارم تلویزیون تماشا می‌کنم. (*right now*) I am watching TV

In English the verb "To Be" is added to form the progressive tense. In Persian, the verb "To Have" is added to form the present progressive tense (see the above example).

In Persian, the present progressive form is only used in spoken form and is thus not considered a full fledged "Tense" in traditional grammar books.

To form the Present Progressive:

1) Conjugate the verb داشتن in the simple present tense.

داشتن

داریم	ما	دارم	من
دارید	شما	داری	تو
دارند	آنها	دارد	او

2) Add the conjugated form of the **main verb** in the **simple present tense**. Stress falls on the می prefix (ex: míkhandidam).

خندیدن

داریم می‌خندیم	ما	دارم می‌خندم	من
دارید می‌خندید	شما	داری می‌خندی	تو
دارند می‌خندند	آنها	دارد می‌خندد	او

The conjugated form of داشتن precedes the compound verbs. Stress falls on the non-verbal component of the compound verb (ex: dāram dárs mikhānam).

درس خواندن

داریم درس می‌خوانیم	ما	دارم درس می‌خوانم	من
دارید درس می‌خوانید	شما	داری درس می‌خوانی	تو
دارند درس می‌خوانند	آنها	دارد درس می‌خواند	او

Note: The two components of the present progressive tense can be separated by other elements such as the direct object. Example:

من دارم [یک فیلم ایرانی] تماشا می‌کنم.

Exceptions: Not all verbs can be used in the present progressive form. In English, you can say "*I am realizing…*"but you cannot say "*I am knowing…*". The restrictions on the usage of the present progressive tense are not the same for English and Persian. For instance, in Persian, you can use the present progressive form to say "*I am thinking*" (دارم فکر می‌کنم) but you cannot use it to say "*I am sitting*". In order to say "*I am sitting*" in Persian, you need to use the present perfect tense (about which we will learn in the next lesson). If you conjugate "*To sit*" in the present progressive form دارم می‌نشینم it would mean "*I am about to sit*".

NEGATION

In Persian, the present progressive does not have a negative form. This is evidence for those who believe that the present progressive form is not a "true" tense in Persian. Example:

* دارم نمی‌خندم   I am not laughing.

In order to say "*I am not laughing*", you need to use the simple present tense (نمی‌خندم).

تمرین ۷

With a classmate, practice reading the conjugations of "To Laugh" and "To Study" in present progressive form. Take turns and listen to each other's reading.

تمرین ۸

Find six verbs in the present progressive form in Dialogue 1 and the passage and write them below:

تمرین ۹

Conjugate the following verbs in the present progressive tense. Read your sentences aloud.

۱. عروس و داماد ــــــــــــــ (غذا خوردن)

۲. ما ــــــــــــــ به ایران ــــــــــــــ (برگشتن)

۳. دانش آموزان ــــــــــــــ (خستگی درکردن)

۴. چرا آنها ــــــــــــــ ؟ (رقصیدن)(Negative)

۵. مادرِ زنِ من ــــــــــــــ (گریه کردن)

۶. مینا کجایی؟ فیلم سینمایی ــــــــــــــ (شروع شدن)

273

تمرین ۱۰

Use a verb in the present progressive form to describe each image. Read your sentences aloud.

۲. آنها ——————— تلویزیون ———————. ۱. لیلی ———————.

۴. بچه‌ها ———————. ۳. آن مرد ———————.

۶. او ———————. ۵. آن زن ———————.

تمرین ۱۱

Listen to the audio file and fill in the missing information:

گوش کنید و پاسخ دهید:

۱. ——————— کمک! ——————— شدم!

۲. من الان دارم ——————— ارشد می خوانم.

۳. ——————— بهترین ——————— تهران را دارد.

۴. لطفاً یک کیلو ——————— با نیم کیلو ——————— بدهید.

۵. پسرم در ——————— و دخترم در ——————— درس می خواند.

۶. مادرِ من امسال ——————— ——————— قشنگی چید.

۷. ——————— شما تا بعد از ——————— تعطیل است؟

۸. دوره‌ی ——————— در ایران ——————— است.

تمرین ۱۲

Write two paragraphs to describe what everyone is doing in the park پارک. Use as many verbs in the present progressive form as possible.

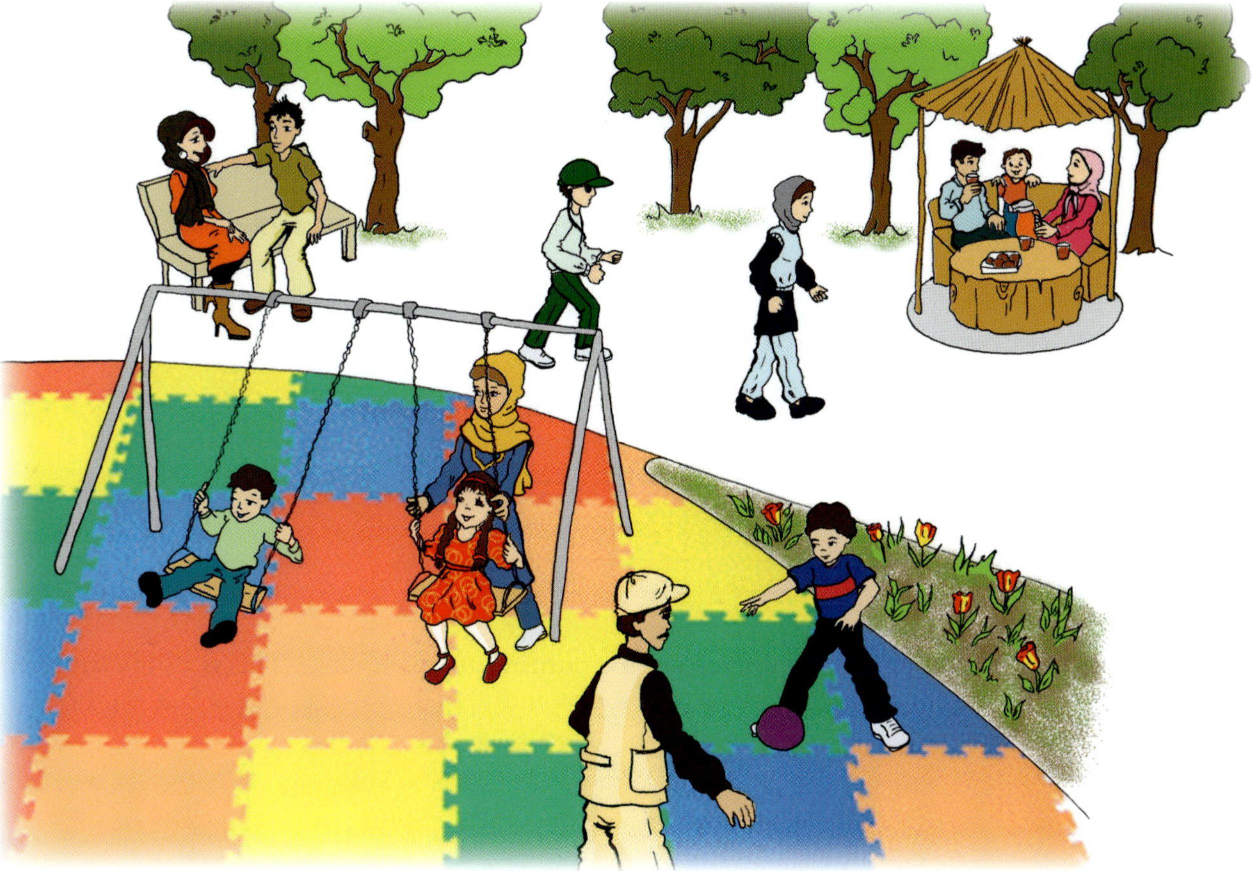

تمرین ۱۳

Fill in the blanks with the appropriate prepositions:

۱. من دارم ———— موبایلِ تو ———— مینا تلفن می‌زنم. (با – به – از – برای – در)

۲. هنرستانِ ما تا بعد ———— «سیزده به در» تعطیل است. (با – به – از – برای – در)

۳. من خیلی ———— دبستان بدم می‌آید! (با – به – از – برای – در)

۴. من می‌خواهم ———— تحصیلاتِ دانشگاهی ———— پایتختِ کشور بروم. (با – به – از – برای – در)

۵. من ———— ایران عاشقِ شیراز شدم! (با – به – از – برای – در)

۶. هم‌کلاسی‌های من می‌خواهند ———— معلّممان جشن تولّد بگیرند. (با – به – از – برای – در)

275

دستور زبان ۲

PAST PROGRESSIVE TENSE گذشته‌ی مَلموس

The past progressive tense describes an action that took place once **for a period of time** in the past, emphasizing the duration of that action. This tense is usually used in conjunction with another tense to describe a situation in a time-frame. Example:

وقتی رسیدی، من داشتم تلویزیون تماشا می‌کردم. When you arrived, I was watching TV.

In Persian, the past progressive form is only used in spoken form and is thus not considered a full fledged "Tense" in traditional grammar books.

To form the Past Progressive:

1) Conjugate the verb داشتن in the simple past tense:

داشتن

داشتیم	ما	داشتم	من
داشتید	شما	داشتی	تو
داشتند	آنها	داشت	او

2) Add the conjugated form of the **main verb** in the **continuous past** tense. This is a little tricky as students tend to add the simple past tense so please be mindful of this usage. Stress falls on the می prefix (ex: dāshtam míkhandidam).

خندیدن

داشتیم می‌خندیدیم	ما	داشتم می‌خندیدم	من
داشتید می‌خندیدید	شما	داشتی می‌خندیدی	تو
داشتند می‌خندیدند	آنها	داشت می‌خندید	او

The conjugated form of داشتن precedes the compound verbs. Stress falls on the non-verbal component of the compound verb (ex: dāshtam dárs mikhāndam).

درس خواندن

داشتیم درس می‌خواندیم	ما	داشتم درس می‌خواندم	من
داشتید درس می‌خواندید	شما	داشتی درس می‌خواندی	تو
داشتند درس می‌خواندند	آنها	داشت درس می‌خواند	او

Note: The two components of the past progressive form can be separated by other elements such as the direct object. Example:

وقتی زنگ زدی، من داشتم یک فیلم ایرانی تماشا می‌کردم.

NEGATION

In Persian, the past progressive does not have a negative form. This is evidence for those who believe that the past progressive form is not a "true" tense in Persian. Example:

*داشتم نمی‌خندیدم   I was not laughing.

In order to say "*I was not laughing*", you need to use the past continuous tense (نمی‌خندیدم).

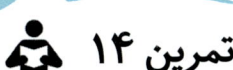

تمرین ۱۴

With a classmate, practice reading the conjugations of "To Laugh" and "To Study" in the past progressive form. Take turns and listen to each other's reading.

تمرین ۱۵

Conjugate the following verbs in the past progressive form.

۱. وقتی نوشین به دبستان رسید، بچّه‌ها ــــــــــــــ (امتحان دادن)

۲. وقتی مادرم را دیدم، او ــــــــــــــ (غذا پختن)

۳. پدر و مادرِ سارا ــــــــــــــ به من ــــــــــــــ (گفتن)

۴. من ــــــــــــــ کتاب فارسی را ــــــــــــــ (خریدن)

۵. وقتی دوست پسرم من را دید، ــــــــــــــ (خستگی درکردن)

۶. من ــــــــــــــ دبیرستان را ــــــــــــــ که برادرم به آلمان رفت. (تمام کردن)

تمرین ۱۶

Form groups of three. Change the verbs into present progressive and then to past progressive. Switch roles after each sentence so that each student reads two sentences. Example:

Student 1 (*book open*):   من درس خواندم.
Student 2 (*book closed*):   من دارم درس می‌خوانم.
Student 3 (*book closed*):   من داشتم درس می‌خواندم.

۱. چرا تو با ماشین به دانشگاه نمی‌روی؟

۲. من کارشناسیِ جغرافی را تمام کردم.

۳. تو با کی حرف می‌زنی؟

۴. دانش آموزان برای امتحان نهایی درس خواندند.

۵. مادرم سفره‌ی هفت سین را می‌چیند.

۶. نوه‌های من از هنرستان بدشان می‌آید.

تمرین ۱۷

Translate the following sentences into Persian. Use the progressive form. Read your sentences aloud.

1. When you arrived, I was not watching TV.

2. My son is studying for the university entrance exam now.

3. I am taking a rest now.

4. When you called, I was preparing food.

5. What were you doing yesterday at four o'clock?

6. Last night, Jim and I were walking and talking together.

7. This morning, I was talking to my grandmother.

8. I am finishing my PhD in the field of Physics.

تمرین ۱۸

Work in pairs, groups, or as a class and ask the following questions of each other. Example:

Student 1 (*book open*): تو مَدرَکِ کارشناسی داری؟

Student 2: (*book closed*): نه، من فوقِ دیپلم دارم.

Group 2	Group 1
۱. دوره‌ی کارشناسیِ تو کِی تموم می‌شه؟	۱. تو داری چه رشته‌ای می‌خونی؟
۲. داری چی تماشا می‌کنی؟	۲. درس‌هات دارن سخت می‌شن؟
۳. وقتی استاد اومد داشتی چی‌کار می‌کردی؟	۳. دیروز ساعت دهِ صبح داشتی چی‌کار می‌کردی؟
۴. داره خوابت می‌گیره؟	۴. تو همیشه داری درس می‌خونی؟
۵. تو راهنمایی رو بیشتر دوست داشتی یا دبستانو؟	۵. بچّه‌ها دارن چی‌کار می‌کنن؟

تمرین ۱۹

الف) به فرمِ نوشتاری تبدیل کنید:

۱. نه، دقیق نتونستم ببینمشون.

۲. زنگ زدم بگم اونارَم دعوت کن.

ب) به فرمِ گفتاری تبدیل کنید:

۱. همسرتان کدام فصل را از همه بیشتر دوست دارند؟

۲. عیبی ندارد. می‌توانی سفره‌ی هفت سین را خودت بچینی؟

درس، هشتم

دستور زبان ۳

پَسوَندها و پیشوَندها SUFFIXES & PREFIXES

Persian uses many suffixes and prefixes to create compound words. We have already seen some of these suffixes and prefixes.

پَسوَندها SUFFIXES

Suffixes of Location		
خوابگاه	دانشگاه	گاه
دبیرستان	هنرستان	ستان
داروخانه (Drugstore)	کتابخانه	خانه

Adverb/Noun-maker Suffix				Agent-maker Suffix		
Manly/For men مردانه	روزانه	صبحانه	انه	هنرمند	کارمند	مند

Noun-maker Suffix			
Greatness بزرگی	Kindness مهربانی	Beauty زیبایی	ی

Note that the above noun-maker suffix /-i/ is different from the non-specific marker /-i/. The former carries stress and the latter does not.

پیشوَندها PREFIXES

Negation Prefix		
Blind	نابینا	
Deaf	ناشِنَوا	نا
Unkind	نامهربان	

With & Without Prefixes				
Emotional	با اِحساس	Tasty	بامزّه	با
Unemotional	بی‌احساس	Flavorless	بی‌مزّه	بی

جمع‌ها PLURALS

Arabic Broken Plurals		
Homework	تَکالیف	← تَکلیف
Verbs	أفعال	← فِعل
Schools	مَدارس	← مدرسه

Other Plural Suffixes				
Sentences	جُمله ← جُمَلات	Words	کَلمه ← کَلمات	ات
Pickled vegetables	تُرشی ← تُرشی‌جات	Vegetables	سبزی ← سبزیجات	جات

تمرین ۲۰

Break down the following words into their suffixes and prefixes and find their meaning.

۳. ناشِناس	۲. خوردنی	۱. بیمارستان‌ها
۶. افغانستان	۵. بی‌کاری	۴. تحصیلات
۹. ناخوش	۸. شیرینی‌جات	۷. ساعات
۱۲. نامردان	۱۱. گلخانه	۱۰. گُلستان

تمرین ۲۱

Look at a Persian dictionary and find six words that contain suffixes/prefixes. Break down each word into its constituents. Share your findings with the class.

تمرین ۲۲

Add any of these prefixes/suffixes to make a word: با - مند - خانه- ستان- گاه - ی - انه - ات

۳. هوش	۲. کار	۱. پاک
۶. بُن	۵. تعطیل	۴. دبیر
۹. غرب	۸. شیرین	۷. زَن

بیشتر بدانیم

Persian Calendar & New Year تَقویمِ ایرانی و نوروز

A. تقویمِ هِجریِ شَمسی The Persian calendar is a solar calendar currently used in Iran and Afghanistan new year نوروز begins on the vernal equinox as determined by astronomical observations. In terms of accuracy, the Iranian calendar is more precise than the Gregorian calendar as it is observation-based, rather than rule-based. The earliest evidence of the Iranian calendar dates back to the second millennium B.C.E.

The first fully preserved Persian calendar is that of the Achaemenids. Throughout history, many modifications have been made to the Persian calendar. Among others, Omar Khayyam عُمَر خَیام (۱۰۴۸-۱۱۳۱) the Persian polymath, philosopher, astronomer, and poet made modifications to the Persian calendar. Iranian months match the Zodiac months.

 **Persian Months** ماه‌های ایرانی

Gregorian Calendar	Zodiac Month	Persian Month	Season
March 21 - April 19	♈	فَروَردین	بهار
April 20 - May 20	♉	اُردیبِهِشت	
May 20 – Jun. 22	♊	خُرداد	
Jun. 20 – Jul. 22	♋	تیر	تابستان
Jul. 23 – Aug. 22	♌	مُرداد	
Aug. 23 – Sept. 22	♍	شَهریور	
Sept. 23 – Oct. 22	♎	مِهر	پاییز
Oct. 23 – Nov. 21	♏	آبان	
Nov. 22 – Dec. 21	♐	آذَر	
Dec. 22 – Jan. 19	♑	دِی	زمستان
Jan. 20 – Feb. 18	♒	بَهمَن	
Feb. 19 - March 20	♓	اِسفَند	

In Afghanistan, the names of the Zodiac months are used instead of the Persian names.

تمرین ۲۳

به پرسش‌های زیر پاسخ کامل دهید:

۱. ماه‌های زمستان را نام ببرید:

۲. تاریخِ تولّدِ تو چیست؟

۳. آخرین ماهِ سال چیست؟

۴. تو در چه ماهی به دنیا آمدی؟

۵. تو کدام فصل را از همه بیشتر دوست داری؟

تمرین ۲۴

متنِ زیر را بخوانید. جاهای خالی زیر را با واژگانِ زیر پر کنید و به پرسش‌های زیر پاسخ دهید:

هفت ـ می‌روند ـ غذای ـ روز ـ می‌پوشند ـ کشورهای ـ بهار ـ است

نوروز

نوروز اوّلین روزِ سالِ جدیدِ ایرانیان و ———— یکمِ فروردین است. سالِ نو در ایران در اوّلین روزِ فصلِ ———— شروع می‌شود. نوروز جشنِ ملّی ایرانیان ———— . در بعضی از ———— همسایه نیز نوروز را جشن می‌گیرند. ———— شبِ عید سبزی‌پلو با ماهی است. در نوروز مردم لباس‌های نو ———— و به دیدن فامیل و دوستان می‌روند. در نوروز بزرگ‌ترها به کوچک‌ترها «عیدی» می‌دهند. عیدی معمولاً پول است. در نوروز مردم سفره‌ی «هفت سین» می‌چینند. در سفره‌ی هفت سین، ———— چیز که با «س» شروع می‌شود می‌گذارند مثل: سِرکه، سُماق، سبزه، سُنبُل، سیب، سیر، سِنجِد، و سِکّه. بیشترِ ایرانیان برای تعطیلاتِ نوروز به مسافرت ———— .

۱. نوروز چیست؟

۲. در چه کشورهایی نوروز را جشن می‌گیرند؟

۳. غذای شبِ عید معمولاً چیست؟

۴. در نوروز مردم چه کار می‌کنند؟

۵. عیدی چیست؟

۶. در سفره‌ی هفت سین چه می‌گذارند؟

The seven items on *haft-seen* are symbolic. Search online to find the significance of each object.

تمرین ۲۵

به فایل صوتی گوش کنید و جاهای خالی را پر کنید. معنی واژگانِ جدید را از لغت‌نامه پیدا کنید. به پرسش‌های زیر پاسخ دهید:

چهارشنبه سوری

چهارشنبه سوری یک جشنِ ———— است که پیش از رسیدنِ نوروز برگزار می‌شود. ———— قبل از آخرین چهارشنبه‌ی سال چهارشنبه سوری ———— . «سور» در فارسی یعنی «جشن» یا «سُرخ». در شبِ چهارشنبه سوری ———— و جوان، همه در خیابان‌ها دورِ هم جمع می‌شوند و ———— می‌گیرند. آنها از روی آتش می‌پرند و به آتش می‌گویند: «زردیِ من از ————، سرخیِ تو از ————» که یعنی «مریضیِ من مالِ تو و سلامتی و قدرتِ تو مالِ من». ———— مراسم دیگری هم دارد مثل «قاشق زنی» و «فال گوش نشستن». همه مخصوصاً بچّه‌ها و جوانان ———— را خیلی خیلی دوست دارند.

۱. چهارشنبه سوری چیست؟

۲. «سور» یعنی چه؟

۳. در شبِ چهارشنبه سوری مردم چه کار می‌کنند؟

۴. «زردیِ من از تو، سرخیِ تو از من» به انگلیسی یعنی چه؟

۵. چهارشنبه سوری چه مراسمِ دیگری دارد؟

تمرین ۲۶

به فایلِ صوتی گوش کنید و با جملاتِ کامل پاسخ دهید:

۱. شبِ یَلدا اوّلین شبِ چه فصلی است؟

۲. شبِ یَلدا آخرین شبِ چه فصلی است؟

۳. شبِ یَلدا در اوّل چه ماهی است؟

۴. در شبِ یلدا ایرانیان چه می‌کنند؟

۵. چند سال است که ایرانیان شبِ یلدا را جشن می‌گیرند؟

IDIOMS, STREET TALK, & DEROGATORY WORDS

The Persian language contains many idiomatic expressions that are used in daily conversations. Most of these idioms have a literal translation that may not necessarily reflect the actual usage. We have already learned some of these idioms throughout the lessons. It is extremely useful for foreign language learners to know these expressions not commonly taught in the classic language textbook. Below are some idioms, street talk, and even derogatory words that are commonly used.

🎧 Idioms

Usage Translation	Literal Translation	
I had so much trouble!	My father came out	پدرم در اومد!
I'd rather be dead!	Dirt on my head	خاک به سرم!
They ripped me off/I was scammed!	They put a hat on my head	کلاه سرم گذاشتن!
I'm tired of repeating (something to someone)!	My tongue grew hair	زبونم مو در آورد!
Cute/Funny	Salty/With salt	با نَمَک
You are so cute/adorable!	May a mouse eat you	موش بخورَدِت!
You've got connections/influence!	Your donkey goes	خَرت می‌ره!
Do you have good news or bad news?	Are you a lion or a fox?	شیری یا روباه؟
Yes Sir/Ma'am! - Whatever you say!	On my eye	رو چِشَم!

Street Talk

Usage Translation	Literal Translation	
You're the bomb!/Good job!	May your breath be warm	دَمِت گَرم!
I've got your back!	I've got your air	هوا تو دارم!
I got shocked/bored	I foamed	کَف کردم
You are lying/You are full of it!	You are closing empty	خالی می‌بندی

Derogatory words

Usage Translation	Literal Translation	
Yeah, right!/B.S!	Your aunt's life	جونِ عمّهات!
Brat/Mean	Father burnt	پدرسوخته
Bastard	Father dog	پدرسگ
Scum	Not a man	نامرد

تمرین ۲۷
Using the Idioms & Slang

What would you say in each of these situations?

1. If you wanted to say to someone that s/he was missed at an event you would say:	جا _____
2. If you wanted to say "I miss you" to someone older than you, you would say:	دلم _____
3. If you wanted to say "thank you" to someone older than you, you would say:	دست _____ _____
4. If someone said "thank you" to you, you would respond by saying:	خوا _____ _____
5. When a guest enters your house, you would say:	خو _____
6. "be salāmat" is the response to:	خد _____
7. If you wanted to say "affectionately" to a close friend, you would say:	قر _____
8. If you were overcharged for a product, you would say:	کلاه _____
9. What do you say to a cute 4-year old child?	موش _____
10. If your friend were going on a trip, you would say to her:	مواظب _____
11. If something bad happened to you, you would say:	پدرم _____

تمرین ۲۸: واژگان

In each line, circle the word that does not match the rest:

آشپزخانه	خیابان	داروخانه	۱. بیچاره
سال	سکّه	سیب	۲. سنبل
مقاله	امتحان نهایی	تحصیلات	۳. سرکه
گلستان	هنرستان	دبیرستان	۴. دبستان
اردیبهشت	خرداد	مهر	۵. فروردین
کنکور	چهارشنبه سوری	نوروز	۶. سیزده به در
کاردانی	کارشناسیِ ارشد	کارگر	۷. کارشناسی
جملات	مهربانی	مدارس	۸. تکالیف

تمرین ۲۹

زیرِ واژه‌ی درست خط بکشید.

۱. من و ساسان با (خود ــ هم) به دریای خزر می رویم.

۲. شما می خواهید با ماشین (خودمان ــ خودتان) بیایید یا با ماشینِ ما؟

۳. نمی توانید این درس را در دفترتان (می نویسید ــ بنویسید).

۴. دوست تو بعد از غذا (خوابش ــ خوابت) گرفت.

۵. هُما (داشت ــ دارد) فیلم می دید که تو آمدی.

۶. افشین یک پپسی (را ــ Ø) به من می دهد.

۷. وقتی آرَش بچّه بود، با پدر و مادرش در کابُل (زندگی می کرد ــ زندگی کرد).

تمرین ۳۰

Write a text about a national holiday in your country. Indicate the name, the date, the history, the traditions of that holiday. Indicate what kinds of food are served on that day. Indicate whether you like/dislike that holiday. Use the written Persian.

REVIEW CORNER	
Points that remain unclear about Lesson 8:	
How I plan to work on these points:	

شعر

Read the following poem about Nowruz attributed to Omar Khayyam and try to find the familiar words. Can you find a Persian month in the poem? Underline the verbs in the imperative form. You will not be evaluated on the content but you can use it for cultural enrichment.

Omar Khayyam's tomb in Neyshabur

بر چهره‌ی گل نسیم نوروز خوش است

در صحن چمن روی دل‌افروز خوش است

از دی که گذشت هر چه گویی خوش نیست

خوش باش و ز دی مگو که امروز خوش است

***

خیام اگر ز باده مستی خوش باش

با ماه‌رخی اگر نشستی خوش باش

چون عاقبت کار جهان نیستی است

انگار که نیستی چو هستی خوش باش

شاعر: عمر خیام (۱۱۳۱ - ۱۰۴۸)

287

Listen to the following song by Farhad on YouTube and find the familiar words. This song talks about the anticipations of a child who is looking forward to Nowruz. Underline the verbs and determine which tense they are. You will not be evaluated on the content but you can use it for cultural enrichment

کودکانه

بوی عیدی، بوی توپ

بوی کاغذ رنگی

بوی تند ماهی دودی، وسط سفره‌ی نو

بوی یاس جانماز ترمه مادر بزرگ

با اینا زمستونو سر می‌کنم ، با اینا خستگیمو در می‌کنم

شادی شکستن قلک پول

وحشت کم شدن سکه عیدی از شمردن زیاد

بوی اسکناس تا نخورده لای کتاب

با اینا زمستونو سر می‌کنم، با اینا خستگیمو در می‌کنم

فکر قاشق زدن یه دختر چادر سیاه

شوق یک خیز بلند از روی بته‌های نور

برق کفش جفت شده تو گنجه‌ها

با اینا زمستونو سر می‌کنم، با اینا خستگیمو در می‌کنم

عشق یک ستاره ساختن با دولک

ترس ناتموم گذاشتن جریمه‌های عید مدرسه

بوی گل محمدی که خشک شده لای کتاب

با اینا زمستونو سر می‌کنم، با اینا خستگیمو در می‌کنم

بوی باغچه، بوی حوض

عطر خوب نذری

شب جمعه، پی فانوس، توی کوچه گم شدن

توی جوی لاجوردی، هوس یه آب‌تنی

با اینا زندگیمو سر می‌کنم، با اینا خستگیمو در می‌کنم

خواننده: فَرهاد (۲۰۰۲ـ۱۹۴۴)

نکته‌ی فرهنگی

Traditional Festivals & Rituals

Iranian festivals are mostly rooted in the ancient traditions of Zoroastrianism which was the religion of Iran before the conquest of Islam in the 7th century AD. These festivals often reflect the closeness of Persian culture with nature. Although these feasts are mainly rooted in Zoroastrianism, religious minorities (including Jews, Christians, Bahai's, etc.) and different ethnic groups (such as Turks, Kurds, Assyrians, Armenians, etc.) celebrate these national festivals especially the Nowruz.

Chārshanbe Suri چهارشنبه سوری means the red or festive Wednesday and is an important prelude to Nowruz. It is the festival of fire and is celebrated on the last Tuesday night before the New Year. The celebrations start in the early evening, with people lighting bonfires on the streets and leaping over them. Chārshanbe suri has other rituals one of which is similar to Halloween's Trick-or-treat. It is the most popular festival amongst the young.

Nowruz نوروز means "new day" and is the first day of the Persian new year. It is usually on March 21st or 20th which corresponds to the 1st day of Farvardin. In preparation for Nowruz people clean their houses ridding them of the winter dust, shop for new clothing and shoes. They prepare the *haft-seen* spread with seven symbolic items beginning with letter "س". Home-made sweets are prepared. At the exact moment of the spring equinox, family members wear their new clothes, gather around the *haft-seen* spread, welcome the New Year and wish for a prosperous year ahead, and forget past grudges. Families make brief visits to each other where tea and sweets are served. People visit their elders first. Children receive *eydi* in the form of brand new cash money. Visits last twelve days and are part of the public holiday.

Sizdah be-dar سیزده به در is the thirteenth day of the New Year. Families gather for a picnic in the parks out of town. They throw away the sabze (greens) that they prepared earlier to get rid of bad luck. This concludes the Nowruz celebrations and people are back to work the day after Sizdah be-dar.

Tirgān is the mid-summer feast usually celebrated on July 2nd and the 13th of Tir. Today, Tirgān is mainly celebrated in the Northern provinces but is gaining popularity among the younger generation. People celebrate Tirgān by dancing, singing, reciting poetry, eating, and swimming.

Mehrgān مهرگان or Jashn-e Mehr جشن مهر is the Persian festival of autumn. It is usually on October 2nd, though traditionally the celebrations lasted six days between 16th-21st of the month of Dey. Mehrgān also corresponded to the day farmers harvested their crops. In the Zoroastrian tradition Mehrgān honors the Yazata of "Mehr" which is responsible for friendship, affection and love. For the Mehrgān celebrations, people set a decorative, colorful table with a mirror, sweets, flowers, fruits (especially pomegranates and apples), and nuts (such as almonds or pistachios).

Yaldā یَلدا means "birth" and is a Syric word imported into Persian by the Syric Christians. It is also referred to as "shab-e chelle" شب چِله, a celebration of the winter solstice on December 21st and 30th of Āzar. Yaldā is the night before winter begins and the longest night of the year in the northern hemisphere. Sweets, fresh fruit (especially pomegranate and watermelon) and nuts are served during the Yaldā night gathering. Families get together and stay up late, talking, reciting poetry, and the elderly tell folk tales.

Sade سَده means hundred. It is the mid-winter feast and celebrates the discovery of fire and its ability to defeat the darkness and cold. Sadeh is usually on January 30th and the 10th of Bahman. Some believe that the name Sadeh is related to the fact that it is 50 days and 50 nights before Nowruz.

ضرب المثل

کار نیکو کردن از پُر کردن است!

Literal translation: *Doing a good job comes with practice!*

(Practice makes perfect!)

Thematic Review of New Vocabulary

Education	
Exam	اِمتِحان
Nationwide final exam	اِمتِحانِ نَهایی
Pre-school	پیش دَبستانی
Education	تَحصیلات
Primary-school	دَبِستان
High/Middle-school teacher	دَبیر
High-school	دَبیرِستان
Doctorate	دُکتُری
High-school diploma	دیپلُم
Middle-school	راهَنمایی
Associate degree	کاردانی – فوقِ دیپلُم
Bachelor's	کارشِناسی – لیسانس
Master's	کارشِناسیِ ارشَد – فوقِ لیسانس
University entrance exam	کُنکور
Degree	مَدرَک
Level	مَقطَع
Vocational school	هُنَرِستان

About Haft-seen	
Greens	سبزه
Vinegar	سِرکه
Coin	سِکّه
Sumac powder	سُماق
Hyacinth	سُنبُل
Seaberry	سِنجِد
Apple	سیب
Garlic	سیر

About Festivities	
Red/Festive Wednesday	چهارشنبه سوری
haft-seen spread (for Persian new year)	سفره‌ی هفت سین
Celebration of the 13th day of the Persian new year	سیزده به در
Nowruz or a religious celebration	عید
Persian New Year	نوروز
Longest night of the year	یَلدا

Suffixes, Prefixes, & Broken Plurals	
Beauty	زیبایی
Greatness	بُزرگی
Blind	نابینا
Deaf	ناشنَوا
Drugstore	داروخانه
Emotional	با احساس
Homework (Plural)	تکالیف
Kindness	مهربانی
One who can hear	شِنَوا
One who can see	بینا
Pickled vegetables	تُرشی‌جات
Schools	مَدارس
Flavorless	بی‌مَزّه
Tasty	بامزّه
Unemotional	بی‌احساس
Unkind	نامهربان
Vegetables	سَبزیجات

Nouns & Adjectives	
Miserable	بیچاره
News	خَبَر
Street	خیابان
Thief	دُزد
Exact	دَقیق
Shape	شکل
Help	کُمَک
Laptop	لَپ تاپ
Article - Paper	مَقاله
Letter (mail)	نامه
Person	نَفَر
Mobile - Cellphone	موبایل

Persian Calendar	
First Persian month	فَروَردین
Second Persian month	اُردیبهشت
Third Persian month	خُرداد
Fourth Persian month	تیر
Fifth Persian month	مُرداد
Sixth Persian month	شهریور
Seventh Persian month	مِهر
Eighth Persian month	آبان
Ninth Persian month	آذر
Tenth Persian month	دِی
Eleventh Persian month	بَهمَن
Twelfth Persian month	اِسفَند
Calendar	تَقویم ــ گاهشُمار
Solar Hejira	هِجریِ شَمسی

Words & Expressions	
Last time	آخَرین بار
From each other	از هم
Hope to see you again	به امیدِ دیدار
Towards	به سمتِ
For God's sake	تو را به خدا
What has happened?	چه شده است؟
What are you doing?	داری چه کار می‌کنی؟
I have missed you	دلم برایت تنگ شده است
Period (of time)	دوره
May you be healthy	سلامت باشی
Duration	مُدَّت
Take care of yourself	مواظبِ خودَت باش!
Right now	همین اَلان
Still/Yet	هَنوز

Derogatory Words	
Brat/Mean	پدر سوخته
Bastard	پدرسگ
Yeah, right!/B.S!	جونِ عمّهات!
Scum	نامرد

Idioms	
Cute/Funny	با نَمَک
I had so much trouble!	پدرم در اومد!
I'd rather be dead!	خاک به سرم!
You've got connections/influence!	خِرت میره!
Yes Sir/Ma'am! - Whatever you say!	رو چِشَم!
I'm tired of repeating (something to someone)!	زبونم مو در آورد!
Do you have good news or bad news?	شیری یا روباه؟
They ripped me off/I was scammed!	کلاه سرم گذاشتن!
You are cute/adorable!	موش بخورَدِت!

Street Talk	
You are lying/You are full of it!	خالی می بندی!
You're the bomb!/ Good job!	دَمِت گَرم!
I got shocked/bored	کَف کردم
I've got your back!	هوا تو دارم!

Verbs & Phrases	
Catch them! (Plural & Formal)	بِگیریدِشان (گِرِفتَن: گیر)
S/he is studying	دارد درس می‌خواند (خواندن: خوان)
I am making …	دارم … دُرُست می‌کنم (کردن: کُن)
I am setting …	دارم … می‌چینم (چیدَن: چین)
I am coming	دارم می آیم (آمدن: آ)
They are/someone is knocking	دارَند دَر می‌زنند (زدَن: زَن)
I was talking	داشتم حرف می زدم (زَدَن: زَن)
I was cooking...	داشتم … می‌پختم (پُختَن: پَز)
I was studying	داشتم درس می‌خواندم (خواندَن: خوان)
I was going	داشتم می‌رفتم (رَفتن: رو)
S/he phoned	زنگ زد (زَدَن: زَن)
Is ready	آماده است (بودن: هست)
S/he stole my bag	کیفَم را زَد (زدَن: زَن)
I see you/See you	می‌بینمت (دیدن: بین)

Instructions for the Exercises	
Text	مَتن
Positive/Affirmative	مُثبَت
Does not match	مُطابقَت ندارد
Meaning	مَعنی
Dialogue	مُکالمه
Negative	مَنفی
Name...! (Plural & Formal)	نام بِبَرید
Written	نِوشتاری
Cognate	هم خانواده
Word(s)	واژه ــ واژگان

Instructions for the Exercises	
Use! (Plural & Formal)	اِستِفاده کنید
Loudly	با صِدای بُلَند
Make! (Plural & Formal)	بِسازید
Answer	پاسُخ
Fill in/out! (Plural & Formal)	پُر کنید
Question	پُرسِش
Find! (Plural & Formal)	پیدا کنید
Convert! (Plural & Formal)	تَبدیل کنید
Translate! (Plural & Formal)	تَرجُمه کنید
Image	تَصویر
Blanks	جاهای خالی
New	جَدید
Sentence(s)	جُمله ــ جُمَلات
Answer	جَواب
Grammar	دَستور زبان
Underline…! (Plural & Formal)	زیرِ... خط بکشید
Question	سُؤال
Change into question form! (Plural & Formal)	سُؤالی کنید
Conjugate! (Plural & Formal)	صَرف کنید
Phrase	عِبارَت
Audio file	فایل صوتی
Verb(s)	فعل ــ اَفعال
Word(s)	کَلَمه ــ کَلَمات
Spoken	گُفتاری
Dialogue	گُفتگو
Listen! (Plural & Formal)	گوش کنید
Dictionary	لُغَت نامه
Synonym	مُتَرادِف
Antonym	مُتَضاد

ایرانگردی
Visiting Iran

Communication Objectives

Making Reservations: Plane Ticket, Hotel Room, etc.
Interacting at the Iranian Airport
Making a Complaint
Asking for Directions
Finding Directions on a Map
Narrating Stories Situated in Time
Talking about Iranian Currency
Using Polite & Modest Forms

Contents

🎧 واژگان ۱

I have applied	دَرخواست کردهام/ دَرخواست کردم (کُن)	End (of)...	آخرِ ...
Passport	گُذَرنامه	Travel agency	آژانسِ مُسافِرَتی
Tax	مالیات	Has expired	باطِل شده است/ باطِل شده (شَو)
You have not gone	نَرفتهاید/ نَرفتین (رَو)	Of course	اَلبَّته
Airline	هَواپیمایی	I have not returned	بَرنَگَشتهام/ بَرنَگَشتم (گَرد)
Homeland	وَطَن	Ticket	بلیت
Both	هَر دو	I have not gone out	بیرون نَرفتهام/ بیرون نَرفتم (رَو)
I get it	میگیرَمَش/ میگیرِمش (گیر)	I am at your service	درخِدمَتِتان هستم/ درخِدمتتون هستم
Stop/Lay over	تَوَقُّف	Airport	فُرودگاه
I am thankful	سِپاسگُزارَم	Approximately	حُدود

کتاب را ببندید و به گفتگو گوش کنید. سپس جاهای خالی را پر کنید.

🎧 گفتگو ۱

در آژانسِ مسافرتی

کاوه: درود بر شما! میخواستم یه ———— برای ایران بخرم.

فروشنده: بله در خدمتتون هستم. چند ساله که ایران نرفتین؟

کاوه: حدودِ شش ساله که به وطنم برنگشتم و پنج ساله که از آمریکا بیرون نرفتم.

فروشنده: پس حتماً گذرنامهی ایرانی و آمریکاییتون هر دو باطل شده.

ولی خوبه که ———— لازم ندارین.

کاوه: بله! برای گذرنامههام درخواست کردم.

فروشنده: برای چه تاریخی میخواین برین ایران؟

کاوه: حدودِ پونزدهِ خرداد میخوام برم و آخرِ تیر برمیگردم.

فروشنده: یه بلیت با هواپیماییِ کی.ال.ام. دارم با یه 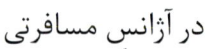 چهار ساعته تو آمستردام.

کاوه: قیمتش چنده؟

فروشنده: هزار و دویست دلار، البّته با مالیاتِ فرودگاه.

کاوه: باشه، میگیرِمش. سپاسگزارم.

فروشنده: خواهش میکنم.

> 💡 The verbs in blue are in the present perfect tense. In spoken form, the pronunciation of the present perfect tense is similar to that of the simple past tense. The difference is the location of stress. We will learn more about it in the grammar section.

نوشتاری

گفتگو ۱

کاوه: درود بر شما! می‌خواستم یک بلیت برای ایران بخرم.

فروشنده: بله در خدمتتان هستم. چند سال است که به ایران ـــــــــــ؟

کاوه: حدودِ شش سال است که به وطنم برنگشته‌ام و پنج سال است که از آمریکا بیرون نرفته‌ام.

فروشنده: پس حتماً گذرنامه‌ی ایرانی و آمریکایی‌تان هر دو باطل ـــــــــــ ولی خوب است که ویزا لازم ندارید.

کاوه: بله! برای گذرنامه‌هایم درخواست کرده‌ام.

فروشنده: برای چه تاریخی می‌خواهید به ایران بروید؟

کاوه: حدودِ پانزده خرداد می‌خواهم بروم و آخرِ تیر برمی‌گردم.

فروشنده: یک بلیت با هواپیمایی کی.ال.ام. با یک توقّفِ چهار ساعته در آمستردام.

کاوه: قیمتش چند است؟

فروشنده: هزار و دویست دلار، البتّه با مالیاتِ فرودگاه.

کاوه: باشد، ـــــــــــ . سپاسگزارم.

فروشنده: خواهش می‌کنم.

تمرین ۱

گفتگوی بالا را با هم‌کلاسی‌تان تمرین کنید:

واژگان ۲ 🎧

I had heard	شِنیده بودم (شِنَو)	I wish	آرزو می‌کنم (کُن)
You have been (Plural & Formal)	بوده‌اید/ بودین	You had come (Plural & Formal)	آمده بودید/ اومده بودین
Customs/ Immigration officer	مأمورِ گُذَرنامه	Here you are	خِدمَتِ شما
Identification card	کارتِ شناسایی	Foreign/Foreigner	خارِجی
S/he had said	گفته بود	Has been	بوده است/ بوده
Have a nice trip!	سفرِ خوشی را برایتان آرزو می‌کنم/ سفرِ خوشی رو براتون آرزو می‌کنم		

کتاب را ببندید و به گفتگوی صفحه‌ی بعد گوش کنید. سپس جاهای خالی را پر کنید.

گفتگو ۲

در فرودگاهِ تهران

مأمورِ گذرنامه: سلام، گذرنامه تون رو لطفاً بدین.

کاوه: گذرنامه‌ی ایرانی یا ـــــــــــــ؟

مأمورِ گذرنامه: ایرانی.

کاوه: بفرمایین. این گذرنامه خدمتِ شما.

مأمورِ گذرنامه: شما ـــــــــــــ ام ایران بودین؟

کاوه: بله! وقتی بچّه بودم با پدر و مادرم اومده بودیم ایران.

مأمورِ گذرنامه: چه سالی اومده بودین ایران؟

کاوه: دقیقاً نمی دونم چون خیلی بچّه بودم. پدرم بهم گفته بود. شاید سال ۱۳۶۲ بوده.

مأمورِ گذرنامه: کارتِ شناسایی‌ام دارین؟

کاوه: بله! ـــــــــــــ ـــــــــــــ که لازم می‌شه، بفرمایین.

مأمورِ گذرنامه: چند وقت ایران می‌مونین؟

کاوه: حدود یک ماه و نیم.

مأمورِ گذرنامه: سفر خوشی رو تو ایران براتون آرزو می‌کنم.

نوشتاری

مأمورِ گذرنامه: سلام، ـــــــــــــ تان را لطفاً بدهید.

کاوه: گذرنامه‌ی ایرانی یا خارجی؟

مأمورِ گذرنامه: ایرانی.

کاوه: بفرمایید. این گذرنامه ـــــــــــــ ـــــــــــــ.

مأمورِ گذرنامه: شما قبلاً هم در ایران بوده‌اید؟

کاوه: بله! وقتی بچّه بودم با پدر و مادرم به ایران آمده بودیم.

مأمورِ گذرنامه: چه سالی به ایران آمده بودید؟

کاوه: دقیقاً نمی دانم چون خیلی بچّه بودم. پدرم به من گفته بود. شاید سال ۱۳۶۲ بوده است.

مأمورِ گذرنامه: ـــــــــــــ هم دارید؟

کاوه: بله! شنیده بودم که لازم می‌شود، بفرمایید.

مأمورِ گذرنامه: چند وقت ایران می‌مانید؟

کاوه: حدود یک ماه و نیم.

مأمورِ گذرنامه: سفر خوشی را در ایران برایتان آرزو می‌کنم.

تمرین ۲

گفتگوی بالا را با هم‌کلاسی‌تان تمرین کنید.

🎧 واژگان ۳

We change/exchange	عَوَض می‌کنیم (کُن)	If possible	اَگر می‌شَوَد/اَگه می‌شه
Credit card	کارتِ اعتباری	I may/should pay	بِپَردازم (پَرداز)
Especially	مخصوصاً	Operator	تِلِفُنچی
I stay	می‌مانم/می‌مونم (مان)	I had wanted/requested	خواسته بودم (خواه)
Hotel	هُتِل	Noise	سَر و صِدا
Elevator	آسانسور	We are not busy (anymore)	سَرمان خلوت شده است/سَرِمون خلوت شده
Single room	اتاقِ یک تخته/اتاقِ یه تخته	We were busy	سَرمان شلوغ بود/سَرِمون شلوغ بود
I should/may make a reservation	رِزِرو کُنَم (کُن)	I am sorry	شَرمَنده‌ام

کتاب را ببندید و به گفتگو گوش کنید. سپس جاهای خالی را پر کنید.

🎧 گفتگو ۳

تلفنچی: هتل نیاوران، بفرمایین.

کاوه: روزتون به خیر. می‌خواستم یه اتاق تو هتلتون رزرو کنم.

تلفنچی: بله، در خدمتتون هستم. برای چه تاریخی؟

کاوه: هیفده خرداد می‌رسم و سه شب اونجا می‌مونم.

تلفنچی: اتاق یه تخته می‌خواین یا دو تخته؟

کاوه: یه تخته. اگه می‌شه دور از ــــــــــ باشه.

تلفنچی: چشم، حتماً.

کاوه: قیمتِ اتاق با صبونه‌ست؟

تلفنچی: بله. صبونه از ساعت هفت تا دهه.

کاوه: می‌تونم با ــــــــــ بِپردازم؟

تلفنچی: بله، حتماً.

در هتل نیاوران

کارمندِ هتل: بفرمایین.

کاوه: سلام، آقا. من دیشب تا صبح نتونستم بخوابم چون سر و صدا خیلی زیاد بود.

کارمندِ هتل: ــــــــــ‌ام جناب. از کجا سر وصدا می‌اومد؟

کاوه: از آسانسور. من مخصوصاً اتاقِ دور از آسانسور خواسته بودم ولی اتاقم کنارِ آسانسوره!

کارمندِ هتل: شرمنده! ما دیشب خیلی سَرِمون شلوغ بود ولی امروز سَرِمون خلوت شده. اتاقتونو همین الان عوض می‌کنیم. پولِ اتاقِ دیشبتون هم مهمونِ ما!

کاوه: چه عالی! ممنون!

کارمندِ هتل: خواهش می‌کنم!

نوشتاری

تلفنچی: هتل نیاوران، بفرمایید.

کاوه: روزتان به خیر. می‌خواستم یک اتاق در هتلتان رزرو کنم.

تلفنچی: بله، در خدمتتان هستم. برای چه تاریخی؟

کاوه: هفده خرداد می‌رسم و سه شب آنجا _____.

تلفنچی: اتاق یک تخته می‌خواهید یا دو تخته؟

کاوه: یک تخته. اگر _____ دور از آسانسور باشد.

تلفنچی: چشم، حتماً.

کاوه: قیمتِ اتاق با صبحانه‌ست؟

تلفنچی: بله، صبحانه از ساعت هفت تا ده است.

کاوه: می‌توانم با کارتِ اعتباری بپردازم؟

تلفنچی: بله، حتماً.

در هتل نیاوران

تلفنچی: بفرمایید.

کاوه: سلام، آقا. من دیشب تا صبح نتوانستم بخوابم چون سر و صدا خیلی زیاد بود.

تلفنچی: شرمنده‌ام جناب. از کجا سر وصدا می‌آمد؟

کاوه: از سمتِ آسانسور. من مخصوصاً اتاقِ دور از آسانسور خواسته بودم ولی اتاقم کنارِ آسانسور است!

تلفنچی: شرمنده! ما دیشب خیلی سرمان شلوغ بود ولی امروز سرمان خلوت‌تر شده است. اتاقتان را همین الان عوض می‌کنیم. پولِ اتاقِ دیشبتان را هم مهمانِ ما _____!

کاوه: چه عالی! ممنون!

کارمندِ هتل: خواهش می‌کنم!

تمرین ۳ 👥

گفتگوی بالا را با هم‌کلاسی‌تان تمرین کنید:

تمرین ۴

شش واژه پیدا کنید که فرمِ نوشتاری و گفتاری‌شان با هم متفاوت است و آنها را در جدولِ زیر بنویسید.

نوشتاری ←	گفتاری	نوشتاری ←	گفتاری

واژگان ۴ 🎧

Handicrafts	صَنایعِ دستی	Turn! (Plural & Formal)	بِپیچید!/ بِپیچین! (پیچ)
Excuse me	عُذر می‌خواهم/ عُذ می‌خوام	Return! (Plural & Formal)	بَرگَردید/ برگردین (بَرگَرد)
Before …	قَبل از	After …	بَعد از
Alley/Residential street	کوچه	House number	پلاک
You have passed	گُذَشته‌اید/ گُذَشتین (گُذَر)	Left	چَپ
Unfortunately	مُتأسِّفانه	Intersection	چهارراه
Straight (direction)	مُستَقیم	Left side	دستِ چپ
Roundabout	میدان/ میدون	Right	راست
I have forgotten	یادم رفته است/ یادم رفته	Passerby	رَهگُذَر

کتاب را ببندید و به گفتگو گوش کنید. سپس جاهای خالی را پر کنید.

گفتگو ۴ 🎧

در خیابان

خانم کامیاب: ببخشین آقا شما می‌دونین فروشگاهِ صنایع دستیِ «آریا» کجاست؟

رهگذر۱: اسمش رو شنیدم ولی یادم رفته. آدرسش چیه؟

خانم کامیاب: خیابونِ وَنَک، میدونِ شیراز، کوچه‌ی یکم.

رهگذر۱: ————— برین، بعد از چهارراهِ دوّم بپیچین دست چپ.

خانم کامیاب: کوچه‌ی یکم قبل از میدونه یا بعد از میدون؟

رهگذر۱: ————— نمی‌دونم، باید اونجا بپرسین.

خانم کامیاب: خیلی ممنون، سپاسگزارم.

در میدان شیراز

خانم کامیاب: عذ می‌خوام جناب، فروشگاهِ صنایع دستیِ «آریا» کجاست؟

رهگذر۲: ازش گذشتین. باید برگردین. قبل از میدونه.

خانم کامیاب: دست چپه یا دست راست؟

رهگذر۲: دست چپه.

خانم کامیاب: ممنون!

خانم کامیاب: ببخشید آقا شما می دانید فروشگاهِ صنایعِ _____ «آریا» کجا است؟

رهگذر۱: اسمش را شنیده‌ام ولی یادم رفته _____. آدرسش چیست؟

خانم کامیاب: خیابانِ ونک، میدانِ شیراز، کوچه‌ی یکم.

رهگذر۱: مستقیم بروید بعد از چهارراهِ دوّم دستِ چپ بپیچید.

خانم کامیاب: کوچه‌ی یکم قبل از _____ است یا بعد از میدان؟

رهگذر۱: متأسّفانه نمی دانم باید آنجا بپرسید.

خانم کامیاب: خیلی ممنون، سپاسگزارم.

در میدان شیراز

خانم کامیاب: عذر می‌خواهم جناب، فروشگاهِ صنایع دستیِ«آریا» کجا است؟

رهگذر۲: از آن گذشته‌اید. باید برگردید. قبل از میدان است.

خانم کامیاب: دستِ چپ است یا دستِ راست؟

رهگذر۲: دست چپ است.

خانم کامیاب: ممنون!

مُتَضاد		مُتَرادف	
چَپ ≠ راست	روادید = ویزا	گُذرنامه = پاسپورت	
قَبل از ≠ بعد از	سپاسگُزارم =مرسی = ممنون	عُذر می‌خواهم = ببخشید	

تمرین ۵

With a classmate, use the instructions provided in the above dialogue and draw a map that shows how to get to the Caspian Hotel.

تمرین ۶ 👥

Task: Use Dialogue 4 as a model and work with a classmate to provide directions for getting from your classroom to your school library. Use the spoken form of Persian.

تمرین ۷ واژگان

جاهای خالی را با واژگانِ جدید پرکنید.

توقّف ــ قبلاً ــ تَحصیلات ــ چهارراه ــ سر و صدا ــ بعد از ــ یک تخته ــ آژانس ــ گذرنامه ــ چپ

۱. لادن در _____ هواپیماییِ پرسپولیس کار می‌کند.

۲. پدر و مادرِ من ———————— در ایران زندگی می‌کردند.

۳. ———————— من باطل شده ولی برای آن درخواست کرده‌ام.

۴. پروازِ شما در آمستردام چند ساعت ———————— دارد؟

۵. اتاقِ ———————— می‌خواهید یا دو تخته؟

۶. ببخشید جناب، بیمارستان قبل از ———————— است؟

۷. آقا ما دیشب تا صبح نتونستیم بخوابیم چون ———————— خیلی زیاد بود.

۸. منزلِ ما کوچه‌ی یکم است که ———————— میدانِ ونک است.

❧ بیشتر بدانیم

🎧 Handicrafts صَنایعِ دَستی

مینا کاری

خاتَم کاری

تِرمه

قَلَم زنی

 تمرین ۸

Task: With a classmate, search online to learn more about the above Persian handicrafts. Describe them in 3-4 sentences. Talk about their colors, size, and fabric. Use comparative and superlative adjectives. Compare them with handicrafts of your country.

دستور زبان ۱

PRESENT PERFECT TENSE گذشته‌ی نقلی

The present perfect (or narrative) tense is used to describe either an action that began in the past and continues in the present, or a past action whose effect still exists. In English, the present perfect tense is formed by using the verb "*To Have*" and the past participle form of the main verb (ex: *I have gone there*). In Persian the short form of "*To Be*" is used with the participle form to constitute the present perfect tense. Example:

من در دانشگاه فارسی خوانده‌ام. I have studied Persian at the University

To form the Present Perfect Tense:

1) Form the **Past Participle** of the verb by adding ﮫ to the **past stem** of the verb:

Past Participle	Past Stem	Infinitive
خندیده	خندید ←	خندیدن
درس خوانده	درس خواند ←	درس خواندن

2) Add the **short form** of the verb بودن in the present tense to the **past participle**.

خندیدن

خندیده‌ایم	ما	خندیده‌ام	من
خندیده‌اید	شما	خندیده‌ای	تو
خندیده‌اند	آنها	خندیده است	او

درس خواندن

درس خوانده‌ایم	ما	درس خوانده‌ام	من
درس خوانده‌اید	شما	درس خوانده‌ای	تو
درس خوانده‌اند	آنها	درس خوانده است	او

In written form, stress falls on the final syllable of the past participle (ex: khandid**é** am). In spoken form, the final syllable of the past participle is shortened and stress falls on the personal ending (ex: khandid**á**m). Thus, the pronunciation of the spoken present perfect tense is very similar to that of the simple past tense.

The difference between the simple past tense and the spoken form of the present perfect tense is that in the former stress falls on the final syllable of the past stem (ex: khand**í**dam), whereas in the latter stress falls on the personal ending (ex: khandid**á**m).

In spoken form, است is dropped from the third person singular form. Example:

Written	خندیده است
Spoken	خندیده

NEGATION

To negate the present perfect tense, add the negative prefix نَ to the beginning of the verb. نَ carries stress (ex: nákhandide am).

خندیدن

نَخندیدهایم	ما	نَخندیدهام	من
نَخندیدهاید	شما	نَخندیدهای	تو
نَخندیدهاند	آنها	نَخندیده است	او

درس خواندن

درس نَخواندهایم	ما	درس نَخواندهام	من
درس نَخواندهاید	شما	درس نَخواندهای	تو
درس نَخواندهاند	آنها	درس نَخوانده است	او

MORE ON THE USAGE

English Present Progressive → Persian Present Perfect

As we saw in Lesson 8, in Persian, if a verb denotes a constant state (such as sitting, standing, being asleep, wearing certain clothes, etc.), as opposed to an activity (laughing, studying, eating, etc.), instead of the **present progressive** form, it would be in **present perfect** tense. Examples:

English		Persian	
I am eating. *(Present Progressive)*	*(Present Progressive)*	۱. من دارم غذا میخورم.	
I am sitting. *(Present Progressive)*	*(Present Perfect)*	۲. من نشستهام.	

Sentence 1 contains an activity verb, so the **present progressive** form is obtained normally.

Sentence 2 has a verb which denotes a constant state (being seated) so the **present progressive** form is replaced with the **present perfect** tense.

Sentence 2 can be used in the **present progressive** form as in 3. However, sentence 3 refers to the process of achieving that state, not the final result (being seated).

I am about to sit.	*(Present Progressive)*	۳. من دارم مینشینم.

English Simple Present → Persian Present Perfect

For certain verbs, a sentence in the **simple present** tense in English has a **present perfect** tense in Persian. These verbs are limited and can be memorized for future use. Examples:

English Usage: Simple Present	Persian Usage: Present Perfect
I miss you.	۱. دلم برایت تنگ شده است. / دلم برات تنگ شده.
I am sad.	۲. دلم گرفته است. / دلم گرفته.
Babak is late.	۳. بابک دیر کرده است. / بابک دیر کرده.
S/he is dead.	۴. او مُرده است. / اون مُرده.

تمرین ۹

فعل‌های بخشِ دستور زبان را با هم‌کلاسی‌تان بخوانید:

تمرین ۱۰

فعل‌های زیر را در زمان گذشته‌ی نقلی صرف کنید:

۱. دوستِ من برای تو نامه _____ . (نوشتن)

۲. پدر و مادرِ من در این خانه _____ .(زندگی کردن)

۳. من از مدرسه به خانه _____ . (برگشتن)

۴. ما آن کتاب‌ها را _____ . (خواندن ـ منفی)

۵. علی و مریم به مدرسه _____ . (رفتن ـ منفی)

۶. شما از مدرسه _____ ؟ (آمدن)

۷. دوست‌های من خیلی _____ . (درس خواندن)

۸. او کتابِ خوبی _____ . (خریدن ـ منفی)

۹. من هم برای گذرنامه‌ام _____ . (درخواست کردن)

۱۰. آنها به پسرشان _____ . (گفتن)

تمرین ۱۱

Describe what you see in each picture. You can write about the position of the people (sitting or standing), what they are wearing, or what they are doing. For the second image indicate that the girl is eating an apple. Remember that sometimes a sentence that requires a present progressive tense in English needs a present perfect tense in Persian.

۲. _____   ۱. _____

_____   _____

۴. _____   ۳. _____

_____   _____

تمرین ۱۲

جملاتِ زیر را به فارسی ترجمه کنید. به فرمِ نوشتاری بنویسید و با صدای بلند بخوانید .

1. I have eaten an ice cream.

2. My parents have never returned to Iran.

3. I think your passport has expired.

4. I have not gone to Tabriz yet.

5. They have told her about me.

6. I have never seen that hotel.

7. Have you watched this film?

تمرین ۱۳ : واژگان

زیر واژه‌ای که با بقیه مطابقت ندارد خط بکشید:

آسانسور	بقّالی	بنگاه	۱. آژانس
کوچه	خیابان	میدان	۲. پلاک
مستقیم	کنار	به سمت	۳. همین الان
حتماً	توقّف	مخصوصاً	۴. دقیقاً
مالیات	کشور	وطن	۵. خارجی
رفته‌ایم	خورده‌ایم	برگشته‌ایم	۶. پیچیده‌ایم
شرمنده‌ام!	ببخشید!	عذر می‌خواهم!	۷. نوش جان!
امیدواریم	دلمان گرفته	دوست داریم	۸. آرزو می‌کنیم

 دستور زبان ۲

PAST PERFECT TENSE گذشته‌ی بَعید

The past perfect tense is used to describe an action that took place prior to another past action or prior to a specific time in the past. In English, the past tense of the verb "*To Have*" is used with the past participle of the main verb to form the past perfect tense (ex: *I had gone there*). In Persian, the past form of the verb "*To Be*" is added to the past participle of the main verb to form past perfect tense. Example:

Before I went to Iran, I had watched this film. قبل از اینکه به ایران بروم، این فیلم را دیده بودم.

To form the Past Perfect Tense:

1) Form the past participle of the verb.

2) Add the conjugated form of بودن in the past tense.

خندیدن

خندیده بودیم	ما	خندیده بودم	من
خندیده بودید	شما	خندیده بودی	تو
خندیده بودند	آنها	خندیده بود	او

Stress falls on the final syllable of the past participle (ex: khandidéh budam).

درس خواندن

درس خوانده بودیم	ما	درس خوانده بودم	من
درس خوانده بودید	شما	درس خوانده بودی	تو
درس خوانده بودند	آنها	درس خوانده بود	او

Exception: بودن cannot be conjugated in the past perfect tense: بوده بوده‌ام *

NEGATION

To negate the past perfect tense, add the negative prefix نَ to the beginning of the verb. نَ carries stress (nákhandideh budam).

خندیدن

نخندیده بودیم	ما	نخندیده بودم	من
نخندیده بودید	شما	نخندیده بودی	تو
نخندیده بودند	آنها	نخندیده بود	او

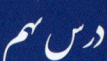

درس خواندن

درس نخوانده بودیم	ما	درس نخوانده بودم	من
درس نخوانده بودید	شما	درس نخوانده بودی	تو
درس نخوانده بودند	آنها	درس نخوانده بود	او

MORE ON THE USAGE

English Past Progressive → Persian Past Perfect

Similar to what we learned for the present perfect, if a verb denotes a constant state (such as sitting, standing, being asleep, wearing certain clothes, etc.), as opposed to an activity (laughing, studying, eating, etc.) the **past perfect** tense is used instead of the **past progressive** form. Examples:

English	Persian
I was eating. (Past Progressive)	(Past Progressive) ۱. من داشتم غذا می‌خوردم.
I was sitting. (Past Progressive)	(Past Perfect) ۲. من نشسته بودم.

Sentence 1 has an activity verb, so the **past progressive** form is obtained normally. Sentence 2 has a verb that denotes a constant state (being seated) so the **past progressive** form is replaced with the **past perfect**. If sentence 2 is used with a **past progressive** verb (as in 3), the sentence refers to the process of achieving that state, not the final result (being seated).

I was about to sit.	(Past Progressive)	۳. من داشتم می‌نشستم.

English Simple past → Persian Past Perfect

For certain verbs, a sentence in the **simple past** tense in English, has a **past perfect** tense in Persian. These verbs are very limited and can be memorzied for future use. Examples:

English Usage: Simple Past	Persian Usage: Past Perfect
I missed you.	۱. دلم برایت/ برات تنگ شده بود.
I was sad.	۲. دلم گرفته بود.
Babak was late.	۳. بابک دیر کرده بود.
He was dead.	۴. او/ اون مرده بود.

تمرین ۱۴

فعل‌های بخشِ دستور زبان را با هم‌کلاسیِ‌تان بخوانید:

تمرین ۱۵

فعل‌های زیر را در زمان گذشته‌ی بعید صرف کنید:

۱. من مخصوصاً به خانم پارسا ـــــــــــــ (گفتن) که به آن هتل نرود.

۲. گذرنامه ایرانی و آمریکایی‌تان حتماً ـــــــــــــ (باطل شدن)

۳. ما برای گذرنامه‌هایمان خیلی دیر ـــــــــــــ (درخواست کردن)

۴. وقتی به ایران ـــــــــــــ (رفتن) کارت شناسایی‌ام را با خودم ـــــــــــــ (بُردن/ منفی)

۵. من تمامِ شب را ـــــــــــــ (خوابیدن)

۶. او هنوز به مکزیک ـــــــــــــ (رسیدن/ منفی)

۷. دوست های من برای امتحان نهایی خیلی ـــــــــــــ (درس خواندن/ منفی)

۸. او کتابِ خوبی ـــــــــــــ (خریدن/ منفی)

تمرین ۱۶ 👄 👤

Work in pairs, groups, or as a class. Change the verb tense into the present perfect and then the past perfect. Example:

Student 1 (*book open*):   کدام فرش را خریدی؟
Student 2: (*book closed*):   کدام فرش را خریده‌ای؟
Student 3: (*book closed*):   کدام فرش را خریده بودی؟

Group 2	Group 1
۱. کریس کارشناسی ارشدش را تمام کرد؟	۱. تو چه غذایی سِفارِش دادی؟
۲. ما داریم درس می‌خوانیم.	۲. کی از این رنگ خوشش می‌آید؟
۳. من از ایران بیرون نمی‌روم.	۳. خانواده‌ی من در ایران زندگی می‌کنند.
۴. سفر خوشی را برایتان آرزو می‌کنم!	۴. گذرنامه‌ات کِی باطل می‌شود؟
۵. چند روز در این هتل می‌مانید؟	۵. جشنِ شبِ یَلدا خوب بود؟

تمرین ۱۷

به تصویرها نگاه کنید و جاهای خالی را با فعلِ مناسب پرکنید. از گذشته‌ی استمراری یا گذشته‌ی بعید استفاده کنید:

۲. می‌خواستم به انگلیس بروم، ولی نتوانستم چون

گذرنامه‌ام _____

۱. وقتی میشل را دیدم، او _____ _____

_____

۴. وقتی تلفن زنگ زد، من _____

_____

۳. وقتی تلفن زنگ زد، من _____

_____

تمرین ۱۸

Underline the present perfect and past perfect verbs in Dialogues 1-3. Explain why you think they are in the present perfect or the past perfect tense.

تمرین ۱۹

Find the verb of each sentence and change it to the **present perfect** and then the **past perfect** tense. Pronounce them aloud. Pronounce the present perfect verb in spoken form.

Past Perfect	Present Perfect	
		۱. ممنون. من غذا نمی‌خورم.
		۲. تاریخِ ایران از کی شروع شد؟
		۳. من به مهمانانِ خارجی کمک می‌کنم.
		۴. دوستِ خارجیِ من به مکزیک برگشت.
		۵. امتحان ساعت چند شروع می‌شود؟
		۶. این کتاب را دیدم ولی نخریدم.
		۷. آنها به فروشگاهِ صنایعِ دستی رفتند.

تمرین ۲۰

متنِ زیر را بخوانید و به پرسش‌های زیر پاسخِ کامل دهید.

هواپیمایی «هُما» از مسافرینِ عزیز خواهش می‌کند که نکاتِ زیر را به هنگامِ رزرو بلیت به ما اطّلاع دهند:

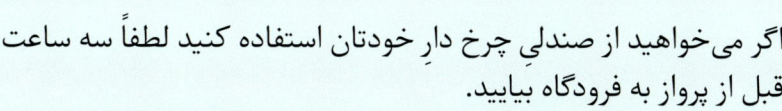

ـ اگر در گروه‌های۷ نفره یا بیشتر مسافرت می‌نمایید.

ـ اگر زبان‌های انگلیسی یا فارسی را نمی‌دانید.

ـ اگر مشکل شنیدن یا دیدن دارید.

ـ اگر با بیشتر از شش بچّه مسافرت می‌کنید.

اگر می‌خواهید از صندلی چرخ دارِ خودتان استفاده کنید لطفاً سه ساعت قبل از پرواز به فرودگاه بیایید.

۱. مسافران باید چه نکاتی را هنگامِ رزرو بلیت اطلاع دهند؟

۲. اگر مسافران مشکل شنیدن یا دیدن دارند باید چه کار کنند؟

۳. اگر مسافران می‌خواهند از صندلیِ چرخدارِ خودشان استفاده کنند باید کی به فرودگاه بروند؟

۴. نام شرکتِ هواپیمایی چیست؟

تمرین ۲۱

Task: Jennifer is staying at the International Persepolis Hotel in Shiraz. Look at the map and provide directions for her to get to Hafez's tomb and from there to Sa'di's tomb and then back to her hotel. Use the directional vocabulary that you learned in Dialogue 4.

What do you think the word بُلوار means?

تمرین ۲۲

با کلمات زیر جمله بسازید:

۱. خیلی ـ امسال ـ شده است ـ هوای تابستانِ تهران ـ گرم

۲. جنوب غربی ـ قرار دارد ـ استان کرمانشاه ـ ایران ـ در

۳. را ـ من ـ پروازِ مستقیم ـ از پروازِ با توقّف ـ بیشتر ـ دوست دارم

۴. رانندگی کرده ام ـ از تهران ـ تا شیراز را ـ در هفت ساعت ـ من

۵. باطل شده است ـ پس حتماً ـ گذرنامه‌ی ایرانی ـ و ـ آمریکایی‌تان

۶. کجاست ـ شما ـ ببخشید آقا ـ صنایع دستی کاسپیَن ـ می‌دانید ـ؟

314

بیشتر بدانیم

 **Money & Currency**

Small change	پولِ خُرد/ پول خورد	Paper money	اِسکِناس
Iran cheque	ایران چِک	Coin	سِکّه
Credit card	کارتِ اِعتِباری	ATM/Bank Machine	عابِر بانک
Currency exchange store	صَرّافی	Bank	بانک
Cash money	پولِ نَقد	Rial	ریال

تمرین ۲۳

گفتگوی زیر را با استفاده از واژگانِ بالا کامل کنید.

در _____ _____

خانم پارسا: سلام. خسته نباشین.

فروشنده: ممنون. روزتون به خیر.

خانم پارسا: ببخشین من کمی دلار داشتم، می‌خواستم به _____ _____ تبدیل کنم.

فروشنده: در خدمتتون هستم. دلارِ کجا هست؟

خانم پارسا: _____ کانادا.

فروشنده: چند دلاره؟

خانم پارسا: حدودِ هزار دلار.

فروشنده: متاسّفانه الان پولِ _____ نداریم. می‌تونم بهتون _____ _____ بدم.

خانم پارسا: همه جا می‌تونم ازش استفاده کنم؟

فروشنده: بله خانوم. ایران چِک دقیقاً مثلِ _____ـه. الان تو خیلی از فروشگاه‌ها از _____ هم می‌تونین استفاده کنین.

خانم پارسا: چه جالب! من نمی‌دونستم! باشه پس چِک بدین. راستی _____ _____ هم دارین؟ می‌خوام این هزار تومنی رو خورد کنم.

فروشنده: بله حتماً. این پولِ خورد و ایران _____ خدمتِ شما.

315

تمرین ۲۴

Below are some of the attractions of Iran. With a classmate, search online to find out about these sites based on your interests. Choose two places that you like and present your findings to the class.

Ski Areas	Beaches, Mineral Waters, & Caves	Monuments & Mausoleums	UNESCO World Heritage
دیزین	دریای خَزَر	نقشِ رستم	پرسپولیس
شِمشَک	جزیره‌ی کیش	مِنار جُنبان	بیستون
توچال	جزیره‌ی قِشم	آرامگاهِ حافظ	پاسارگاد
آبعلی	جزیره‌ی چاه بهار	آرامگاهِ سَعدی	چُغازَنبیل
	غارِ عَلی صَدر	آرامگاهِ فِردوسی	تختِ سلیمان
	آبگرمِ سَرعین	آرامگاهِ خَیّام	قَره کلیسا
		آرامگاهِ عَطّار	باغِ فینِ کاشان

تمرین ۲۵

Read the following passage and try to understand the gist of it. Find four verbs in present perfect tense and answer the following questions. *Hint:* اِمپراطور means "emperor", یَهودی means "Jewish", and اِعلامیّه‌ی حُقوقِ بَشَر means "declaration of human rights".

کوروشِ بزرگ

«کوروشِ بزرگ» اوّلین امپراطورِ «هَخامَنِشی» بوده است. پدر و پدر بزرگِ کوروش هر دو از پادشاهانِ ایران بودند. کوروش یک مردِ بزرگ بود. درسالِ ۵۳۷ پیش از میلاد، کوروش شهرِ «بابِل» را گرفت و بیشتر از چهل هزار یَهودی را که در زندان‌های «بابِل» بودند آزاد کرد. نامِ کوروش در کتابِ مقدّس یهودیان آمده است. کوروش اوّلین «اِعلامیّه‌ی حقوق بشر» را نوشته است. اِعلامیّه‌ی حقوق بشر کوروش به چندین زبان ترجمه شده است. آرامگاهِ کوروشِ بزرگ در «پاسارگاد» در نزدیکیِ شهر شیراز است. پاسارگاد یکی از چهار پایتختِ امپراطوریِ «هَخامَنِشی» بوده است.

۱. کوروش چه کسی است؟

۲. نامِ کوروش در چه کتابی آمده است؟

۳. کوروش چه چیزی را نوشته است؟

۴. آرامگاهِ کوروشِ بزرگ درکجا و در نزدیکیِ چه شهری است؟

بیشتر بدانیم

POLITE, DEFAULT, & MODEST FORMS

We have already learned that in Persian, pronouns can have different forms to show respect, distance, and politeness. For instance the second person plural pronoun is used instead of the singular form to show respect and distance. In Lesson 4, we learned that the verb تشریف داشتن (To be present) is used instead of بودن to show respect and distance. In Lesson 7, we learned that the verb میل داشتن (To want) is used instead of خواستن to show respect. In the charts below, you can see that there is also a **modest** form for some of the verbs and pronouns. **When a speaker is using the polite form to show respect or distance, s/he may also use the modest form to refer to her/himself.** Therefore, the modest forms are mainly used for the first person singular. This concept does not exist in western culture so it may need some time to be absorbed. Examples:

Verbs

	Modest	Default	**Polite**
To be		بودن	تَشریف داشتن
To go		رفتن	تَشریف بُردَن
To come		آمدن	تَشریف آوردن
To say	عَرض کردن	گفتن	فَرمودن
To eat		خوردن	میل کردن
To want		خواستن	میل داشتن
To give	تَقدیم کردن	دادن	مَرحِمَت کردن

Pronouns

	Modest	Default	Polite
I	بَنده	من	
You (singular)		تو	جِناب ـ جنابعالی ـ سَرکار ـ شما
S/he		او	ایشان/ایشون

بَنده literally means "servant". سَرکار is used for females.

تمرین ۲۶

Underline the modest or polite forms in the following sentences and provide the other form/s:

۱. خوشحال می‌شیم فردا بیاین منزلِ ما.

۲. جناب، نوشیدنی چی میل دارین؟

۳. بنده عرض کردم که شرمنده‌ام!

۴. گذرنامه تون رو لطفاً مرحمت کنین.

۵. این ترانه را به وطنم تقدیم می‌کنم.

317

تمرین ۲۷

متنِ زیر را با استفاده از واژگانِ زیر کامل کنید و به پرسش‌های زیر پاسخ دهید:

دقیقه ــ شهر ــ آخرین ــ زیباترین ــ هنری ــ اتاق ــ خارجی

مهمانسرای عبّاسی

مهمانسرای عبّاسی یا «هتل شاه عبّاس» قدیمی‌ترین هتلِ ایران و یکی از قدیمی‌ترین هتل‌های جهان است.

مهمانسرای عبّاسی اوّلین هتلِ پنج ستاره‌ی ــــــــــــــ اصفهان است که بیشتر از سی صد سال قدمت دارد.

مهمانسرای عبّاسی از نوعِ معماری دوران صفوی است که بسیار تاریخی و زیباست. «شاه سُلطان حسینِ صَفَوی» که

ــــــــــــــ پادشاهِ صفوی بود این مهمانسرا را به مادرِ خود هدیه کرد. در قدیم نام این مهمانسرا «کاروانسَرای

مادرِ شاه سُلطان حسین» بود. در زمانِ حمله‌ی افغان‌ها این مهمانسرا ویران شد. در زمانِ «رضا شاهِ پَهلَوی» این

مهمانسرای با معماری ــــــــــــــ و تاریخیِ دورانِ صفَویّه بازسازی شد.

مهمانسرای عبّاسی صد و هشتاد و شش ــــــــــــــ و بیست و هفت سوئیت و نه آپارتمان دارد. این هتل

سالن‌های بسیار زیبایی به سبک دورانِ صفوی دارد. هر سال هزاران مهمان ــــــــــــــ از کشورهای مختلف به

دیدنِ هتل عبّاسی می‌آیند. مهمانسرای عبّاسی با ماشین چهل و پنج ــــــــــــــ با فرودگاه فاصله دارد.

Caravanserai of the mother of Shah Sultan Hussein by Pascal Coste, 1840.

۱. مهمانسرای عبّاسی چند سال قدمت دارد و نامِ دیگرِ آن چیست؟

۲. «شاه سُلطان حسینِ صَفَوی» این مهمانسرا را به چه کسی هدیه کرد؟

۳. در زمانِ چه کسی مهمانسرای عبّاسی بازسازی شد؟

۴. مهمانسرای عبّاسی چند ستاره است و چند سوئیت دارد؟

۵. مهمانسرای عبّاسی چقدر با فرودگاه فاصله دارد؟

تمرین ۲۸

به فایل صوتی گوش کنید و به سوال‌های زیر پاسخ کامل دهید . به زبان نوشتاری بنویسید.

۱. مسافرین می‌توانند چه چیزهایی را به داخل هواپیما ببرند؟

۲. ساعت حضور در ترمینال چیست؟

۳. اگر مسافرین در ساعات معیّن شده در ترمینال حاضر نباشند

بلیت آنها چه می شود؟

۴. آیا مسافرینی که بیمه‌ی سفر دارند می‌توانند از پروازِ بعدی استفاده کنند؟

۵. بیمه به انگلیسی یعنی چه؟

تمرین ۲۹

Task: John wants to visit Iran. He reads the following information on the visa application website.

- امور گذرنامه
- امور ثبت و احوال
- امور دانشجویی
- امور اجتماعی
- روادید
- فهرست هزینه‌ها
- پرسش و پاسخ
- پیوند آدرس الکترونیکی
- وضعیت پرونده

Which option is about visa-related issues? What does وضعیت پرونده mean? Which option is about students' affairs? What is the general idea of the sentence below? Underline the verbs and indicate what tense they are.

خوشنودیم به اطلاع برسانیم هم اکنون وضیعت پرونده خود را در این نمایندگی

از طریق اینترنت می‌توانید ببینید.

تمرین ۳۰

الف: به زبان نوشتاری تبدیل کنید:

۱. بله در خدمتتون هستم. چند ساله که نرفتین ایران؟

۲. مستقیم برین، بعد از چهار راهِ دوّم بپیچین دست چپ.

ب: به زبان گفتاری تبدیل کنید:

۱. چند سال است که به ایران نرفته‌اید؟

۲. سفر خوشی را در ایران برایتان آرزو می‌کنیم.

تمرین ۳۱ 👥

Task: With a classmate work on the following dialogue taking place at a travel agency. Improvise the answers. Use the spoken from and include **polite** and **modest** verbs and pronouns:

1. Ask if Mr. Kamyab is present. Ask when he will be back.

2. Ask if she is busy.

3. Tell the agent that you want to buy a ticket for Iran.

4. Ask if the price of the ticket includes the airport tax.

5. Ask for clarification by saying "what did you say?" using the polite form.

6. Find out if they have a student discount.

7. Ask if you can get a discount because you are a foreigner.

8. Ask if they can help you book a hotel room for 3 nights in Tehran and for 4 nights in Kish Island.

9. Tell the agent that you are a student and you want a three star hotel.

10. Tell her that you also want a quiet room.

11. Ask her if you can pay with a credit card.

12. Say thank you and good bye.

REVIEW CORNER	
Points that remain unclear about Lesson 9:	
How I plan to work on these points:	

شعر

Read the following poem by Rumi and try to find the familiar words. Underline the verbs in the present perfect tense. You will not be evaluated on the content but you can use it for cultural enrichment.

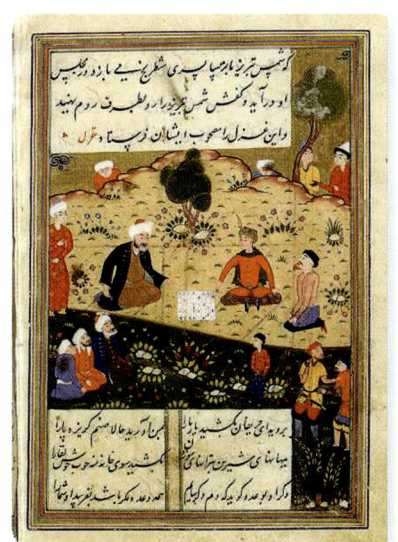

Illustration of a scene from Rumi's poetry, 1503.

هین کژ و راست می‌روی، باز چه خورده‌ای بگو

مست و خراب می‌روی، خانه به خانه کو به کو

با که حریف بوده‌ای، بوسه ز کی ربوده‌ای

زلف که را گشوده‌ای، حلقه به حلقه مو به مو

نی تو حریف کی کنی، ای همه چشم و روشنی

خفیه روی چو ماهیان، حوض به حوض جو به جو

راست بگو به جان تو، ای دل و جانم آن تو

ای دل همچو شیشه‌ام، خورده میت کدو کدو

راست بگو نهان مکن، پشت به عاشقان مکن

چشمه کجاست تا که من، آب کشم سبو سبو

شاعر: مولوی (رومی) (۱۲۷۳ـ۱۲۰۷)

321

ترانه

Listen to the following song by Kourosh Yaghmaie on YouTube and try to find the familiar words. Underline the verbs in the present perfect tense. Find at least five words in spoken form and provide their written counterpart. You will not be evaluated on the content but you can use it for cultural enrichment.

گلِ یخ

غم میون دو تا چشمون قشنگت، لونه کرده
شب تو موهای سیاهت، خونه کرده

دو تا چشمون سیاهت، مثل شب‌های منه
سیاهی‌های دو چشمت، مثل غم‌های منه

وقتی بغض از مژه‌هام پایین می‌آد، بارون میشه
سیل غم آبادیمو ویرونه کرده

وقتی با من می‌مونی تنهاییمو، باد می‌بره
دو تا چشمام بارونِ شبونه کرده

بهار از دستای من پر زد و رفت
گل یخ توی دلم جَوونه کرده

تو اتاقم دارم از تنهایی آتیش می‌گیرم
ای شکوفه توی این زمونه کرده

چی بخونم جوونیم رفته، صدام رفته دیگه
گل یخ توی دلم جوونه کرده

چی بخونم جوونیم رفته، صدام رفته دیگه
گل یخ توی دلم جوونه کرده

خواننده: کوروش یَغمایی

322

نکته‌ی فرهنگی

Tips on Traveling to Iran:

The majority of Iran's population is young. A high percentage are college graduates and many of them have post-graduate degrees. Iranians have great reverence for the literary traditions of the country and the shrines of the great poets are mobbed. Even the illiterate elderly know the poetry of Hafez and Sa'adi by heart. Family connections are at the heart of Iranian culture. Iranians are among the most hospitable people in the world. Tourists often are asked to join people for tea, lunch, or on a picnic.

The best time to travel to Iran is in spring or fall. Summers are too hot and winters are mild or cold. The south of Iran enjoys a nice climate in the winter so traveling to the south in the winter can be very pleasant. Driving in Iran can be risky so it is not a good idea for tourists to rent a car and drive. Due to the current Islamic laws, women and girls above the age of nine must cover their hair with a scarf and wear non-transparent clothing. Light colors and red are not put on during national mourning days. The chādor is not mandatory but it is required for visiting mosques. Men put on non-transparent clothing too. They may wear short-sleeved shirts but not shorts in public. The choice of color is the same for men as well. Health and hygiene are highly observed in Iran. However, public toilets on the roads may not be clean. Most of the public restrooms have Turkish toilets (as shown in the picture below). Some private residences have western style toilets. Pubic restrooms may or may not have toilet paper but there is running water for cleaning up instead.

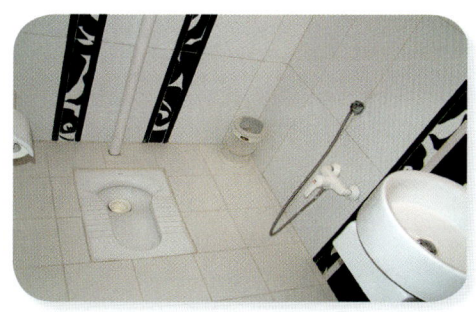

The currency is called the Iranian Rial (IR). However, the word Toman is used more often in interactions (10 IR = 1 Toman). International credit cards cannot be used in Iran but Iranian banks offer debit cards that can only be used in Iran. The use of a certain kind of travelers' cheque issued by the Central Bank of Iran (Iran Cheque) has recently become widespread. Here are some of the Iranian bills and coins.

Ten Thousand Rials

Hundred Thousand Rials

Iran Cheque

Different Coins

ضرب المثل

Literal translation: *What came with the wind went with the wind!*

(Easy come, easy go!)

باد آورده را باد می‌بَرَد!

324

Thematic Review of New Vocabulary

Traveling	
Travel agency	آژانسِ مُسافَرَتی
Ticket	بلیت
Passport	پاسپورت
Flight	پَرواز
Stop/Lay over	تَوَقُّف
Foreign/Foreigner	خارجی
Visa	رَوادید ـ ویزا
Airport	فُرودگاه
Passport	گُذَرنامه
Tax	مالیات
Hotel	هتل
Airline	هَواپیمایی
Homeland	وَطَن

Asking for Directions	
After...	بعد از ...
House number	پِلاک
Left	چَپ
Intersection	چهارراه
Left side	دستِ چَپ
Right	راست
Passerby	رَهگُذَر
Before ...	قَبل از ...
Alley/Residential street	کوچه
Straight (direction)	مُستَقیم
Roundabout	میدان

Nouns & Adjectives	
Single room	اتاقِ یک تخته
Elevator	آسانسور
Insurance	بیمه
Date/History	تاریخ
Operator	تِلِفُنچی
Noise	سَر و صدا
Page	صَفحه
Handicrafts	صَنایع دستی
Identification card	کارتِ شناسایی
Customs/Immigration officer	مأمورِ گُذَرنامه

Expressions	
Here you are	خِدمتِ شما
We are not busy (anymore)	سَرمان خَلوَت شده است
We were busy	سَرمان شُلوغ بود
Have a nice trip!	سَفَر خوشی را برایتان آرزو می‌کنم
I am thankful	سِپاسگُزارَم
I am sorry	شَرمَنده‌ام
I am at your service	درخِدمَتِتان هستم
Excuse me	عُذر می‌خواهم

About Currency	
Paper money	اِسکِناس
Iran cheque	ایران چِک
Bank	بانک
Small change	پولِ خُرد
Cash money	پولِ نَقد
Rial (Iranian currency)	ریال
Coin	سِکّه
Currency exchange store	صَرّافی
ATM/Bank Machine	عابِر بانک
Credit card	کارتِ اِعتِباری

Handicrafts	
Persian handicraft	تِرمه
Persian handicraft	خاتم کاری
Persian handicraft	قَلَم زنی
Persian handicraft	مینا کاری

Words & Phrases	
If possible	اگر می‌شَوَد
End of...	آخِرِ...
Of course	اَلبَتّه
Approximately/About	حُدود
Unfortunately	مُتِأسِّفانه
Especially	مَخصوصاً
Both	هَر دو

Verb	Modest	Default	Polite
To come		آمدن	تَشریف آوَردن
To go		رفتن	تَشریف بُردَن
To be		بودن	تَشریف داشتن
To say	عَرض کردن	گفتن	فَرمودن
To give	تَقدیم کردن	دادن	مَرحَمَت کردن
To want		خواستن	میل داشتن
To eat		خوردن	میل کردن

Pronoun	Modest	Default	Polite
I	بَنده	من	
You (Singular)		تو	جِنابعالی – جِناب ـ سَرکار ـ شما
S/he		او	ایشان

Verbs	
I wish	آرزو می‌کنم (کردن: کُن)
You had come (Plural & Formal)	آمده بودید (آمَدن: آ)
Has expired	باطل شده است (شُدَن: شَو)
I may/should pay	بپردازم (پرداختن: پَرداز)
Turn! (Plural & Formal)	بپیچید (پیچیدن: پیچ)
Return! (Plural & Formal)	برگَردید (برگَشتن: گَرد)
I have not retuned	برنگشته‌ام (برگَشتن: گَرد)
Has been	بوده‌است (بودن: هَست)
You have been (Plural & Formal)	بوده‌اید (بودن: هَست)
I have not gone out	بیرون نرفته‌ام (رَفتن: رَو)
I had wanted/requested	خواسته بودم (بودن: هست)
I have applied	درخواست کرده‌ام (کردن: کُن)
I should/may make a reservation	رِزرو کنم (کردن: کُن)
I had heard	شنیده‌بودم (شَنیدن: شِنَو)
We change/exchange	عوض می‌کنیم (کردن: کُن)
You have passed	گُذَشته‌اید (گُذَشتن: گُذَر)
He had said	گفته بود (گفتن: گو)
I get it	می‌گیرَمش (گرفتن: گیر)
I stay	می‌مانم (ماندن: مان)
You have not gone	نرفته‌اید (رَفتن: رَو)
I have forgotten (Psychological verb)	یادم رفته است (رَفتن: رَو)

ورزش و سرگرمی
Sports & Entertainment

 واژگان ۱

You're the bomb! (Slang)	چاکِرتَم	Awful	اِفتِضاح
We will see	خواهیم دید	This much!	این قَدر / انقَد
I had missed…	دِلَم تَنگ شده بود	Cool (Slang)	باحال
Boss	رَئیس	Game - Match	بازی
How much do you bet?	شَرطِ چند می‌بندی؟	You do not believe	باوَرَت نمی‌شَوَد! / باوَرِت نمی‌شه! (شَو)
Fan - Follower	طَرَفدار	Winner	بَرَنده
What luck!	عَجب شانسی!	Let's go (Slang)	بِزَن بِرویم / بِزَن بِریم
Match	مُسابقه	Shake on it! (Slang)	بِزَن قَدِش!
Sure - Certain	مُطمَئِن	Childhood	بَچِّگی
How is that possible?	مَگَر می‌شود؟ / مَگه می‌شه؟	Accidental - Accidentally	تصادُفی
Favorite	موردِ عَلاقه	Team	تیم
For (Spoken)	واسه	Serious - Seriously	جدّی
I have heard	شنیده‌ام / شنیدم	Swear to you	جانِ تو / جونِ تو

کتاب را ببندید و به گفتگو گوش کنید. سپس جاهای خالی را پر کنید.

🎧 گفتگو ۱

کامران: باورت نمی‌شه چی شده! امروز یکی از بهترین روزای زندگیمه!

کیارَش: بابا چی شده که انقد خوشحالی؟

کامران: خیلی باحال شد جونِ تو! رئیسم بهم دو تا بلیت داده واسه مسابقه‌ی جمعه شبِ «پرسپولیس» و «اِستقلال»!

کیارَش: _____ می‌گی؟ عجب شانسی! پس بزن بریم! دلم واسه تیمِ موردِ علاقه‌ام تنگ شده بود! من عاشق تیم استقلالم!

کامران: نه بابا! من نمی‌دونستم! مگه می‌شه؟یعنی تو طرفدارِ تیمِ پرسپولیس نیستی؟

کیارَش: من آبی آبی‌ام. تمام فامیلِ ما قرمزَن ولی من از _____ عاشقِ تیمِ استقلال بودم؛ هنوزم هستم!

کامران: شنیدم که بازیِ هفته‌ی پیششون خیلی _____ بوده!

کیارَش: اون که تصادفی بوده ولی من مطمئنم که جمعه استقلال برنده می‌شه!

کامران: خواهیم دید! شرطِ چند می‌بندی؟

کیارَش: یه چلو کباب! _____!

کامران: چاکرتم!

> In English, the word "cool" can be used by itself as in "Cool!". But in Persian, it cannot be used alone.

The written forms are provided for educational purposes as slang is not used in the written form.

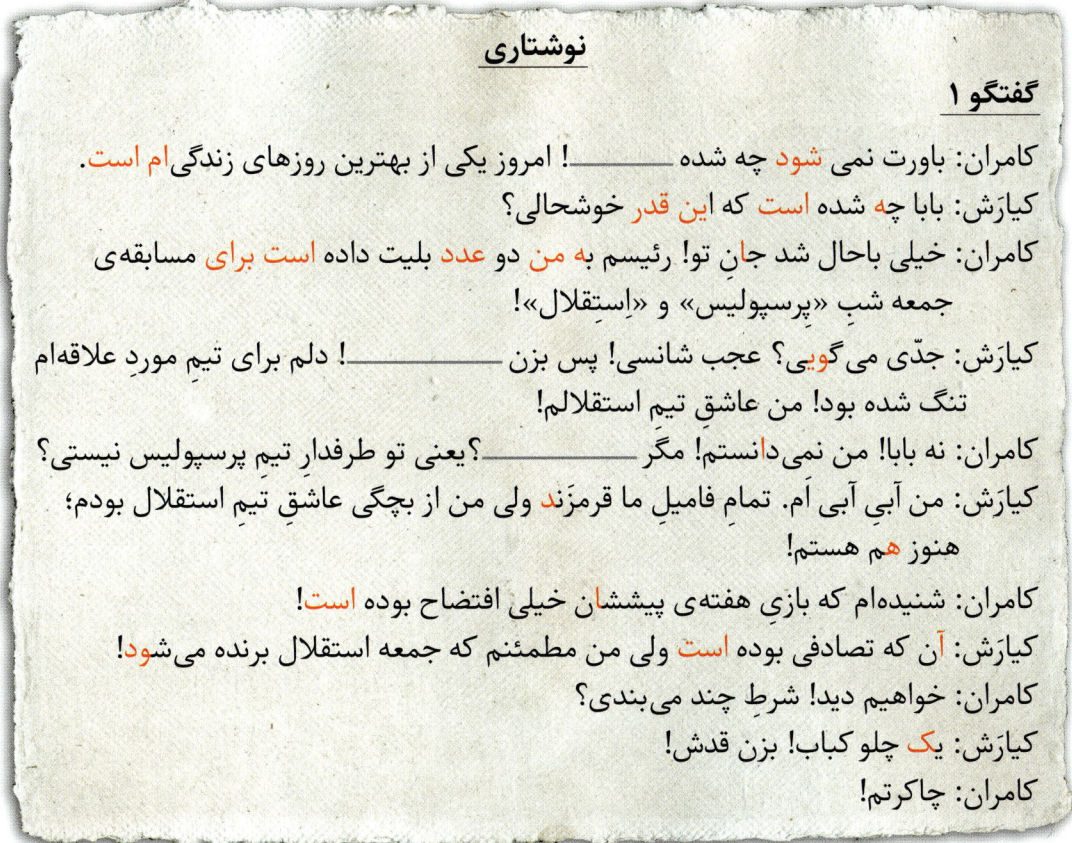

نوشتاری

گفتگو ۱

کامران: باورت نمی شود چه شده _____! امروز یکی از بهترین روزهای زندگی‌ام است.

کیارش: بابا چه شده است که این قدر خوشحالی؟

کامران: خیلی باحال شد جانِ تو! رئیسم به من دو عدد بلیت داده است برای مسابقه‌ی جمعه شبِ «پرسپولیس» و «استقلال»!

کیارش: جدّی می‌گویی؟ عجب شانسی! پس بزن _____! دلم برای تیمِ موردِ علاقه‌ام تنگ شده بود! من عاشق تیم استقلالم!

کامران: نه بابا! من نمی‌دانستم! مگر _____؟ یعنی تو طرفدارِ تیمِ پرسپولیس نیستی؟

کیارش: من آبی آبی‌ام. تمامِ فامیلِ ما قرمزند ولی من از بچّگی عاشقِ تیمِ استقلال بودم؛ هنوز هم هستم!

کامران: شنیده‌ام که بازیِ هفته‌ی پیششان خیلی افتضاح بوده است!

کیارش: آن که تصادفی بوده است ولی من مطمئنم که جمعه استقلال برنده می‌شود!

کامران: خواهیم دید! شرطِ چند می‌بندی؟

کیارش: یک چلو کباب! بزن قدش!

کامران: چاکرتم!

تمرین ۱

گفتگوی بالا را با هم‌کلاسی‌تان تمرین کنید:

واژگان ۲ 🎧

At work	سَرِ کار	Incidentally	اِتّفاقاً
Line - Queue	صَف	If you want	اَگر بخواهی/اگه بخوای
Director	کارگَردان	This way	این طوری
We may/should catch/find	گیربیاوَریم/گیربیاریم	After that (Spoken)	بَعدِش
Do you feel like…? (Slang)	حال داری؟	Positive reply to a negative question	چرا
I stand	می‌ایستم/وای می‌سَم	Festival	جَشنواره
		Late (time)	دیر وقت

کتاب را ببندید و به گفتگوی صفحه‌ی بعد گوش کنید. سپس جاهای خالی را پر کنید.

🎧 گفتگو ۲

رخشان بنی اعتماد

تهمینه میلانی

کاوه: فردا شب برنامه داری عزیزم؟ ————— بریم سینما؟

پریسا: من فکر کردم تا دیر وقت کار می‌کنی!

کاوه: نه ————— زود می‌آم خونه. اگه بخوای می‌تونیم بریم. جشنواره‌ی فیلم «فَجر» داره تموم می‌شه. فردا شب آخَرِشه!

پریسا: می‌گن فیلمای امسال خیلی عالی بوده! حالا فیلمش چیه؟ می‌دونی که من عاشقِ فیلمای تَهمینه میلانی‌ام!

کاوه: متأسّفانه کارگردانِ فیلم فردا تَهمینه میلانی نیست. رَخشان بَنی‌اعتماده. از کارای اون خوشت نمی‌آد؟

پریسا: چرا! خیلی کاراشو دوست دارم! فکر می‌کنی بتونیم بلیت گیر بیاریم؟ حتماً خیلی شلوغ می‌شه!

کاوه: آره. من از سرِ کار مستقیم می‌رم سینما تو ————— وای می‌سَّم تا تو بیای.

پریسا: این طوری عالیه! بعدش می‌تونیم بریم رستورانِ موردِ علاقه‌ی من!

نوشتاری

گفتگو ۲

کاوه: فردا شب برنامه داری عزیزم؟ حال داری به سینما برویم؟

پریسا: من فکرِ کردم تا دیر وقت کار می‌کنی!

کاوه: نه اتفاقاً زود به خانه می‌آیم. اگر بخواهی می‌توانیم برویم. ————— فیلمِ «فَجر» دارد تمام می‌شود. فردا شبِ آخرش است!

پریسا: می‌گویند فیلم‌های امسال خیلی عالی بوده است! حالا فیلمش چی است؟ می‌دانی که من عاشقِ فیلم‌های تَهمینه میلانی‌ام!

کاوه: متأسّفانه ————— فیلم فردا تَهمینه میلانی نیست. رَخشان بنی‌اعتماد است. از کارهای او خوشت نمی‌آید؟

پریسا: چرا! خیلی کارهایش را دوست دارم! فکر می‌کنی بتوانیم بلیت گیر بیاوریم؟ حتماً خیلی شلوغ می‌شود!

کاوه: بله. من از سرِ کار مستقیم به سینما می‌روم و در صف ————— تا تو بیایی.

پریسا: این طوری عالی است! بعدش هم می‌توانیم به رستورانِ موردِ علاقه‌ی من برویم!

💡
The affirmative answer to a negative question requires چرا:

از کارهای او خوشت نمی‌آید؟ چرا، خیلی!

تمرین ۲

گفتگوی بالا را با هم‌کلاسی‌تان تمرین کنید:

تمرین ۳ 👄 ✏

شش واژه پیدا کنید که فرمِ نوشتاری و گفتاری‌شان با هم متفاوت است و آنها را در جدولِ زیر بنویسید.

گفتاری	← نوشتاری	گفتاری	نوشتاری ←

خواندن 🎧

جشنواره‌ی بین‌المللیِ فیلمِ «رُشد»

جشنواره‌ی بین‌المللیِ فیلمِ رشد قدیمی‌ترین جشنواره‌ی فیلم در ایران است که هر سال در آبان ماه در تهران برگزار می‌شود. جشنواره‌ی فیلم رشد جشنواره‌ی فیلم‌های برترِ آموزشی است. این جشنواره نخستین بار در سال ۱۳۴۲ هجریِ شمسی برگزار شد. امسال بیشتر از بیست و شش کشور در این جشنواره شرکت خواهند کرد و سازمانِ «یونیسف» به فیلم های برنده جایزه خواهد داد. جشنواره‌ی بین‌المللیِ فیلم رشد بخش‌های مختلفی دارد مثلِ بخشِ فیلم‌های آموزشیِ کوتاه و بلند، بخشِ فیلم‌های مستندِ کوتاه و بلند، بخشِ فیلم‌های انیمیشنِ کوتاه و بلند، و بخشِ فیلم‌های داستانیِ کوتاه و بلندِ کودک و نوجوان.

Story - Fiction	داستان	Animation	اَنیمِیشن
Organization	سازمان	Educational	آموزِشی
They will attend	شِرکَت خواهَند کرد	Section - Part	بَخش
Old (for inanimates)	قَدیمی	Is organized	بَرگُزار می‌شود
Short	کوتاه	Was organized	بَرگُزار شد
Child	کودَک	Long	بُلَند
Various	مُختَلِف	International	بِین اُلمِلَلی
Documentary	مُستَنَد	Prize - Award	جایِزه
Adolescent	نوجَوان	Will give	خواهَد داد

تمرین ۴

به پرسش‌های زیر پاسخِ کامل دهید.

۱. جشنواره‌ی بین المللی فیلم رشد در کجا و کی برگزار می‌شود؟

۲. جشنواره‌ی فیلم رشد درباره‌ی چه فیلم‌هایی است؟

۳. جشنواره‌ی بین المللی فیلم رشد نخستین بار در چه سالی برگزار شد؟

۴. امسال چند کشور در این جشنواره شرکت خواهند کرد؟

۵. جشنواره‌ی بین المللی فیلم رشد چه بخش‌هایی دارد؟

۶. «یونیسف» چیست؟

۷. آیا کشورِ شما جشنواره‌ی فیلم‌های آموزشی دارد؟ نامِ آن جشنواره چیست؟

Antonyms			Synonyms	
قَدیمی ≠ جدید	کوتاه ≠ بلند	برنده ≠ بازَنده	داستان = قِصّه	کودَک = بچّه
	متأسّفانه ≠ خوشبَختانه	آخَر ≠ اوّل		بَخش = قِسمَت

تمرین ۵ واژگان

جملات زیر را با واژگان مناسب از لیستِ زیر کامل کنید:

شرط ــ طرفدار ــ کارگردان ــ مستند ــ برنده ــ شرکت خواهند کرد ــ حال داری ــ قدیمی‌ترین ــ بین المللی

۱. جشنواره‌ی بین المللی فیلم «رشد» ـــــــــــــ جشنواره‌ی فیلم در ایران است.

۲. فردا شب برنامه داری عزیزم؟ ـــــــــــــ بریم سینما؟

۳. امسال بیشتر از بیست کشور در این جشنواره ـــــــــــــ

۴. «رخشان بنی اعتماد» ـــــــــــــ موردِ علاقه‌ی من است.

۵. من نمی‌دانستم! یعنی تو ـــــــــــــ تیمِ پرسپولیس نیستی؟

۶. جشنواره‌ی فیلم «رشد» یک جشنواره‌ی ـــــــــــــ است.

۷. خواهیم دید! ـــــــــــــ چند می‌بندی؟

۸. سازمانِ «یونیسف» به فیلم‌های ـــــــــــــ جایزه خواهد داد.

درس دهم

دستور زبان ۱

FUTURE TENSE زمانِ آینده

In Lesson 3, we learned that the simple present tense can be used to describe actions taking place in the future. Persian also has a future tense, which is not commonly used in spoken form and is mainly used in the written form. The usage is similar to the English "will/shall" in a sentence such as "We shall see". The future tense may also be used for emphasis and clarity in the spoken form.

To form the Future Tense:

1) Conjugate خواستن in the **present tense** for the appropriate subject, but **do not** add the می prefix.

2) Add the **past stem** of the main verb (with no verb ending). Example: خواهم + خندید

خندیدن

خواهیم خندید	ما	خواهم خندید	من
خواهید خندید	شما	خواهی خندید	تو
خواهند خندید	آنها	خواهد خندید	او

For compound verbs, the conjugated خواستن is placed closest to the verbal component.

درس خواندن

درس خواهیم خواند	ما	درس خواهم خواند	من
درس خواهید خواند	شما	درس خواهی خواند	تو
درس خواهند خواند	آنها	درس خواهد خواند	او

NEGATION

To negate the future tense, attach the negative prefix نَ to the conjugated form of خواستن in the present tense.

خندیدن

نخواهیم خندید	ما	نخواهم خندید	من
نخواهید خندید	شما	نخواهی خندید	تو
نخواهند خندید	آنها	نخواهد خندید	او

درس خواندن

درس نخواهیم خواند	ما	درس نخواهم خواند	من
درس نخواهید خواند	شما	درس نخواهی خواند	تو
درس نخواهند خواند	آنها	درس نخواهد خواند	او

تمرین ۶

فعل‌های بخشِ دستور زبان را با هم‌کلاسی‌تان بخوانید.

تمرین ۷

فعل‌های زیر را در زمانِ آینده صرف کنید:

۱. کلاسِ مینا ساعت هفت ــــــــــــــــــــ . (تمام شدن)

۲. خانه‌ی آقا و خانم کریمی سه طبقه ــــــــــــــــــ . (بودن)

۳. تو امروز چه ــــــــــــــــــ . (کار کردن)

۴. من غذای چینی ــــــــــــــــــ . (خوردن – منفی)

۵. آنها از هواپیمایی هُما ــــــــــــــــــ . (استفاده کردن – منفی)

۶. شما با آقای مدیر ــــــــــــــــــ . (مسافرت کردن)

۷. من در آینده در ایران ــــــــــــــــــ . (زندگی کردن)

۸. آیا شما آلکس را در آنجا ــــــــــــــــــ ؟ (دیدن)

۹. من در تعطیلات به کارم ــــــــــــــــــ . (فکر کردن – منفی)

۱۰. پدر و مادرِ من ــــــــــــــــــ . (فهمیدن)

تمرین ۸

به فارسی ترجمه کنید. از فرم نوشتاری استفاده کنید.

1. Next year, will you not come to Iran? Yes, I will come to Iran.

2. Will you not go to the Perspolis match? Yes, I will go to Perspolis match.

3. Will you marry me? No, I will not marry you.

4. Will you not eat this food? Yes, I will eat it.

5. Will the Fajr Film Festival be organized in Shiraz next year? No, it will not be organized in Shiraz next year.

6. Your airplane ticket will expire next month? Yes, it will expire next month.

تمرین ۹

Change the verbs into the future tense. Change the adverbs to match the tense. Work in pairs, groups, or as a class. Example:

Student 1 (*book open*): من در ایران زندگی می‌کنم.

Student 2: (*book closed*) من در ایران زندگی خواهم کرد.

Group 2	Group 1
۱. ما در کشورِ سردی زندگی می‌کنیم.	۱. این درس سخت است.
۲. من مطمئنم که جمعه استقلال برنده می‌شود.	۲ دلم برای تیمِ موردِ علاقه‌ام تنگ شده بود.
۳. فرشِ ابریشم گران‌تر است.	۳. من نمره‌ی بدی گرفتم.
۴. حتماً گذرنامه‌ی ایرانی‌تان باطل شده است.	۴. این جشنواره در تهران برگزار می‌شود.
۵. تو به جشنواره‌ی فیلم رشد می‌روی؟	۵. به نظرِ تو ایران کشورِ خوبی است؟

تمرین ۱۰

The following text is part of a play called آرش, written by Bahram Beyzai. It is about an ancient heroic figure. The text is written in archaic style so it may be difficult to understand. Underline familiar words and find a verb in the future tense.

نمایشنامه‌ی آرش

و او «کشواد» گفت: یک فرسنگ.

و خروش از سپاهیان برخاست. ایشان به فریاد بلند می‌گفتند: ای کشواد پیش برو، به سوی تورانیان که گروهشان به گروه دیوان می‌ماند. و به ایشان بگوی که تو تیر خواهی انداخت. تا هر کجا که تیرِ تو برود تا همانجا از آنِ ایران است. تا هر کجا تیر تو برود ای کشواد!

سردار می‌گوید: اینک فرمان!

و کشواد می‌غرّد: نمی‌برم!

پس سردار از دلِ آن غبار سرخ به او می‌نگرد: ای کشواد باد می‌وزد، و من پاسخ تو نشنیدم.

نویسنده: بَهرام بیضائی

337

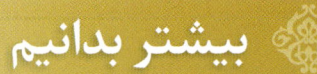

بیشتر بدانیم

ورزشِ موردِ علاقه‌ات چیه؟

والیبال

دو و میدانی / دو میدانی

کُشتی

تِنیسِ روی میز – پینگ پُنگ

تِنیس

اِسکی

وَزنه‌بَرداری

شِنا

هنرهای رَزمی

ورزشِ باستانی

بَسکِتبال

فوتبال

تمرین ۱۱

جملات زیر را با واژگانِ مناسب از لیستِ زیر کامل کنید:

اسکی – بین المللی – تنیس – فوتبال – جشنواره – بسکتبال – باستانی – سازمان – تنیس

۱. من به کلاس ــــــــــــ روی میز می روم.

۲. رنگِ یونیفورم تیمِ ــــــــــــ استقلال آبی است.

۳. ورزشِ ملّیِ کشورِ ایران ورزشِ ــــــــــــ است.

۴. در نزدیکِ تهران سه پیستِ ــــــــــــ است: «دیزین»، «شمشَک» و «آبعلی».

۵. در ورزشِ ــــــــــــ نباید توپ را با پا پرت کنیم.

۶. ورزشِ ــــــــــــ کمی مثلِ تنیس است.

تمرین ۱۲

Talk with three of your classmates about their favorite sports. Present your findings to the class.

تمرین ۱۳

Name one or two sports that each of these countries is famous for. Write in Persian:

۲. پاکستان		۱. آمریکا	
۴. چین		۳. روسیه	
۶. کانادا		۵. برزیل	

پیستِ اسکیِ دیزین درنزدیکیِ تهران

تمرین ۱۴

Look at the following advertisement and answer the following questions:

- What kind of facilities are offered in گل نرگس sports complex?
- What kind of classes do they have for women and men?
- What are the credentials of the manager?

دستور زبان ۲

USES OF "ke" «که» انواع

که is used **in** several constructions:

a) که in Conjunction

که can be used in conjunction form and can be optionally omitted as in English.

I think that he is Nima.	۱. فکر می‌کنم که او نیما است.
I think he is Nima.	۲. فکر می‌کنم او نیما است.

b) که in Relative Clauses

که can be used as a relative pronoun. The English words *Who, Whom, Whose, Which, That,* and *Where* can be replaced by که in Persian. In a relative clause, the noun that appears before که requires a non-specific suffix /i/. Examples:

The girl who is laughing is my sister.	۳. دختری که می‌خندد، خواهر من است.
The book that/which I read was not so good.	۴. کتابی که خواندم، خیلی خوب نبود.
The man whom you saw is my brother.	۵. مردی که دیدی، برادر من است.
The girl whose car is here, is my friend.	۶. دختری که ماشینش اینجاست، دوستِ من است.

c) که as "So that" or "In order to"

I go to class (in order) to learn Persian.	۷. من به کلاس می‌روم که فارسی یاد بگیرم.
Mina went to Iran (in order) to visit her homeland	۸. مینا به ایران رفت که وطنش را ببیند.

When که means "so that" or "in order to", it is followed by a verb in **subjunctive** form (ex. 7 & 8). که can be replaced by تا when it means "so that" or "in order to". We will learn about تا on the next page.

341

USES OF "tā" انواع «تا»

تا is used in the following constructions some of which we have already learned:

a) تا For counting

In spoken form, تا can be used after a number to show counting and quantification.

١. من پنج تا کلاس دارم.   I have five classes.

b) تا as "So that" or "In order to"

As we saw on the previous page, تا can replace که when it means: "so that" or "in order to". In this construction the verb that follows تا must be in **subjunctive** form. Examples:

٢. من به کلاس می روم تا فارسی یاد بگیرم.   I go to class (in order) to learn Persian.

٣. مینا به ایران رفت تا پدرش را ببیند.   Mina went to Iran (in order) to visit her father.

c) تا as a preposition

تا can function as the prepositions "until/till", "as long as", or "as soon as". Examples:

٤. من تا ساعتِ پنج در دانشگاه هستم.   I am/will be at the university till five o'clock.

٥. تا تو نگاه می کنی، کارِ من آه کردن است. (شعری از شهریار)   As long as you gaze, my job is to sigh.

تمرین ۱۵

Connect the two sentences with که. Look at the example below. Note which element is removed and pay attention to the usage of the non-specific suffix /i/.

آن مرد آمد. آن مرد برادرِ من است. ← مردی که آمد برادرِ من است.

١. آن کتاب را خواندم. آن کتاب افتضاح بود.

٢. یک فیلم دیدی. آن فیلم چطور بود؟

٣. یک خانه خریدیم. آن خانه خیلی بزرگ است.

٤. من یک کارگردان را خیلی دوست دارم. آن کارگردان «تهیمنه میلانی» است.

٥. مسافرانِ خارجی به ایران آمدند. مسافران خارجی خیلی از ایران خوششان آمد.

تمرین ۱۶

جاهای خالی را با (که ــ تا ــ Ø) پرکنید:

۱. می‌خواهم درس بخوانم _____ دکتر بشوم. (که ــ تا ــ Ø)

۲. کتابی _____ خوانده بودی این کتاب است؟ (که ــ تا ــ Ø)

۳. جشنواره‌ی فیلم رشد _____ چه روزی خواهد بود؟ (که ــ تا ــ Ø)

۴. _____ _____ تو غذا نخوری من نمی‌خورم. (که ــ تا ــ Ø)

۵. ورزشی _____ همیشه دوست داشتم فوتبال بوده است. (که ــ تا ــ Ø)

۶. خیلی وقت است _____ تو را ندیده‌ام. (که ــ تا ــ Ø)

۷. خواهیم دید _____ چه تیمی برنده می‌شود! (که ــ تا ــ Ø)

تمرین ۱۷

جملات زیر را به فارسی ترجمه کنید. از فرمِ نوشتاری استفاده کنید:

1. I went to the bank (in order) to get money.

2. The man who is driving is my father.

3. This is the woman whom I saw.

4. I am at home until afternoon.

5. She told me that her child is hungry.

6. John works hard (in order) to become rich.

تمرین ۱۸

Write a short essay about a film festival in your country. Describe the festival and talk about what kinds of films are shown in that festival. Indicate how often that festival is organized and in which city. Indicate whether you like or dislike that film festival. Support your ideas with concrete reasons. Use at least two relative clauses (with که). Include a sentence with a verb in the future tense.

تمرین ۱۹

Below is a monologue from a popular Iranian film "Ali Santoori", written by Dariush Mehrjoui and Vahidéa Mohammadi:

1. Underline the familiar words.

2. Underline the verbs and indicate which tense they are.

3. Find at least one psychological verb.

4. Find two instances of که and determine what is the English equivalent of them (*who, whose, whom, which, that* or *where*).

5. What is the gist of the text?

6. Write a short summary of this text and use your own words.

فیلمِ علی سَنتوری

وقتی از ایستگاهِ مترو اومدم بالا آسمون مثلِ همیشه کِدِر و بدرنگ بود. توی هوا پر از دود بود و من نمی‌دونستم که این آخرین باریه که این هوای کثیفو به ریه‌های سوخته‌ام می‌دم. از وقتی هانیه همسرم گذاشته رفته، دیگه دلم به کار نمی‌ره. بعضی از برنامه‌ها رو قبول نمی‌کنم. با بعضی‌هاش بدقولی می‌کنم و نمی‌رم. یا سرِ مجلس خوابم می بره یا می‌زنم زیرِ گریه.

مثِ اون شب تو کنسرت تو نمایشگاه که انقدر پاتیل بودم که یادم نبود هانیه رفته! خیال می‌کردم مثلِ همیشه تو ردیف جلو نشسته و با نگاهِ شیفته به من خیره شده. تو میکروفون گفتم:

مرسی، ممنون. امشب یه موجود خیلی عزیزی اینجاس که باید ازش تشکر کنم: هانیه، همسرم! واقعیّتش تالاپ خورد تو کلّه‌ام. هانیه اونجا نبود!

این روزا همش مست و پاتیل بودم. خراب کاریایی کردم، چه جور! که باعث شد شهرتم کم‌کم ضایع بشه و دیگه کسی بهم کار نده...

نویسندگان: داریوش مهرجویی و وحیده محمّدی
کارگردان: داریوش مهرجویی

344

بیشتر بدانیم

سَرگَرمیِ موردِ علاقه‌ات چیه؟

	Cooking	آشپزی	
	Singing	آواز خواندن/خوندن	
	Computer games	بازی‌های کامپیوتری	
	Gardening	باغبانی	
	Theater	تئاتر	
ه / ٥	Calligraphy	خوش‌نویسی	سَرگَرمیِ موردِ علاقه‌ام
	Sewing	خَیّاطی	
	Dance (Traditional)	رَقص (سُنَّتی)	
	Cinema	سینَما	
	Chess	شَطرنج	
	Reading	کتاب خواندن/خوندن	
	Music (Traditional)	موسیقی (سُنَّتی)	
	Painting	نَقّاشی	

تمرین ۲۰

Task: Interview your classmate and ask about his/her favorite hobbies. Then interview a second classmate and ask the same. Ask the second classmate whether or not s/he likes the hobbies mentioned by the first classmate. Prepare a report comparing and contrasting the hobbies that your two classmates like/dislike. Example:

سرگرمی مورد علاقه‌ی ماریا موسیقی است. او از رقص هم خوشش می‌آید. او به آشپزی هم علاقه دارد و هر روز آشپزی می‌کند. ماریا از بازی‌های کامپیوتری خیلی بدش می‌آید ولی کریس عاشق بازی‌های کامپیوتری است. کریس از شطرنج هم خیلی خوشش می‌آید ولی متاسّفانه وقت برای شطرنج ندارد.

Calligraphy & Handwriting خوش‌نویسی و دست خَط

Calligraphy has a long history in Iran which goes back to the Zoroastrian roots of Iran. There are several types of Persian calligraphy such as Nasta'ligh نَستَعلیق and Cursive Nasta'līgh نَستَعلیقِ شِکسته. Here are some samples of Persian calligraphy.

نَستَعلیقِ شِکسته

نَستَعلیق

346

تمرین ۲۱

By now, you know that Persian handwriting is in many ways different from Persian fonts that are used in typing. Here are the handwritten forms of the نَستَعلیق text on the previous page. With a classmate, explore the differences between the following handwritings.

تمرین ۲۲

Practice reading the following handwritten text:

تمرین ۲۳

الف: به فرم نوشتاری تبدیل کنید:

۱. می‌خوای من برم سینما تو صف وای‌سم تا تو بیای؟

۲. خیلی کارای این کارگردانو دوس دارم! یعنی می‌شه بتونیم بلیتِ فیلمشو بگیریم؟

ب: به فرم گفتاری تبدیل کنید:

۱. باورت نمی شود چه شده است!

۲. جدّی می گویی؟ پس بعدش هم به رستورانِ موردِ علاقه‌ی من برویم.

347

تمرین ۲۴

به فایل صوتی گوش کنید و جاهای خالی را پر کنید:

زَرتُشت

زَرتُشت _____ پیامبرِ _____ بود _____ سال‌ها پیش

از مَسیح _____ _____ . هیچکس _____ دقیقِ

_____ زرتشت را نمی‌داند. _____ قبل از حمله‌ی اعراب

_____ بودند. بعد از حمله‌ی اعراب بعضی از _____ به _____

_____ رفتند، _____ مسلمان شدند، و بعضی _____

_____ زرتشتی ماندند. هنوز هم بعضی از ایرانیانِ زرتشتی در ایران _____

_____ ولی تعداد _____ بسیار _____ است. زرتشتیانی که بعد از حمله‌ی اعراب،

از ایران به هند رفتند پارسی نامیده _____ . زرتشتیان ایران بیشتر در _____

شهرهای _____ ، یزد، کرمان، اصفهان، _____ و اهواز زندگی می‌کنند.

تمرین ۲۵

جملات زیر را با حرف اضافه‌ی مناسب کامل کنید:

۱. من هر روز _____ اتوبوس به کلاسِ رقص می‌روم. (با ـ به ـ از ـ برای ـ در)

۲. مسافرانِ خارجی _____ جشنواره‌ی رشد به ایران آمده‌اند. (با ـ به ـ از ـ برای ـ در)

۳. من _____ شطرنج خیلی خوشم آمده است. (با ـ به ـ از ـ برای ـ در)

۴. جشنواره‌ی بین‌المللیِ فیلمِ فجر _____ تهران برگزار می‌شود. (با ـ به ـ از ـ برای ـ در)

۵. من _____ سرِ کار به سینما می‌روم و _____ صف می‌ایستم. (با ـ به ـ از ـ برای ـ در)

۶. فردا یکی _____ بهترین روزهای زندگی من خواهد بود. (با ـ به ـ از ـ برای ـ در)

تمرین ۲۶

فعل‌های زیر را در زمان داده شده صرف کنید:

۱. شاهین ــــــــــــــ (درس خواندن) (Present progressive)

۲. کتابِ فارسیِ ما خوب ــــــــــــــ (بودن) (Present/Negative)

۳. با من ــــــــــــــ (حرف زدن) (Negative/Imperative/Singular)

۴. من تو را ــــــــــــــ (دیدن) (Present perfect)

۵. او همیشه مادرش را ــــــــــــــ (دوست داشتن) (Past perfect)

۶. آنها ــــــــــــــ (خندیدن) (Past continuous)

۷. آنها ــــــــــــــ (خوردَن) (Past progressive)

۸. آنها می‌خواهند ــــــــــــــ (دعوت کردن) (Subjunctive)

۹. کلاس شما چند ساعت ــــــــــــــ (طول کشیدن) (Future)

۱۰. ما به ایران ــــــــــــــ (رفتن) (Negative/Future)

۱۱. تو هم ــــــــــــــ ؟(رقصیدن) (Future)

۱۲. من از هوای ابری ــــــــــــــ (بد + آمدن) (Psychological verb/Present)

تمرین ۲۷ 🎧

Listen to the audio file and fill in the blanks. Next, underline the verbs in the text and identify what tense they are:

ماریا پانزده سال است که درایران زندگی ــــــــــــــ او دانشجوی زبان فارسی ــــــــــــــ و از

بچّگی از زبان و ادبیاتِ فارسی خیلی ــــــــــــــ . ماریا به ایران ــــــــــــــ تا زبان فارسی یاد بگیرد.

همسایه‌های او که افغانی هستند، فارسیِ دَری ــــــــــــــ ماریا به راحتی می تواند لهجه‌ی آنها را

ــــــــــــــ . ماریا می خواهد سالِ آینده به کابل برود. او بعداز دیدنِ کابل به تهران ــــــــــــــ .

ماریا به موسیقیِ ــــــــــــــ ایرانی و ــــــــــــــ ایران هم ــــــــــــــ دارد. فیلم‌های ــــــــــــــ

ــــــــــــــ او فیلم‌های ــــــــــــــ و ایرانی هستند. ماریا معتقد است سینمای ایران و سینمای ایتالیا

از ــــــــــــــ و هنری‌ترین سینماهای ــــــــــــــ هستند.

تمرین ۲۸

جاهای خالی را با شکل درست فعل پُر کنید:

۱. مادر: غذا حاضر است. برادر و خواهرت را ــــــــــ ــــــــــ . (صدا کردن)

مینا: چشم، مامان جان!

۲. من فردا ساعتِ شش به مینا ــــــــــ (تلفن کردن) و از او ــــــــــ ــــــــــ (پرسیدن) که آیا دوست

دارد با ما به مسابقه ــــــــــ . (آمدن)

۳. مادرم می‌گوید که مطمئن است که فیلمِ «علی سنتوری» در جشنواره ــــــــــ (برنده شدن) ولی

من زیاد امیدوار ــــــــــ . (بودن / منفی)

۴. سینا از شطرنج خیلی خوشش می‌آید. او با چند دانشجو ــــــــــ (دوست شدن) که برنده‌ی

مسابقات شطرنج ــــــــــ (بودن) و می‌خواهد از آنها شطرنج ــــــــــ . (یاد گرفتن)

۵. دیروز نگین خیلی ناراحت ــــــــــ (بودن) چون باید در هوای ابری و بارانی پیاده به خانه

ــــــــــ . (رفتن)

۶. هم‌کلاسی‌های لادن می‌خواهند برای او جشنِ تولّد ــــــــــ . (گرفتن)

۷. من حدود شش سال است که به وطنم ــــــــــ (برگشتن / منفی) و پنج سال است که از کانادا ــــــــــ

ــــــــــ . (بیرون رفتن / منفی)

تمرین ۲۹

Task: Your friend wants to start learning a new sport. He is considering learning how to ski. You want to convince him that skiing is not a good sport for him because he dislikes (Psychological verb) cold places and the cold. Suggest that you think he should learn martial arts because it is good for his body and his soul. Support your ideas with concrete reasons.

REVIEW CORNER	
Points that remain unclear about Lesson 10:	
How I plan to work on these points:	

شعر

The following poem is by Mohammad Kazem Kazemi, the Afghan Poet residing in Iran. It is about Afghan refugees in Iran. Underline the verbs in the future tense. Find two past participle forms. You will not be evaluated on the content but you can use it for cultural enrichment.

بازگشت

غروب در نفسِ گرمِ جاده خواهم رفت

پیاده آمده بودم، پیاده خواهم رفت

طلسم غربتم امشب شکسته خواهد شد

و سفره‌ام که تهی بود، بسته خواهد شد

و در حوالی شبهای عید، همسایه!

صدای گریه نخواهی شنید، همسایه!

همان غریبه که قلک نداشت، خواهد رفت

و کودکی که عروسک نداشت، خواهد رفت

منم که تمام افق را به رنج گردیده

منم که هر که مرا دیده، در گذر دیده

منم که نانی اگر داشتم، از آجر بود

و سفره‌ام ـ که نبود ـ از گرسنگی پر بود

به هرچه آینه، تصویری از شکست من است

به سنگ سنگ بناها، نشان دست من است

اگر به لطف و اگر قهر، می‌شناسندم

تمام مردم این شهر، می‌شناسندم

من ایستادم، اگر پشت آسمان خم شد

نماز خواندم، اگر دهر ابن ملجم شد

شاعر: محمّد کاظم کاظمی

351

Listen to the following song by Shahram Nazeri on YouTube. The lyrics are from Rumi. Underline the verbs in the future tense. Find one verb in the present perfect tense. You will not be evaluated on the content but you can use it for cultural enrichment.

یادگار دوست

دل در غم عشق مبتلا خواهم کرد

جان را سپر تیر بلا خواهم کرد

عمری که نه در عشق تو بگذاشته ام

امروز به خون دل قضا خواهم کرد

تا با غم عشق تو مرا کار افتاد

بیچاره دلم در غم بسیار افتاد

بسیار فتاده بود اندر غم عشق

اما نه چنین زار که این بار افتاد

شاعر: مولوی (رومی) (۱۲۷۳-۱۲۰۷)

 نکته‌ی فرهنگی

Ancient Iranian Sport and Zurkhāne

The ancient Persian sport is called varzesh-e bāstāni ورزش باستانی (ancient sport), also known as pahlevāni پهلوانی or Zurkhāne'i زورخانه‌ای . This is a traditional sport originally used to train warriors. Bāstāni is not just a sport to train the body but it is a lifestyle in which the athlete learns to exercise high moral values in life. It contains elements of martial arts, calisthenics, wrestling, and strength training, which are accompanied by song, music, and Sufi and epic poetry. UNESCO recognized this sport as one of the ancient forms of athletics and training, with its roots possibly going back to pre-Islamic Persian culture.

The space where this sport is practiced is called Zurkhāne زورخانه (house of strength) and is a domed structure with a lowered stage where the audience can sit around and observe the rituals. Music is an important element of Bāstāni sport. Usually a live performance by a Tombak (Persian goblet drum) or Daf (Persian frame drum) with special songs accompanies the Bāstāni ritual.

Iranian Cincma

Iranian cinema has become one of the world's most flourishing cinemas within the past several decades and many critics have praised Iranian Cinema as one of the world's most important artistic cinemas. Iranian directors and script writers have received prestigious awards at many international film festivals around the world. There are also a substantial number of Iranian women filmmakers who produce exceptional work.

Here are some images from popular Iranian films:

قیصر ۱۹۶۹

خداحافظ تهران ۱۹۶۶

بچّه‌های آسمان ۱۹۹۷

آتش بَس ۲۰۰۶

ضرب المثل

مار از پونه بدش می‌آد، دِر لونه‌اش سبز می‌شه!

Literal translation:
Snake dislikes pennyroyal and it grows in front of his nest.

This proverb means that if you detest something, you may even attract it more to your life.

354

Thematic Review of New Vocabulary

Nouns & Adjectives	
Awful	اِفتِضاح
Ancient	باستانی
Childhood	بَچّگی
Section	بَخش
Long	بُلَند
International	بِینُ المِلَلی
Prize/Award	جایزه
Serious/Seriously	جِدّی
Boss	رَئیس
Organization	سازمان
Traditional	سُنّتی
Line/Queue	صَف
Old (for inanimates)	قَدیمی
Section/Part	قِسمَت
Short	کوتاه
Child	کودَک
Various	مُختَلِف
Sure	مُطمَئِن
Favorite	موردِ عَلاقه
Grade/Mark	نُمره
Adolescent	نوجَوان

Sports	
Ski	اِسکی
Basketball	بَسکِتبال
Tennis	تِنیس
Table Tennis	تِنیس روی میز ـ پینگ پُنگ
Track and Field	دو و میدانی
Swimming	شِنا
Soccer	فوتبال
Wrestling	کُشتی
Volleyball	والیبال
Sport	وَرزِش
Ancient Sport	وَرزِش باستانی
Weight-lifting	وَزنه بَرداری
Martial Arts	هنرهای رَزمی

Film & Theater	
Animation	اَنیمِیشن
Educational	آموزشی
Festival	جَشنواره
Story/Fiction	داستان
Story/Tale	قِصّه
Director	کارگَردان
Documentary	مُستَنَد
Play	نَمایشنامه

About Sport	
Loser	بازَنده
Game/Match	بازی
Winner	بَرَنده
Team	تیم
Fan/Follower	طَرَفدار
Match	مُسابقه

Words & Expressions	
Incidentally	اِتّفاقاً
If you want	اَگَر بخواهی
This way	این طوری
This much	این قَدر
After that (Spoken)	بَعدِش
Accidental/Accidentally	تَصادُفی
Positive reply to a negative question	چِرا
Fortunately	خوشبَختانه
Late (time)	دیر وَقت
At work	سَرِ کار
How much do you bet?	شَرطِ چند می بَندی؟
What luck!	عَجَب شانسی!
How is that possible?	مَگَر می شوَد؟

Hobbies	
Cooking	آشپزی
Singing	آواز خواندن
Computer games	بازیهای کامپیوتری
Gardening	باغبانی
Theater	تئاتر
Calligraphy	خوشنویسی
Sewing	خَیّاطی
Dance	رَقص
Cinema	سینما
Chess	شَطرنج
Reading	کتاب خواندن
Music	موسیقی
Painting	نَقّاشی

Slang/Street Talk	
Cool	باحال
Let's go	بِزَن بریم!
Shake on it!	بِزَن قَدِش!
Swear to you	جانِ تو
You're the bomb!	چاکِرتَم!
Do you feel like…	حال داری؟

Verbs & Phrases	
You do not believe (Psychological verb)	باوَرِت نمی شَوَد! (شُدن: شَو)
Was organized	بَرگُزار شُد (شُدن: شَو)
Is organized	بَرگُزار می‌شود (شُدن: شَو)
S/he will give	خواهَد داد (دادن: دَه)
We will see	خواهیم دید (دیدن: بین)
I had missed… (Psychological verb)	دِلَم تَنگ شده بود (شُدن: شَو)
They will attend	شِرکَت خواهَند کرد (کردن: کُن)
We may/should catch/find	گیربیاوَریم (آوردن: آوَر)
I have heard	شنیده‌ام (شنیدن: شِنَو)
I stand	می‌ایستم (ایستادن: ایست)

Prepositions	
Except	غِیر از
For (Spoken)	واسه

APPENDIX A: VERB CHARTS

Translation	Preposition	Past stem of verbal element	Present stem of verbal element	Infinitive
To greet	با	کَرد	کُن	اَحوال‌پرسی کردن
To wish		کَرد	کُن	آرِزو کردن
To marry	با	کَرد	کُن	ازدواج کردن
To rest		کَرد	کُن	استراحت کردن
To use	از	کَرد	کُن	استفاده کردن
To make a mistake		کَرد	کُن	اشتباه کردن
To fall	از	اُفتاد	اُفت	اُفتادن
To be prepared		بود	هَست	آماده بودن
To prepare		کَرد	کُن	آماده کَردَن
To take an exam			دَه	امتحان دادن
To come	از / به	آمَد	آ	آمَدَن
To be hopeful		بود	هست	اُمیدوار بودن
To choose		کَرد	کُن	انتخاب کردن
To perform		داد	دَه	انجام دادَن
To bring	برای	آوَرد	آوَر	آوَردَن
To stand (up)	در	ایستاد	ایست	ایستادن
To expire		شُد	شَو	باطِل شدن
To take	از / به	بُرد	بَر	بردن
To take	از / به	بُرد	بَر	بُردَن
To return	به / از	گَشت	گَرد	برگَشتَن
To know (language/skill)		بود	هَست	بَلد بودَن
To be		بود	هَست	بودَن
To kiss		بوسید	بوس	بوسیدن
To wake up		شُد	شَو	بیدار شُدَن
To wake someone up		کرد	کن	بیدار کردن
To cook		پُخت	پَز	پُختَن
To accept		پذیرفت	پذیر	پذیرفتن
To pay	به	پرداخت	پَرداز	پرداختَن
To ask	از	پُرسید	پُرس	پُرسیدَن
To spread		کردن	کُن	پَهن کَردن

Translation	Preposition	Past stem of verbal element	Present stem of verbal element	Infinitive
To wear/put on clothes		پوشید	پوش	پوشیدَن
To walk (on foot)		رفت	رو	پیاده رفتن
To turn		پیچید	پیچ	پیچیدَن
To find		کرد	کُن	پِیدا کَردَن
To give a discount	به	داد	دَه	تخفیف دادن
To get a discount	از	گرفت	گیر	تخفیف گرفتن
To translate		کرد	کُن	ترجمه کردن
To come (Polite)	برای	آوَرد	آوَر	تَشریف آوَردن
To go (Polite)	از / به	بُرد	بَر	تَشریف بُردَن
To be present (Polite)		داشت	دار	تَشریف داشتَن
To thank	از	کرد	کُن	تَشَکُّر کردن
To decide		گرفت	گیر	تصمیم گرفتن
To do Tārof		کرد	کُن	تعارف کردن
To offer	به	کرد	کُن	تقدیم کردن
To make a call	به	زَد	زَن	تلفن زدن
To make a call	به	کرد	کُن	تلفن کردن
To watch		کرد	کُن	تَماشا کَردَن
To finish (It...)		شُد	شَو	تَمام شُدَن
To finish (something)		کرد	کُن	تَمام کَردَن
To clean		کَرد	کُن	تمیز کردن
To have to use the toilet		داشت	دار	توالت داشتن
To go to the toilet	به	رفت	رَو	توالت رفتن
To be able to/Can		تَوانِست	تَوان	تَوانِستَن
To describe		کَرد	کُن	توصیف کردن
To explain	به	داد	دَه	توضیح دادن
To register		کرد	کُن	ثبت‌نام کردن
To celebrate		گِرِفت	گیر	جَشن گِرِفتَن
To gather	با	شُد	شَو	جَمع شُدَن
To respond	به	داد	دَه	جَواب دادن
To haggle	با	زد	زَن	چانه زدن
To chat	با	کَرد	کُن	چَت کردن

Translation	Preposition	Past stem of verbal element	Present stem of verbal element	Infinitive
To set/display		چید	چین	چیدَن
To get ready		شُد	شَو	حاضِر شُدَن
To speak/talk	با	زَد	زَن	حَرف زَدَن
To count/calculate	برای/با	کَرد	کُن	حِساب کردن
To take a bath/shower		کَرد	کُن	حَمّام کردن
To get embarrassed	از	کَرد	کُن	خِجالت کشیدن
To say good bye	با	کَرد	کُن	خدا حافظی کردن
To buy/shop		کَرد	کُن	خَرید کردن
To buy		خَرید	خَر	خَریدَن
To take a rest		درکَرد	دَرکُن	خَستِگی دَر کردن
To laugh		خَندید	خَند	خَندیدَن
To dream		دید	بین	خواب دیدن
To sleep		خوابید	خواب	خوابیدَن
To want	از	خواست	خواه	خواسﺘَن
To read		خواند	خوان	خواندَن
To plead	از	کَرد	کُن	خواهش کردن
To eat		خورد	خور	خوردَن
To have a good time	به	گُذَشت	گُذَر	خوش گُذَشت
To give	به	داد	دَه	دادَن
To have		داشت	دار	داشتَن
To know (something)		دانِست	دان	دانِستَن
To knock		زَد	زَن	دَر زَدَن
To request	برای/به	کرد	کن	دَرخواست کردن
To study		خواند	خوان	دَرس خواندَن
To give a lesson	به	داد	دَه	دَرس دادَن
To invite	به	کرد	کن	دَعوَت کردن
To prepare/make	برای/با	کَرد	کُن	دُرُست کردن
To shake hands	با	داد	دَه	دست دادن
To look for		گَشت	گَرد	دُنبالِ ... گَشﺘَن
To review		کَرد	کُن	دوره کردن
To gather/get together	با	شُد	شَو	دورِهم جَمع شُدَن
To like		داشت	دار	دوست داشﺘَن

Translation	Preposition	Past stem of verbal element	Present stem of verbal element	Infinitive
To take a shower		گرفت	گیر	دوش گرفتن
To see		دید	بین	دیدَن
To get/become late		شُد	شَو	دیر شُدَن
To drive	با	کرد	کُن	رانَندگی کَردَن
To walk		رَفت	رَو	راه رَفتَن
To make a reservation		کرد	کُن	رِزرو کردن
To arrive	از/به	رسید	رس	رِسیدَن
To go	از/به	رَفت	رَو	رَفتَن
To dance	با	رَقصید	رَقص	رَقصیدن
To pour/through/shed/fall	روی	ریخت	ریز	ریختن
To hit	به	زد	زَن	زدن
To fall down		خورد	خور	زمین خوردن
To get a wife		گرفت	گیر	زن گرفتن
To live	با	کرد	کُن	زِندِگی کَردَن
To buzz/call		زَدَن	زَن	زَنگ زَدن
To build		ساخت	ساز	ساختن
To be quiet		بود	هست	ساکِت بودن
To convey greetings	به	رسان	رس	سلام رساندن
To say hello	به	کَرد	کُن	سلام کردن
To get on/in - To board		شد	شَو	سوار شدن
To have a question	از	داشت	دار	سؤال داشتن
To ask a question	از	کَرد	کُن	سؤال کردن
To get one's fill		شُد	شَو	سیر شُدَن
To smoke		کشید	کِش	سیگار کشیدن
To become		شُد	شَو	شُدَن
To begin		شُد	شَو	شُروع شُدَن
To start		شُروع کَرد	شُروع کُن	شُروع کَردَن
To wash		شُست	شو	شستن
To count (numbers)		شمرد	شُمار	شمردن
To know (someone)		شِناخت	شِناس	شِناختَن
To hear		شِنید	شِنَو	شِنیدَن

Translation	Preposition	Past stem of verbal element	Present stem of verbal element	Infinitive
To get a wife		کَرد	کُن	شوهر کردن
To have patience		داشت	دار	صَبر داشتَن
To wait	برای	کَرد	کُن	صَبر کَردَن
To speak	با	کَرد	کُن	صُحبَت کردن
To call (someone)		کَرد	کُن	صِدا کردن
To line up/get in a queue		بَست	بَند	صف بستن
To line up/get in a queue		کِشید	کِش	صف کشیدن
To last		کِشید	کِش	طول کِشیدَن
To apologize	از	خواست	خواه	عُذر خواستن
To say (Modest)	به	کَرد	کُن	عَرض کردن
To wed/marry	با	کَرد	کُن	عروسی کردن
To change/exchange	با	کرد	کن	عَوَض کردن
To matter		داشت	دار	عیب داشتَن
To put on glasses		زد	زَن	عینک زدن
To cook food	با/برای	پُخت	پَز	غذا پختن
To eat	با	خورد	خور	غذا خوردن
To graduate	از	شُد	شَو	فارغ‌التحصیل شدن
To forget		کَرد	کُن	فراموش کردن
To forget		کَرد	کُن	فَراموش کَردَن
To send	به	فِرستاد	فِرست	فِرستادَن
To say/command (Polite)	به	فرمود	فَرما	فَرمودن
To sell	به	فروخت	فُروش	فروختن
To think		کَرد	کُن	فِکر کَردَن
To make one understand	به	فَهمید	فَهم	فهماندن
To understand		فَهمید	فَهم	فَهمیدَن
To be located	در	داشت	دار	قرار داشتن
To work		کَرد	کُن	کار کَردَن
To do		کَرد	کُن	کَردَن
To pull		کشید	کِش	کشیدن
To help	به	کَرد	کُن	کمک کردن
To get help	از	گِرفت	گیر	کمک گرفتن

361

Translation	Preposition	Past stem of verbal element	Present stem of verbal element	Infinitive
To steal ones bag		زَد	زَن	کیف زدن
To put/allow		گذاشت	گُذار	گذاشتن
To spend time		گذراند	گُذاران	گذراندن
To pass	از	گُذَشت	گُذَر	گُذَشتَن
To stroll	به	کَرد	کُن	گردش کردن
To take/get/hold/catch	از	گِرِفت	گیر	گِرِفتَن
To cry		کَرد	کُن	گریه کردن
To tell	به	گُفت	گو	گُفتَن
To listen	به	داد	دَه	گوش دادن
To listen	به	کَرد	کُن	گوش کردن
To catch/find		آوَرَد	آوَر	گیرآوردن
To put on clothes		پوشید	پوش	لباس پوشیدن
To stay		ماند	مان	ماندَن
To give (Polite)	به	کَرد	کُن	مَرحِمَت کردن
To die		مُرد	میر	مُردَن
To be sick		بود	هست	مریض بودن
To become sick		شد	شَو	مریض شدن
To travel	با	کَرد	کُن	مُسافِرَت کردن
To brush one's teeth	با	زَد	زَن	مسواک زدن
To believe	به	بود	هست	مُعتَقِد بودن
To apologize	از	خواست	خواه	معذرت خواستن
To be careful		بود	هست	مواظب بودن
To want (Polite)		داشت	دار	مِیل داشتن
To eat/want (Polite)		کَرد	کُن	میل کردن
To name		بُرد	بَر	نام بُردَن
To sit	روی	نِشَست	نِشین	نِشَستَن
To look/glance	به	کَرد	کُن	نگاه کردن
To write	با/به	نِوشت	نِویس	نِوشتَن
To drink		نوشید	نوش	نوشیدَن
To teach/train	به	داد	دَه	یاد دادَن
To learn	از	گِرِفت	گیر	یاد گرفتن

Psychological Verbs

Translation	Preposition	Past stem of verbal element	Present stem of verbal element	
To believe (something)		شد	شَو	باور + شدن
To dislike	از	آمَد	آ	بَد + آمَدن
To be thirsty		بود	هست	تِشنه + بودن
To feel sleepy		آمَد	آ	خواب + آمَدن
To like	از	آمَد	آ	خوش + آمَدن
To miss (someone/something)	برای	شد	شَو	دل + تَنگ شُدَن
To be down/To feel blue	از	گرفت	گیر	دل + گِرفتن
To feel cold		بود	هست	سَرد + بودن
To be hungry (Spoken)		بود	هست	گشنه + بودن
To be hungry		بود	هست	گرسنه + بودن
To feel warm		بود	هست	گرم + بودن
To remember	به	آمَد	آی	یاد + آمَدن
To remember		بود	هست	یاد + بودن
To forget	از	رفت	رَو	یاد + رَفتَن

APPENDIX B: GLOSSARY

Lesson	English	Persian
4	Eyebrow	اَبرو
6	Cloudy	اَبری
5	Silk	اَبریشَم
4	Bedroom	اُتاقِ خواب
4	Dining room	اُتاقِ ناهارخوری
4	Living room	اُتاقِ نِشیمَن
9	Single room	اتاقِ یک تخته
10	Incidentally	اِتّفاقاً
3	Bus	اُتوبوس
4	Rent (noun)	اِجاره
2	Literature	اَدَبیات
8	Second Persian month	اُردیبهِشت
5	Cheap	اَرزان
5	Sell it for less so that we become customers	اَرزان بِدهید مُشتَری بِشَویم
6	Europe	اُروپا
3	From	اَز
8	From each other	از هم
7	To get married	اِزدِواج کردن
3	Spanish	اِسپانیایی
8	Exam - Nationwide final exam	اِمتحان – اِمتحان نهایی
1	Is	اَست
1	Professor	اُستاد
6	Province	اُستان
6	Australia	اُستُرالیا
8	Use! (Plural & Formal)	اِستفاده کنید
8	Twelfth Persian month	اِسفَند
9	Paper money	اِسکناس
10	Ski	اِسکی
1	Name	اِسم
5	Cursor	اِشاره‌گر
10	Awful	اِفتِضاح
1	Afghan	اَفغانی
10	If you want	اَگَر بخواهی
9	If possible	اگر می‌شَوَد (شُدَن: شَو)
4	Now	اَلان

9	Of course	اَلبَتّه
4	Word to answer phone	اَلو
3 & 6	Today	اِمروز
3 & 6	Tonight	اِمشَب
5	We hope	اُمیدواریم (بودن)
7	Pomegranate	اَنار
4	Finger - Toe	اَنگُشت
1, 2 & 3	English	اِنگلیسی
10	Animation	اَنیمیشن
1	She/He	او
4	First	اَوّل
4	First	اَوَّلین
1	Where from	کُجا اَهلِ
3	Italian	ایتالیایی
9	Iran cheque	ایران چِک
1	Iranian	ایرانی
4	Bus stop/Station	ایستگاه
1	They (Plural & Formal)	ایشان
4	We email	ایمِیل می کنیم (کردن: کُن)
2	This	این
10	This way	این طوری
10	This much	این قَدر
5	Internet	اینترنِت
4	Here	اینجا
3	Water	آب
6	Weather/Climate	آب و هوا
8	Eighth Persian month	آبان
7	Sister/Sis (Slang)	آبجی
4	Blue	آبی
4	Apartment	آپارتِمان
7	Hooray! - Yay!	آخ جان!
9	End of…	آخرِ…
5	What is the final price?	آخَرِش چند؟
8	Last time	آخَرین بار
4	Email address	آدرسِ اِلکترونیکی
8	Ninth Persian month	آذر
6	Tomb	آرامگاه

1	Yes (Informal)	آره
9	Travel agency	آژانسِ مُسافِرَتی
2	Easy	آسان
9	Elevator	آسانسور
6	Asia	آسیا
1	Cook	آشپَز
4	Kitchen	آشپزخانه
10	Cooking	آشپزی
6	Sunny	آفتابی
6	Africa	آفریقا
7	Bravo!/Good job!l	آفَرین
1	Mr./Sr.	آقا
1 & 3	German	آلمانی
9	You had come (Plural & Formal)	آمده بودید (آمَدن: آ)
6	America	آمریکا
1	American	آمریکایی
10	Educational	آموزشی
2	That	آن
6	Those times/days	آن وَقت‌ها
4	There	آنجا
1	They	آنها
10	Singing	آواز خواندن
7	You brought	آوَردی (آوَردن: آوَر)
5	Icon	آیکُن
3	With/By	با
8	Emotional	با احساس
1	Polite	با اَدَب
8	Loudly	با صدای بُلَند
8	Cute/Funny	با نَمَک
3	With each other	با هَم
2 & 6	Dad/Man (Slang)	بابا
6	Grandpa	بابا بزرگ
10	Cool	باحال
7	Eggplant	بادِمجان
6	Suffix to count how many times	بار
6	Rainy	بارانی
10	Loser	بازَنده

10	Game/Match	بازی
10	Computer games	بازیهای کامپیوتری
10	Ancient	باستانی
5	OK (Spoken)	باشه
9	Has expired	باطل شده است (شُدَن: شَو)
10	Gardening	باغبانی
7	Lima bean, rice & meat	باقالی پُلو با گوشت
3	Above	بالا
8	Tasty	بامزّه
9	Bank	بانک
10	You do not believe (Psychological verb)	باوَرت نمی شَوَد! (شُدَن: شَو)
1	Intelligent	باهوش
5	Must	بایَد
3	Excuse me	بِبَخشید
3	Sorry to bother you	بِبَخشید مُزاحِم شُدَم
9	I may/should pay	بپردازم (پَرداختن: پَرداز)
5	I should/may ask	بپُرسَم (پُرسیدَن: پُرس)
9	Turn! (Plural & Formal)	بپیچید (پیچیدن: پیچ)
10	Childhood	بَچّگی
2	Baby/Child/Kid	بَچّه
5	I should/must buy	بخَرَم (خَریدَن: خَر)
10	Section	بَخش
1	Bad	بَد
1	I am not bad	بَد نیستَم
6	Worse	بَدتر
6	The worst	بَدترین
7	I dislike	بَدَم می‌آید (آمدن: آ)
7	I do not dislike	بَدَم نمی‌آید (آمدن: آ)
5	We should/may give	بدَهیم (دادَن: دَه)
2	Brother	بَرادَر
6	Brother's child	برادرزاده
4	For	بَرای
7	Kind of bread	بَربَری
6	Snowy	بَرفی
9	Return! (Plural & Formal)	برگردید (برگَشتن: گَرد)
10	Was organized	بَرگُزار شُد (شُدَن: شَو)
10	Is organized	بَرگُزار می‌شود (شُدَن: شَو)

3	Program/Plan/Schedule	بَرنامه
10	Winner	بَرَنده
9	I have not retuned	برنگشته‌ام (برگَشتن: گَرد)
5	S/he should/may go	بِرَوَد (رَفتَن: رَو)
5	Go! (Plural & Formal)	بِرَوید (رَفتَن: رَو)
7	Lamb	بَرّه
1	Big/Large	بُزُرگ
8	Greatness	بُزُرگی
10	Let's go! (Slang)	بِزَن بِریم!
10	Shake on it! (Slang)	بِزَن قَدش!
8	Make! (Plural & Formal)	بِسازید
7	Ice cream	بَستَنی
5	Per box	بَسته‌ای
10	Basketball	بَسکِتبال
7	Plate	بُشقاب
3	Afternoon	بَعد از ظهر
3	After...	بعد از...
10	After that (Spoken)	بَعدش
4	Come in/Here you go (Informal)	بِفَرما
3	Here you go/are Come in/Response to hello on phone	بِفَرمایید
5	Small grocery store	بَقّالی
5	Search	بِگَرد
8	Catch them! (Plural & Formal)	بِگیریدشان (گِرفتَن:گیر)
3	You know (skill/language)	بَلَدی (بودَن: هَست)
10	Long	بُلَند
5	Blouse	بلوز
1	Yes	بَله
9	Ticket	بلیت
9	Servant/I (Modest)	بَنده
4	Purple	بَنَفش
4	Real estate agency	بُنگاه
5	Boutique	بوتیک
4	Budget	بودجه
6	I was	بودم (بودن: هَست)
6	They were	بودند (بودن: هَست)
9	Has been	بوده‌است (بودن: هَست)

368

9	You have been (Plural & Formal)	بوده‌اید (بودن: هست)
6	You were	بودی (بودن: هست)
3	To	به
2	Plus	به اِضافه(ی)
8	Hope to see you again	به اُمید دیدار!
3	Wow!/Yum Yum!	بَه بَه!
7	To be born	به دُنیا آمدن
5	Quickly/Soon	به زودی
3	Be safe	به سَلامَت
8	Towards	به سمتِ
6	In my opinion	به نظرِ من
6	Spring	بَهار
8	Eleventh Persian month	بَهمَن
1	Impolite	بی اَدب
8	Unemotional	بی احساس
8	Flavorless	بی مَزّه
8	Miserable	بیچاره
3	S/he wakes up	بیدار می‌شَوَد (شُدَن: شَو)
9	I have not gone out	بیرون نرفته‌ام (رَفتن: رَو)
2	Twenty	بیست
2	Twenty five	بیست و پَنج
2	Twenty four	بیست و چهار
2	Twenty two	بیست و دو
4	Twenty Second	بیست و دوُّم ـ بیست و دوُّمین
2	Twenty three	بیست و سه
2	Twenty six	بیست و شش
2	Twenty nine	بیست و نُه
2	Twenty eight	بیست و هَشت
2	Twenty seven	بیست و هَفت
2	Twenty one	بیست و یک
4	Twenty first	بیست و یکُم ـ بیست و یِکُمین
4	Twentieth	بیستُم ـ بیستُمین
6	More	بیشتَر
6	The most	بیشتَرین
5	Sick/Ill	بیمار
5	Hospital	بیمارستان
9	Insurance	بیمه

3	Between		بِین
10	International		بِینُ المِلَلی
8	One who can see		بینا
4	Nose		بِینی
4	Leg/Foot		پا
5	Fabric		پارچه
5	Fabric store		پارچه فروشی
4	Garage/Parking space		پارکینگ
7	Paris		پاریس
9	Passport		پاسپورت
8	Answer		پاسُخ
2	Fifteen		پانزَده
4	Five hundred		پانصد
6	Capital city		پایتَخت
6	Fall/Autumn		پاییز
3	Below		پایین
7	Pepsi		پپسی
2	Father		پدَر
8	Brat/Mean		پدر سوخته
2	Parents		پدَر وَ مادَر
6	Grandfather		پدربزرگ
6	Grandparents		پدربزرگ و مادربزرگ
8	Bastard		پدرسگ
6	Husband's father		پدرشوهَر
8	I had so much trouble! (Slang)		پدرم در اومد!
8	Fill in/out! (Plural & Formal)		پُرکنید
7	Orange		پُرتقال
1	Nurse		پَرستار
8	Question		پُرسِش
7	Per portion		پُرسی
9	Flight		پَرواز
6	The day before yesterday		پَریروز
6	The night before last		پَریشَب
2	So		پَس
6	Two days before yesterday		پَس پَریروز
6	Two nights before last		پَس پَریشَب
6	The day after tomorrow		پَس فَردا

6	The night after tomorrow night	پَس فَردا شَب
5	Email	پُستِ اِلِکترونیکی
7	Pistachio	پِسته
2	Boy/Son	پِسَر
6	Maternal aunt's son	پسر خاله
6	Paternal aunt's son	پسر عَمّه
6	Maternal uncle's son	پسردایی
6	Paternal uncle's son	پسرعَمو
3	Behind/Back	پُشت
3	Pashto	پَشتو
9	House number	پِلاک
7	Steamed rice	پُلو
1	Police	پُلیس
2	Five	پَنج
4	Five hours	پنج ساعت
3	Thursday	پنج شَنبه
2	Fifty	پَنجاه
4	Fifth	پَنجُم – پَنجُمین
7	Cheese	پَنیر
5	Clothes	پوشاک
5	Money	پول
9	Small change	پول خُرد
9	Cash money	پول نَقد
7	Spread!	پَهن کُن! (کردن: کُن)
3	On foot	پیاده
7	Onion	پیاز
8	Find! (Plural & Formal)	پیدا کنید
5	I should/may find it	پِیدایَش کُنَم (کردن: کُن)
1	Old	پیر
5	Dress	پیراهَن
6	Previous	پیش
8	Pre-school	پیش دَبِستانی
10	Ping-pong	پینگ پُنگ
5	Links	پیوَندها
2, 4, 5, & 10	Until/Till/So that/As long as/As soon as/For counting	تا
6	Summer	تابِستان
1	Tajik	تاجیکی

5	Website	تارنَما
2, 8 & 9	Date - History	تاریخ
7	Kind of bread	تافتون
3	Taxi	تاکسی
8	Convert! (Plural & Formal)	تَبدیل کنید
7	Congratulations - To congratulate	تَبریک ــ تَبریک گفتن
8	Education	تَحصیلات
2	Board	تَخته
5	Discount	تخفیف
5	Student discount	تَخفیفِ دانشجویی
5	Egg	تُخم مُرغ
7	Radish	تُربچه
8	Translate! (Plural & Formal)	تَرجُمه کنید
8	Pickled vegetables	تُرشی‌جات
1	Turkish (person)	تُرک
3	Turkish	تُرکی
2	Term	تِرم
7	To offer condolences	تَسلیَت گفتن
4	Are present (Polite verb)	تَشریف دارند (داشتن: دار)
7	Thirsty	تِشنه
7	I am thirsty	تِشنه‌اَم است (بودن: هست)
10	Accidental/Accidentally	تصادُفی
8	Image	تَصویر
6	Off/Not working	تَعطیل
2	Division	تَقسیم
2	Divided (by)	تَقسیم (بَر)
8	Calendar	تَقویم
8	Homework (Plural)	تَکالیف
2	Homework	تَکلیف
9	Operator	تِلِفُنچی
5	Contact us	تماس
6	Entire/All	تَمام
3	Finishes (something)	تَمام می‌شَوَد (شُدَن: شَو)
1	Exercise	تَمرین
1	Lazy	تَنبل
6	Lonely	تَنها
10	Tennis	تِنیس

10	Table Tennis	تنیس روی میز
1	You	تو
2 & 3	In/Inside/At	تو(tu)
8	For God's sake	تو را به خدا
9	Stop/Lay over	تَوَقُّف
7	Birthday	تَوَلُّد
4	Puppy	توله سَگ
9	Toman (Iranian Currency)	تومان
1	Tehran	تِهران
1	From Tehran	تهرانی
5	T-shirt	تی شِرت
8	Fourth Persian month	تیر
10	Team	تیم
10	Theater	تئاتر
8	Blanks	جاهای خالی
2	Sociology	جامِعه شناسی
2	Dear	جان
10	Swear to you	جانِ تو
6	You were missed	جایَت خالی
10	Prize/Award	جایِزه
10	Serious/Seriously	جِدّی
8	New	جَدید
5	Search	جُستُجو
7	Celebration	جَشن
7	They should/may celebrate	جَشن بِگیرند (گیر)
10	Festival	جَشنواره
2	Geography	جُغرافی
5	Pair	جُفت
3	Front	جُلو
2	Addition	جَمع
3	Friday	جُمعه
8	Sentence(s)	جُمله ــ جُمَلات
5	Sir/Excellency/You (Singular/Polite)	جناب
9	You (Singular/Polite)	جِنابعالی
6	South	جُنوب
6	South East	جنوبِ شرقی
6	South West	جنوبِ غربی

373

8	Answer		جَواب
1	Young		جَوان
7	Baby chicken		جوجه
5	Sock		جوراب
8	Yeah, right!/B.S! (Slang)		جون عمّه ات!
5	Denim/Jeans		جین
5	Chador		چادُر
10	You're the bomb! (Slang)		چاکِرتَم!
5	They should/may haggle		چانه بزنند (زَدن: زَن)
7	Tea		چای
7	Tea would be nice!		چای می چَسبَد!
9	Left		چَپ
2 & 4	Why		چرا
10	Positive reply to a negative question		چرا
1	Positive response to a request		چَشم
4	Eye		چَشم
4	How/How come		چطور
1	How are you?		چطوری؟
1	How are you? (Plural & Formal)		چطورید؟
4	How much		چِقَدر
4	How		چِگونه
7	Steamed rice with ...		چُلو
7	Soltāni rice and Kabab		چلوکَبابِ سُلطانی
7	Cholo Kabab specialty restaurant		چلوکَبابی
1	Several		چَند
2 & 4	How many		چَند (تا)
2	How old...?		چند ساله...؟
4	How many times		چَندبار
4	N/A		چَندُم ــ چَندُمین
4	How many people		چَندنَفَر
4	How long		چَندوقت
7	Fork		چَنگال
3	Because		چون
2 & 4	What		چه
4	Which		چه ...... ی
6	What's up?		چه خبر؟
1	How nice!		چه خوب!

8	What has happened?		چه شده است؟
2	How excellent!		چه عالی!
6	What did you do?		چه کار کردی؟
4	Who		چه کسی
7	What kind		چه نوع
3	What do you do?		چه کاری می‌کُنی؟
2	Four		چهار
9	Intersection		چهار راه
2	Fourteen		چهاردَه
3	Wednesday		چهارشَنبه
4	Four hundred		چهارصد
4	Fourth		چهارُم - چهارُمین
2	Forty		چِهل
4	Fortieth		چِهلُم – چِهلُمین
1	What is		چیست
1 & 3	Chinese		چینی
4	I get ready		حاضِر می‌شَوَم (شدن: شَو)
4	Are you not ready?		حاضِر نیستی؟
6	Famous Persian poet		حافِظ
10	Do you feel like…		حال داری؟
1	How are you? (Plural & Formal)		حالِ شَما چِطور اَست؟
6	Now		حالا
1	Definitely/For sure		حَتماً
9	Approximately/About		حُدود
5	I should/may count		حساب کُنَم (کردن: کُن)
7	Sweet roasted flour & butter		حَلوا
4	Bath		حَمّام
4	Yard		حَیاط
9	Foreign/Foreigner		خارِجی
8	I'd rather be dead!		خاک به سرم!
6	Maternal aunt		خاله
8	You are lying/You are full of it!		خالی می بندی!
1	Mrs./Ms./Lady		خانُم
2	Family		خانِواده
3	House/Home		خانه
5	OK/Well		خُب
8	News		خَبَر

375

7	Funeral	خَتم
1	Good bye	خُدا نِگَهدار
1	Good bye	خُداحافِظ
9	Here you are	خِدمتِ شما
4	Donkey	خَر
8	You've got connections/influence! (Slang)	خَرِت می رِه!
8	Third Persian month	خُرداد
4	Rabbit	خَرگوش
5	Dates	خُرما
6	Caspian	خَزَر
1	Tired	خَسته
3	May you not be tired	خَسته نَباشید
6	More tired	خَسته تر
6	Gulf	خَلیج
3	Dormitory	خوابگاه
7	I am sleepy	خوابَم می آید (آمدن: آ)
9	I had wanted/requested	خواسته بودم (بودن: هست)
1	Singer	خوانَنده
10	S/he will give	خواهَد داد (دادن: دَه)
2	Sister	خواهَر
6	Sister's child	خواهرزاده
3	You are welcome/Please	خواهِش می کُنَم
10	We will see	خواهیم دید (دیدن: بین)
1	Good/Fine	خوب
5	To get well	خوب شُدن
1	I am well	خوبَم
1	Are you well?	خوبی؟
1	Are you well? (Plural & Formal)	خوبید؟
7	Yourself	خودَت
2	Pen	خودکار
7	Food	خوراک
7	Stew	خورِش
4	Welcome! (Informal)	خوش آمدی!
2	Good for you	خوش به حالَت
6	Had a good time	خوش گُذَشت (گُذَر)
10	Fortunately	خوشبَختانه
1	Happy	خوشحال

1	Beautiful/Pretty	خوشگِل
7	I like	خوشَم می‌آید (آمدن: آ)
7	I do not like	خوشَم نمی‌آید (آمدن: آ)
1	Delicious	خوشمَزه
10	Calligraphy	خوشنویسی
1	Good to meet you	خوشوَقتَم
8	Street	خیابان
7	Cucumber	خیار
10	Sewing	خَیّاطی
5	May it bring you luck	خِیرش را ببینید
1	A lot/Very	خِیلی
7	Brother/Bro (Slang)	داداش
8	S/he is studying	دارد درس می‌خواند (خواندن: خوان)
2	I have	دارم
8	I am making…	دارم … دُرُست می‌کنم (کردن: کُن)
8	I am settinng...	دارم … می‌چینم (چیدَن: چین)
8	I am coming	دارم می‌آیم (آمدن: آ)
2	They have	دارَند
8	They are/someone is knocking	دارَند دَر می‌زنند (زدَن: زَن)
8	Drugstore	داروخانه
2	You have	داری
8	What are you doing?	داری چه کار می‌کنی؟
10	Story/Fiction	داستان
8	I was talking	داشتم حرف می‌زدم (زَدَن: زَن)
8	I was cooking…	داشتَم … می‌پختم (پُختَن: پَز)
8	I was studying	داشتم درس می‌خواندم (خواندَن: خوان)
8	I was going	داشتم می‌رفتم (رَفتن: رَو)
6	Son in law/Groom	داماد
4	Veterinary	دامپزشکی
5	Skirt	دامَن
1	K-12 student	دانِش آموز
1	University student	دانشجو
1	University	دانِشگاه
5	Each	دانه‌ای
6	Maternal uncle	دایی
2	Girl/Daughter	دُختَر
6	Daughter of maternal aunt	دختر خاله

6	Daughter of paternal aunt	دختر عَمّه
6	Daughter of maternal uncle	دختردایی
6	Daughter of paternal uncle	دختر عَمو
8	Doctorate	دُکتُری
8	High/Middle school teacher	دَبیر
1, 2, & 3	In/Inside/At/Door	دَر
5	About/Concerning	درباره(ی)
9	I am at your service	درخِدمَتِتان هستم
3	Tree	دِرَخت
9	I have applied	درخواست کرده‌ام (کردن: کُن)
5	We should/may study	دَرس بخوانیم (خواندَن: خوان)
7	Passing (away)	دَرگُذَشت
7	Hello to you	دُرود بَر شما
6	Sea	دَریا
6	Lake	دَریاچه
8	Thief	دُزد
8	Primary school	دَبِستان
8	High school	دَبیرِستان
3 & 4	Hand/Arm	دَست
3	Thank you	دَستِتان دَرد نَکُنَد
4	Washroom	دَستشویی
8	Grammar	دَستور زبان
2	Notebook	دَفتَر
8	Exact	دَقیق
4	Minute	دَقیقه
1	Doctor	دُکتُر
5	Button	دُکمه
8	I have missed you	دلم برایت تنگ شده (است)
10	I had missed... (Psychological verb)	دِلَم تَنگ شده بود (شُدن: شَو)
4	Nose	دَماغ
8	You're the bomb!/Good job! (Slang)	دَمِت گَرم!
4	You look for...	دُنبالِ ... می‌گردید (گَشتن: گَرد)
4	Tooth	دَندان
7	World	دُنیا
2	Two	دو
4	Two million	دو میلیون
10	Track and Field	دو و میدانی

2	Twelve	دوازَده
4	Twelfth	دَوازدَهُم - دَوازدَهُمین
3	Bicycle	دوچَرخه
4	Two-bedroom	دوخوابه
3	Far	دور
8	Period (of time)	دوره (dowre)
6	We used to get together	دورِهَم جَمع می‌شُدیم (شُدن: شَو)
2	Friend	دوست
7	Boy friend	دوست پسر
2	I like (I have a liking)	دوست دارم (داشتن: دار)
6	You liked	دوست داشتی (داشتن: دار)
7	Girlfriend	دوست دختر
3	Monday	دوشَنبه
7	Yoghurt drink	دوغ
4	Second	دوّم - دوّمین
4	Two thousand	دوهزار
4	Two hundred	دویست
4	Hundred Second	دویست و دوّم - دویست و دوّمین
2	Ten	دَه
4	Tenth	دَهُم - دَهُمین
8	Tenth Persian month	دِی
8	High-school diploma	دیپلُم
6	I saw	دیدَم (دیدَن: بین)
6	You saw	دیدی (دیدَن: بین)
4	Late	دیر
4	I am late	دیر کَردَم (کردن: کُن)
10	Late (time)	دیر وَقت
4	It gets late	دیرمی‌شَوَد (شدن: شَو)
6	Yesterday	دیروز
6	Last night	دیشَب
7	Next - Other	دیگر
2	Wall	دیوار
2	Specific direct object suffix	را
9	Right	راست
7	By the way	راستی
8	Middle school	راهنَمایی
2	Computer	رایانه

379

4	Quarter/15 minutes	رُبع
9	I should/may make a reservation	رِزرو کنم (کردن: کُن)
4	Restaurant	رِستوران
3	Academic field	رِشته
6	Mountain range	رِشته کوه
6	They went	رفتند (رَفتن: رَو)
10	Dance	رَقص
5	Password	رَمز عبور
4	Rainbow	رَنگین کَمان
3	On top	رو
8	Yes Sir/Ma'am! - Whatever you say!	رو چشَم!
9	Visa	رَوادید
2	Psychology	رَوان شِناسی
3	Facing	روبِرو
5	Ladies' long coat	روپوش – مانتو
6	River	رود
1	Good day	روز به خِیر
3	Daily	روزانه
5	Scarf	روسَری
9	Passerby	رَهگُذَر
2	Mathematics	ریاضی
9	Rial (Iranian Currency)	ریال
10	Boss	رَئیس
3	Tongue/Language	زَبان
8	I'm tired of repeating (something to someone)!	زبانم مو در آورد!
4	Yellow	زَرد
1	Smart	زِرَنگ
6	Winter	زِمِستان
2	Woman/Wife	زَن
6	S/he used to live	زندگی می کرد (کردن: کُن)
3	You live	زِندِگی می کُنی (کَردَن: کُن)
8	S/he phoned	زنگ زد (زَدَن: زَن)
4	Quickly/Early/Fast	زود
5	A lot/Many	زیاد
1	Beautiful	زیبا
6	More beautiful	زیباتَر
6	The most beautiful	زیباترین

8	Beauty		زیبایی
3	Under/Underneath		زیر
8	Underline! (Plural & Formal)		زیر ...خَط بکشید
2	Biology		زیست شِناسی
1 & 3	Japanese		ژاپُنی
5	Cardigan		ژاکَت
10	Organization		سازمان
4	Hour/Time/Clock/Watch		ساعَت
4	Five o'clock		ساعتِ پنج
4	It is five o'clock		ساعت پنج است
1	Quiet		ساکِت
2	Year		سال
7	Salad		سالاد
4	Green		سَبز
7	Fresh greens		سَبزی خوردَن
7 & 8	Vegetables		سَبزیجات
5	Light (weight)		سَبُک
9	I am thankful		سِپاسگُزارَم
9	You (Singular/Polite/Female)		سَرکار
10	At work		سَر کار
9	Noise		سَر و صِدا
1	Soldier		سَرباز
6	Cold		سَرد
7	I am cold		سَردَم است (بودن: هست)
9	We are not busy (anymore)		سَرمان خَلوَت شده است
9	We were busy		سَرمان شُلوغ بود
4	Navy		سُرمه‌ای
6	Famous Persian poet		سَعدی
7	We should/may order		سِفارِش بِدَهیم (دادن: دَه)
6	Travel/Trip		سَفَر
9	Have a nice trip!		سَفَر خوشی را برایتان آرزو می کنم
7	Tablecloth (for eating on the floor)		سُفره
4	White		سِفید
9	Coin		سِکّه
4	Dog		سَگ
1	Hello		سَلام
1	Say hello		سَلام بِرسانید

8	May you be healthy		سلامت باشی
5	Taste		سَلیقه
10	Traditional		سُنَّتی
7	Kind of bread		سَنگَک
5	Heavy		سَنگین
5	Supermarket		سوپرمارکت
4	Third		سِوُّم – سِوُّمین
2	Three		سه
3	Tuesday		سه شَنبه
8	Question		سُؤال
8	Change into question form! (Plural & Formal)		سُؤالی کنید
2	Thirty		سی
4	Thirtieth		سی اُم - سی اُمین
4	Black		سیاه
5 & 7	Apple		سیب
7	Potato		سیب زَمینی
7	Per skewer		سیخی
7	Full (not hungry)		سیر
7	Garlic		سیر
7	I got/became full		سیر شُدَم (شُدَن: شو)
2	Thirteen		سیزدَه
4	Three hundred		سیصد
10	Cinema		سینما
1	Poet		شاعِر
3	Dinner		شام
2	Sixteen		شانزدَه
5	Egg crates		شانه
3	Night		شَب
10	How much do you bet?		شَرطِ چند می بندی؟
6	East		شَرق
10	They will attend		شِرکَت خواهَند کرد (کردن: کُن)
7	To attend		شِرکَت کردن
9	I am sorry		شَرمَنده‌ام
2	Six		شِش
4	Six hundred		ششصد
4	Sixth		شِشُم - شِشُمین
2	Sixty		شَصت

10	Chess	شطرنج
8	Shape	شکل
5	Pants	شَلوار
3	Busy/Crowded	شُلوغ
1	You (Plural & Formal)	شُما
1	How about you?	شما چطور؟
3 & 6	North	شُمال
6	North East	شمالِ شرقی
6	North West	شمالِ غربی
10	Swimming	شنا
3	Saturday	شَنبه
8	One who can hear	شِنَوا
9	I had heard	شنیده‌بودم (شَنیدن: شِنَو)
2	Husband	شوهَر
3	City	شَهر
8	Sixth Persian month	شهریور
7	Milk	شیر
1	From Shiraz	شیرازی
8	Do you have good news or bad news?	شیری یا روباه؟
7	Pastry	شیرینی
2	Chemistry	شیمی
3	You are the valuable one	صاحِبش قابِل دارد
3	Morning	صُبح
1	Good morning	صُبح به خیر
3	Breakfast	صُبحانه
5	Wait! (Plural & Formal)	صَبرکُنید (کردن: کُن)
2 & 4	Hundred	صد
4	Hundred first	صد و یَکُم ــ صد و یَکُمین
4	Hundred thousandth	صد هِزارُم ــ صد هِزارُمین
7	Call!	صِدا کُن! (کردن: کُن)
4	Hundredth	صَدُم ــ صَدُمین
4	Hundred thousand	صدهزار
4	Hundred thousand and one	صدهزار و یک
9	Currency exchange store	صَرّافی
8	Conjugate! (Plural & Formal)	صَرف کنید
10	Line/Queue	صَف
9	Page	صَفحه

5	First page	صَفحه نُخُست
2	Zero	صِفر
9	Handicrafts	صَنایع دستی
2	Chair	صَندَلی
4	Face	صورَت
7	Bill/Invoice	صورَتِحساب
4	Pink	صورَتی
2	Multiplication	ضَرب
2	Multiplied (by)	ضَرب (دَر)
4	Storey/Floor	طَبَقه
10	Fan/Follower	طَرَفدار
4	Parrot	طوطی
3	Noon	ظُهر
9	ATM/Bank Machine	عابِر بانک
6	I fell in love with	عاشِقِ .... شُدَم (شَو)
8	Phrase	عِبارَت
10	What luck!	عَجَب شانسی!
7	Formal word used after numbers (for inanimates)	عَدَد
9	Excuse me	عُذر می‌خواهم
3	Arabic	عَرَبی
6	Daughter in law/Bride	عَروس
7	Wedding	عَروسی
7	My dear	عَزیزَم
3	Later afternoon/Evening	عَصر
1	Good afternoon	عَصر به خِیر
5	Spice & herb store	عَطّاری
7	Religious ceremony of marriage	عَقد
6	Paternal uncle	عَمو
6	Paternal aunt	عَمّه
9	We change/exchange	عوض می‌کنیم (کردن: کُن)
4	No problem	عِیب نَدارد
3	Food	غَذا
6	West	غَرب
10	Except	غِیر از
2 & 3	Persian	فارسی
7	Sweet noodles with rose water	فالوده
6	Extended family	فامیل

2	Last/Family name	فامیلی (fámily)
8	Audio file	فایلِ صوتی
7	You forgot	فَراموش کردی (کردن: کُن)
7	I did not forget	فَراموش نکردم (کردن: کُن)
1 & 3	French	فَرانسَوی
3 & 6	Tomorrow	فَردا
6	Tomorrow night	فَردا شَب
5	Rug	فَرش
9	Airport	فُرودگاه
8	First Persian month	فَروَردین
5	Store	فُروشگاه
5	Seller	فروشنده
1	Sales person	فُروشنده
8	Verb(s)	فِعل – اَفعال
1	Bye for now	فعلاً خُداحافظ
6	I used to think	فکر می کردم (کردن: کُن)
7	To pass away	فُوت کردن (fowt)
10	Soccer	فوتبال
2	Physics	فیزیک
3	This is not valuable	قابِلی نَدارَد
6	Continent	قارّه
7	Spoon	قاشُق
5	Rug	قالی
9	Before	قَبل از
6	Previously	قَبلاً
10	Old (for inanimates)	قَدیمی
6	Is located	قرار دارد (داشتن: دار)
3	Affectionately (Formal)	قُربانِ شُما
2	Affectionately (Informal)	قُربانَت
4	Red	قِرمِز
10	Section/Part	قِسمَت
1	Beautiful/Pretty	قَشَنگ
6	More beautiful	قَشَنگ تر
6	The most beautiful	قَشَنگ ترین
10	Story/Tale	قِصّه
6	Antarctica	قُطبِ جُنوب
6	Peak	قُلّه

7	Herbs, beans, and meat stew	قورمه سَبزی
1	Strong (physical)	قَوی
4	Brown	قَهوه‌ای
5	Price	قِیمَت
5	Winter coat	کاپشن
7	Gift/Present	کادو
3	Work/Job	کار
8	Associate degree	کاردانی – فوقِ دیپلُم
8	Bachelor's	کارشِناسی – لیسانس
8	Master's	کارشِناسی ارشَد – فوق لیسانس
3	I do not work	کار نِمی کُنَم (کَردَن: کُن)
9	Credit Card	کارتِ اِعتِباری
9	Identification card	کارتِ شناسایی
1	Worker	کارگَر
10	Director	کارگَردان
1	Employee (office)	کارمَند
2	Computer	کامپیوتر
1	Canadian	کانادایی
7	Lettuce	کاهو
3 & 7	Kabab (Fillet mignon - Ground beef)	کَباب (بَرگ – کوبیده)
5	Coat	کُت
5	Suit	کُت و شَلوار
2	Book	کِتاب
10	Reading	کتاب خواندن
5	Bookstore	کتاب فروشی
2	Library	کتابخانه
4	Where	کُجا
1	Where from	کُجایی (kójāyi)
4	Which	کُدام
4	Cream	کِرم
7	Butter	کَره
4	Foal	کُرّه خَر
10	Wrestling	کُشتی
6	Country	کِشور
8	I got shocked/bored! (Slang)	کَف کردم!
5	Shoe store	کَفّاشی
5	Shoe	کَفش

386

2	Class/Classroom	کِلاس
5	Hat	کُلاه
8	They ripped me off/I was scammed!	کَلاه سرم گذاشتند!
8	University entrance exam	کُنکور
8	Word(s)	کَلَمه ـ کَلَمات
8	Help	کُمَک
3	A little	کَمی
3	Next to/Beside	کِنار
10	Short	کوتاه
1	Small	کوچَک
9	Alley/Residential street	کوچه
10	Child	کودَک
6	Desert	کَویر
5, 8, & 10	That/Which/Who/When/Where/Whose/Whom	که
2 & 4	Who	کی
4	When	کِی
8	S/he stole my bag	کیفَم را زَد
5	Per Kilogram	کیلویی
4	Garage	گاراژ
7	Server	گارسُن
4	Cow/Cattle	گاو
8	Calendar	گاهشُمار
5	Gabbeh	گَبِّه
2	Chalk	گَچ
5	Password	گُذَر واژه
9	Passport	گُذَرنامه
6	Past/Previous	گُذَشته
9	You have passed	گُذَشته‌اید (گُذَشتن: گُذَر)
5	Expensive	گِران
4	Cat	گُربه
7	Walnut	گِردو
7	Hungry	گُرسنه
6	Warm/Hot	گَرم
7	Hungry	گُشنه
7	I am hungry	گُشنه‌اَم است (بودن: هست)
8	Spoken	گفتاری
8	Dialogue	گُفتگو

9	He had said	گفته بود (گفتن: گو)
3	Flower	گُل
7	Pear	گُلابی
5	Qilim	گِلیم
7	Tomato	گوجه فَرَنگی
4	Heifer	گوساله
7	Mutton	گوسفَند
4	Ear	گوش
8	Listen! (Plural & Formal)	گوش کنید
7	Meat	گوشت
7	Beef	گوشتِ گاو
7	Vegetarian	گیاه خوار
10	We may/should catch/find	گیربیاوَریم (آوردن: آوَر)
2	I need	لازم دارم
4	Lip	لَب
5	Clothes	لِباس
7	Dairy	لَبَنیّات
8	Laptop	لَپ تاپ
5	Moment	لَحظه
3	Kind of you	لُطف دارید
3	Please	لُطفاً
8	Dictionary	لُغَت نامه
7	Kind of bread	لَواش
4	List	لیست
7	Cup/Glass	لیوان
1	We	ما
2	Mother	مادَر
6	Grandmother	مادربزرگ
6	Wife's mother	مادرزَن
6	Husband's mother	مادرشوهَر
7	Yoghurt	ماست
7	Yoghurt and (minced) cucumber side dish	ماست و خیار
3	Car	ماشین
4	Whose	مالِ چه کسی – مالِ کی
9	Tax	مالیات
2	Mom	مامان
6	Grandma	مامان بزرگ

9	Customs/Immigration officer	مأمورِ گذرنامه
6	You stayed	ماندی (ماندن: مان)
6	Month/Moon	ماه
7	Fish	ماهی
5	Congratulations	مُبارَک است!
7	Congratulations	مُبارَک باشد
4	Sofa/Love seat	مُبل
9	Unfortunately	مُتأسِّفانه
3	I am sorry	مُتِأسِّفَم
1	Married	مُتأهِّل
8	Synonym	مُتَرادِف
5	Per meter	مِتری
1	Thanks	مُتشَکِّرم
8	Antonym	مُتَضاد
8	Text	مَتن
8	Positive/Affirmative	مُثبَت
5	For example	مَثَلاً
1	Single	مُجَرَّد
7	Formal party	مَجلِس
10	Various	مُختَلِف
9	Especially	مَخصوصاً
8	Degree	مَدرَک
8	Level	مَقطَع
2	Pencil	مِداد
5	Medical Treatment	مُداوا
8	Duration	مُدَّت
5	School -Schools	مَدرِسه ــ مَدارِس
1	Manager/Principal	مُدیر
7	Ceremony	مَراسِم
3	Man	مَرد
8	Fifth Persian month	مُرداد
1	Thanks	مِرسی
7	Chicken	مُرغ
6	Provincial capital	مَرکَزِ اُستان
5	Shopping center	مرکزِ خرید
5	Sick/Ill	مَریض
4	Eyelash	مُژه

389

10	Match		مُسابِقه
6	Travel/Trip		مُسافَرَت
2	Equal (to)		مُساوی (با)
9	Straight (direction)		مُستَقیم
10	Documentary		مُستَنَد
5	Client		مُشتَری
4	Black		مِشکی
8	Does not match		مُطابِقَت ندارد
10	Sure		مُطمَئِن
1	Teacher		مُعَلِّم
3	Usually		مَعمولاً
8	Meaning		مَعنی
5	Shop		مَغازه
8	Article/Paper		مَقاله
5	Firm/Fixed price		مَقطوع
8	Dialogue		مُکالِمه
10	How is that possible?		مَگِر می شود؟
6	Mild		مُلایِم
1	Thanks		مَمنون
1	I		مَن
7	Me too		من هم هَمینطور
4	House/Home		مَنزِل
1	Secretary		مُنشی
8	Negative		مَنفی
5	Main menu		منوی اَصلی
2	Subtraction		منها
2	Minus		مِنها(ی)
4	Hair		مو
8	Take care of yourself		مواظِب خودَت باش!
10	Favorite		مورِد عَلاقه
7	Banana		موز
10	Music		موسیقی
3	Mouse		موش
8	You are cute/adorable! (Slang)		موش بخورَدت!
8	Seventh Persian month		مِهر
1	Kind		مِهرَبان

8	Kindness	مهربانی
7	Guest	مِهمان
7	Party	مِهمانی
1	Engineer	مُهَندِس
7	You drink	می نوشی (نوشیدن: نوش)
10	I stand	می ایستم (ایستادن: ایست)
7	I bring	می‌آوَرَم (آوَردن: آوَر)
3	You come	می‌آیی (آمَدَن: آ)
8	I see you/See you	می‌بینمت (دیدن: بین)
5	You wear	می پوشی (پوشیدَن: پوش)
5	I can/I am able to	می تَوانَم (تَوانِستَن: تَوان)
6	We used to laugh	می خَندیدیم (خَندیدن: خَند)
3	I sleep	می‌خوابَم (خوابیدَن: خواب)
3	S/he reads	می‌خوانَد (خواندَن: خوان)
5	I want	می خواهم (خواستَن: خواه)
5	We want	می خواهیم (خواستَن: خواه)
3	I eat	می‌خورَم (خوردَن: خور)
3	You know (something)	می دانی (دانِستَن: دان)
6	S/he used to see	می‌دیدیم (دیدَن: بین)
4	We arrive	می‌رسیم (رسیدَن: رس)
3	I go	می‌رَوَم (رَفتَن: رَو)
3	You know (someone)	می‌شناسی (شناخْتَن: شناس)
3	You do	می کُنی (کَردَن: کُن)
6	We used to talk/say	می گُفتیم (گُفتن: گو)
9	I get it	می گیرَمش (گرفتن: گیر)
9	I stay	می‌مانم (ماندن: مان)
1	Middle aged	میانسال
9	Roundabout	میدان
2	Table/Desk	میز
7	You want (Polite verb)	مِیل دارید (داشتن: دار)
7	Fruit	میوه
5	Fruit store	میوه فروشی
8	Blind	نابینا
1	Upset/Sad	ناراحَت
4	Orange	نارنجی
8	Deaf	ناشِنَوا
2	Name	نام

6 & 8	Name...! (Plural & Formal)		نام بِبَرید (بُردَن: بَر)
2	Last/Family name		نامِ خانوادِگی
5	User name		نامِ کاربَری
8	Scum		نامَرد
8	Letter (mail)		نامه
8	Unkind		نامهربان
3	Bread		نان
5	Bakery		نانوایی
3	Lunch		ناهار
5	It should/may not be		نَباشَد (بودَن: هَست)
4	First		نُخُست
4	First		نُخُستین
2	I do not have		نَدارَم
6	They did not go		نَرَفتَند (رَفتَن: رَو)
9	You have not gone		نرفته‌اید (رَفتَن: رَو)
4	Close by/Near		نَزدیک
6	Near each other		نَزدیکِ هَم
8	Person		نَفَر
1	Painter		نَقّاش
10	Painting		نَقّاشی
6	Map		نَقشه
5	Icon		نَمادِ تَصویری
10	Play		نَمایشنامه
10	Grade/Mark		نُمره
5	Don't you give...?		نمیدَهید؟ (دادَن: دَه)
10	Adolescent		نوجَوان
2	Ninety		نَوَد
2	Nineteen		نوزدَه
7	Good appetite!/Eat heartily!		نوشِ جان!
8	Written		نِوشتاری
7	Beverage		نوشیدَنی
6	Grandchild		نَوه
1	Writer/Author		نِویسَنده
1	No		نَه
2	Nine		نُه
4	No (Formal/Emphatic)		نه‌خیر
4	Nine hundred		نُهصد

4	Ninth		نُهُم – نُهُمین
1	I am not		نیستَم
4	Half		نیم
3	Midnight		نیمه شب
2	And		وَ
8	Word(s)		واژه – واژگان
10	For (Spoken)		واسه
6	Really		واقِعاً
10	Volleyball		والیبال
5	Website		وِبگاه
10	Sport		وَرزِش
10	Ancient Sport		وَرزش باستانی
5	Enter		وُرود
10	Weight-lifting		وزنه بَرداری
3	Middle		وَسَط
9	Homeland		وَطَن
2	Have you got time?		وَقت داری؟
4	We have got time		وَقت داریم (داشتن: دار)
6	When (in declarative sentence)		وَقتی
3	But/Though		وَلی
9	Visa		ویزا
9	Hotel		هتل
2	Eighteen		هِجدَه
8	Solar Hejira		هِجری شَمسی
5	Present/Gift		هِدیه
9	Both		هَر دو
3	Every day		هَر روز
6	Each one/Anyone		هَرکَسی
4	One thousand		هزار
4	One thousand one		هزار و یک
4	Thousandth		هِزارُم – هزارُمین
1	(There) is/exits		هَست
1	I am		هَستَم
1	You are		هَستی
1	You are (Plural & Formal)		هَستید
2	Eight		هَشت
2	Eighty		هَشتاد

4	Eight hundred		هشتصد
4	Eighth		هَشتُم
4	Eighth		هَشتُمین
2	Seven		هَفت
2	Seventy		هَفتاد
4	Seven hundred		هفتصد
4	Seventh		هَفتُم
4	Seventh		هَفتُمین
3	Week		هفته
2	Seventeen		هِفدَه
6	Also		هَم
8	Cognate		هم خانواده
6	Neighbor(s)		هَمسایه ـ هَمسایگان
2	Spouse		هَمسَر
5	Co-worker		هَمکار
7	Classmate		هَم‌کلاسی
4	All		هَمه
5	All kinds		هَمه نوع
3	Always		هَمیشه
8	Right now		همین اَلان
7	Watermelon		هِندِوانه
3	Hindi		هِندی
2	Arts		هُنَر
8	Vocational school		هُنَرِستان
1	Artist		هُنَرمَند
10	Martial Arts		هنرهای رزمی
4 & 8	Still/Yet		هَنوز
6	Air/Weather forecast		هوا
8	I've got your back (Slang)		هوا تو دارم!
3	Airplane		هَواپیما
9	Airline		هَواپیمایی
7	Carrot		هَویج
6	Or		یا
7	You forgot		یادَت رَفت (رَفتن: رو)
6	Good old days		یادش به خیر
7	I remember		یادَم است (بودن: هست)
9	I have forgotten (Psychological verb)		یادم رفته است (رَفتن: رَو)

2	Eleven	یازدَه
4	Eleventh	یازدهُم - یازدهُمین
5	Results	یافته ها
4	It means	یَعنی
2	One	یِک
4	One billion	یک میلیارد
4	One million	یک میلیون
4	One million and one	یک میلیون و یک
4	One Millionth	یک میلیونُم ــ یک میلیونُمین
3	Sunday	یکشَنبه
4	One Hundred	یَکصد
4	First	یِکُم ــ یکُمین

APPENDIX C: GRAMMAR REVIEW

Simple Present حالِ ساده (Lesson 3)

I laugh	می‌خندم	← Verb ending م	+ Present stem خَند	+ می

Imperative اَمر (Lesson 5)

Laugh! (sg.) Laugh! (pl.)	بخند بخندید	← Ø ← 2nd person pl.	+ Present stem خَند	+ بـ

Present Subjunctive حالِ التزامی (Lesson 5)

I should/may laugh	بخندم	← Verb ending م	+ Present stem خَند	+ بـ

Simple Past گذشته‌ی ساده (Lesson 6)

I laughed	خندیدم	← Verb ending م	+ Past stem خَندید

Past Continuous گذشته‌ی استمراری (Lesson 6)

I used to laugh/ I was laughing	می‌خندیدم	← Verb ending م	+ Past stem خَندید	+ می

Present Progressive حالِ مستمر (Lesson 8)

I am laughing	دارم می‌خندم	← Verb ending م	+ Present stem خَند	+ می	{ Verb ending + دار } دارم

Past Progressive گذشته‌ی مستمر (Lesson 8)

I was laughing	داشتم می‌خندیدم	← Verb ending م	+ Past stem خَندید	+می	{ Verb ending + داشت } داشتم

Present Perfect   گذشته‌ی نقلی   (Lesson 9)

I have laughed	خندیده‌ام	Simple present of *"To Be"* (short form) اَم	Past participle { ه + Past stem } خندیده

Past Perfect   گذشته‌ی بعید   (Lesson 9)

I had laughed	خندیده بودم	Simple past of *"To Be"* بودم	Past participle { ه + Past stem } خندیده

Future   آینده   (Lesson 10)

I will laugh	خواهم خندید	Past stem + خندید	{ Verb ending + خواه } خواهم

Psychological Verbs   فعل‌های احساسی   (Lesson 7)

I like... I am sleepy	خوشم می‌آید خوابم می‌آید	Verb in 3rd person sing. می‌آید	Suffix pronoun + م	Noun/Adjective خوش/خواب

Iranian Studies Series

J.C. Bürgel & C. van Ruymbeke (eds.)
Nizāmī: A Key to the Treasure of the Hakim
ISBN 978 90 8728 097 0

J. Coumans
The Rubáiyát of Omar Khayyám. An Updated Bibliography
ISBN 978 90 8728 096 3

N. Fozi
Reclaiming the Faravahar: Zoroastrian Survival in Contemporary Tehran
ISBN 978 90 8728 214 1

R. Harris and M. Afsharian
A Journal of Three Months' Walk in Persia in 1884 by Captain John Compton Pyne
ISBN 978 90 87282 622

F. Lewis & S. Sharma (eds.)
The Necklace of the Pleiades. 24 Essays on Persian Literature, Culture and Religion
ISBN 978 90 8728 091 8

M.A. Nematollahi Mahani
The Holy Drama. Persian Passion Plays in Modern Iran
ISBN 978 90 8728 115 1

C. Pérez González
Local Portraiture. Through the Lens of the 19th-Century Iranian Photographers
ISBN 978 90 8728 156 4

L. Rahimi Bahmany
Mirrors of Entrapment of Emancipation: Forugh Farrokhzad and Sylvia Plath
ISBN 978 90 8728 224 0

R. Rahmoni & G. van den Berg
The Epic of Barzu as Narrated by Jura Kamal
ISBN 978 90 8728 116 8

A. Sedighi
Agreement Restrictions in Persian
ISBN 978 90 8728 093 2

A. Sedighi
Persian in Use: An Elementary Textbook of Language and Culture
ISBN 978 90 8728 217 2

A.A. Seyed-Gohrab
Courtly Riddles. Enigmatic Embellishments in Early Persian Poetry
ISBN 978 90 8728 087 1

A.A. Seyed-Gohrab (ed.)
The Great Umar Khayyam: A Global Reception of the Rubáiyat
ISBN 978 90 8728 157 1

A.A. Seyed-Gohrab & S.R.M. McGlinn (eds.)
One Word—Yak Kaleme. 19th-Century Persian Treatise Introducing Western Codified Law
ISBN 978 90 8728 089 5

A.A. Seyed-Gohrab & S.R.M. McGlinn (eds.)
Safina Revealed. A Compendium of Persian Literature in 14th-Century Tabriz
ISBN 978 90 8728 088 8

A.A. Seyed-Gohrab, F. Doufikar-Aerts & S. McGlinn (eds.)
Embodiments of Evil: Gog and Magog. Interdisciplinary Studies of the 'Other' in Literature
& Internet Texts
ISBN 978 90 8728 090 1

P. Shabani-Jadidi
Processing Compound Verbs in Persian: A Psycholinguistic Approach to Complex Predicates
ISBN 978 90 8728 208 0

B. Solati
The Reception of Hāfiz: The Sweet Poetic Language of Hāfiz in Nineteenth and Twentieth Century
Persia
ISBN 978 90 8728 197 7

S. Tabatabai
Father of Persian Verse. Rudaki and his Poetry
ISBN 978 90 8728 092 5

K. Talattof & A.A. Seyed-Gohrab (eds.)
Conflict and Development in Iranian Film
ISBN 978 90 8728 169 4

R. Zipoli
Irreverent Persia: Invective, Satirical and Burlesque Poetry from the Origins to the Timurid Period
(10th to 15th centuries)
ISBN 978 90 8728 227 1

M. van Zutphen
A Story of Conquest and Adventure. The Large Farāmarznāme
ISBN 978 90 87282 721